| DATE | | | |
|---|---|---|---|
| MAR 19'84 | | | |
| JUL 1 5 2009 | | | |
| | | | |
| | | | |
| | | | |
| | | | |
| | | | |
| | | | |
| | | | |
| | | | |
| | | | |

© THE BAKER & TAYLOR CO.

# JAY'S TREATY

A Study in Commerce and Diplomacy

by SAMUEL FLAGG BEMIS

GREENWOOD PRESS, PUBLISHERS
WESTPORT, CONNECTICUT

Library of Congress Cataloging in Publication Data

Bemis, Samuel Flagg, 1891-1973.
    Jay's treaty.

    Reprint of the ed. published by Yale University
Press, New Haven.
    Appendix VI (p.    ):  A.  Definitive treaty of peace
and independence, 1783.--B.  Jay's treaty (treaty of
amity, commerce, and navigation) 1794.
    Includes bibliographical references and index.
    1.  Jay's Treaty, 1794.  2.  United States--Foreign
relations--Great Britain.  3.  Great Britain--Foreign
relations--United States.  I.  United States.  Treaties,
etc., 1789-1797 (Washington)  II.  Great Britain.
Treaties, etc., 1760-1820 (George III)
III.  Title.
[E314.B453  1975]            341.7'54            75-11844
ISBN 0-8371-8133-X

This study in American history was awarded the first prize in the competition, open to teachers of history in American colleges, conducted by the Knights of Columbus in 1922 to encourage investigation into the origins, the achievements, and the problems of the United States; to interpret and perpetuate the American principles of liberty, popular sovereignty, and government by consent; to promote American solidarity; and to exalt the American ideal. The author was then on the faculty of Whitman College, Walla Walla, Washington.

This edition published in 1962 by Yale University Press
New Haven

Reprinted with the permission of Yale University Press

Reprinted in 1975 by Greenwood Press,
a division of Williamhouse-Regency Inc.

Library of Congress Catalog Card Number 75-11844

ISBN 0-8371-8133-X

Printed in the United States of America

To the Memory of

My Father and Mother

# Preface to the Second Edition

JAY'S TREATY, or the Jay Treaty, as historians have commonly called the convention signed at London on November 19, 1794, by plenipotentiaries of the United States and Great Britain, was the first treaty negotiated by the new government of the United States, according to the Constitution of 1787, under the administration of President George Washington. It received the advice and consent of the Senate by a bare two-thirds majority of the Senators present on June 24, 1795, after long debate, and aroused passionate political controversy throughout the new nation. The President after anxious deliberation finally ratified it on August 14, 1795, and ratifications were exchanged in London on October 28, 1795.

Fortunate it was for me that in my student days Professor Edward Channing in 1915 assigned to me the negotiation of the treaty as a doctoral dissertation. The subject of my investigation was not the political storm that followed publication of the convention[1] but

1. The late Josiah N. Newcomb, Ph.D., of Poughkeepsie, New York, wrote a capable study of the ratification and execution of Jay's Treaty which was never printed following his death in 1944. More recent, published studies of this interesting subject are to be found in Irving Brant, *James Madison: Father of the Constitution, 1787–1800* (Indianapolis, 1950); in the last and seventh volume of Douglas Southall Freeman's *George Washington,* written after Freeman's death by John Alexander Carroll and Mary Wells Ashworth (New York, 1957); and in Alexander DeConde, *Entangling Alliance: Politics and Diplomacy under George Washington* (Durham, N. C., 1958).

rather the background of issues which led to the treaty, and the negotiation itself. Hitherto historians had studied the diplomacy of Jay's Treaty only from the American sources and principally from the diplomatic documents printed in *American State Papers*. Before the dissertation was completed my researches led me first to the Canada Archives in Ottawa, then to the Public Record Office in London. As is generally the case with such dissertations, in later years I worked over the subject more extensively, with supplementary inquiries in the archives of the United States and in French and Scandinavian archives, and reshaped it in form and substance, before presenting it in the anonymous contest offered by the Knights of Columbus in 1922.

Fortunate I say it was that I embarked upon this subject because it carried me further into multiarchival study of the diplomacy of President Washington's Administration, and of the foundations of American foreign policy, indeed to the whole diplomatic history of the United States. These studies in turn led me to certain general interpretations, which I have suggested elsewhere, of the success of the foreign policy of the United States during its rise to world power.

Since this monograph was first written the bibliography of the subject has expanded during some forty years of fruitful American historiography. Numerous excellent books and articles have appeared to embellish or correct my chapters. These titles can easily be found in the annual *Writings on American History*, published by the American Historical Association through 1953 (there is still a gap for the years 1941–47, which is being made up by a volume in preparation) ; *Guide to*

*the Diplomatic History of the United States, 1775–
1921,* published for the Library of Congress by the
Government Printing Office, Washington, 1935; and
the *Harvard Guide to American History* (Cambridge,
Mass., Belknap Press of Harvard University Press,
1954). Given the existence of these finding media,
which so readily supplement the original bibliography,
I have limited the "bibliography" at the end of this
volume to an extensive note on manuscript sources.
The new printed material, whether sources or historical writings, I have presented in footnotes throughout
this new edition (e.g. *Simcoe Papers,* etc., etc.).

Of the historical works published since the first edition of the present study, the most significant, at least
for my study, is of course Professor A. L. Burt's
magisterial work on *The United States, Great Britain,
and British North America from the Revolution to the
Establishment of Peace after the War of 1812* (New
Haven, Yale University Press, 1940). In the pertinent
chapters of Mr. Burt's book I see reflected some
thoughts that must have been common to both of us;
on the other hand, I am grateful to him for corrections
to which I now have an opportunity to pay attention,
notably in Chapter 8, "The Frontier Crisis."

In presenting this new edition I repeat my thanks
in the acknowledgments listed in the original edition
of 1923, and further take occasion to express my obligation to Miss Helen C. Boatfield for skillful assistance in checking, revising, and proofreading. Miss
Ruth Anna Fisher has rechecked from photocopies in
the Library of Congress citations to and quotations
from documents in the Foreign Office and Colonial
Office papers in the Public Record Office. Mrs. Marian

Neal Ash and Mrs. Elizabeth F. Hailey of the Yale Press have been of great help in getting the copy ready for the printer.

This second edition is now published by the Yale University Press, with the generous sanction of the Knights of Columbus, the original sponsors. I here renew the expression to that organization of my appreciation for a helping hand at the beginning of my historical labors.

S. F. B.

*New Haven, 1962*

# Introduction to the First Edition

BY GAILLARD HUNT*

MRS. JANET MONTGOMERY, the widow of General
Richard Montgomery who was killed in 1775 before
the walls of Quebec, writing to James Monroe, then
on his mission in France, on August 29, 1796, said
that she lamented the "infamous" treaty which John
Jay had made with Great Britain, and, with thousands
of others, had wept over the sale of her country.[1]
There were no women politicians in those days, and
women did not lightly express their views on public
questions. Mrs. Montgomery's remarks, therefore,
show the deep interest which all classes felt in Jay's
Treaty. The indignation meetings and riotous demon-
strations against the treaty which occurred throughout
the nation found an echo in the voice of a quiet lady
living in the country. The condemnation which the
treaty called forth even extended to the President,
who had appointed Jay and had reluctantly sent the
treaty to the Senate. A prominent Virginian, John
Beckley, wrote to James Madison, September 10,
1795: "You can have no idea how deeply the public
confidence is withdrawing itself from the President,

---

* Historian of the Department of State, the late Gaillard Hunt was
one of the judges in the Knights of Columbus competition in which
this book was awarded first prize.

1. Monroe MSS in possession of the Gouverneur family.

and with what avidity strictures on his conduct are received." [2]

Before Jay went on his mission there was widespread prejudice against him. His nomination was confirmed by a divided Senate—18 votes for him and 8 against him. Some opposed him because they did not think it proper that the Chief Justice of the United States should also hold a diplomatic office; but most of the opposition was based upon the belief that his sympathies were with England. It was believed, also, that the party to which he belonged was not true to the republican idea and that a number of leading members desired to see the republican form of government give place to a monarchy on the British plan. Thus Jay, going on his mission with suspicions behind him, could not expect to return to a welcoming constituency. Nevertheless, the denunciation which was hurled at him when the terms of his treaty became known was more severe than he had expected it to be and far more severe than he deserved. No man could have brought home a satisfactory or fair treaty at that time.

Disaster would have been the fate of the treaty if it had not been that Washington wished it to be accepted. With him still dwelt the voice of power. However lukewarm or even hostile the feeling toward him had become in some quarters no one could truthfully accuse him of foreign partialities or of desertion of the American experiment in government. He sent the treaty to the Senate, which advised its ratification by the necessary two-thirds vote, but without a single vote to spare. The absence of one Senator who favored it would have resulted in its rejection. The British Govern-

2. Madison MSS, Library of Congress.

ment having accepted it, Washington proclaimed it on February 2, 1796. Then he transmitted a copy of it to the Senate and the House. The House was a stronghold of the opponents of the treaty and they precipitated a savage debate which lasted a month. The House requested the President to send it copies of the instructions on which the treaty had been negotiated, but this he promptly refused to do, saying that under the Constitution he, with the Senate's advice and consent, negotiated treaties, and that the House had nothing to do with their making. The debate brought forward leaders on both sides and marked the beginning of a number of public careers. The forensic battle swayed back and forth. The majority, at first, was with the opponents of the treaty, but on a test vote in the committee of the whole the parties were evenly divided until the chairman cast his vote with the supporters of the treaty. A few days later on the same question in the House the treaty party won by three votes. Then there were more desertions from the Republicans. There was still force in the cry "to follow where Washington leads." Outside of Congress there was some reaction for the treaty. The violence of the opposition expended itself, and many people, on sober reflection, found some good points in the treaty. Especially they saw one good point, namely, that it would prevent, for a time at any rate, a war between the United States and Great Britain. Intelligent people knew that a war would be dangerous to the very existence of the United States.

Washington did not pretend to like the treaty. After Jay had delivered it he kept it for four months before he could bring himself to submit it to the Senate. He knew it would provoke a storm of protest and that the protest would have grounds to support it. He believed that he could not get a better treaty and that some treaty was necessary. We are not called upon to pronounce upon the merits of the treaty. Most of the provisions were bad, but England would not grant better terms to such a weak country as the United States then was. The Government was only six years old. It had not yet won the affections of its citizens. The belief was common that it would not last.

The ratification and the Federalist victory in the House which followed had a far-reaching effect upon the future of the United States. The Federalists, encouraged by having overcome a powerful opposition, went on with a program which was designed to render the opposition powerless. Because several prominent Republicans were of foreign birth and edited newspapers which attacked the Federalists a new naturalization law was passed on June 18, 1798, prescribing fourteen years as the probationary period of residence before an alien could become an American citizen. Then, on June 25, it was enacted that the President might expel any alien whose presence he deemed to be dangerous to the United States. Then, on July 14, the Sedition Act was passed, making it a criminal offense for any one to publish false or malicious writings against the Government or its officers. Apparently, the dominant party had the opposition by the throat and could strangle it at will.

But it had gone too far. Many men who believed in the federal system of government were unwilling to remain members of a party which had made a bold attempt at tyranny. The membership dwindled. The party had, in fact, committed suicide and was smothered under the indignation which its own laws had produced. The way was made clear for the triumphant entry into power of the Republican hosts with Thomas Jefferson at their head.

Vital national questions entered into the negotiation of Jay's Treaty. The surrender by the British of the frontier posts affected our relations with the Indian population on our northern border; the boundary question involved the extent of the Republic; the navigation regulations bore directly upon occupations in which much American capital was invested and in which thousands of Americans earned their living; to define contraband affected large groups of producers. European international relations, British internal politics, American politics, the strength and adaptability of the American Government were all involved in the events leading up to the negotiation of the treaty, in the negotiation itself, in the ratification and the enforcement of the treaty.

Into all the questions surrounding the negotiation of the treaty and the treaty itself Professor Samuel Flagg Bemis has examined with indefatigable industry, exhaustive research, and trained intelligence and skill. The result is an historical monograph which is not only a credit to American scholarship but a notable contribution to American history.

*Washington, D. C.*
*January 11, 1923*

# Contents

# Key to Abbreviations in Footnotes

A.H.A.          American Historical Association.

*A.H.R.*         *American Historical Review.*

Arch. Aff.
Étrang.         Archives des Affaires Étrangères.

*A.S.P.,F.R.*    *American State Papers, Foreign Relations.*

*A.S.P.,I.A.*    *American State Papers, Indian Affairs.*

C.A.          Canadian Archives. Series letter, volume number, and page follow consecutively, viz.: C.A., Q, 41, 16 indicates Canadian Archives, Series Q, Volume 41, page 16. Sometimes the volume is in two parts, as C.A., Q, 41–2, 16, indicating Canadian Archives, Series Q, Volume 41, Part 2, page 16.

             C.A., *Rept. 1890,* or other years, refers to the printed report of the Canadian Archivist on the Archives for the year designated.

*M.P.C.*       *Michigan Pioneer and Historical Collections* (40 vols. Lansing, 1877–1929).

P.R.O.        Public Record Office, London.

P.R.O.,C.O.   Public Record Office, Colonial Office Papers, followed consecutively by series number and volume number as in P.R.O.,F.O.

P.R.O.,F.O.   Public Record Office, Foreign Office Papers. In referring to F.O. papers, the series number follows consecutively after F.O., next the volume number, viz.: P.R.O.,F.O., 115, 8, indicating Series 115, Volume 8, the pagination to bound volumes of MSS not being given in this instance. The enumeration of series and volume follows the official *List of Foreign Office Rec-*

*ords to 1837 Preserved in the Public Record Office.*

S.P.       *Simcoe Papers:* E. H. Cruikshank, ed., *The Correspondence of Lieut. Governor John Graves Simcoe, with Allied Documents Relating to His Administration of Upper Canada* (5 vols. Toronto, 1923–31).

# CHAPTER 1

# The Anglo-American Frontier

ANGLO-AMERICAN diplomatic history from the treaty of independence to the signature of Jay's Treaty is concerned definitely with the frontier and overseas commerce. The complications which arose from these two factors at an epochal period of European as well as of American history help to interpret the first decade of the independence of the United States.

The familiar "critical period" of our constitutional history was followed, after ratification of the Constitution in 1788, by an equally critical period for the newly established nation. The Constitution gave body to American nationality. It was the instrument fashioned by the Fathers to rescue the people from anarchy. The administrative genius of Alexander Hamilton endowed the body with life and kept it functioning. Under Hamilton's system the infant nation nursed at the breast of commerce. Without commerce life would have been impossible, because the revenue which vitalized the nation came from imposts. Most of the commerce of the United States in those years was with Great Britain. Therefore the life of the new nation depended on the tranquillity of Anglo-American relations. For this reason these relations become an important field of investigation.

Let us first consider the Anglo-American frontier.

The peace treaty of 1783 recognized American possession of an immense domain northwest of the Ohio
River. From the point where the parallel of 45 degrees
meets the River St. Lawrence, as far west as the Lake
of the Woods, the political frontier coincided with a
definite and natural water boundary. It gave both
nations complete access to the magnificent system of
lake navigation, highway for future economic exploitation of a large part of the continent. The "Old
Northwest" thus contained within United States territory was practically untouched by civilization.
Scarcely an American settler had carried his ax across
the Ohio when the treaty of peace was signed. Save for
a few hundred *habitants* in the old French towns along
the Illinois the only white men within this immense
territory were Canadian traders with the Indians. Add
to them the farmers who made a scanty living by
supplying produce to the British frontier garrisons
and the trading population clustered about them, and
the census is complete. All that continental stretch of
forest land and prairie to the north and west of the
Ohio was still the aboriginal domain of savages and
fur-bearing animals. Through it journeyed the traders
and fur-collectors of the Montreal merchants, exchanging with the natives, for the furs so precious
to Europeans, cheap articles of English manufacture.
This traffic lifted the Indian abruptly into the iron
age and centered the satisfaction of his rapidly increasing wants about the trading stations at the frontier
posts. All but one of these fortified positions were on
the American side of the boundary—proof of the

prodigious ability of the peace negotiators of the United States.

The posts served both as military guaranty of the jurisdiction of civilized nations over that wild woodland and as protection for the only industry of the interior, the fur trade. They were located along the extensive inland water frontier at a few strategic points necessary to control the major routes of transportation and communication. Two of the forts, at Dutchman's Point and Pointe-au-Fer, secured the outlet of Lake Champlain and the old military passage from Montreal to Albany. These positions possessed additional importance because this military route was developing into a valuable pathway of trade. It was attracting the commercial if not the political affiliations of the inhabitants of the Champlain watershed of Vermont and New York.[1] The three posts of Oswegatchie, Oswego, and Niagara controlled the navigation of the St. Lawrence River, Lake Ontario, and the connection with Lake Erie. At the eastern end of Lake Erie was located another post, Fort Erie, on the left (west) bank of the Niagara River, on the British side of the treaty boundary. A glance at the map demonstrates the obvious importance of the post at Detroit on the straits between Lakes Erie and Huron. The little fortified island of Michilimackinack, off the northern tip of the Michigan peninsula, controlled the entrance to three lakes, Huron, Michigan, and Superior. Garrisoned by a few hundred British troops and supported by a horde of savage allies, these eight forts had

1. See documents published by the author in *A.H.R.*, XXI, 547–61. See maps on pp. 151–52.

enabled England to protect Canada during the American Revolution. They had helped her to harass the whole line of settlements south of the Ohio and in western New York and Pennsylvania. Held in British possession at the peace, they became important military positions in the rear of the American states. They protected the fur trade. They overawed the souls of the savage allies who more and more were coming to depend on purchasing with their furs their luxuries, even their very subsistence, from the traders sheltered under the guns of the forts. Seven of the posts were on American soil south of the boundary fixed by the treaty of peace of 1783.

Article II of the treaty of peace stipulated the evacuation of American soil by British troops with "all convenient speed." Ratification of the treaty was completed May 12, 1784.[2] General Sir Guy Carleton withdrew his army from New York City December 3, 1783, but evacuation of the frontier posts was not begun either at that time or at any other time before the year 1796, twelve years after the peace. Therein lay one of the two major issues between the United States and Great Britain. The United States had won the war, but the troops of a defeated power still held American territory, as a gauge, England asserted, for the proper performance of its treaty obligations by the victorious party. Had the United States won its first war only to lose its first peace?

American demands for the execution of the terms

2. The treaty was proclaimed as ratified by the United States, Jan. 14, 1784. It was proclaimed by King George III, April 9, 1784. Exchange of ratifications was completed May 12, 1784; Francis Wharton, *The Revolutionary Diplomatic Correspondence of the United States* (6 vols. Washington, 1889), VI, 757–58, 806.

of the definitive treaty[3] were not severe in construing the words "all convenient speed." It was seven months after the departure of Sir Guy Carleton from New York and two months after the final exchange of ratifications of the treaty when Lieutenant Colonel Hull, bearing a proper commission from the United States Secretary of War, arrived in Canada in July, 1784, to fix details of evacuation. He was told by General Haldimand, the Governor General of British North America, that no orders had been received which would sanction a surrender of the posts. Haldimand vouchsafed to Hull his "private opinion" that one reason why the posts were not relinquished was the harsh treatment which returning Loyalists were receiving in the United States.[4] "That there was a settled policy to refuse delivery of the posts, notwithstanding the terms of the treaty, is evident," wrote Mr. Douglas Brymner, the eminent Canadian archivist.[5] General Haldimand's remark to the effect that the United States was not loyally fulfilling its obligations under the treaty is the first expression of a recrimination— soon to become only too well established in fact—

3. General Washington had tried to arrange for evacuation following signature of the preliminaries of peace and cessation of hostilities. He sent General von Steuben to Canada to arrange with General Haldimand details of evacuation in July, 1783, but the British general, who had received no orders to evacuate, refused to treat on the matter. The Governors of New York and Vermont also had demanded evacuation of positions within their respective states, but Haldimand easily evaded this by stating that Great Britain had treated in the peace negotiations with all the United States jointly and could not discuss the subject with individual states. A. C. McLaughlin, "Western Posts and British Debts," A.H.A., *Ann. Rept. 1894,* 413–14; Haldimand to Washington, Aug. 11, 1783, C.A.,Q, 21, 405.

4. Haldimand to Sydney, July 16, 1784, C.A.,Q, 23, 329.

5. C.A., *Rept. 1890,* xxxii.

which American representatives encountered during
the next ten years whenever delivery of the posts was
demanded. John Adams, first American Minister in
London, constantly met this answer to his statements,[6]
until discouraged and disgusted, he withdrew from the
Court of St. James's and thereby severed diplomatic
relations. "It was on such grounds, therefore," noted
Mr. Brymner, "that the British Government declined to
give up possession of the posts within the boundaries
agreed on by the treaty. The justice or otherwise of
this action may now be determined with more calm-
ness and impartiality than was possible at the time
the question was in agitation." [7]

The real reason for this "settled policy to refuse
delivery of the posts, notwithstanding the terms of the
treaty," lies in the fur trade, at that time the greatest
and most profitable single industry in North America.
Failing to find on the Atlantic coast of North America
the mines of gold and silver which they sought, the
European explorers of the seventeenth century next
devoted their abundant energies to the prosecution of
the fur trade of the interior and the quest for the
Northwest Passage. Together trader and explorer
made their trails across the continent. When finally
the fabled Northwest Passage was pushed off the contemporary maps the men who had paddled and por-
taged through the wilderness and over the mountains
in search of the Western Sea had found in the furs of
North America more riches than ever might have

6. C. F. Adams, ed., *The Works of John Adams* (10 vols. Boston,
1850–56), VIII, 394.
7. C.A., *Rept. 1890,* xxxiii.

floated from China and the spice islands through such a passage.

The conquest of New France by Great Britain in 1760 marked an epoch in the history of the fur trade,[8] which had languished under the restrictions which the French King had laid on the traders and pathfinders of his American domains. Although interrupted by the Seven Years' War and by the Conspiracy of Pontiac which followed the war, the trade speedily developed, under the business instinct and untiring energy of the shrewd Scotch immigrants to Montreal, into the richest commerce of the continent. The first Scotch nabob returning from America in his old age was not an iron-master but a prosperous Montreal fur magnate. He was Sir Alexander Mackenzie,[9] whose well-earned title, fame, and fortune all came from this lucrative business. Within twenty years after the English conquest, that is, by the time of the treaty of peace with the United States, the trade had risen to the amount of £200,000 annually,[10] which is a reasonable estimate of its annual value for the next ten years.[11] Montreal was the depot of export for practically all this

8. G. C. Davidson, *The North West Company* (Berkeley, 1918), p. 3.

9. See his *Voyages through North America* (London, 1801) for the earliest account of the fur trade. See the recent studies: Wayne E. Stevens, *The Northwest Fur Trade, 1763–1800* (Urbana, Ill., 1926), and Harold A. Innis, *The Fur Trade in Canada* (rev. ed. Toronto, 1956).

10. Report to General Haldimand on the Northwest trade, 1780. Br. Museum, Additional MSS, 21,759, printed in appendix to Davidson, pp. 256–59.

11. "Importation of Skins from Canada, 1788," Report to Grenville on the Fur Trade, dated London, Nov. 1789, C.A.,Q, 43,826; Account of the Fur Trade of Canada furnished by John Inglis to Lord Grenville, Mark Lane, May 31, 1790, C.A.,Q, 49, 287; "Memoir in

great traffic. It went exclusively to England.[12] The
peltries were there prepared for the European market.
The commerce furnished huge profits for the Montreal
traders, valuable freight for English navigators, rich
tariffs to the English exchequer, a lucrative turnover
to the London importers. The whole industry fitted
admirably into the mercantile system and the dominant
economic theory of the day. It was a national asset
well worth protecting.

The furs which came down to Montreal were trap-
ped by Indians who roamed the millions of acres between the Ohio River and Lake Athabasca, between
the lower St. Lawrence and the front ranges of the
Rocky Mountains. This magnificent country was being
exploited by a combination of Montreal traders. In
order to eliminate the evils of cut-throat competition
(not always a figurative term in the early rivalries of
the trade) they had amalgamated their individual
interests into the famous North West Company, an
enterprise well remembered if only through the roister-
ing passages of Washington Irving. The principal part
of the fur trade of the interior thus dominated by the
Nor'westers was with Indians who dwelt south of the
newly established American boundary line. Judging

Regard to the Fur Trade, *circa* 1794" in Chatham MSS, Bdl. 346.
These three documents have been printed by Davidson, *North West
Company;* James McGill to Hamilton, Montreal, Aug. 1, 1785, C.A.,Q,
25, 111.

12. "Q. Have we the whole of this Trade, or does any part of it
go to the people of the United States?

"A. We have the whole at present, and we take great pains to
preserve it." Extract from the testimony of Thomas Ainslee before
the Board of Trade, Dec., 1788–Jan., 1789, printed in *North West
Company,* p. 267.

from an estimate made for the British Ministry in 1790, one-half of the annual yield was collected in the "countries to the southward of the Great Lakes." Moreover, furs to the value of £40,000 annually were then coming in from the "Country generally called the North West"—the territory to the south, west, and north of Lake Superior.[13] The product of this country was just beginning to be tapped when the treaty of peace was concluded. These furs came in over the Grand Portage, a necessary link in the connection with the Lake of the Woods across the height of land, to Lake Superior. To their disappointment the men of the North West Company now discovered that the Grand Portage was also included within the American boundary!

Thus if the terms of the treaty should be carried out and the new boundary should be recognized without some provision for the protection of the fur trade the commercial prosperity of all Canada would be threatened. Substitution of American for British garrisons would turn the Indian country over to the process of American settlement and eventually wipe out the richest portion of the fur preserves. It would admit the Americans to the navigation of the Great Lakes. From thence it would not be difficult for them to divert the furs to Albany and New York. Possession by the United States of the Grand Portage meant the possibility of choking off that great artery of commerce to the new Northwest country.[14] All these dangers the

13. "Account of the Fur Trade of Canada furnished by John Inglis to Lord Grenville," May 31, 1790.

14. Benj. Frobisher to Mabane, Montreal, April 19, 1784, *M.P.C.*, XX, 219–22.

traders contemplated. Their importunities against execution of the treaty speedily found the ears of Government.[15] Added to the anxiety of British importers of
American peltries, such objections had great influence
in determining the Ministry to retain the posts. Even
before these petitions began to be formulated, Governor Haldimand realized another difficulty inseparable
from reliquishment of the posts. He dreaded to inform
the Indians dwelling within American territory of the
new boundary line. The land to the north and west of
the Ohio and west of a line drawn from the Allegheny
River to Fort Stanwix in western New York had been
recognized definitely as Indian territory by treaty with
the western tribes before the American Revolution.[16]
Now the Indians beheld it ceded to their enemies, the
Americans. The British Canadian officials found themselves under the necessity of repudiating this colonial
Indian treaty or of failing to fulfill an obligation of
the treaty of peace with the United States.

The Indian allies of Great Britain could not understand the legal abstractions which were assumed by the
negotiators of the treaty of 1783—fine distinctions as
to the nature of a division of empire and the relationship of the sovereignty of civilized nations to the territory of savage tribes. They were likely to regard
transfer to the United States of sovereignty over their
territory as downright betrayal of their interests to
their enemy.[17] Haldimand had no doubt as to the

15. Benj. & Joseph Frobisher to Haldimand, Montreal, Oct. 4, 1784,
C.A., *Rept. 1890*, 50–52.

16. Haldimand to Lord North, June 2, Aug. 20, 1783, C.A.,Q, 21,
229, 388.

17. Brig. Gen. A. Maclean to Haldimand, Niagara, May 18, 1783,
C.A.,B, 103, 175; *M.P.C.*, XX, 117–21.

proper course for England to follow. Because of the economic and political interests of British subjects his recommendations were in favor of the Indians. Persuaded that the Indians would resent the treaty as a piece of treachery, he gave orders to the officers commanding the western posts not to divulge the boundary line when announcing the fact of peace. Despite this caution rumors of the new boundary soon reached the western tribes,[18] much to the uneasiness of British officers residing among them. They could not help sympathizing with their savage allies. They did not consider it impossible that the Indians might prove uncontrollable even to the danger of the British themselves should native interests be betrayed by delivery of the posts. The commanding officer at Fort Niagara was careful to tell the Six Nations not to listen to rumors brought by "evil birds"; the King would still protect the tribes with all his power,[19] an assurance which was incorporated in General Haldimand's instructions to the British Indian agents in the interior.[20]

Despite these forebodings, Governor Haldimand, the subordinate army officers on the frontier, officials of the Indian Department, and the fur traders of the interior expected evacuation of the posts according to the terms of the treaty. This is evident from the correspondence between them immediately after receipt of the preliminaries of peace in Canada. It is equally evident that they hoped for postponement of evacuation

18. Maj. De Peyster to Brig. Gen. Maclean, Detroit, May 17, June 18, 1783, *M.P.C.*, XX, 116, 128.

19. Maclean to Haldimand, May 18, 1783, ibid., 121: "I do from my soul Pity these people and should they commit outrages at giving up the Posts, it would by no means surprise me."

20. Haldimand to Sir J. Johnson, May 26, 1783, ibid., 123.

as a means of easing the dreaded difficulties with the
Indians and the damage to the fur trade.[21]

As early as August 20, 1783, the Governor General
had voiced these fears and hopes and his own reluctance to yield the posts, in a dispatch to Lord North.
The longer evacuation might be delayed, he advised,
the more time the traders would have to get their
merchandise out of the country or to convert it into
furs; meanwhile there would be opportunity to reconcile the Indians to the delivery of the posts and proclamation of the new boundary, "a measure for which
they entertain the greatest abhorrence."

In this dispatch Haldimand included news that the
tribes were forming a general confederacy which might
be used against the British as well as against the
Americans. He made no mention of American infractions of the treaty as a reason for holding the posts.[22]
Rather than alluding to American infractions the
whole Canadian correspondence during these months,
1783–1784, is alive with chagrin at the boundary
which the United States had secured. Letters of British

21. Benj. Frobisher to Adam Mabane, Montreal, April 19, 1784,
ibid., 219. Cf. Haldimand to Robertson, May 6, 1784, ibid., 226. It took
two years from the time goods for the Indian country left Montreal
for them to come back in the shape of furs for shipment to England.
Thus an immediate evacuation of the posts and withdrawal of fur
traders from American territory would mean a total loss of the year's
trade for which the goods were brought into the country and even
the loss of those goods themselves.

22. C.A.,Q, 21, 388. Nine months afterward in a letter to Lord
North, May 12, 1784, Haldimand suggested that evacuation be delayed a year, as a means of prolonging by twelve months the time
granted to Loyalists by the treaty to solicit recovery of their estates
in America. C.A.,Q, 23, 161.

subjects in Canada also are full of lament at the non-chalance or ignorance as to the western country which His Majesty's peace commissioners displayed at Versailles.[23] The embarrassments of the new boundary were thus brought home to the Ministry before there was any question of American violation of the treaty of peace.[24]

The dispatch which laid the foundation of British policy on the frontier for the next ten years was written April 8, 1784, by Lord Sydney, Secretary of State for Home Affairs in the Pitt Cabinet, and addressed to Haldimand. Sydney noted that the second article of the treaty stipulated for evacuation "with all convenient speed," no definite time being fixed. Since the United States had not complied with even one article of the treaty, he maintained that evacuation might be delayed "at least until we are enabled to secure the fur traders in the Interior Country and withdraw their property." [25] The following day, April 9, George III proclaimed ratification of the treaty, promising that "we will sincerely and faithfully perform and observe all and singular the things which are contained in the aforesaid treaty, and that we will never suffer it to be

23. For example, Frobisher to Mabane, April 19, 1784, *M.P.C.,* XX, 219.

24. For direct solicitations of the fur traders to Government see Benj. and Jos. Frobisher to Haldimand. Montreal, Oct. 4, 1784, C.A., *Rept. 1890,* p. 50; Haldimand to Townshend, May 7, 1783, C.A.,Q, 21, 220; unsigned letter to Nepean, Detroit, Sept. 1, 1784, *M.P.C.,* XXIV, 17.

25. C.A.,B, 50, 142. This dispatch must have arrived in Canada by the time Lt. Col. Hull appeared there in July to arrange for delivery of the posts.

violated by any one or transgressed in any manner." [26]

Whatever may have been the original reason for their retention, a convenient excuse for holding the posts soon arose when it became evident that the weak American Confederation was powerless to restrain individual states from putting obstacles in the way of the collection of British debts guaranteed by the treaty. This was an *ex post facto* excuse, as we now know, but a strong one. Even had the treaty been executed punctually and completely by Great Britain it is doubtful whether the Congress of the Confederation would have been able to compel adherence to it. No appreciable time elapsed after ratification by the United States before state laws began to harass the collection of British debts. Before the adoption of the Constitution there was no Supreme Court to declare unconstitutional state legislation violating a treaty. While it is true that both sides failed to execute the treaty, American failure is to be explained by political incapacity to carry out obligations rather than by a secret executive order to disregard the instrument. There was at least an honest effort on the part of Congress to secure obedience to the treaty until it became evident that the posts were not being evacuated.

It is fruitless to attempt to attach the burden of prior infraction to either party. Nevertheless we should not lose sight of the real motive of the British Government in its original refusal to deliver. As Professor Alfred L. Burt so justly comments in the latest review of the whole frontier controversy: "The American

26. Wharton, *Diplomatic Corres.*, VI, 757 n. Technically the United States of course was not bound to carry out the treaty until after formal exchange of ratifications had been effected. Congress, however, proclaimed the treaty as in force, Jan. 14, 1784, as above noted.

object did not extend to the British side of the boundary agreed upon in 1783, whereas the British object lay on the American side of that line." [27]

Once the policy of continued occupation had been adopted, it came to have intimate relations to the campaigns undertaken by the United States Government against the hostile Indians in the Ohio Valley. It gave the authorities in Canada interest in the outcome of this bloody frontier warfare, the result of reluctance of the western tribes to recognize a peace which had left their enemies in possession of their tribal lands. This determination was not unacceptable to the Government of British North America, because of the fact that an American conquest of the Indians would bring the troops of the new republic uncomfortably close to the occupied posts. The reports of the commanding officers of the posts and the correspondence with the home government of Governor Haldimand and his successor, Lord Dorchester, afford abundant testimony to chronic nervousness regarding the possibility of a defeat of the Indians or an unsatisfactory peace between them and the Americans. Either event, it was feared, would be the natural preliminary to occupation of its own posts by the United States, with all the attendant consequences.[28]

27. A. L. Burt, *The United States, Great Britain, and British North America from the Revolution to the Establishment of Peace after the War of 1812* (New Haven, Toronto, 1940), p. 135. See also McLaughlin, "Western Posts and British Debts," A.H.A., *Ann. Rept. 1894*, 418–20.

28. For specific citations see Haldimand to Sydney, Dec. 2, 1784, C.A.,Q, 24-1, 43; same to same, Jan. 23, 1785, ibid., 258; St. Leger to Sydney, Feb. 14, 1785, ibid., 191; Caldwell to Ancrum, Detroit, Sept. 6, 1785, C.A.,Q, 25, 212; Dorchester to Sir J. Johnson, Dec. 14, 1786, C.A.,Q, 27–1, 86; same to Sydney, Jan. 16, 1787, ibid., 34.

"Policy as well as gratitude demands of us an attention to the sufferings and future situation of these unhappy people," Governor Haldimand had written at the close of the Revolution, explaining that during the war the Indians had been receiving provisions and supplies and that to discontinue these at this time would encourage the natives to bite the hand that had fed them. Moreover, if the United States were able to reach a separate agreement with the tribes, the latter might be alienated and rendered useless for defense in case of the fancied ever-imminent American attack on the posts.[29]

It was noticed with concern in Canada that immediately after the proclamation of peace, the United States had announced a policy of conciliation with the western Indians; even before the signature of the definitive treaty of peace, commissioners had been dispatched to the hostile tribes by the Secretary of War, following a resolution by Congress.[30] To say the least, the American commissioners received no cooperation from British officers in the western part of the United States. The commandant at Detroit, having induced them to come into the post where they could be safely under his eyes, maneuvered them quickly out of the settlement before they could read their instructions to the few Indian chieftains who happened to be there. Detroit was "by no means a settlement for American deputies to reside in," he wrote to his superior officer.[31] That officer, Brigadier General Allan Maclean com-

---

29. Haldimand to Townshend, Feb. 14, 1783, C.A.,Q, 21, 184; same to North, Aug. 20, 1783, ibid., 388.

30. Resolution of May 1, 1783, *M.P.C.,* XX, 111.

31. De Peyster to Maclean, Detroit, July 7, 1783, ibid., 138.

manding the western posts, has left a terse and human comment illustrative of the opinion he and his brother officers shared as to American efforts for peace with the natives:

> The Indians get this day from the King's stores the bread that they are to eat tomorrow, and from his magazines the clothing that covers their nakedness: in short they are not only our allies, but are a part of our family; and the Americans might as well (while we are in possession of these Posts) attempt to seduce our children from their duty and allegiance, as to convene and assemble all the Indian nations, without first communicating their instructions to His Majesty's Representative in Canada.[32]

It was soon evident that the peace policy would not be generally accepted. Led by the famous Mohawk chieftain, Joseph Brant, the tribes of the Old Northwest in a loose confederacy repudiated the peace treaties accepted in 1784 by some of the Six Nations. Consent of the whole Indian confederacy was held necessary for the cession of lands. They pointed to the Treaty of Fort Stanwix of 1768 as the only treaty to which the tribes had given unanimous consent.[33]

To this decision the hostile natives were encouraged by the local commandants at the posts, by the highest Canadian officials, and, as we shall see, by the responsible minister of the British Cabinet at Whitehall.

---

32. Maclean to De Peyster, Niagara, July 8, 1783, ibid.
33. W. L. Stone, *Life of Joseph Brant* (2 vols. New York, 1838), II, 245–69; *A.S.P.,I.A.,*I, 10; Max Farrand, "The Indian Boundary Line," *A.H.R.,* X, 782–91.

In handling the native tribes the Government of British North America was at great advantage because of its well-organized Department of Indian Affairs. This department, under the superintendency of Sir John Johnson, son of Sir William Johnson of colonial fame, was a legacy from the pre-Revolutionary administration of the interior country created in 1755 to replace by a uniform imperial control the decentralized method of dealing with the natives through the governments of the individual colonies.[34] During the war the Department had been the instrument by which the cooperation of the Indian allies was stimulated and managed. After the peace its agents continued to wield their influence over the natives north of the Ohio. Its very efficient personnel was composed of survivors of the old colonial department and of Tory renegades and partisan leaders, some of whom feared for their lives to return within patriotic American communities because of popular hatred for inciters of Indian warfare during the late hostilities.[35] The managing of the savages and the weaving of native intrigue opened up a field congenial to the taste of such notorious characters as Alexander McKee and John Butler, who found in it almost unlimited opportunity to indulge their peculiar genius. From Detroit, the great distributing point of the fur trade and the strategic military position of the West, the Canadian Indian Department extended its operations over the Michigan, Indiana, and Ohio country, even over western New York by means of bases at the occupied posts of Niagara and Oswego.

34. C. E. Carter, *Great Britain and the Illinois Country, 1763-1774* (Washington, 1910), pp. 78-81.

35. Clark to Dundas, Quebec, June 13, 1792, C.A.,Q, 59-2, 393.

American readers seldom realize that for years after the winning of independence the agents of a carefully organized branch of the British colonial government received and carried out their orders in territory scores of miles south of the boundary line and among tribes continually and actively hostile to the United States.[36]

When reproached by the natives for the surrender of their lands, the agents of the Indian Department— still awaiting definite instructions on Indian policy— hastened to assure the tribes that the King still cherished their affections and would not abandon them to the resentment of the Americans.[37] Though perfunctorily advising them to desist from hostilities and warning that they could no longer expect the aid of the King, who was now at peace with his former enemy, the Indian Department strove in every possible way to keep the tribes from a peace with the Americans which would yield land north and west of the old line of 1768. Every honest man, declared Sir John Johnson to a delegation of chiefs in 1785, must admire their determination to support their rights against the bad faith and encroachments of the United States. By united action they could succeed, he told them.[38]

A definite policy as to Indian hostilities within the United States was reached by Pitt's Ministry at the time of the visit of Brant to London in the winter of 1785–1786. That energetic and intelligent chieftain

36. For salaried list of the Indian Department, officers and personnel, and stations on American soil, see C.A., Upper Canada Sundries, 1791–1797.

37. Haldimand to Sir J. Johnson, May 26, 1783, *M.P.C.*, XX, 123.

38. Speech of Sir J. Johnson to the Six Nations, at Montreal, Nov. 18, 1785, C.A.,Q, 26–2, 378.

crossed the ocean to ask active aid from England for
the Indian confederacy against the United States and
to present claims for losses incurred by his tribe
of Mohawks during the Revolution. While evading
Brant's request for direct aid Lord Sydney encouraged
the confederacy to "stick to their rights," and, following an interview with Brant, wrote secret instructions to the British representatives at Quebec to guide
their administration of Indian affairs. This dispatch
mirrors British Indian policy for the next several years.
"No open encouragement" was to be given to the
Indians in their hostilities, declared Sydney in these
orders, but it would not be consistent with justice to
leave them to the "mercy of the Americans." As
material means of helping Brant's Indians to stand
firmly enough "to preserve the possession of the Upper
Country and the Fur Trade," Sydney disclosed that
he had promised that chieftain the payment of his
claims.[39]

These instructions from London were carried out
by the Superintendent of Indian Affairs and the under-
officials of the Canadian administration, pending the
arrival of the new Governor General, Lord Dorchester. No encouragement to hostilities had been
given, Lieutenant Governor Hope was able to report
in the summer of 1786.[40]

An examination of the papers of the Indian Department convinces us that this meant no "open encouragement." For example, we read in a letter to Brant from
the Indian Superintendent in 1787:

39. Sydney to Hope, April 6, 1786, C.A.,Q, 26–1, 73.
40. Hope to Sydney, July 1, 1786, C.A.,Q, 26–2, 493.

> Do not suffer an idea to hold a place in your mind, that it will be for your interests to sit still and see the Americans attempt the posts. It is for your sakes chiefly, if not entirely, that we hold them.

The letter went on to state that the American Union was falling to pieces (Shays's Rebellion), and that the eastern states were desirous of returning to British allegiance (a reference to the intrigues of the Vermont separatist party).[41] Though there may have been no "open encouragement," the agents of the Indian Department, working among the tribes in United States territory, promised that the new Governor General would bring ammunition for them.[42] Before the arrival of Dorchester ammunition had been plentifully distributed from the occupied posts. "Provisions," "supplies," and "merchandise" were constantly given out by the Indian Department from its various stations. The nature of such "supplies" is indicated by a "List of merchandize absolutely necessary for the savages depending on Detroit" made out by Lieutenant Colonel De Peyster at that post in 1784. It included "10,000 ball and shot 'A'," "500 lbs. gunpowder 2/3 fine," and "100 riffle guns." Similar items run through the Department's accounts.[43]

Lord Dorchester took possession of his new office with no wish to stir up the natives to warfare against the United States. One of his first acts was to write to Sir John Johnson that he had no desire to "begin a war

41. Sir J. Johnson to Brant, Mar. 22, 1787, Stone, *Brant,* II, 267–69.
42. Butler to Hope ( ? ), Niagara, Oct. 5, 1786, C.A.,Q, 26–2, 594.
43. Memorandum of Col. A. S. De Peyster, *M.P.C.,* XX, 271.

that might involve half the globe." He expressed a
belief that if the Indians were indifferent to the posts
there was little reason for England to hold them,
though if they were attacked "war must be repelled
by war"—·a sentence which had some importance in
subsequent border history.[44] Dorchester had not been
long in his new station before he came to share the
fears of the frontier officials that surrender of the
posts to the Americans would be followed by prostration of the fur trade. He adopted the reasoning of the
Montreal fur merchants and his military subordinates
that control of the Indians and the most profitable industry of the continent depended on British occupation, and he governed the frontier accordingly.[45]

The policy of Great Britain to bolster defense of the
occupied posts by an Indian buffer hostile to the advance of the Americans can be read in another dispatch of Sydney to Dorchester in the spring of 1787.
Considering a movement against the posts as the natural sequel of any successful campaign against the
Indians, Sydney expressed the hope that the tribes
would succeed in holding back their adversaries, for in
case the posts were attacked by the Americans,

> the assistance to be derived from the Indians
> would be extremely desirable. . . . To afford
> them active assistance would be a measure ex-
> tremely imprudent, but at the same time it would
> not become us to refuse them such supplies of
> ammunition as might enable them to defend them-
> selves. I observe by Captain Brant's letter that
> they are in great want of that article, and, cir-

44. Dec. 14, 1786, C.A.,Q, 27–1, 36.
45. Dorchester to Sydney, Jan. 16, 1787, ibid., 34.

cumstances as they are, there can be no objection to furnishing them with a supply, causing it to be done in a way less likely to alarm the Americans, or to induce the Indians to think there is a disposition to excite them to hostile feelings.[46]

Dorchester was instructed five months later that the posts must be held at all costs, recaptured if taken; that the expense of clothing and provisioning the Indians was preferable to loss of the fur trade and the endangering of Quebec, "particularly at a moment when their native assistance may be called for, which may happen if the posts are attacked." [47]

One other factor we must not lose sight of in analyzing the frontier question as it existed at the installation of Washington's Administration. That is the relation to the British Government of the separatist parties of the rising young commonwealths of the American West, Kentucky and Tennessee, and of Vermont, which, though an older community, showed the political attributes and sectional interests common to the newer settlements of the West.

The geography of the West in 1789 explains a separatist tendency on the part of the back-country settlements which it is not always easy to appreciate readily in the twentieth century. The Appalachians and the Green Mountains before the day of rail and motor were barriers far more formidable than the Rockies today. It was actually easier for farmers in western Pennsylvania, on the upper Ohio, to send their heaviest

46. Sydney to Dorchester, April 5, 1787, C.A.,Q, 27–1, 44.
47. Same to same, Sept. 14, 1787, C.A.,Q, 28, 28. This letter is calendared in C.A., *Rept. 1890,* with omission of reference to above quotation.

produce to Philadelphia by way of New Orleans than directly overland.[48] The thousands of miles of easy waterway were preferable to the axle-breaking roads across the mountains. The people of the young commonwealths of Kentucky and Tennessee were altogether dependent on the water carriage afforded by the Mississippi, which Spain controlled at the delta. Jay's proposals to the Spanish Minister, Gardoqui, in 1786, to surrender for twenty-five years the American claim to the free navigation of the river in exchange for commercial privileges in European harbors, valuable only to eastern shipping interests, had been esteemed a significant exhibition of negligence of western interests. Two years later the adoption of the United States Constitution was nearly wrecked in the ratifying convention of Virginia. In that pivotal state the delegates from the Kentucky counties feared to intrust their most vital interest to a remote central government which had already demonstrated itself so careless of the interests of the "men of the western waters." [49]

Under these circumstances it seemed expedient for foreign powers to hold forth to western settlers inducements to loosen their allegiance to the Congress of the Confederation. Spain did this by opening the

48. E. R. Johnson et al., *History of Domestic and Foreign Commerce of the United States* (2 vols. Washington, 1915), I, 205.

49. Jonathan Elliot, *The Debates, Resolutions, and Other Proceedings in Convention, on the Adoption of the Federal Constitution* (6 vols. Washington, 1827–35), II, 127, 266; W. C. Ford, "Charles Pinckney's Reply to Jay, Aug. 16, 1786, regarding a Treaty with Spain," *A.H.R.*, X, 817–27; Monroe to Patrick Henry, Aug. 12, 1786, S. M. Hamilton, ed., *The Writings of James Monroe* (7 vols. New York, 1898–1903), I, 144.

Mississippi at New Orleans to free passage for the tobacco and other exports of the smooth-quilled American apostate, General James Wilkinson, and his friends in Kentucky.[50] England similarly intrigued with the Allen brothers of Vermont, which until 1791 considered itself a sovereign independent state unattached to the United States though its territory was included within the boundaries recognized by the treaty of peace. To the Vermont separatists the British Government granted special commercial privileges for exports and imports by way of the Richelieu River and Lake Champlain, a much easier route to England than by the cumbersome land carriage to the harbors of Massachusetts and New Hampshire. Thus the inhabitants of western and northern Vermont and northeastern New York were enabled to evade in part the restrictions of the English navigation laws encountered by the United States. The story of the intrigues of Ethan, Levi, and Ira Allen with the British Government at Quebec and London and their efforts to use this economic dependence of Vermont on Canada to achieve a political union hardly sustains the popular impression of the hero of Ticonderoga and his kin. There was also a good deal of well-covered intrigue going on between British agents in the Ohio Valley and dissatisfied westerners, to whom was held forth the lure of a commercial connection with Canada by way of the navigation of the Great Lakes and the St. Lawrence at

50. C.A., *Rept. 1890*, 99, 100, 107; Chatham MSS, Bdl. 343; F. J. Turner, "English Policy toward America in 1790–1791," *A.H.R.*, VII, 706–35, VIII, 78–86, gives abundant references in footnotes; see also W. R. Shepherd, "Wilkinson and the Beginnings of the Spanish Conspiracy," *A.H.R.*, IX, 490–506.

a time when Congress did not seem anxious to open the
navigation of the Mississippi.[51] This argument had the
same practical appeal for a minority of these restless
frontiersmen that the economic inducement of the
Champlain water route had for ambitious intriguers
in Vermont.

That these western communities would continue to
pull within the weak orbit of the American Confederation was by no means certain. Secret observers employed by the Foreign Office and stationed in the
United States studded their dispatches to Downing
Street with prophecies of approaching dissolution of
the American Union,[52] prophecies which most students
of the "critical period" would agree were well founded.
In this event the secret connections already fostered
in the back-country settlements of the United States
might prove an attraction strong enough to bring
back these communities within the sovereignty of the
Empire, while control already existing over the Indians and the country north of the Ohio had never
been released by Great Britain. The possibility was
not small that because of sheer inability to govern
themselves and to reconcile their various interests, the
United States might dissolve their feeble union and

51. For documents showing relation between Vermont separatists
and Great Britain, see *A.H.R.*, XXI, 547–61. For the Ohio Valley, see
W. H. Smith, ed., *The St. Clair Papers: The Life and Public Services
of Arthur St. Clair* (2 vols. Cincinnati, 1882), I, 156, II, 101–06;
Charles Gayarré, *History of Louisiana* (4 vols. 4th ed. New Orleans,
1903), III, 235–37; Theodore Roosevelt, *The Winning of the West*
(4 vols. New York, 1899–1900), III, 129; C.A., *Rept. 1890,* 124; W. P.
Palmer, *Calendar of Virginia State Papers* (11 vols. Richmond, 1875–
93), IV, 555–56.

52. See reports of the British secret agent, "P. Allaire," or "P.A.,"
alias "R.D.," scattered through P.R.,F.O., 4, 4–11.

slip back, section by section, within the dominion of the King of Great Britain.

Such was the situation of the Anglo-American frontier when George Washington took oath in 1789 as first President of the United States. One of the tasks which he faced was to emancipate the American hinterlands. They must be released from the control which a foreign power, beaten in war, had nevertheless been able to maintain in the peace that followed, because of the pitiful military weakness and political impotency of the American Confederation. Another task of Washington's Administration in the field of foreign affairs was to set aside the sinister influence of foreign intrigue in the American West and to fasten to the central government the allegiance of those remote communities.

Before we proceed to trace the diplomatic negotiations in which this policy was put forward, we must notice, in the next chapter, the other equally important field of Anglo-American relations, the commerce of the Atlantic.

# CHAPTER 2

# Anglo-American Commerce

WITH the return of peace the former colonists eagerly looked forward to the rewards of hard-won independence. One of the greatest, they confidently expected, would be freedom from the shackles of the celebrated Navigation Laws which had made the island of England the European depot for colonial produce and had fenced in the colonies as closed markets for English manufactures. In independence the Americans beheld the open sesame to bounteous commercial expansion.[1] They believed that automatically it would bring liberation from the restrictions of the British mercantilist system and would open on most favorable terms the markets of the world. In this fond expectation they were destined to disappointment. European nations extended not very much more favorable commercial privileges to the United States as an independent nation than they had given to it as a British dominion.[2]

1. This expectation can be read in the instructions of Congress to the Commissioners sent in 1783 to negotiate treaties of commerce with the nations of Europe. Wharton, *Diplomatic Corres.*, VI, 717, 802.

2. France allowed to the United States most-favored-nation privileges by virtue of the terms of the treaty of commerce of 1778; American ships could enter French harbors with goods not generally prohibited. A royal ordinance of 1784 opened the French West Indies to foreign ships bringing enumerated goods to specified ports, products which included the principal American exports to the West

True, the new republic was free from the restrictions which the Navigation Laws had placed on its exports to countries other than Great Britain, but it was at the same time stripped of the economic advantages attaching to the British Empire; for example, the prosperous unrestricted traffic of ante-bellum days with the sugar islands of the British West Indies. Moreover, it was soon evident that the greater part of American foreign commerce continued to be with England, as it had been before the war, this despite the fact that the former colonies were now foreign to the Empire and free, supposedly, from the working of the Navigation Laws.

Until Jay's Treaty went into operation in 1796 there was no commercial treaty between the United States and Great Britain. Until that year, therefore, the com-

Indies. A large portion of the ships plying to the French islands were American. They were allowed to take back rum and molasses, so essential to the prosperity of New England, and these exports were encumbered with only nominal duties. By France there was no discrimination, direct or indirect, against American shipping either in her European or colonial dominions, but France took only a small share of the total American trade. See Isambert de Crusy Jourdan, *Recueil général des anciennes lois françaises* (29 vols. Paris, 1822–33). XXVII, 459–64. The imports which were permitted into the French West Indies were: wood, coal, cattle on the hoof, pickled beef, salt fish, rice, maize, green and tanned leather, skins, tar, and pitch. A duty of 3 livres per cwt. was levied on salt fish to form a fund to be given as premium to the French fisheries for cod and other fish. In times of dearth the colonial governments might suspend the law. See also Act of the King's Council of State for the encouragement of commerce with the United States, Dec. 29, 1787.

Treaties of commerce were negotiated by Congress with Prussia and Holland, both of whom granted most-favored-nation privileges; but the trade with Prussia was very small and the Dutch tariffs were uniformly high to all nations. Report by Jefferson on regulations affecting American commerce, *A.S.P.,F.R.,* I, 300.

merce of the two countries was controlled by the
municipal laws of each government. In England an
Act of Parliament of April, 1783, renewed commercial
intercourse on a peace footing and made it subject to
orders-in-council issued under authority of that act.
The nature of these orders may best be seen in the
general order of December, 1783, which codified such
orders as had been issued previously. It permitted to
come into England unmanufactured goods or merchandise, the importation of which was already allowed by
law, except oil and other whale products, and in addition naval stores produced in the United States, for
the supply of which the British navy was obliged to
depend on foreign sources. Such goods might be carried to England directly in British or in American ships
on the same terms as if from a British colony—a
status similar to pre-Revolutionary conditions. To
counteract the direct shipments to Europe of American
tobacco, which were now possible, it was provided that
the product might be admitted and warehouse free of
all duty in England if destined for re-exportation—a
provision designed to retain for the English jobber the
turnover profit which had been his in the colonial period when the weed could reach the European con-
sumer only through his hands.[3] The laws controlling
trade between the United States and the remaining
British provinces in North America may be reviewed
conveniently in the summary of them which was incorporated into an act of 1788. This allowed imports

3. 23 Geo. III, c. 39; see orders-in-council of May 14, June 6, July 2,
1783, in W. L. Grant, James Munro, A. W. Fitzroy, *Acts of the Privy
Council of England, Colonial Series* (6 vols. Hereford and London,
1908–12), V, 527–32; and John Reeves, *A History of the Law of Shipping and Navigation* (London, 1792), pp. 341–77, Appendix I.

exclusively in British ships of tobacco, provisions, and naval stores from the United States into the British West Indies. No other products of the United States could be received by the islands. Even these enumerated ones could not be brought in American vessels; and, of course, no exports could be taken thence by Americans, except salt from Turk's Island, on which a heavy export duty was levied. Thus were American ships which in colonial days had plied a prosperous traffic with the British West Indies now excluded as a result of that independence which had been so extolled as a boon to freedom of trade. To make sure that exclusion should not in fact be frustrated by ferrying across from the Dutch and French colonies (to which American ships and goods were admitted) of products of the United States, the importation from foreign islands of the enumerated goods—tobacco, naval stores, provisions—was prohibited absolutely, though in emergencies the local governors might suspend this prohibition to allow such importation if in British ships by British subjects.[4] Similarly the trade of Canada was restricted to British ships and no importation of American goods was allowed except under special executive proclamation in time of emergency.[5] These laws always were limited to one year in duration but were annually extended by acts of Parliament and subordinate orders-in-council.[6]

Thus during the first ten years of independence the

4. 28 Geo. III, c. 6.
5. 25 Geo. III, c. 1.
6. Earl of Crawford, ed., *Bibliotheca Lindesiana* . . . *Handlist of Proclamations Issued by Royal and Other Constitutional Authorities, 1714–1910*, Vol. VIII (Wigan, Gt. Brit., 1913); *Journal of House of Commons* for annual acts.

greater part of the foreign commerce of the United
States was subject to the prescription of ephemeral and
uncertain regulations of the British Government whose
sole aim was its own advantage. Legislation of this
temporary character was necessary, it was asserted
in England, because the divided nature of the American Government provided no authority for the making of national treaties of commerce.[7] If Americans
were irritated at such trade laws and disappointed in
the first commercial fruits of independence, loyal
Englishmen regarded it as quite proper requital for a
people who had dared to withdraw from the Empire.

The Navigation Laws were the concern of all true
sons of Britain. Primarily their purpose was protection
of national sea power and not the convenience of
foreign nations. English observers were careful to point
out that most American products coming into England
proper were much favored in contrast to the products
of European nations, because they enjoyed the same
footing as imports from the British colonies, though
in truth the reason for this was not indulgence for the
United States but solicitude for cheap supply of raw
materials for British factories. Whatever the theory
of the matter, the exclusion of American ships and
goods from the British West Indies was a blow to
merchants and shipowners of the United States. They
demanded that the laws of their own country be shaped
to retaliate effectively.

Retaliation was soon resorted to by some of the

7. Report of the committee of the Privy Council on trade between the
British dominions and America (1791), in *Collection of Interesting and
Important Reports and Papers on Navigation and Trade* (London,
1807), p. 50.

several American states. The states had not hesitated to legislate against the commerce of each other; it was easy for many of them in their exasperation to retaliate against England. Massachusetts, New Hampshire, and Rhode Island actually prohibited British vessels or those owned by British subjects to load any goods or merchandise the product or growth of the United States, under penalty of seizure and condemnation. Other states contented themselves with retaliatory tariff and tonnage duties; Maryland and North Carolina put a tax of a shilling a ton on all foreign shipping except British, which paid four shillings; Virginia bore twice as heavily on British as on other foreign craft; Pennsylvania at one time laid five shillings sixpence on ships of all nations not having treaties of commerce with the United States, which principally hit Great Britain; the New England states, except Connecticut, all charged sixpence a bushel on salt imported in British vessels, a retaliation against the Turk's Island export duties on salt; in New York and Maryland the cargoes of such ships paid twice the duty placed on other foreign cargoes; and Virginia also levied heavier duties on British than on other imports.[8]

These retaliations were not effective, because they lacked uniformity and unanimity. There were always among the thirteen one or more states, such as Connecticut, which would receive British commerce free of duty at a time when the others were excluding it from their harbors or heavily discriminating against it in their efforts to force a satisfactory commercial agreement with England. John Adams, while first

8. For summary of these state laws, see ibid., pp. 55–58.

American Minister in London, continually urged the
adoption of some uniform system of retaliation. The
action of Massachusetts in prohibiting exports in
British ships was of more avail, he stated, than any
amount of diplomatic representation.[9] Attempts were
made by several of the states to confer on Congress
power to legislate during a period of fifteen years on
commercial affairs. Massachusetts, Pennsylvania, and
Rhode Island passed resolutions making over this
power after consent should have been received from
the nine states. The rivalry and petty bickering among
the thirteen made impossible the adoption of any such
amendment to the Articles of Confederation. This
unstable commercial condition, as is well known, was
one of the chief arguments for the formation and
adoption of a new, national constitution. In the words
of Washington in 1788 after the Philadelphia convention: "It would be idle to think of making commercial
regulations on our part. One State passes a prohibitory
law respecting some article, another State opens wide
the avenue for its admission. One Assembly makes a
system, another Assembly unmakes it." [10]

The impotency of the confederation in this respect
was fully recognized in England. "It will not be an
easy matter to bring the American States to act as
a nation," observed contemptuously one of the most
acute and influential students of Anglo-American commerce; "they are not to be feared as such by us. It
must be a long time before they can engage, or will

9. Adams to Jay, June 17, 26, July 19, 1785, *Works,* VIII, 268–83.
10. W. C. Ford, ed., *The Writings of George Washington* (14 vols.
New York, 1889–92), XI, 254.

concur in any material expence. . . . We might as
reasonably dread the effects of combinations among the
German as among the American States, and depricate
the resolves of the Diet, as those of Congress." [11]
English opinion assumed that the United States were
not and never could be united, wrote Adams.[12]

In England there were two schools of opinion as to
the proper regulation of the Anglo-American trade.
One of these followed the ideas of Adam Smith, who
then had no wide influence. By attacking what he considered the fallacy of colonial and commercial monopoly, Adam Smith made the first hole in the great
dykes of the mercantile system. He approved the
Navigation Laws in so far as they furnished a nursery
for seamen and bulwarked British sea power, but when
he applied his commercial liberalism and the lucidity
of his powerful mind to questions of American commerce he could not defend those laws in their entirety.
Immediately after peace with America, Adam Smith
expressed himself in favor of unrestricted commercial
intercourse. Admit the United States to the West
Indies on the same terms as before the war, he advised,
remedying as they might occur any resulting inconveniences. "The lumber and provisions of the United
States are more necessary to our West India Islands
than the rum and sugar of the latter are to the former." To give any extraordinary encouragement or discouragement to the trade of any country more than to
that of another was a "complete piece of dupery" by

11. Lord Sheffield, *Observations on the Commerce of the American
States* (6th ed. London, 1784), pp. 245, 246.
12. *Works,* VIII, 290.

which the interest of the nation was sacrificed to some particular class of traders.[13]

It was apparently with some such theory that William Pitt, who was a close student of the *Wealth of Nations*,[14] introduced into Parliament his trade bills early in 1783, bills which would have established intercourse between the United States and Great Britain, including the colonies, on terms of entire equality. This liberal-minded proposal immediately stirred up protest from the shipowners of the Empire and from the American Loyalists settled in Canada, who wanted a monopoly of supplying the West Indies. The opposition was too strong for Pitt. Several times amended, the bill was finally killed and restrictive legislation enacted in its place.[15] When Pitt came to power in 1784 he did not again take up the subject. John Adams describes a noteworthy interview in which the young Prime Minister insisted that the navigation system of Great Britain had to be preserved.[16] This victory of the "shopkeepers of the nation" over Pitt's attempt at commercial liberalism was a triumph over the ideas of Adam Smith. In regard to foreign commerce the great theorist was half a century ahead of his times; as to

13. Adam Smith, *An Inquiry into the Nature and Causes of the Wealth of Nations* (2 vols. 1st ed. London, 1776), II, 190–224; Adam Smith to Mr. Eden, Dec. 15, 1783, R. Eden, ed., *The Journal and Correspondence of Lord Auckland* (4 vols. London, 1861–62), I, 64; A. T. Mahan, *Sea Power in Its Relations to the War of 1812* (2 vols. Boston, 1905), I, 49.

14. W. H. Lecky, *A History of England in the Eighteenth Century* (8 vols. London, 1878–90), V, 36.

15. W. C. Ford, ed., *Report of a Committee of the Lords of the Privy Council . . .* (Washington, 1888), pp. 64–76; E. C. Burnett, "London Merchants on American Trade, 1783," *A.H.R.*, XVIII, 769–80.

16. *Works*, VIII, 306.

colonial policy more than a hundred years in advance.

The controversy over Pitt's bills crystallized the other school of opinion, dominated by the writings of Lord Sheffield. Following his lead a group of publicists in numerous tracts opposed the gratuitous liberalism of Pitt's bills and stressed the disadvantages which would follow further extension of privileges to the United States. These writers based their arguments on the mercantile theory of commercial monopoly and upon present expediency. It was their belief that Parliament had but to "sit still" and do nothing and the Empire would retain as much of the American trade as was for its interest to keep.[17] By "prudent management" few of the advantages of the trade of the former colonies would be lost, while the cost of their defense had disappeared. Prudent management consisted in holding steadfastly to the Navigation Laws and relying on the community of Anglo-American civilization to keep the bulk of American trade in the old colonial channels. The Sheffieldites recognized the overwhelming affinity of the mother country with American merchants. They pointed out that American customs, traditions, religion, and language were all similar to those of England, that in the competition for American trade there was inestimable advantage in the bonds of that empire of culture "as wide as Shakespere's soul." Prudent management could retain the profitable exploitation of a commercial situation which was already sufficiently favorable to England.

One of the advantages of this situation was the credit system. Sheffield declared that British merchants were the only ones able to extend sufficient credit to

17. Sheffield, *Observations,* p. 157.

capture American orders. Some of them, in fact, had already overstretched their transatlantic accounts and were so involved that he doubted whether it were wise to cultivate too close relations with purchasers who could not pay in specie.[18] The trading correspondence of the time well reflects Sheffield's doubts, in the hesitation of British merchants to extend more credit in the United States. For the first few years after the peace, when so many prewar debts lay unpaid and cash was scarce, only merchants with the highest-class credentials could buy in England.[19]

Credit was hard to get in England. It could not be had elsewhere. With sad results French merchants had loaded cargoes for the United States; for, refusing to extend the necessary long-term credit, they had soon become involved in the maelstrom of financial entanglement that followed the American Revolution.

18. Sheffield, *Observations,* p. 248.

19. For example, a London firm, because of intimate knowledge of the integrity of a Newport correspondent, is induced against its rule of business to fill an order, "notwithstanding we have made a determination not to open up any new account in America that requires any credit whatsoever." Their agent in the United States was instructed to recommend no new person for credit. A commercial house in Bristol, beginning a business with an American firm in 1786, describes the situation thus: "Numberless have been the applications made to us to ship goods to different parts of America, but hitherto we have declined executing a single order, knowing the difficulty which people there must labor under in making their remittances, however well inclined they may be; but the knowledge we have of Mr. Wright and the great regard he has for our interest, will occasion our executing with much pleasure the order you have sent us." Lane, Son, and Frazer to Christopher Champlain, London, Mar. 30, 1786; Prothero and Claxton to Christopher Champlain, Bristol, Jan. 23, 1786. In this latter letter it is stated that the insurance on American bottoms is $3\frac{1}{2}$ guineas per cent, on British bottoms 2 per cent. Westmore Papers, Mass. Hist. Soc.

British credit cut away what little trade they might try to secure. American tastes refused to be converted to French goods. During his American exile Talleyrand noticed this and later expounded the subject in a pamphlet written in Paris. In the Anglo-American trade the payment of the first debt, he said, brought credit for the second, the interest of which was gained from the profit on the next order as well as on the former one. The first debt established a connection between the English merchant and the American correspondent against which it was hard to compete. The merchant feared that if he failed to send goods he would overwhelm a debtor whose prosperity was his only security. The American buyer was afraid of quitting a creditor with whom he had too many old accounts to settle.[20] Confronted by these discouragements, scarcely a French merchant had embarked successfully on the American trade.[21]

Turning from the monopoly of long credits, Sheffield exultantly pointed to the superiority and cheapness

20. C. M. Talleyrand-Périgord, *Memoir Concerning the Commerical Relations of the United States with England* (London, 1806), p. 34. For other French observations on American commerce see J. P. Brissot de Warville, *Nouveau Voyage dans les États-Unis* (3 vols. Paris, 1791), which explains the English monopoly of American commerce and analyzes in detail (Vol. III), as does Sheffield, the articles of the American trade and how they might be captured for French merchants.

21. The American *chargé d'affaires* in France, writing to the Secretary of State as to the attitude of the National Assembly, states that body considered American commerce as much less important than they would at some future time. The experience of seven years accounted for this lack of enthusiasm. "They are supported in this opinion by many of their merchants, who tell them that there is no instance of a French house having undertaken that commerce, without losing by it." Short to Jefferson, Oct. 21, 1790, *A.S.P.,F.R.,* I, 121.

of English goods and the supremacy of English skill
and ingenuity in manufacturing, advantages which Talleyrand also acknowledged. These qualities would
compel Americans to buy in England whether or not
they had a treaty of commerce. That American ships
were permitted to carry goods only to England was
enough. Sheffield indulged in a long analysis of the
different articles of American commerce with a view to
English control of the trade. For example, some of the
goods sold in America would meet no competition by
producers anywhere outside of England. Such included
wool, iron and steel manufactures, clothing, shoes,
glassware, copper goods, cordage, drugs, books. England could not supply wines and brandy, he admitted,
but consoled himself with the fact that there appeared
to be little consumption of brandy in the United States,
the inhabitants being inveterate rum-drinkers. He
further stated that British legislation could control
channels of American exportation, to the interests of
the Empire. Products of the American whale fisheries,
for instance, should be excluded from England so as to
encourage the maintenance of a British whaling fleet
as a nursery for seamen. American lumber and grain
should be shut out of the British West Indies in order
to furnish a market for similar Canadian products. On
the other hand, Government ought to allow the free importation of naval stores, indispensable to the British
navy, as well as tobacco, rice, fur and peltries, flaxseed,
pot and pearl ash, etc., in order to prevent the loss of
their profits to the English middleman.[22]

The great question of all English economic speculation was that of the West India Islands. It was there

22. *Observations*, pp. 7–120.

that the shippers and navigators of the United States demanded unrestricted trading privileges with the British colonies It was there that the planters cried for permission to import American provisions and lumber. They saw themselves overwhelmed by the competition of the French and Dutch islands to which American provisions and lumber went freely and cheaply in vessels of the country in which they were produced.[23] The scanty products of Canada, arriving in British ships which made the three-cornered voyage, England to Canada, to the West Indies, to England, cost enormously more than the products of the United States so easily landed at the other sugar islands. The planters considered direct trading with the United States in American bottoms vitally necessary. Because they could pay for their imports only with their produce they naturally desired also to be permitted to sell directly to the United States, especially since they had no adequate market in Europe. The complaints of the planters were directly antagonistic to the theory of the Navigation Laws, which diverted to England the exports of the colonies and commanded exclusively British ships for the colonial carrying trade for reasons of national security and the prosperity of English merchants.[24]

Such a petition was duly forwarded to London and referred to a committee of the Privy Council which advised against opening the West Indies to foreign commerce. It argued that exclusive and reciprocal commerce

23. Representation of a Committee of West Indian Merchants held at the London Tavern, Nov. 26, 1783, P.R.O.,F.O., 4, 3.

24. Bryan Edwards, *The History, Civil and Commercial, of the British Colonies in the West Indies* (2 vols. London, 1793), II, 496–501.

between the different colonies and the mother country
if properly conducted would meet all demands of ordinary times. It was enough that the planters already
could import provisions, lumber, and live stock from
the United States if in British bottoms.[25] The committee denied that the number of available craft was in-
sufficient, and advised, inconsistently, that the colonies
would do well to build ships to put into a trade which
by law was reserved to British vessels. There is little
doubt to one who studies the report that it was in-
fluenced throughout by the erudite and scholarly work
of Lord Sheffield, *Observations on the Commerce of
the American States,* which had first appeared in 1783
and quickly went through several editions. The reasoning of the Lords of the Privy Council followed un-
swervingly the path of his arguments. To those who
lived in England instead of the British West India
Islands, who sold manufactures instead of sugar and
molasses, who depended for their existence not on
slaves and provisioning them but on a proper equipment of well-armed and well-manned ships-of-the-line,
the logic of Sheffield, exponent *par excellence* of the
mercantilist theory, was irresistible, despite the striking
lesson of the American Revolution.[26] If Sheffield him-

25. Report of a Committee of the Privy Council, May 31, 1784, in
*Collection of Interesting and Important Reports,* pp. 1–43.

26. John Stevenson wrote in 1784, in his *Address to Brian Edwards,
Esq.,* p. 90: "Whoever deeply considers the national importance of our
manufactures, our ship-carpenters and our seamen, must wonder how
any Briton can openly attempt to reduce their numbers: but his
astonishment must be greatly increased, by seeing our West Indian
planters and merchants straining every nerve to effect that ruinous
purpose!" There were some pamphleteers who championed the cause
of the planters. The most powerful of these was Bryan Edwards, who
had lived long and observed sharply in the islands. The fruit of his

self admitted that the interest on the debt incurred in the American Revolution was double the annual value of English manufactures sent to those colonies,[27] no one feared that the feeble West India plantations would cause Britain to pile up another such debt.

Sheffield shaped the opinion of the British public and the policy of the Government. "The Navigation Act, the palladium of Britain," wrote his intimate friend, the historian Gibbon, "was defended, and perhaps, saved by his pen, and he proves, by the weight of fact and argument, that the mother-country may survive and flourish after the loss of America." [28]

Any commercial liberalism that may have existed in 1783 was soon smothered by the multitude of tracts and newspaper articles that flooded England, grandiloquently extolling the Navigation Laws and warning against any lessening of their rigor in favor of the United States, which now was a foreign nation and ought to be treated as such. The United States, contended these writers, had no equivalent to offer in return for commercial favors, and its economic position

---

observations was the excellent *History of the British Colonies in the West Indies*. See also his *Thoughts on the Late Proceedings of Government Respecting the Trade of the West India Islands with the United States of North America* (London, 1784). Sheffield denied that the planters suffered. Professor Channing found a note in the Sheffield Papers in the John Carter Brown Library at Providence, R. I., which asserts that Jamaica was almost twice as prosperous in 1786 as in 1776. Edward Channing, *A History of the United States* (6 vols. New York, 1905–25), III, 418. For other tracts in favor of free intercourse see J. G. Kemeys, *Free and Candid Reflections Occasioned by the Late Additional Duties on Sugar and Rum* (London, 1783) ; *A Free and Candid Review, of a Tract, Entitled* [Lord Sheffield's] *"Observations on the Commerce of the American States"* (London, 1784).

27. *Observations*, p. 329 n.

28. Edward Gibbon, *Autobiography* (World Classics ed.), p. 206.

was such that it could take no legal steps without promoting the commercial interests of Great Britain. Let the American people refuse, if indeed they could enforce such a prohibition, to allow their exports (that is, such of them as were permitted by England) to be sent to the British West Indies in British ships and they would cripple their own market and place a bounty on the produce of Nova Scotia and Canada. Did they place a high tax on imports from England, as consumers of necessities they themselves would have to pay the tax.[29] They were bound by the ties of custom and the necessities of the situation. John Adams wrote home bitterly: "Now, the boast is, that our commerce has returned to its old channels, and that it can follow in no other; now, the utmost contempt of our commerce is freely expressed in pamphlets, gazettes, coffee-houses, and in common street talk." [30]

The influence of the Sheffieldites impels us to inquire into the comparative value to the United States and to Great Britain of the Anglo-American commerce, for these economic factors might be expected to affect the diplomatic history of the two nations.

To the United States the trade was vitally important. It composed by far the greater part of the total volume of American commerce. The precise percentage which Great Britain shared of the total trade of the United States cannot be determined because American customs records do not begin until 1789, and the

29. G. Chalmers, *Opinions on Interesting Subjects of Public Law and Commercial Policy Arising from American Independence* (London, 1784), pp. 126–40 ff.

30. *Works,* VIII, 289.

English statistics have been destroyed by fire.[31] In 1790 of the total American exports valued at $20,194,794 there were sent to British ports $9,246,562; but of a total value of $15,388,409 of imports paying *ad valorem* duties $13,797,168 were from Britain,[32] that is, about ninety per cent. These last figures do not show comparisons with the whole of American imports of that year, because there were other imports, value not estimated, which paid specific duties. If England possessed this amount of the trade in 1790, it is fair to assume that she held at least such a proportion in the six years preceding 1789. Of shipping amounting to 90,420 tons clearing from ports in the British Isles for the United States in 463 ships in 1790, 50,979 tons went in 245 British ships: 39,441 tons were classed as in 218 American vessels. Of 109,431 tons entering from America, 64,197 tons were in 312 British ships, and 246 American ships carried 45,234 tons.[33] The trade to Great Britain, restricted as it was, thus continued over seventy-five per cent of all the foreign commerce of the United States. British writers were not wrong when they concluded that the United States could not prosper without it. Moreover, British ships carried over half the commerce between the two countries.

If England dominated American commerce, the

31. J. G. McCulloch, *Dictionary of Commerce* (London, 1871), pp. 726–27; Henry Atton and H. H. Holland, *The King's Customs* (2 vols. London, 1908–10), Introduction.

32. *A.S.P.,Commerce and Navigation,* I, 34–35. Exports for the Year Ending 1790.

33. *Collection of Interesting and Important Reports and Papers,* Supplement XXIV, p. ccx.

United States was the greatest single foreign customer of England. The ravages of fire have hindered any accurate information to establish this fact; but the writer of this study, made curious by the great public interest in the subject, as shown by the contemporary pamphleteers, examined the public papers of William Pitt in a search for evidence. Happily Pitt left copies, now preserved in the Chatham Manuscripts in the

RELATION OF THE AMERICAN TRADE TO TOTAL BRITISH COMMERCE, 1788–1794, INCLUSIVE

A. *Exports and Imports*

|  | 1788 | | | 1789 | | | 1790 | | |
|---|---|---|---|---|---|---|---|---|---|
|  | £ | s | d | £ | s | d | £ | s | d |
| Total British Exports | 17,472,283 | 8 | 3 | 19,333,565 | 5 | 9 | 20,120,121 | 17 | 2 |
| Total British Exports to U. S.[1] | 1,886,142 | 2 | 10 | 2,525,299 | 9 | 2 | 3,431,778 | 17 | 7 |
| Total British Exports to Greatest Foreign Customer other than U. S.[2] | (Germany) 1,473,309 | 1 | 9 | (Holland) 1,636,063 | 4 | 9 | (Germany) 1,694,522 | 8 | 5 |
| Total to British West Indies[3] | 1,684,038 | 8 | 11 | 1,695,975 | 2 | 6 | 1,877,211 | 12 | 3 |
| Total British Imports | 18,027,170 | 1 | 3 | 17,821,170 | 1 | 3 | 19,130,886 | 5 | 3 |
| Total British Imports from U. S. | 1,023,789 | 13 | | 1,050,199 | 4 | | 1,191,072 | 1 | 9 |
| Total British Imports from Russia[4] (the only greater vendor to Great Britain) | 1,916,221 | 8 | 9 | 1,471,251 | 14 | | 1,710,374 | 4 | 10 |
| Total from British West Indies | 4,053,154 | 8 | 3 | 3,876,506 | 9 | 3 | 3,854,204 | 12 | 7 |

B. *Exports of British Manufactures*

|  | 1788 | | | 1789 | | | 1790 | | |
|---|---|---|---|---|---|---|---|---|---|
| Total Exports of British Manufactures | 12,724,719 | 17 | 9 | 13,779,506 | 2 | 6 | 14,921,084 | 9 | 7 |
| Total Exports of British Manufactures to U. S. | 1,682,588 | 5 | 1 | 2,301,194 | | | 3,178,594 | 19 | 9 |
| Total Exports of British Manufactures to Greatest Foreign Customer other than U. S. | (France) 884,100 | 7 | 1 | (Germany) 858,443 | | | (Italy, including Venice) 803,884 | 15 | 7 |
| Total Exports of British Manufactures to British West Indies | 1,467,938 | 12 | 8 | 1,490,943 | 5 | 8 | 1,697,156 | 1 | 7 |

1. The exports to America, in striking contrast to those of the biggest European customer, comprised almost wholly "British manufactures." The amount of "foreign merchandise" included in the total exports to the United States was: 1789, £224,105/5/6; 1790, £253,183/17/10; 1791, £295,676/18/4; 1792, £296,591; 1793, £241,956; 1794, £270,682/10/4.
2. Of these exports to Germany from England, £4,309,695/3/4 was "foreign merchandise," representing entrepot traffic. In 1793, the "foreign merchandise" exported from England to Germany was £1,764,221/10; in 1792, £1,327,970/15/6; in 1791, £1,111,532/11/11; in 1790, £902,920/13/4; in 1789 (Holland), £835,464/7/10. The increased exports to "Germany," in 1794, must be regarded as due in all probability to trade with France by way of German states, avoiding British prohibitions against trading with the enemy.
3. As in the case of the United States, the exports from Great Britain to the British West Indies were almost wholly "British manufactures." Of the total exports thence each year, the "foreign merchandise" was: 1789, £205,031/16/10; 1790, £180,055/10/8; 1791, £221,929/11/11; 1792, £233,665/13/2; 1793, £247,943/7/7; 1794, £531,172/6/1.

Public Record Office, of customs receipts for the years 1788–1794, precisely the years which interest us here. These tabulations were made for the Prime Minister by the Inspector-General of the Customs. We cannot overemphasize their importance to this study. They are apparently the only statistics that remain to demonstrate the real importance to the British Empire of the American trade. Immediately below are set forth in

| 1791 £ | s | d | 1792 £ | s | d | 1793 £ | s | d | 1794 £ | s | d | 1795 £ | s | d |
|---|---|---|---|---|---|---|---|---|---|---|---|---|---|---|
| 22,731,995 | 7 | 3 | 24,905,200 | 3 | 5 | 20,390,180 | 8 | 10 | 26,340,699 | 15 | 4 | 27,270,553 | | 5 |
| 4,225,448 | 11 | | 4,271,418 | 9 | 3 | 3,514,681 | 10 | 11 | 3,859,518 | 7 | 2 | | | |
| (Germany) 1,889,745 | 15 | 1 | (Germany) 2,139,111 | 1 | 6 | (Germany) 2,482,695 | | | (Germany) 5,943,569 | 15 | 10 | | | |
| 2,530,055 | 15 | 6 | 2,784,310 | 9 | 5 | 2,540,762 | 6 | 8 | 3,741,285 | 5 | 9 | | | |
| 19,669,782 | 13 | 7 | 19,659,358 | 6 | 7 | 19,256,717 | 9 | 8 | 22,288,894 | | 5 | | | |
| 1,194,232 | 16 | 3 | 1,083,707 | 9 | | 904,040 | 7 | 8 | 625,723 | 13 | 8 | | | |
| 1,548,677 | 12 | 6 | 1,708,671 | 9 | 5 | 1,804,025 | 12 | 11 | 1,789,448 | 7 | 9 | | | |
| 3,651,611 | 6 | 6 | 4,128,047 | 5 | 1 | 4,339,613 | 16 | 9 | 5,294,742 | 6 | 9 | | | |

| £ | s | d | £ | s | d | £ | s | d | £ | s | d | £ | s | d |
|---|---|---|---|---|---|---|---|---|---|---|---|---|---|---|
| 16,870,018 | 16 | 4 | 18,336,851 | 6 | 11 | 13,892,268 | | | 16,341,944 | 4 | 4 | | | |
| 3,929,771 | 2 | 8 | 3,974,827 | 9 | 3 | 3,272,725 | 10 | 11 | 3,588,835 | 16 | 10 | | | |
| (Italy, etc.) | | | (Germany) | | | (Germany) | | | (Germany)[5] | | | | | |
| 932,148 | 9 | 1 | 811,140 | 6 | | 718,474 | | 11 | 1,633,874 | 12 | 6 | | | |
| 2,308,126 | 3 | 7 | 2,550,644 | 16 | 3 | 2,298,818 | 19 | 1 | 3,209,493 | 19 | 8 | | | |

4. Exports to Russia: 1788, "British manufactures," £273,032/7, "foreign merchandise," £82,253/6/1; 1789, "British manufactures," £212,792/12/7, "foreign merchandise," £95,725/18/5; 1790, "British manufactures," £265,920/8/10, "foreign merchandise," £188,369/5/5; 1791, "British manufactures," £281,243/1/1, "foreign merchandise," £212,113/15/6; 1792, "British manufactures," £428,774/6/2, "foreign merchandise," £371,987/16/10; 1793, "British manufactures," £197,683/17, "foreign merchandise," £123,144/2/8; 1794, "British manufactures," £240,520/9/9, "foreign merchandise," £255,287/8/5.

5. Probably much of this went to France, evading the trading-with-the-enemy regulations after war began on February 1, 1793.

These tables are compiled from statistics in the Chatham MSS entitled "A Comparative Statement of the Value of the Imports and Exports of Great Britain during the Last Six Years, etc.," dated "Inspector General's Office, Customs House, London, April 10, 1794" (Bdl. 286), and "A Comparative Statement of the Value of the Imports into and the Exports from Great Britain in the Following Years (1789–1794), Distinguishing the Countries, and Distinguishing the British Manufactures from Foreign Merchandise," dated "From Mr. Irving, April 3, 1795" (Bdl. 287).

detail the figures for the years 1788–1794 inclusive, as
an illustration of the part played by commerce in Anglo-
American diplomatic history.

These figures show not only that the United States
was the greatest single foreign purchaser of British
exports but that the proportion of exports taken was
increasing steadily, at least up to the beginning of the
French Revolutionary wars, if we except a slight drop
in 1792. In 1788 it was approximately 10 per cent of
the total; in 1789, 13 per cent; in 1790, 17 per cent; in
1791, 18.5 per cent; in 1792, 17 per cent.

The importance of this trade to people living in
England was even greater than the figures indicate;
of the British exports to Europe a great proportion
represented an *entrepôt* trade; that is, they consisted
of re-exportations of articles imported first to England
mostly from the colonies, the United States, and the
East Indies. On the other hand, the exports to the
United States consisted almost wholly of English *manufactures*. The German states, Britain's greatest foreign market next to the American republic (with the
exception of Holland in the year 1789), took only one-
half their imports in English manufactures. The rest
was an *entrepôt* traffic; profitable, to be sure, to English shipping interests and commercial houses but not
to the important manufacturing interests. The figures
further show that from consuming roughly one-twelfth
of the manufactures of England in the year 1788 the
United States had increased its demand so that it took
nearly one-fifth of the whole in 1793 and 1794, the last
years for which the figures are available. For the purchase of the products of English factories the United

States was the greatest and most profitable customer, foreign or colonial.

The Anglo-American commerce in 1789 was indispensable to the prosperity of England. The loss of her greatest foreign customer at a time when the Industrial Revolution was creating heavy demands for more and larger markets would have entailed great hardship. It was a commerce worth far more to the Empire in general and to English manufacturers and factory operatives in particular than all the furs of Canada. Should it become a question of choosing between the complete loss of the Canadian fur trade and a serious injury to the American market for English manufactures, an English Ministry at this time could choose but one way: no government could survive an inexcusable destruction of the American market.

If Anglo-American commerce was indispensable to British prosperity in 1789 it was vitally necessary for the national existence of the United States. By that year a complete recovery had been made from the collapse of commerce that accompanied the Revolution, and the new government was heavily dependent on that prosperity in making the experiment of nationalism in the Constitution. Ninety per cent of American imports came from Great Britain and the American revenue came mostly from tariff on imports. Suddenly to have upset commercial relations with Great Britain, no matter how unfair and humiliating the British discriminations against American commerce, would have meant the destruction of three-fourths of American foreign commerce. To use a later expression of Alexander Hamilton, it would have cut out credit by the roots. Without financial credit the new national government must have reverted to the pitiful impotency of the old Confederation. The experiment of the Constitution would have ended in failure. It is this very real fact which dominated the foreign policy of the United States in the period we are to study.

# CHAPTER 3

# Informal Negotiations

BEFORE the adoption of the United States Constitution American nationality had found expression in the Declaration of Independence and successful revolution against the British Empire; but the national vigor had not been strong enough in the hour of victory to bring together in permanent union the thirteen sovereign states, nor had there been a Prussia among the states nor a Bismarck among the statesmen of the Revolution to strike such a union while the irons were hot. National unity was finally achieved through the peaceful deliberations of a representative body of American statesmen and businessmen who had gone through the trying experience of seven years of unconstructive government under the Articles of Confederation and were face to face with foreign contumely, domestic anarchy, and business chaos.

Great Britain's continued occupation of the frontier forts and her disinclination to enter into a treaty of commerce had been due to the ineffectiveness and weakness of the American Confederation and to the uncertainty of its continued existence. The new Constitution by giving the power of commercial legislation to the federal Government now made possible a national commercial policy and the enactment of navigation laws in reprisal against the systems of foreign nations. By instituting a Supreme Court and pronouncing treaties the law of the land, it gave a guaranty of their execution which had not been possible when each state clung to its pristine sovereignty, including the right to make its own tariff and navigation laws. It was now possible for the United States Government, through the jurisdiction of the Supreme Court, to remove the obstructions which some of the states in their exasperation had put upon the recovery of British ante-bellum debts.

A demonstration to foreign nations of the practical force of the new national government was the enactment of tariff and tonnage laws. The first Congress in its first session adopted the most successful shipping policy the United States has ever had,[1] a policy which followed the principle of the British Navigation Laws by giving to American vessels certain advantages over those of other nations. The debates provoked by the introduction of these laws reveal the first alignment under the new government of the representatives of the trading and shipping communities, which had feared to disturb Anglo-American commerce, versus the agrarian and frontier constituencies which had least to lose in any commercial disturbance or in the collapse of a strong central government based on commercial prosperity and the full protection of private property. Curiously enough, it was James Madison, Alexander Hamilton's collaborator in the writing of *The Federalist*, who introduced the bills, so worded as to place a heavy discrimination on British commerce. Thereby he

1. J. P. Baxter, III, "Our First National Shipping Policy," *U. S. Naval Inst. Procs.*, XLVI (1920), 1251.

aroused the fears of merchants and shipowners and made nervous the men, like Hamilton, who were looking to tariff revenue as a means of maintaining the credit of the Government. These people considered the principal purposes of tariff and tonnage legislation to be first the production of revenue[2] and second the protection of infant manufactures, and they did not want laws which might provoke such commercial hostility with the biggest foreign customer as to defeat these primary purposes. Madison's support of the bills in their discriminating character marks the political parting of the ways between him and Hamilton. The cleavage of opinion in this debate presages the birth of American political parties under our present form of government and shows how closely our political and economic life and our new-born nationality were connected with Anglo-American relations.

"The policy of Parliament," said Madison, "has been to seize every advantage which our weak and unguarded situation exposed. She [England] has bound us in commercial manacles and nearly defeated the object of our independence." His bill called for a higher tariff on importations from countries having no treaties of commerce with the United States than from those having such treaties and for heavier tonnage duties on the ships of such nations entering American ports. After a lively debate Madison succeeded in carrying only a part of his program through the House of Representatives, that which levied six cents a ton on ships of American registry, thirty cents a ton on ships of nations in "commercial alliance" with the United States, and fifty cents a ton on the ships of nations hav-

2. Hamilton referred to them as "revenue laws."

ing no commercial treaties with this country. Though
the tonnage discriminations passed the House, Madison's original tariff discriminations were toned down
to the innocuous provision for lighter duties on spir-
ituous liquors imported from countries "in alliance" as
distinguished from other countries.

It was only against nations not having treaties of
commerce with the United States, and not specifically
against any one nation, that the discriminations of
Madison's original tariff bill were directed. But the
fact remained that in practice such a tariff would have
operated principally against British commerce, which,
as has been shown, constituted over three-fourths of
all American foreign trade. The House of Representatives did not believe in the expediency of such perfectly
justifiable action against a nation which excluded
American vessels altogether from some of its ports.
The Senate was even more cautious about presuming,
under the existing circumstances, to put pressure on
England in this way. As enacted with Senate amendments the tariff act made no discrimination among foreign nations, whether or not they had treaties of commerce with the United States, but allowed a discount of
ten per cent in imposts on all goods imported in 'American ships. The Senate also threw out the House discrimination in tonnage duty in favor of nations in "commercial alliance." In its final form the tonnage act
levied six cents a ton on American vessels, thirty cents
a ton on vessels built in the United States but owned in
part by foreign subjects, and on all other foreign ships
fifty cents a ton.

"The Senate, God bless them, as if designated by
Providence to keep rash and frolicome brats out of the

fire, have demolished the absurd, impolitic, mad discrimination of foreigners in alliance from other foreigners," wrote Fisher Ames of the shipping city of Boston, in his satisfaction at the adoption of the amendments.[3]

The benefits thus judiciously extended to American shipping continued to be the basis of national policy until 1815, when they were removed insofar as they affected nations having reciprocity treaties with the United States. The operation of this policy, therefore, was restricted to practically the period of the great struggle between France and England which began with the wars of the French Revolution, and consequently it is impossible to tell just how much it helped to shift Anglo-American commerce to American ships or how much this transfer was due to the protection enjoyed by neutral flags. Such a transfer did take place. In 1790 American vessels carried less than fifty per cent of the commerce between Great Britain and the United States, but by 1800 they were carrying nearly the whole of it, ninety-five per cent; and the shift to the American flag is noticeable even before the outbreak of war between France and England in 1793, as a glance at the figures in the footnote below will indicate.[4]

3. Seth Ames, ed., *Works of Fisher Ames* (2 vols. Boston, 1854), I, 45. For the debates in the House see *Annals of Congress,* 1789, 106–382. For tariff and tonnage acts of July 4, July 20, 1789, amended July 20 and Aug. 10, 1790, see *U. S. Statutes at Large,* I, 24, 27, 135, 180.

4. A gradual transfer of freight between Great Britain and the United States from British to American bottoms began in 1790. It was already markedly under way before the war between Great Britain and France accelerated the movement. It is shown by the following table presented by the London Society of Shipowners in 1806:

What interests us particularly in connection with this study is the reaction which this national shipping policy produced in England. No sooner was it in prospect of enactment than the letters of British consuls in America[5] began to teem with apprehension as to its effect on the carrying trade of England. Lord Grenville,[6] Pitt's Secretary of State for Home Affairs (an office which for a few years after the separation of the Colonies also included the portfolio of Colonial Affairs), read

*Account of the number of Vessels and Tonnage which cleared inwards and outwards, between Great Britain and the United States in the following years:*

|      |          | British | | American | |
|------|----------|---------|---------|---------|---------|
|      |          | *Ships* | *Tonnage* | *Ships* | *Tonnage* |
| 1790 | Outwards | 245 | 50979 | 218 | 39441 |
|      | Inwards  | 312 | 64197 | 246 | 45234 |
| 1791 | Outwards | 253 | 55328 | 291 | 55806 |
|      | Inwards  | 247 | 53102 | 318 | 62253 |
| 1792 | Outwards | 223 | 50963 | 285 | 59414 |
|      | Inwards  | 197 | 42035 | 313 | 64035 |
| 1799 | Outwards | 57  | 14627 | 354 | 78683 |
|      | Inwards  | 42  | 9796  | 343 | 75225 |
| 1800 | Outwards | 62  | 14381 | 507 | 112596 |
|      | Inwards  | 77  | 27144 | 550 | 124015 |

This "shews the deep and well digested policy of America, in imposing a duty on *British* manufactures exported into America in *British* ships, which is not counteracted by any adequate duty on American produce, &c., exported into *Great Britain* in *American* bottoms." (Supplement XXIV, p. cxx, to *Collection of Interesting and Important Reports and Papers on Navigation and Trade.*)

5. P. Bond to Carmarthen, Phila., April 29, 1789; Sir John Temple to Carmarthen, N. Y., May 17, 1789; Geo. Miller to Carmarthen, Charleston, May 20, 1789; P.R.O.,F.O., 4, 7.

6. William Wyndham Grenville (1759–1834), elected to Parliament, 1782; Paymaster General, 1783; Secretary of State for Home Affairs, 1789–1791; created Baron Grenville, 1790; Secretary for Foreign Affairs, 1792–1801; Prime Minister, 1806–1807.

the dispatches from America with quickened interest. Copies of the tariff and tonnage laws he referred for study and report to the Committee of the Privy Council on Trade and Plantations (of which he himself was one of the ablest members), and forthwith he summoned the one Englishman in London who was thoroughly familiar with current political conditions in the United States, an army officer by the name of Beckwith who had just returned from a confidential visit to the seat of the new American Government.

Lieutenant Colonel George Beckwith had made his first acquaintance with America as a subaltern during the Revolution. By the end of the war he had risen to the rank of Lieutenant Colonel attached to the staff of General Sir Guy Carleton, commander-in-chief. Three years later when the General, raised to the peerage as Lord Dorchester, was appointed Governor General of British North America, Beckwith accompanied him to Canada and was soon employed as a confidential agent operating in the United States. In 1787 Beckwith passed six months secretly observing political conditions in America, particularly the movement for a stronger government which culminated in the Philadelphia Convention. His voluminous reports to Dorchester, which were straightway transmitted to Whitehall, together with the consular reports of more local content, constituted, in the absence of any legation in the United States, the medium by which the British Ministry kept in touch with American affairs. Beckwith made a second trip in 1788 to gather opinions of leading American personalities and their attitude toward England and to observe the effect of the Constitution—the adoption of which he esteemed a political event of consequence, though he was not sanguine as to its chances of success. On this trip in 1788 he was not required to disclose his official identity. He devoted himself quietly to studying the trend toward nationalism and to analyzing the factors which might be of use to offset the force of this movement should it prove inimical to England's interests. One such makeweight he discerned in the separatist sentiment of the back countries. Through the medium of an emissary whom he sent to Pittsburgh for the purpose, he succeeded in opening "an unsuspecting communication" with settlers in the Ohio valley. The reports which he received from this source led him to anticipate an "harmonious understanding in point of commercial interest between Great Britain and these rising settlements." The dissatisfaction of the Vermont separatists, who long since had been negotiating secretly with British representatives at Quebec,[7] also appealed to him forcibly. Aside from the political possibilities of the loosely attached frontier settlements of the United States, Beckwith noted the development everywhere of an increasing "British interest." He concluded it would be expedient to speak a friendly language and to show a disposition to negotiate a treaty of commerce, "whenever they shall have established a government and shown that they have something solid to bestow in return." [8]

7. *A.H.R.*, XXI, 547.

8. The best source for Beckwith's personal history before 1792 is to be found in a memorial to Henry Dundas, Secretary for Home Affairs, dated June 20, 1792, describing his past services for Government. This is among the "Papers of Lt. Col. Beckwith" in the Public Record Office, Foreign Affairs, 4, Vol. 12 (see Appendix I to this study). The volume contains nineteen letters of Beckwith to Grenville during 1790 and 1791 and is one of the most valuable sources for the informal negotiations of those years. Other Beckwith papers have

It was fresh from these observations that Beckwith had arrived in England toward the end of 1788. During the next few months he was frequently closeted with the Government's advisers on American affairs, particularly with Lord Hawkesbury and Lord Sydney, and with Lord Grenville when he took over the department of Home Affairs. As above noted, he was still in England when Grenville received the new American tariff and tonnage acts, and there followed several conferences between the two as to the possible consequences of such legislation. Grenville was especially disturbed by the attempts manifested in Congress to create a navigation system which, had it been wholly enacted, would have discriminated severely against British commerce. The upshot of his reflections and of his conferences with Beckwith was to send the latter back to the United States informally to convey to the new American "ministers" the advice that England could not look with indifference upon the passage of laws discriminating against her commerce, in the event of which retaliation by Parliament would surely follow.[9]

Commercial retaliation was not the only recourse which Grenville had in mind to meet this new condition

been printed in C.A., *Rept. 1890.* The latter are the letters sent by Beckwith to Dorchester, who forwarded them to England. One of the letters to Grenville, that of April 7, 1790, is in C.A.,Q, 49, 283 (calendared but not printed). A less important letter from Beckwith of Dec. 2, 1791, not included in either of the above sources, is published by F. J. Turner, in "English Policy toward America," *A.H.R.,* VII, 734, who cites it as "F.O., America, K." Mr. Brymner, in his introduction to C.A., *Rept. 1890,* gives Beckwith's history after 1792. For his rank during the American Revolution see W. C. Ford, *British Officers Serving in the American Revolution, 1774–1783* (Brooklyn, 1897), p. 26. See also *Dictionary of National Biography.*

9. Beckwith's Memorial. See Appendix I to this volume.

of affairs in the United States. In case the constitutional reformation should develop a strong government and a national policy incompatible with British commercial interests and hostile to the existing frontier situation, he looked forward to utilizing the forces of western separatism as a means of weakening the national strength which appeared to be developing under Washington's Administration. In addition to Beckwith's former reports, other information recently had been forwarded from Canada concerning the increasingly independent attitude of some of the "men of the western waters" and their desire to secure foreign aid, either French or Spanish, to open the navigation of the lower Mississippi to their commerce.[10] On October 21, 1789, before any word had come from Beckwith since his departure from London, Grenville wrote Dorchester that this news in regard to the Kentucky settlements was highly important. It was desirable, he declared, that the western settlements should establish a government distinct from that of the Atlantic states. In this event "means should be taken to cultivate a closer connection with them." Intercourse with leading men in

10. See "Desultory Reflexions by a Gentleman of Kentucky," C.A., *Rept. 1890,* 107. This was probably written by James Wilkinson, and disseminated in Kentucky, whence a copy was dispatched to Dorchester by a secret informant, whom the writer has decided to be the ex-Tory Dr. John Connolly. The authorship is evident by comparing the document with Wilkinson's letter to Miró of Feb. 12, 1789. Wilkinson and the "Spanish Conspiracy" have received much attention. For extensive coverage of Spanish-American relations and the Spanish-American frontier, see S. F. Bemis, *Pinckney's Treaty: A Study of America's Advantage from Europe's Distress, 1783–1800* (2nd ed. New Haven, 1960); and A. P. Whitaker, *The Spanish-American Frontier 1783–1795: The Western Movement and the Spanish Retreat in the Mississippi Valley* (Boston and New York, 1927).

Kentucky ought to be established if only to prevent the growth of a close connection between them and Spain, but Dorchester was cautioned not to "make any promise of eventual and still less of immediate assistance against the Atlantic states." [11]

Beckwith reached New York, then the seat of government, in October, 1789. Washington's Cabinet still lacked the presence of the Secretary of State. Jefferson, appointed to that office, had not arrived from France and did not actually take up his place in the Government until the following March.[12] For this reason, aside from his irregular diplomatic character, Beckwith was unable to have any contact with the "minister" whose office was the administration of foreign affairs. This did not prevent him from establishing relations with other persons of official character. One of the first ready listeners to his message was the thoroughly anglophile Senator William Samuel Johnson of Connecticut. Beckwith soon made the acquaintance of at least twenty-three (according to his ciphered enumeration) political personalities of more or less influence, most of them federal office-holders or members of Congress. His greatest achievement in this respect was Alexander Hamilton, who had just taken up the office of Secretary of the Treasury. Hamilton's father-in-law, General Schuyler, one of Beckwith's first acquaintances, introduced him. Their first interview has great significance for us here, because it marks the beginning of

11. C.A.,Q, 42, 153.

12. Washington did not inform Jefferson of his appointment until Oct. 13, 1789, which letter was acknowledged Dec. 15. Jefferson accepted Feb. 14, 1790. He reached New York to take office March 21, 1790. P. L. Ford, ed., *The Writings of Thomas Jefferson* (10 vols. New York, 1892–99), V, 140, 143, 148.

a diplomatic *liaison* which became the controlling personal factor in Anglo-American relations for at least the next seven years. In the absence of Jefferson, Hamilton assumed to be the spokesman of the Administration's foreign policy. When Jefferson some months later arrived at his desk the relation thus established in an informal way between Hamilton and this unaccredited agent of the British Government had grown so intimate and at the same time so subtle that the real Secretary of State was never able to conduct his office with thorough independence. But of this more later.

We have the interview almost verbatim in Beckwith's dispatches. Hamilton began by stating that the United States Government was now established on principles which made it safe for any nation to enter into treaty relations with it. He declared that there was a strong desire to negotiate a treaty of commerce with Great Britain which should include the privilege of entrance for American ships of limited tonnage to trade in the ports of the British West Indies. *"We think in English,"* he declared, alluding to the cultural solidarity between the two countries, and went on to say that "we are now so circumstanced as to be free to enter into a discussion of this sort, from our condition in regard to the other maritime powers; this may not be the case hereafter," whereupon he hinted at a possible connection with the House of Bourbon to secure the free navigation of the Mississippi River.

"On the other hand," he continued, "connected with you, by strong ties of commercial, perhaps of political, friendships, our naval exertions, in future wars, may in your scale be greatly important and decisive. These are my opinions, they are the sentiments, which I have long entertained, on which I have acted, and I think them suited to the future welfare of both countries. I am not sufficiently authorized to say so, it is not in my department, but I am inclined to think a *person will soon be sent to England to sound the disposition of your Court upon it.*" [13]

Beckwith replied that his "private views" were that it would be reasonable in any such negotiation to settle the matters still unadjusted with respect to the treaty of peace, to which Hamilton agreed, adding that two such matters in which the United States was interested were the frontier posts and the status of Negro slaves which had been carried away by British troops at the evacuation of New York and other Atlantic ports.[14] Beckwith hoped that the person to be sent to England would be free from such a bias toward any other foreign power as to frustrate his mission.

"I beg leave however to suggest," he said, "how much such a measure may be promoted, or impeded, by the predilections, possibly by the prejudices, of an individual so circumstanced."

13. The spelling and the punctuation of reports of these conversations by Beckwith have been preserved in this text.

14. It was the claim of the United States that Article VII of the treaty of peace which provided for evacuation without "carrying away any Negroes or other Property" required the delivery by Great Britain of the Negro slaves who had escaped within British lines during the war and who were taken away on British transports when the troops left the United States; that in lieu of restitution of their persons a money compensation should be given to their owners. General Sir Guy Carleton maintained that the slaves were free men from the time they entered British lines and were manumitted thereby, and that therefore the treaty did not apply to them. For thorough discussion of this dispute, see F. A. Ogg, "Jay's Treaty and the Slavery Interests of the United States," A.H.A., *Ann. Rept. 1901,* I, 275–98.

"Undoubtedly," replied Hamilton, "we have not in
some former instances been exempt from this sort of
inconvenience, to which the manner of naming to public
appointments under our old government not a little
contributed. The case is now altered, these nominations
originate with General Washington, who is a good
judge of men, and the gentleman, to be employed in this
business, is perfectly master of the subject, and if he
leans in his bias towards any foreign country, it is
decidedly to you."

In this conversation as in the interviews he had with
other Americans, Beckwith was careful to carry out
his instructions to give warning as to the effect on
Parliament of tariff laws discriminating against Great
Britain.

"I cannot think Commercial Hostility with us, the
mode to obtain Commercial Friendship," he observed.

Hamilton assured him that "whilst the Revenue and
Tonnage Bills were under discussion, I was decidedly
opposed to those discriminating clauses, that were so
warmly advocated by some gentlemen."

"I think I clearly comprehend the scope of the communication that you have been pleased to make to me,"
said Beckwith at the close of the interview. "Pray what
use do you intend me to make of it? Is it with the view
of my mentioning it to Lord Dorchester?"

"Yes," replied Hamilton, "and by Lord Dorchester
to your Ministry, in whatever manner His Lordship
shall judge proper; but I should not chuse to have this
go any further in America." [15]

15. Beckwith's Memorial; Dorchester to Grenville, Oct. 25, 1789,
enclosing communications, C.A., *Rept. 1890,* 121. For key to numbers
describing persons interviewed see Introduction to C.A., *Rept. 1890,* xli.

What was disclosed in this conversation concerning a person to be sent to the British Court had already been decided at a conference of the President with Hamilton and John Jay, the former Secretary for Foreign Affairs of the Continental Congress, and now Chief Justice. Washington records in his Diary under date of October 7 that he discussed with them the matter of an informal mission to England to sound that court upon the question of a commercial treaty and the status of the western posts. At the suggestion of Hamilton[16] it was decided to intrust the business to Gouverneur Morris, who then happened to be in France on private affairs. Instructions to him were dispatched a few days later by the President.[17] Beckwith, his work for the present completed, soon departed for Canada.[18]

16. Jay suggested Dr. Edward Bancroft. Bancroft was no man to be intrusted with American affairs. Throughout the American Revolution he had been a most successful salaried spy of the British Foreign Office in Paris. Never were diplomatists more duped than the American negotiators of the treaty of alliance with France in 1778; Bancroft claimed that he got word to London concerning the content of the treaty within forty-eight hours after its signature. B. J. Lossing, in his notes to *The Diary of George Washington, from 1789 to 1791* (New York, 1860), p. 15, says: "Edward Bancroft, M.D., was . . . intimate with Dr. Franklin, and a friend to the American cause during the War for Independence. He was with Silas Deane, in Paris, for some time; and in the diplomatic operations of the United States, during the war, he was an efficient auxiliary. Dr. Bancroft was a Fellow of the Royal Society of London, and gained much repute as author of 'An Essay on the Natural History of Guiana,'" etc., etc. For an account of his services as a spy see his Memorial to Carmarthen, September 17, 1784, P.R.O.,F.O., 4, 3. In 1784 he was in the United States engaged in sending secret information to Leeds. S. F. Bemis, "British Secret Service and the French-American Alliance," *A.H.R.*, XXIX, 474–94.

17. *A.S.P.,F.R.*, I, 121.

18. The Memorial does not say at what time he left, but no more communications from him appear until the next year.

There is nothing to indicate that he had ascertained who was to be expected in London. His final reports were duly forwarded from Quebec by Lord Dorchester.

What Hamilton had said of the man to be appointed as being personally fitted for the mission we should remember as we follow the negotiation of Gouverneur Morris, which marks the first attempt of President Washington's Administration to clear up the outstanding issues with England, a solution of which was so important to American commercial prosperity and territorial integrity.

Governeur Morris was one of the most brilliant Americans then living. He was acknowledged by his countrymen, and by foreigners who knew him, as a man of great talents if not genius. From 1789 to 1796 he passed most of his time in the great capitals of Europe, where during tumultuous years he acquired an exceptional reputation as a perspicacious political observer.[19] Already his personality had attracted notice in France. The prominent part which he had played in the Continental Congress during the American Revolution, his able work for the federal cause in the Philadelphia Convention, his trenchant pen which had worded most of the Constitution, all were achievements to win the respect of statesmen. More than this, Morris's pleasing personality, from which flowed without interruption a sparkling and gallant conversation and conduct, had launched him as a great favorite into the midst of French society. In spite of his leanings toward mild aristocratic government, a penchant which did not coincide with the liberal cult then fashionable among

19. *The Manuscripts of J. B. Fortescue, Esq., preserved at Drop-more* (3 vols. London, 1892–99), III, index. Cited as *Dropmore Papers.*

French philosophers, he soon became a social lion and achieved a reputation as a *homme d'esprit* probably never equaled by any other American in France, Franklin excepted. He on his part was delighted though by no means enthralled by the *monde* of French drawing-rooms, wherein his heart warmed as quickly as it cooled when he mingled in English society. "I consider France as the natural ally of my country," he said at this time, "and of course, that we are interested in her prosperity; besides, to say the truth, I love France." [20]

Undoubtedly Morris was a shrewd observer of European affairs; nevertheless the accuracy of his observations occasionally suffered from overconfidence in his own diplomatic prowess, if we are to judge by his diary and his correspondence with the President.[21] He mentions with no little satisfaction the way in which he handled the British Foreign Minister, the Duke of Leeds, tells of the embarrassment he caused in obliging him to "play an awkward part," relates with some assurance his analysis of the latter's mind while putting him probing questions, and speaks of touching Pitt's pride. What reacted particularly against Morris in

20. Jared Sparks, *The Life of Governeur Morris* (3 vols. Boston, 1832), II, 62.

21. The printed sources for the Morris mission are Washington's *Diary; Writings* or *Works* of Jefferson, Washington, Hamilton; A. C. Morris, ed., *Diary and Letters of Gouverneur Morris* (2 vols. New York, 1888); Sparks, *Life of Morris; A.S.P.,F.R.,* I; and a few miscellaneous allusions in *Dropmore Papers,* the private correspondence of Grenville. There are several Morris letters, comparatively unimportant, not printed, in U. S. State Dept. Records, National Archives, Dispatches, France, 3,B. Beatrice Cary Davenport published an unexpurgated edition of Morris's *Diary,* up to January 1793, where the reader may find details of Morris's racy gallantries: *A Diary of the French Revolution* (2 vols. Boston, 1939).

London was the lack of tact which he displayed in cultivating the intimacy of the French Ambassador, La Luzerne, at a time when war was imminent between England and the Bourbon allies, France and Spain. Morris dined with La Luzerne and was a frequent visitor at his house, while he purposely avoided introductions to anyone connected with the English Court and was reputed to be on very friendly terms with Charles James Fox, leader of the parliamentary opposition.[22] It is certain that this affected the attitude of Leeds and Grenville, and of the Prime Minister, toward Washington's confidential agent, for Beckwith (who was again in New York in 1790) complained to Hamilton about Morris's conduct before the latter's mission was ended.[23]

An example of this lack of discretion was the disclosure to La Luzerne by Morris of the nature of his instructions. These instructions, as briefly penned by Washington, had directed him to inquire whether there now existed objections to executing the still unfulfilled articles of the treaty of peace and whether there were any disposition for a treaty of commerce, and what terms might be acceptable in any such treaty. He was to ask the reason for the retention of the posts and to ascertain what action was contemplated by the British Government in regard to the deported Negro slaves.

22. *Diary and Letters of G. Morris,* I, 309–48. Morris denied he was intimate with Fox, whom he had seen but twice; see H. C. Lodge's note to his edition of *The Works of Alexander Hamilton* (9 vols. New York, 1885–86), IV, 49; cited as Hamilton, *Works* (Lodge ed.).

23. Hamilton to Washington, Sept. 30, 1790, J. C. Hamilton, ed., *The Works of Alexander Hamilton* (7 vols. New York, 1850–51), IV, 73; cited as Hamilton, *Works.*

He was also to sound the Ministry on its attitude as to an exchange of regular diplomatic representatives.[24] Morris explained to the President that he had thought it best to make this communication confidentially to the French Ambassador "because the thing itself cannot remain a secret; and by mentioning it to him, we are enabled to say with truth, that, in every step relating to the treaty of peace, we have acted confidentially in regard to our ally." That Morris then considered himself bound to the confidence of France in the matter of a treaty which the original negotiators had signed in defiance of their instructions to go hand in hand with the French Foreign Minister must be the wonderment of every reader of his letters. The confidence with which La Luzerne treated the ill-advised revelation— entirely unjustified by anything in Morris's instructions —is testified by the fact that his own words were echoed back to Morris the very day of his conversation with the Ambassador.[25]

Morris presented to Leeds his personal letter from Washington describing the purpose of his mission, on March 29, 1790.[26] The Minister received him with

24. *A.S.P.,F.R.*, I, 122.

25. Morris to Washington, April 7, 1790, ibid.; *Diary and Letters,* I, 310.

26. *A.S.P.,F.R.*, I, 123. "I received from Major Hasgill who arrived here on the twenty-first Instant the two letters which you did me the honor to write me on the thirteenth of October. I shall in consequence set off for London as soon as I possibly can. When last in that City I saw the Duke of Leeds at the french Embassadors, and from some slight Circumstances was induced to believe that the british Court are better disposed towards a connection with the United States than they were some eighteen months ago—The principal difficulty will I imagine arise from the personal character of the King, which is that of Perseverance, and from the personal dislike which he bears towards his former subjects." Morris to Washington, Paris, Jan. 22, 1790, Wash-

"much warmth and gladness in his appearance," but Morris could get no definite statement from him. The matter of appointing a minister to the United States was difficult; America was a "great way off," thought Leeds, though he promised to communicate later on that point.[27] A month thereafter Morris received a short note of the kind that had been handed to John Adams in former years: a statement that England's object in holding the posts was to secure fulfillment of the treaty by the United States or proper compensation for the lack of such fulfillment. As to a commercial treaty Leeds professed a "sincere wish . . . to cultivate a real and bona fide system of friendly intercourse," which noncommittal statement meant to Morris that no treaty was desired.[28]

At this first meeting on March 29, the personal agent of President Washington believed he discerned from the Duke's "countenance and manner on the perusal" of Washington's letter that he derived "that sort of pleasure, which a man feels at the removal of something, which every now and then brings to his mind disagreeable ideas." Even the astute Morris could not fathom the source of this emotion, but he guessed it was due to "some disquietude respecting the part, which the United States might take in case of a general war." [29]

His guess was correct. Behind the doors of the Foreign Office the sensational Nootka Sound controversy had been developing for several weeks and was about

ington Papers, State Department (now in Library of Congress), Vol. 245, p. 32853.

27. *A.S.P., F.R.,* I, 123.
28. Ibid.
29. Morris to Washington, April 13, 1790, Sparks, *Morris,* II, 9.

to assume the proportions of a possible general European war. After two hundred years of opposition the rival colonizing systems of England and Spain had come again into conflict. Under the guidance of the "heaven-born" Pitt the Government had made an issue of the capture by a Spanish officer of some English merchant ships on the northwest coast of America and stood determined to deny at whatever cost that the Pacific was a Spanish ocean. Leeds, a month before the meeting with Morris, had demanded in very strong words to the Spanish Ambassador immediate satisfaction for the captures and had refused to admit the Spanish claim to exclusive jurisdiction over the Pacific Ocean and its American shores, the grounds on which the vessels had been seized at Nootka.[30] In Madrid the outlook was ominous for peace. In London Pitt had been closeted with Miranda, the South American revolutionist,[31] planning details of a war which with the aid of a general insurrection was to tear loose from Spain her colonies in two continents and open up another great domain to the felicities of constitutional government and the products of English factories. In such a war, what would be the attitude of the United States, whose territory lay in a strategic position between Spanish Louisiana and British North America, a nation which had against Spain the grievance of the Mississippi cloture and against England that of the occupied posts?[32] It was this question which caused the force of Gouverneur Morris's informal representations

30. W. R. Manning, "Nootka Sound Controversy," A.H.A., *Ann. Rept. 1904*, 363–87.

31. W. S. Robertson, "Francisco de Miranda and the Revolutionizing of Spanish America," A.H.A., *Ann. Rept. 1907*, I, 272.

32. Turner, "English Policy toward America," *A.H.R.*, VII, 706.

to fluctuate in proportion to the danger of war between Spain and England.

The formal reply of Leeds to Morris, described above, was written on April 28. Two days afterward a Cabinet meeting was held at which it was decided to recommend to the King to demand immediate and adequate satisfaction for the Nootka seizures and a naval armament to support such demands from Spain. A great press of seamen to equip the new armament took place on the fourth of May. The next morning the Duke of Leeds replied to the last Spanish note (which had passed over British claims for redress) with an emphatic assertion of England's intention to protect the rights of her subjects on the Pacific Ocean. The same day Pitt had another meeting with Miranda and further elaborated their plans for war, plans which that evening were submitted to the Cabinet. Simultaneously the King appeared before Parliament to request funds for the new naval armament. The Nootka crisis was laid bare to an astonished public.[33] Pitt had nailed his flag to the masthead.

As the crisis became acute and war seemed likely the Government began to mobilize the military and diplomatic resources of the Empire. Holland and Prussia stood ready to fight at the side of England in a war against Spain and France, and the diplomatic situation was such that most of the powers of Europe would be ranged on one side or the other in case of hostilities.[34]

33. Manning, "Nootka Sound Controversy," 380–82. The opposition had no inkling of the Government's Spanish policy until the affair was published, May 6. It supported the Government. See *A.S.P.,F.R.,* I, 123; Morris, *Diary and Letters,* I, 325.

34. Manning, ch. 8.

As to the United States, two possibilities were open. One was to encourage that country to join in a colonial war against Spain by promising the free navigation of the Mississippi in the event of the reduction of Spanish Louisiana. For such a privilege the "men of the western waters," if not the whole country, would go to great lengths. The other was the exploitation of western separatism in order to paralyze any possible hostility expected by Canadian officials, who were sure that the United States would not scruple to use an opportunity to occupy the frontier posts by military force. To a certain extent both of these prospects were contemplated by Pitt's Ministry, but the final adjustment of the Nootka crisis made it unnecessary to choose definitely either one.

Under these circumstances the Ministry considered it opportune to extend a hand to the Vermont separatists, in whose interests the shrewd Green Mountain intriguer, Levi Allen, for some months past had been in London trying to negotiate a separate commercial treaty between Great Britain and the "sovereign" state of Vermont, a treaty which would provide for free trade with the province of Quebec. Such a trade already existed to a considerable extent as a result of ordinances issued by Lord Dorchester with the sanction of the home government. Allen, however, wanted the recognition of separate independence which would result from a treaty and undoubtedly was looking forward to reunion with the British Empire. The British Government was not averse to a secession of Vermont and Kentucky, and wished to see a buffer community under British protection extending all along the frontier between the Atlantic states and Canada. This de-

vice would secure control of the Great Lakes and the
fur trade to the south of them and would prevent Spain
from marching, with or without American cooperation,
across the Northwest Territory against Canada. It
would also afford a big market for English manufactures imported by means of the water communication
of the Great Lakes and the Champlain system.

Such was the gist of a report of the Privy Council
based on the information of the Government's observers of western separatism. Nevertheless the report,
which appeared during the Nootka crisis, expressed
doubt whether it were "politically prudent, all circumstances considered, by a separate treaty with Vermont
to risk offending the United States Congress, but the
Lords of the Privy Council were of the opinion that it
would be well for the benefits of this country commer-
cially to prevent Vermont and Kentucky and all the
other settlements now forming in the interior part of
the great continent of North America, from being dependent upon the Government of the United States or
on that of any other foreign country." At any rate,
Allen was "taken by the hand" and encouraged.[35]
Simultaneously the American overtures through Morris presented a possible opportunity for the bestowal
of timely diplomatic favors to attach the United States
to British interest should the occasion require it.

To drive the United States into the arms of Spain
by meeting Washington's very proper overtures with
too cool an attitude was obviously to be avoided. In a
dispatch which Grenville directed to Dorchester on this
same critical May 6[36] (the day of the conference be-

35. See documents in *A.H.R.*, XXI, 555; VII, 705.

36. Grenville to Dorchester, May 6, 1790, Nos. 22, 23, 24, secret,
C.A., *Rept. 1890*, 132.

tween Pitt and Miranda and of the special Cabinet meeting on the Spanish business), he alludes to the prospect of war and the possibility of the United States' taking advantage of that circumstance to attack the frontier posts. Because of this, Dorchester was requested to defer an intended visit to England. Another dispatch of the same date reviewed the recent conversations with Levi Allen. Allen had been "encouraged" so that his influence might be used if expedient; Vermont's friendship would be a "considerable acquisition of strength." A third dispatch dwelt more particularly on relations with the United States proper. The Morris mission, it stated, had seemed to indicate a desire for closer connection with Great Britain. It had been necessary at first to be firm with Morris because of the nonexecution of the treaty by the United States and the inadequate response by that nation to British commercial "liberalities"; nevertheless it would certainly be worth while to establish if possible a greater degree of sympathy for Great Britain than had previously existed in that country. Some one should be sent to sound American opinion and get the earliest information as to any hostile designs in the present situation. It might even be possible to bring the Americans over to the British side in case of a Spanish war, for to promise them the navigation of the Mississippi would be to offer something quite as important to them as possession of the posts. Grenville concluded with a wish to be kept closely informed of developments.[37]

It is not surprising, therefore, to note that when Morris, this time at Leeds's request, appeared for

37. Some minor additional trade concessions were extended to Vermont and adjacent Champlain country in 1790. Ibid., 732–33.

another conference,[38] May 21, with the Foreign Minister, at which he found Pitt also present, he was greeted
with considerable warmth, to which the American
did not respond with much enthusiasm. In the unex-
pected European crisis Morris beheld an uncommonly
fortunate opening for American diplomacy. War between Spain and Great Britain, he wrote Washington,
seemed inevitable. "If it does happen, then they will
give a good price for our neutrality; and Spain I think
will do so too." Both Pitt and Leeds again assured
Morris that he had misunderstood the Duke's letter in
regard to a treaty of commerce.

"I answered coolly," records Morris, "that it was
easy to rectify the mistake; but it appeared idle to form
a new treaty, until the parties should be thoroughly
satisfied about that already existing."

The Prime Minister then took up the conversation,
which drifted into a fruitless discussion of the violations by both parties of the treaty of peace. The
dialogue grew quite brisk and the point of national
honor, concerning the occupied posts, was raised by
Morris, and returned by Pitt, who held that British
honor demanded the posts be retained until the treaty
should be fully complied with by the United States.

38. In the press of May 4 several American citizens had been taken
—the first instance of impressment of Americans by the British navy.
Though Morris had no specific power to this effect he had on May 20
successfully interceded with Leeds for their release. Leeds at this
time took occasion to say that Morris had misunderstood his letter of
April 28 (see above p. 70), that by it he had certainly meant to
express a willingness to enter into a treaty of commerce. Morris
showed some indifference and affected to be concerned at this interview only with the fate of the impressed seamen, but Leeds requested
a conference the following day, pending which he promised to confer
with the King's law officers in regard to the impressments. *A.S.P.,F.R.,*
I, 123; Sparks, *Morris,* II, 21.

"We do not think it worth while to go to war with you for these posts," retorted Morris, *"but we know our rights, and will avail ourselves of them when time and circumstances may suit."*

Pitt asked if Morris had any powers to treat and was informed that the United States could not appoint a minister as long as England had neglected to send one. to America. The Prime Minister then inquired whether the United States would send a minister if England did. Morris responded that he could "almost promise that we should, but was not authorized to give any positive assurance." He suggested the appointment of a minister and the delaying of his departure from England until news should arrive of a similar appointment in the United States. A short discussion of the commercial privileges extended by each country to the other ended this notable interview, at the close of which the two ministers promised to consult together and to inform the American agent of the result of their deliberations.[39]

Pitt had left the matter at a point from which he could advance or retreat according to the turn of the Spanish business. Morris's opinion was that in case Spain should yield the English would demand impossible terms in any treaty of commerce: in case war should come England would yield the posts; in fact, he had reliable information that Grenville had that very day consulted with some persons familiar with the American fur trade, and he supposed it was in regard to the possibility of relinquishing the posts.[40]

This supposition is corroborated by the records of

39. *A.S.P.,F.R.,* I, 123–25.
40. Ibid.

the Colonial Office which show reports made to Grenville in May, 1790, by both military and commercial advisers that it would be possible to withdraw the garrisons from United States territory and to install them in forts across the boundary from the old positions without endangering their strategical value, while at the same time some treaty provision might be made to secure the fur trade to British subjects. Grenville has left on record an opinion agreeing with this advice.[41]

Four days after the interview, above described, of Morris with Pitt and Leeds there arrived interesting news from Beckwith in New York. As will be narrated in the next chapter, Beckwith had been sent to the United States again, from Quebec, by Lord Dorchester, before the arrival at that capital of Grenville's dispatches of May 6, for the purpose of observing American political and military affairs. In a dispatch dated April 7 he reported that the American Government had resolved to send an expedition against the western Indians, and the Creeks, with whom negotiations for peace had not been satisfactory. The objects of this effort were threefold:

> The first is an Indian war: the second, the strengthening of the general Government of the

41. C.A.,Q, 287; Answers by Capt. Shank, May, 1790, to memoranda of Lord Grenville concerning the posts, C.A.,Q, 49, 297; Memoranda from Lord Grenville, *M.P.C.,* XXIV, 91. An opinion by another officer took a contrary view: "Without posts of strength in this country it cannot be expected that much of the trade will remain with us, and how far it may be preserved by forming posts in lieu of those we now are occupying is, I think, very problematical. The Indians have ever since the Peace dreaded our relinquishing the posts, and will assuredly take the alarm, whenever that happens, after which their friendship will no longer be depended on." Mathews to Nepean, July 9, 1790, ibid., 309.

Union, by an encrease in the Military establishment; and the last, leads to the idea of possessing
hereafter in the Western Territory, a force not
only equal to overawe the neighbouring Indian
tribes, but with such assistance as may be derived
from the growing population and resources of
that new world, the being in a condition to undertake offensive war, although I have reason to
think that this object is not in immediate contemplation, on the contrary, I have grounds to believe
that there is a wish to cultivate a connexion infinitely important, in my humble apprehension, to
the genuine interests and future prosperity of this
country.[42]

Grenville's interpretation of this news is recorded in
his dispatch of June 5 to Dorchester. The information
from Beckwith and other[43] secret communications led
him to believe that no attack would be made this year
on the posts by the United States, but the report of the
weakness of these posts and preparations of the Americans gave ground to apprehend that they might not be
secure in the event of a war with Spain. Latest dispatches from Madrid would not admit any opinion of
the eventual issue of the Nootka affair; meanwhile
British armaments would continue, making it difficult
to send out troops to Canada. Should war occur, how-

42. Beckwith to Grenville, N. Y., April 7, 1790, P.R.O.,F.O., 4, 12. See
also copy of same sent via Quebec, indorsed as received May 25, 1790,
C.A.,Q, 49, 283; and Beckwith to Grenville, N. Y., April 24, 1790,
P.R.O.,F.O., 4, 12. This latter dispatch, which estimated the number
of troops *to be employed against the Indians* at 3,000, did not arrive
until June 25.

43. See Dorchester to Grenville, Mar. 8, 1790, C.A.,Q, 44–1, 121.

ever, re-enforcements, either additional corps of Loyalists or "foreign troops," would be provided for Dorchester.[44]

This dispatch shows that Morris's thinly veiled threat and generally truculent attitude could not but have been disturbing, under the circumstances. But at no time during the Morris mission did the Pitt Ministry advance any further than the position taken in the interview of May 21. During the summer instructions were sent to Dorchester to restrain the Indians from depradations on the Ohio against American settlers, "particularly on account of the embarrassment and Danger which may arise from the Americans sending an army against them." [45]

Immediately after this admonition had been given there arrived at Whitehall (August 5) news that Spain had acceded to the first demands of England and had agreed to give compensation for the seizures at Nootka. This yielding on the part of the Spanish monarchy indicated a probability of peace, which was dissipated when the concession was promptly followed by demands that Spain recognize England's equal right to commerce and settlement in the unoccupied regions of the Pacific, a direct challenge to the monopoly hitherto asserted since the ancient Treaty of Tordesillas (1494). The full issue of the Nootka controversy was now apparent, and peace or war depended on the adherence of the National Assembly of revolutionary France to the Bourbon Family Compact.[46]

44. Grenville to Dorchester, June 5, 1790, C.A.,Q, 44–1, 161.
45. Grenville to Dorchester, Aug. 4, 1790, C.A.,Q, 45–2, 510. For the carrying out of these radically new instructions, see Motz to Sir J. Johnson, Quebec, Sept. 27, 1790, C.A.,Q, 46–2, 529.
46. Manning, ch. 11.

While in London they were still uncertain whether France would unreservedly support the Spanish alliance, Gouverneur Morris had an interview with Leeds which for all practical purposes may be said to have terminated this remarkable and first of American "personal" missions. Having received no word as to any decision which the Ministry might have reached as a result of the conference of May 21, Morris, who had "patiently waited" nearly four months, on September 10, wrote a formal note expressing his disappointment and intimating that continued silence might be construed as an unconditional refusal to execute the peace treaty except on some specific condition the nature of which was withheld. Interpretation of this attitude in America, he suggested, might lead to measures of "reciprocal injury" rather than mutual advantage. As a result of this note a final interview with Leeds took place on September 15. The Secretary for Foreign Affairs had just received news of an informal communication of the United States Government to Beckwith, in New York, that threats of individual officers on the frontier against the occupied posts were unauthorized; and that the United States, while as yet having no diplomatic understanding with Spain, was keeping its freedom of action in the event of war.[47] Again the Duke repeated the verbal assurances of the previous May, that England was anxious for a "real *bona fide* connexion, not merely by the words of a treaty, but in reality." He stated that he hoped soon to fix upon a minister to America who would be

47. Beckwith to Grenville, N. Y., Aug. 5, 1790. Indorsed "rec'd Sept. 14." P.R.O.,F.O., 4, 12, printed in *A.H.R.*, VII, 719. A fuller account is printed in C.A., *Rept. 1890*, 145–46.

sent over with letters of credence in his pocket (i.e., presumably to hold pending the appointment of a diplomatic representative by the United States), an expedient which Morris cordially approved. There were two points of difficulty which the Foreign Secretary wished might be gotten out of the way. He did not immediately state what these might be, and Morris, "with an air of serious concern," thereupon asserted his own conviction that the detention of the western posts would form an insurmountable barrier to any treaty. Though he professedly was no judge of "the great circle of European politics," he suggested that while England was doubtful of the attitude of the United States she could not act with decisive energy towards the neighbors of that country. He took it for granted that *"they* [i.e., the British] *would naturally square their conduct towards us by their position in respect to other nations."* This conduct, he inferred to Leeds, naturally depended on the attitude of the French National Assembly: he supposed that by this time final dispositions had been made in regard to the House of Bourbon and that England would now be able to make some definite reply to the United States; it was in the power of that country to throw the possession of the West India Islands to whomever it pleased. Morris, recalling the tendency toward anti-British discrimination which had been manifested in Congress, ended the interview with a request to be apprised speedily of any decision. Leeds promised to communicate with him in Paris, but the American refused this, suggesting a direct reply to the United States Government by way of British packets. He himself departed for France, after addressing his dispatches to President Washington.[48]

During the first week in October news arrived in London that Spain would probably not go to war. It was interpreted as proof of the weakness of the Bourbon alliance. A British ultimatum had left for Madrid on October 2, and on November 4 there came the news that the Spanish King had bowed to its terms. The Family Compact had not been able to stand the strain of the French Revolution. Spain dared not meet the British navy alone.[49] Without a war English diplomacy had won the fruits of one—that those fruits were never fully gathered on the shores of the Pacific was due to the long train of European difficulties that followed the French Revolution between the year 1793 and the pronouncement of the Monroe Doctrine in 1823.

Spain's surrender in the Nootka affair automatically removed all English anxiety as to American action in case of a Spanish war. It also rendered it unnecessary for Leeds to have any further intercourse with Gouverneur Morris. When Morris returned to London in December he was unable to see the Foreign Minister. Two conversations with the Undersecretary developed the fact that matters were in the same pass at which they had stood in September; the Government hoped soon to appoint a minister, but as yet that official was not selected nor had it been determined what the nature of his instructions should be. The subject had been referred some three months previously to the

48. *A.S.P.,F.R.,* I, 126–27.
49. Manning, ch. 13.

consideration of Lord Hawkesbury, who had made no report. The Government was as desirous as the United States for a treaty, said the Undersecretary, and if Morris could return in the spring then more progress might be possible. Morris replied that "perhaps he might" be in England in the spring, but it was of "no consequence"; the Ministry could easily find a channel of its own through which to communicate with the American Executive.[50]

A complete study of the sources of the Morris mission, supplemented by Manning's excellent exposition of the Nootka controversy, leads to the conclusion that the mission had very small direct results, that it rather hindered than advanced any Anglo-American *rapprochement*. Morris's untactful behavior made him *persona non grata* both to the Government and the Court. The Foreign Office treated him with cold propriety and responded to his overtures only when the exigencies of the Spanish crisis made it expedient to do so. The appointment of a minister to the United States

50. "There was nothing in this which at all surprised me. It needs no comment, and is, indeed, exactly what I expected. *Next spring* they will know better what to look for from their present negotiations." Morris to Jefferson, Dec. 28, 1790. Morris reported that a "Mr. Elliot" had told one of his friends "during the height of the [Nootka] armament" that he had been appointed as Minister to the United States. This appointment, said Morris, had been suspended upon the termination of the Nootka affair. Sparks, *Morris*, II, 55. Joshua Johnson to Thomas Jefferson, London, March 26, April 18, July 2, 1791. Department of State Records, Consular Dispatches, I, National Archives. Andrew Elliot was a former Loyalist of Scotch origin who enjoyed high personal connections in the British Government after the Revolution. Eugene Devereux, "Andrew Elliot, Lieutenant Governor of the Province of New York," *Pa. Magazine of History and Biography*, XI, 129–50. See also J. G. Simcoe to Henry Dundas, London, August 12, 1791, *S.P.*, I, 48.

may or may not have been seriously discussed in 1790. The present investigation has discovered no evidence,[51] other than that already cited from Morris's correspondence, to show that this busienss took definite shape before January, 1791. What alarmed the Government particularly was not the possible action of the United States in the case of a Spanish war; the evidence points to the conclusion that Pitt had deliberately weighed the situation in the spring of 1790 and was quite ready to go to war. If necessary the Americans in that event could be taken care of either by fanning a backfire of western separatism or by voluntarily relinquishing the posts if the United States appeared to be ready and able to take them by force. It was rather the danger to British commerce at the hands of Congress that had quickened the attention of the Ministry and had led to the sending of Beckwith late in 1789.

This possibility continued to agitate the minds of the Cabinet and to indicate the desirability of establishing a regular representative in Philadelphia. Meanwhile an informal negotiation had been proceeding in America. It will be necessary in the following chapter to consider more closely the details of that negotiation and to analyze the repercussion on the other side of the Atlantic of the Nootka affair and of the failure of the Morris mission.

51. The Foreign Office papers have been consulted.

# CHAPTER 4

# Informal Negotiations (*Continued*)

WE recall that in the autumn of 1789 Lord Grenville had sent Beckwith from London to New York as an informal agent, without powers, to warn the American "ministers" of the danger of an anti-British commercial policy.

After Beckwith had interviewed a number of prominent Americans, notably Alexander Hamilton, whose conversation has been set forth at length in the preceding chapter, he reported in person to Lord Dorchester at Quebec. Hamilton's statements, together with the other conversations, were straightway transmitted by Dorchester to the British Cabinet. Beckwith was soon sent back to the United States, in March, 1790, "to thank 'No. 7'" (Hamilton was thus represented in the cipher) for his suggestions and to make further observations. This was before news had arrived in Canada of the Nootka trouble and before orders had been issued by Dorchester, at Grenville's direction, to restrain the Indians from depredations on the frontier in order not to encourage any American advance into the Indian country. The reason for sending Beckwith again to the United States was anxiety as to the purpose of the frontier troops which the American Government was organizing. The posts had been repaired and supplied, but Dorchester was uncertain whether the local militia could be relied on for an adequate defense in case the true purpose of the American forces should be, as he apprehended, to possess the forts by force. He wrote Grenville that the United States ought to bring forward a frontier treaty and a treaty of commerce, but he feared that the new government might do something "less solid and more brilliant . . . to captivate its citizens."[1] It was while on this trip that Beckwith had sent from New York information of the new troops being mobilized for Indian campaigns and of the desire of influential Americans for a British "connexion," which news, as we have seen, proved timely and useful to Grenville during the Nootka crisis and the Morris conversations.

Beckwith's stay in New York was limited to a few weeks in March and April, 1790. He renewed intercourse with the men whose acquaintance he had already made, not neglecting further long conversations with Senator William Samuel Johnson of Connecticut. He told Johnson that Lord Dorchester had not yet been able to hear from England as to the reaction of the Cabinet to the Senator's expressions in their first interview. The report had been forwarded to London: meanwhile the Governor General "judged it necessary to defer no longer expressing his approbation of the principles which had been laid down in the previous autumn"; namely, that "a solid friendship should be established between the two countries."[2] It was for Johnson to decide whether he judged it expedient, in

1. Dorchester to Grenville, Mar. 8, 1790, C.A.,Q, 44–1, 121.
2. Ibid., 252. This is printed but badly garbled in C.A., *Rept. 1890*, 133.

the present state of the business, to make any further
communications to Lord Dorchester. The Senator did
not refuse to go on to express the desire of many
Americans for a "commercial friendship" which would
include a share of the West Indian trade. He said that
he opposed the party which wished to adopt in its
entirety the principle of the British Navigation Laws
and to turn against England her own invention. "As
to our adopting any hostile measures against you, or
with a view to seize the Forts by arms, I can assure
you it is not in our contemplation at present; there
may be individuals in the House of Representatives
who have such wild ideas, but I do not think there is
a single member in the Senate who would not repro-
bate such a proceeding, and *without our approbation
no such measure can be undertaken*. We know that you
have put the Forts in repair."

The moment was very favorable for a commercial
treaty, thought the Senator, and he would like to see
an exchange of ministers between the two countries.
These matters, however, now lay in the department
of Mr. Jefferson, who had just taken up his office.
Nevertheless, Johnson gave his opinions on the persons from whom any American minister to 'Great
Britain was likely to be chosen. If Adams were selected,
"things would not go well." Nor would they succeed
if Jefferson or Madison should be appointed. If the
choice of the President should be Jay, Hamilton,
Rufus King, or General Knox, the mission ought to be
successful so far as the personal factor was concerned.
"Will you send us a Minister?" Johnson asked, apparently without being vouchsafed any answer (so far
as one gathers from Beckwith's notes), "perhaps we

shall not wish to send a second time without assurances of this nature, or your taking a lead in it, it would be a popular measure and would tend greatly to set everything in motion in a good humored way."

The remarks of the voluble Senator from Connecticut, though informing to the British Government as to personal sentiments of influential Americans, had nothing authoritative in them, but they revealed the disposition of a party in the Senate. They did nevertheless convey a measure of the "British interest" which was so strong in Federalist districts, and Johnson summed up for Beckwith the political situation in words which the purpose of this study justifies quoting in some length:

> There are two parties in our Legislature, both have it in view to form a friendly connexion with Great Britain, differing in their ideas as to means; the one is desirous of very moderate measures on our part, and the shunning everything that may wear the appearance of commercial warfare, observing that although Great Britain has excluded us from her American and West India possessions, yet that she has granted us certain advantages in her ports of Europe, that in Asia she treats us with kindness, that hers is the best market for our exports, and that, if we are intemperate, we may naturally look for an alteration in these points; the other is of opinion that prompt and spirited resolutions are best calculated to effect this purpose and that the interests of the States essentially require them. These gentlemen think that in placing all the maritime powers of Europe

under similar restrictions, and treating their shipping in our ports precisely as they treat ours in
their American and West Indian possessions, or
in excluding them from ours, if they shall continue to exclude our from theirs, the States in such
a struggle will have the best of it; for one of two
things must happen, either some European power
will give way in order to form an advantageous
treaty with us, to the disadvantage of the others,
or if not, we shall consume less in future, set seriously about the introduction of domestic manufactures and take our chances for a market for
our raw material. Such is the language of the two
parties; which may preponderate I cannot tell, but
those who are the advocates for strong measures
carry with them an air of popularity.[3]

This is a good description of the two parties then
crystallizing in Congress over the issue of the proper
policy toward Britain. A comment which Beckwith
records as coming from "a Mr. Telfair, a British Merchant resident in New York," neatly supplements
Johnson's words:

I greatly doubt whether the States are in a condition to take such steps as these [i.e., the measures
proposed by "Jefferson, Mr. Madison, and that
party"], *their present Government is supported
by the impost and tonnage duties;*[4] they are wholly
English, is it then to be supposed that they will
put everything to the hazard at once and risk the
dangerous necessity of direct taxation on such a

3. C.A., *Rept. 1890*, 136–38.
4. Ibid., 140.

question as this where there is a difference of opinion even among themselves, many gentlemen thinking they are not yet in a situation to attempt any sort of marine establishment and that foreign shipping carrying their bulky productions, particularly in the Southern States is both advantageous and desirable.

Beckwith had other conversations, with business men and minor political characters, including one Scott, representative to Congress from the "western waters" of Pennsylvania, who shared the feeling of other settlers in the Ohio Valley for a "British connexion" which might help them open the navigation of the Mississippi, but the writer of these lines has not discovered any record of a conversation with "No. 7" on this visit to New York. Beckwith returned to Quebec the last of April with information which caused his chief to advise the Superintendent of Indian Affairs that there appeared no hostile designs of the United States against the posts, though it would be necessary to strengthen those positions and to prepare for mobilization of the provincial militia for any emergency.[5]

Beckwith had not been long at Quebec when Grenville's dispatches of May 6, 1790, revealing the gravity of the Nootka crisis, arrived. In conformity with these instructions, already noted,[6] Dorchester immediately issued orders to the Indian Department to restrain the

5. Dorchester to Sir J. Johnson, May 31, 1790, C.A.,Q, 46–2, 440. Beckwith's reports to Dorchester are printed in full in C.A., *Rept. 1890,* 134–42. Two letters direct to Grenville, already cited in the last chapter, are in P.R.O.,F.O., 4, 12, "Corres. of Lt. Col. Beckwith."
6. See above pp. 75–76.

natives of the Ohio Valley from their depredations on American settlers,[7] and sent Beckwith again to the United States. He was now furnished with two sets of instructions, signed by the Governor General.[8] The first consisted of a letter obviously for exhibition and designed to give the appearance of endowing him with a certain diplomatic character. It directed him to express a hope that "neither the appearance of a war with Spain nor its actually taking place, will make any alteration in the good disposition of the United States to establish a firm friendship and *alliance*[9] with Great Britain to the mutual advantage of both countries." Dorchester had heard with satisfaction, continued the letter, of the negotiation in London by Morris, though it had not been so "explicit and formal as the case may require," the agent having been equipped

7. "On reading your instructions to Mr. Gautier of the 31st of July, 1790, Lord Dorchester observes, among the reasons directed to be given to the Indians for preserving peace among themselves, the following expression: 'and at a time, too, when it is most probable that they may be called upon by that part of their confederacy bordering on the American states to defend their country, should it be invaded, as they are apprehensive it will.' Considering that we are at present at peace with the American States, with a prospect of continuing so, it would seem to be desirable to avoid everything that might be construed as a mark of unfriendly disposition on our part. For this reason His Lordship wishes you to recall the above-mentioned instructions out of Mr. Gautier's hands in the safest and most expeditious manner, and to substitute others, omitting any expressions which might appear unfriendly to the United States." Motz (Secretary to Dorchester) to Sir J. Johnson, Sept. 27, 1790, C.A.,Q, 46–2, 526. Sir John had inserted the clause in question because he feared the Americans would attack the posts. Sir J. Johnson to Motz, Sept. 30, 1790, ibid., 529.

8. Dated June 27, 1790. See C.A., *Rept. 1890,* 143–44.

9. Italics inserted.

only with a personal letter from the President. In case of war, the Governor General suggested, the United States could be better served by a junction with Great Britain than otherwise. Dorchester had also heard of hostilities by some Indians on the Ohio "at the instigation of some southern tribes, supposed to be under the influence of Spain." He represented that he himself had always endeavored to preserve peace since his arrival in Canada and could not approve of such hostilities.

The secret set of instructions displays the real purpose of Beckwith's mission: to learn the disposition of the Government and of the people towards the approaching war with Spain, the nature of the negotiations being conducted with the western Indians, and the state of military preparedness.

> As there may be a difference of opinion concerning the western country, and the navigation of the Mississippi, you will be cautious in advancing anything specific on that head, but rather lead them to explain the different lines of policy, each party may have in view, endeavouring to ascertain the extent and importance of the adherents of each particular system. In general you may assert it as your own opinion that in case of a war with Spain you see no reason why we should not assist in forwarding whatever their interests may require.

He was to send full accounts back to Quebec and to Whitehall on these heads and on any other matters of interest and was to remain in the United States as long as his presence there might be of advantage to the King's interests.[10]

Beckwith reached New York in July, 1790, and immediately got in touch with Alexander Hamilton.[11] As a proof of his official connections the Englishman began by mentioning Morris's negotiations, stating that the latter had not produced any regular credentials but only a personal letter from the President. Delays "on account of Mr. Morris's absence on a trip to Holland . . . and other circumstances" [12] might have given the impression of "backwardness" on the part of the Ministry. Dorchester had directed Beckwith to state that any such impression was not well founded "as he had reason to believe that the cabinet of Great Britain entertained a disposition not only towards a friendly intercourse, but towards an alliance with the United States." Beckwith pointed out that it would be to the interest of the United States to join England in any war against Spain. He produced the letter of Dorchester corroborating these statements. Hamilton observed that such were merely Dorchester's sentiments. Beckwith stated that it should be presumed Dorchester knew well the consequences of making such statements without higher authority. He went on to mention his lordship's concern at the Indian depredations on the frontier. Nothing of the kind received the countenance of the Governor General: messages, in fact, had been

10. C.A., *Rept. 1890,* 144.

11. July 8, 1790, according to Hamilton's memorandum, *Works,* IV, 30, corroborated by an entry for that date in Washington's *Diary.*

12. Leeds, in his letter of April 28, alludes to having heard that Morris was in Holland. Morris, in his letter of May 1 to Washington, says, "I might in reply have made some strictures upon the information that I was in Holland." Sparks, *Morris,* II, 11, 15.

sent to the natives to restrain them. The conversation
ended by Beckwith's allusions to threats against the
posts by American army officers on the frontier, which
Dorchester was prone to consider rather as "effusions
of individual feelings than as the effects of any instruction from authority." [13]

A memorandum containing the substance of the
interview was immediately handed to the President by
Hamilton. Beckwith's presence in New York in this
semi-official character had become the cause of some
perturbation to the Administration; first as to whether
he should be accorded any diplomatic status; second,
as to what action to take in case of an Anglo-Spanish
war. For such a war seemed imminent from the nature
of Beckwith's statements to Hamilton and from the
predictions which meanwhile had arrived from Gouverneur Morris.[14] On July 5 Washington recorded in his
diary a rumor that "the Traitor Arnold" had reviewed
the British militia at Detroit. This act, he noted, "had
occasioned much speculation in those parts—and with
many other circumstances, though trifling in themselves, led strongly to the conjecture that the British
had some design on the Spanish settlements on the
Mississippi and of course to surround these United
States." It was three days after this entry that the
President received Hamilton's memorandum. "The aspect of this business," he noted, "in the moment of its
communication to me, appeared simply, and no other
than this;—We did not incline to give any satisfactory
answer to Mr. Morris, who was *officially* commissioned
to ascertain our intentions with respect to the evacua-

13. Hamilton, *Works,* IV, 31–32.
14. Washington's *Diary,* July 1–8, 1790.

tion of the Western Posts within the territory of the United States and other matters . . . until by this unauthorized mode we can discover whether you will enter into an alliance with us and make common cause against Spain. In that case we will enter into a Commercial Treaty with you and *promise perhaps* to fulfil what [we] already stand engaged to perform."

He discussed the question with his cabinet advisers, who then included the Vice President, John Adams, and on this occasion the Chief Justice, John Jay. It was decided to treat Beckwith's communication courteously but to intimate that the agent carried no credentials nor did he give any definite specifications to his irregular proposals for an alliance. Hamilton was commissioned to extract as much information as he could from him and report to the President, without committing the Government in any way. This Hamilton did the following day. The Secretary of the Treasury also took occasion to add, perhaps gratuitously, that there existed no diplomatic connection between the United States and Spain, and that the menaces which Beckwith mentioned as having been thrown out by individual officers with respect to the western posts were entirely unauthorized, "proceeding probably from a degree of irritation which the detention of the posts had produced in the minds of many." When Beckwith alluded to possible British operations against Spanish South American possessions, Hamilton hinted cautiously the dislike of the United States for "any enterprise on New Orleans." As to an alliance, Beckwith was unable to state anything definite.[15]

15. Hamilton, *Works,* IV, 33, 34.

A record of the conversation was forwarded [16] direct to London, where it arrived, as the reader has noted, one day before Gouverneur Morris's interview (of September 15) with the Duke of Leeds.[17] Hamilton appended to his record of the conversation with Beckwith—which tallies with the Englishman's account—a note stating "Mr. Jefferson was privy to this transaction." Since Beckwith failed to record the latter's presence during the interview, we assume that Jefferson knew about the interview but was not present, for the Secretary of State consistently carried out the decision of the Government not to extend any official recognition to Dorchester's aide, who carried no proper credentials.[18]

That Hamilton noted the privity of the Secretary of State to the interview of July 15 is interesting because it contrasts significantly with many other interviews before and after that date to which Jefferson was not privy. It had been at the first interview in 1789, knowledge of which Hamilton did not wish to go any further in America,[19] that the latter had spoken to Beckwith of a possible "political connexion" with England and complementary "naval exertions" of the United States. This remark may well have encouraged Dorchester to resort to this easily effaceable

16. Beckwith to Grenville, N. Y., Aug. 5, 1790, Rec'd Sept. 14, P.R.O.,F.O., 4, 12. The same information was also relayed by way of Dorchester. Dorchester to Grenville, Sept. 25, 1790. C.A., *Rept. 1890,* 145.

17. See above, pp. 81–82.

18. "Besides, what they are saying to you, they are talking to us through Quebec; but so informally, that they may disavow it when they please." Jefferson to the U. S. Informal Agent in Great Britain (G. Morris), Aug. 12, 1790, *Writings,* V, 224.

19. Above, p. 64.

maneuver of sounding Washington's Government as to an alliance in case of war with Spain.

After deciding not to recognize Beckwith there remained the question of what attitude to take if Great Britain in any invasion of Spanish Louisiana should demand a passage across the Northwest Territory. As a matter of fact, the British plans of attack on Louisiana appear to have been based on naval operations; the researches for this essay have revealed no idea of a descent in 1790 on that province from Canada; really the Ministry feared an American attack on the posts during the Spanish crisis as much as the President apprehended an advance through the territory of the United States.[20] But Washington imagined such an invasion to be imminent, as Dorchester fancied an attack on the posts to be dangerously near, and the President dreaded the British encirclement of American territory which the conquest of Louisiana would mean. So much did he fear this that he made to his Cabinet

20. Sir A. Campbell to Pitt, Upper Harley St., Oct. 28, 1790, Chatham MSS, Bdl. 120, printed by Turner in *A.H.R.,* VII, 716; see also Robertson, "Francisco de Miranda," in A.H.A., *Ann. Rept. 1907,* I, 266. Professor Turner also printed the correspondence of Pitt's secret informants, identity unknown, whose information as to Florida and Louisiana, a "second India," the "granary of America," was reaching the Prime Minister during the Nootka negotiations. Professor Turner thinks the letters signed "R. D." were sent direct to Pitt. The fact that some of them are also contained in the correspondence of the British consuls in America suggests an indirect transmission as well. The very confidential nature of these communications makes it impossible to say just how they found their way into Pitt's papers. Whoever received them had previously been corresponding with the informant. "R. D." speaks of "receiving your two letters" in his of November 4, 1790. "R. D." was a pseudonym for "P. Allaire"; see above, Ch. I, n. 52.

officers the well-known request for written opinions on what answer to make in case Dorchester should ask permission to send troops across American soil.

The advice which Washington received shows much confusion of opinion and no determination to resist such an aggression. Jefferson appreciated the fatal results of a conquest of Louisiana but had in mind no resolute course of action. He would refuse to answer any such demand. If the passage were then made, nevertheless, he would keep alive an altercation on the subject until events should decide whether it were more expedient to accept apologies or to profit by the incident as a cause for war. Adams would refuse passage; in case the refusal should be overridden he recommended an energetic negotiation as the utmost action for redress. Jay, whose opinion was also requested, would not go to war if the passage were forced; he thus practically agreed with Adams. Knox, Secretary of War, gave an indefinite answer counseling strict neutrality and yet speaking of the possibility of sufficient inducements which might be accepted to enter the war on the more profitable side. Hamilton took much time and molded his answer into a long state paper. There was a right by international law to refuse or to consent to such a passage; the choice should be made solely according to the interests of the United States. A middle course, that of withholding an answer, was timidly evasive, he believed, undignified and impolitic. Refusal would involve the nation in either war or disgrace; if it could not be backed effectively by force it ought not to be made. All things considered, he believed it would be best to grant the request; there was more to be gained by cultivating the friendship of England than of Spain.[21]

Fortunately these opinions, which would have been so interesting to the Foreign Office during the Nootka crisis, remained unknown to Beckwith.

While the general tenor of Jefferson's counsel dictated neutrality in case of a European war, he characteristically attempted to exploit the situation for the interests of the United States, in order to secure from Great Britain evacuation of the posts and from Spain opening of the Mississippi. In instructions to Morris, written after receiving the latter's account of the notable interview of May 21 with Leeds and Pitt, the Secretary of State declared that if England should formally propose an exchange of diplomatic representatives the United States would appoint a minister. It was the wish of the United States to be neutral, and it would be so if Great Britain would execute the treaty fairly and attempt no conquest adjoining its territory. Simultaneously instructions, also based on the assumption of war, were dispatched to the American *chargés* in Spain and France. In case of hostilities Carmichael, in Madrid, was to press firmly for the opening of the Mississippi and to magnify the unrest of the western citizens whom the United States was endeavoring to quiet with expectations of attaining their object by peaceful means. Short, in Paris, was instructed that in case France should join her ally, she might reasonably be expected to do everything to diminish the number of Spain's enemies: "she cannot doubt that we will be

21. The written opinions may be found in Jefferson, *Writings*, V, 238; J. Adams, *Works*, VIII, 497; W. C. Ford, *The United States and Spain in 1790* (Brooklyn, 1890), pp. 50, 103, for Jay and Knox; Hamilton, *Works*, IV, 48–69.

among them if she does not yield our right to navigate the Mississippi." Through the influence of Lafayette, Short was to induce France to urge Spain to open the river.[22] Thus Jefferson, in the event of war being declared, would have threatened Spain with a rush on New Orleans of irate western citizens; to France he would have spoken openly of placing the United States among Spain's enemies; but to England, the enemy of France and Spain, he would have promised neutrality upon conditions. "Peace and profit" would be the aim of the neutral United States in case of war in Europe, he caused it to be made known to the British Government through a private correspondent of his own, Benjamin Vaughan of London: "A high price and sure market for our productions, and no want of carrying business will I hope enable my countrymen to pay off both their private and public debts." [23]

The question also came up at this time of the expediency of apprising Lord Dorchester of the purpose of the proposed campaign against the Indians. Jefferson's writings contain an opinion against giving such notice.

22. For Jefferson's instructions to Short, Carmichael, and Morris, to be used in the event of war between England and Spain, see his *Writings*, V, 216, 218, 224. They are dated Aug. 2 to 12, 1790, and were taken to Europe by a special messenger, Colonel Humphreys, who sailed for London on September 4. See Beckwith to Grenville, Sept. 4, 1790, P.R.O.,F.O., 4, 12; Jefferson to the United States Secret Agent, Aug. 11, 1790, *Writings*, V, 221. Humphreys did not reach Europe until after the Nootka affair had been settled.

23. Jefferson's letter of June 27, 1790, was conveyed by Vaughan to Evan Nepean, Undersecretary for War in the British Government, on Sept. 8, 1790. I am indebted to Dr. Julian Boyd, editor of the definitive publication of Thomas Jefferson's correspondence, for this document, out of the Public Record Office, F.O., 4, 8.

For, if the notification be early, he [Dorchester] will get the Indians out of the way, and defeat our object. If it be so late as not to leave him time to withdraw them before our stroke be struck, it will then be so late also as not to leave him time to withdraw any secret aids he may have sent them. And the notification will betray to him that he may go on without fear in his expedition against the Spaniards, and for which he may yet have sufficient time after our expedition is over.[24]

Nevertheless the British commandant at Detroit was informed officially by General St. Clair, under whose command the American frontier troops were placed, that the President desired assurances to be given of the peaceful disposition of the United States toward Great Britain and that the military expedition was not against Detroit or any other post in possession of the British: the sole object was to chastise savage tribes, perpetrators of outrages on the American people and humanity in general. The President trusted, therefore, that the savages would receive no assistance nor encouragement and that traders would be restrained from inciting them.[24a] Hamilton already had told Beckwith that an expedition was under way against the western Indians, which, said Beckwith, had been mentioned in order "to prevent any alarm at our Posts, although he relied on my not speaking of it here." [25]

This confidence illustrates the diplomatic intimacy

24. *Writings,* V, 240, Aug. 29, 1790.

24a. St. Clair to Maj. Murray, Marietta, Sept. 19, 1790, C.A.,Q, 49, 105.

25. Beckwith to Dorchester, rec'd, Quebec, Sept. 11, 1790, C.A., *Rept. 1890,* 159.

which had grown up between Hamilton and Beckwith. Until the arrival in October, 1791, of a regularly accredited British Minister, Beckwith kept constantly in close touch with the Secretary of the Treasury. If it was not possible, for lack of proper credentials, to establish any official contact with the Secretary of State, it was easy to communicate informally with the influential Federalist leader who had frankly declared and who continued to declare himself an advocate of a political as well as a commercial connection with England.

In a case of a European war Hamilton would have chosen the side of England if it proved impossible to get both the posts and the Mississippi navigation in return for American neutrality. He had advised Washington that the continued possession of New Orleans by Spain meant in the near future "infallibly . . . a war with Spain, or separation of the Western Country." But

> in regard to the possessions of Great Britain on our left [east] it is at least problematical, whether the acquisition of them will ever be desirable to the United States. It is certain that they are in no shape essential to our prosperity. Except, therefore, the detention of our Western posts, (an object, too, of far less consequence than the navigation of the Mississippi,) there appears no necessary source of future collision with that power.[26]

It was his prime object of foreign policy to adjust as soon as possible all differences with Great Britain and he was impatient at anything or anybody who

26. Hamilton to Washington, Sept. 15, 1790, *Works,* IV, 64, 65.

stood in the way of such an adjustment. To communicate his idea to the British Government he made use of Beckwith, and these communications, always oral and confidential,[27] were frequent, full, and free. After winter closed the river route to Quebec, Beckwith, on whose letters we rely for the revelation of these secret efforts for an Anglo-American *rapprochement,* sent his dispatches direct to England as well as to Quebec, and continued to do so during the remainder of his sojourn in America. Hamilton thus got a quick and ready hearing in London. It is safe to say that this informal diplomacy was far more effective in securing an eventual exchange of regular diplomatic representatives than was the negotiation of Gouverneur Morris. The Secretary of the Treasury early explained to Beckwith that any minister regularly appointed as resident in America would have to negotiate directly with the Secretary of State, who would then become the channel of communication to the President:

> in the turn of such affairs the most minute circumstances, mere trifles, give a favorable bias or otherwise to the whole.
>
> The President's mind I can declare to be perfectly dispassionate on this subject. Mr. Jefferson . . . is a gentleman of honor and zealously desirous of promoting . . . the interests of his country . . . but from some opinions which he has given respecting your Government, and possible

27. *Beckwith:* "You are going from hence [New York] to Philadelphia, if anything should happen that I might wish to communicate to you, you can point out a mode of doing it by letter?"

*Hamilton:* "That would be precarious, there seems a necessity of my seeing you." C.A., *Rept. 1890,* 164.

predilections elsewhere, there may be difficulties which may possibly frustrate the whole, and which might be readily explained away.

In case such difficulties should occur, Hamilton, who had constant access to the President, wished to know of them, in order that they might be "clearly understood and candidly examined." [28]

Hamilton told Beckwith that Morris had been a "little too shy" in responding to Leeds's question whether the United States would send a minister if Great Britain did. He agreed with Beckwith's explanation of the aloofness of the Ministry during the Morris negotiation, that Morris's conduct and attitude had been untactful,[29] and he repeated this to Washington, who replied, sententiously, that "the motives, however, by which the author of the communication to you was actuated, although they *may* have been pure, and in that case praiseworthy, do also (but it may be uncharitable to harbour the suspicion) admit of a different

---

28. Ibid., 149.

29. "If '23' [Morris] has cultivated an intimacy with the Ministers, of any other power in Europe, or has caused suspicion on that ground with respect to France, or elsewhere, he has no authority for so doing, it occurs to me that he was very intimate with Mons. de la Luzerne the Ambassador of France now in London, when he was Minister in this Country; possibly from that circumstance he may have been more frequently there, than prudence ought to have dictated, and the knowledge of this circumstance may have produced a greater reserve on the part of your Administration; these ideas strike me, although I have no ground to go upon." Hamilton to Beckwith, as recorded by the latter. Received by Dorchester Oct. 27, 1790, C.A., *Rept. 1890,* 161. Hamilton's letter to Washington, conveying the gist of the conversation, is dated Sept. 30, *Works,* IV, 73. See also David Humphreys to George Washington, London, Oct. 31, 1790, and F. L. Humphreys, *Life and Times of David Humphreys* (New York and London, 1917), II, 52.

interpretation, and by an easy and pretty direct clue may be developed." [30]

One of Hamilton's statements to Beckwith which illustrates the general nature of what passed between the two men, was made in October, 1790, after news had been received of the first Spanish concession (of July) to England and when the prospect of war had diminished for the moment:

> I have already explained my opinions very fully on the mutual advantages that must result to the two countries from an approximation in commercial matters in the first instance, foreign nations in commerce are guided solely by their respective interests in whatever concerns their intercourse; between you and us there are other circumstances; originally one people, we have a similarity of tastes, of language and general manners. You have a great commercial capital and an immense trade, we have comparatively no commercial capital, and are an agricultural people, but we are a rising country, shall be great consumers, have a preference for your manufactures, and are in the way of paying for them; you have considerable American and West India possessions, our friendship or enmity may soon become important with respect to their security, and I cannot foresee any solid grounds of national difference between us; I do not think the posts are to be considered in this light, and we have no desire to possess anything to the northward of our present boundaries as regulated by the peace; but

30. Washington to Hamilton, Oct. 10, 1790, *Writings*, XI, 501.

the navigation of the river Mississippi we must have, and shortly, and I do not think the bare navigation will be sufficient, we must be able to secure it by having a post at the mouth of the river, either at New Orleans or somewhere near it; there are reports, that the Spanish Government are disposed to change their system, but this I doubt, for it is so different from their national character.

You know we have two parties with us; there are gentlemen who think we ought to be connected with France in the most intimate terms, and that the Bourbon compact furnishes an example for us to follow; there are others who are at least as numerous, and influential, who evidently prefer an English connection, but the present condition of Great Britain and the States is favourable to the former party, and they are zealous to improve it, the present therefore is the moment to take up the matter seriously and dispassionately, and I wish it done without loss of time.

We consider ourselves perfectly at liberty to act with respect to Spain in any way most conducive to our interests, even to the going to war with that power, if we shall think it advisable to join you.[31]

A few weeks later the European mails brought intelligence of the continued preparation of Europe for war and the increased armaments of England.

"We have now a probability of a Spanish war," Beckwith informed the Secretary, "and a possibility

31. C.A., *Rept. 1890,* 162–63; Beckwith to Grenville, Nov. 3, 1790, rec'd Dec. 6, 1790, P.R.O.,F.O., 4, 12. See also Beckwith to Dorchester, C.A., *Rept. 1890,* 165.

of a French one, I trust it will not interrupt our tranquillity with you?"

Hamilton, speaking as an individual, replied that the United States would preserve an honorable attention to its engagements with foreign powers. This, however, did not mean taking the part of France, "in a contest in which she is altogether an auxiliary," and it might be considered expedient to use the circumstances to secure those points which were in contest with Spain. "Certain points have occurred since the peace which leave us perfectly free with respect to France, *even if she should go to war as a principal.*"

He further declared that there existed no secret agreement with France.

Beckwith trusted the United States courts would render justice to complaints against state laws "which impede the ordinary course of justice between debtors and creditors."

"Undoubtedly," assured Hamilton, "for our judiciary has declared treaties with foreign powers to be the law of the land. Nothing but an insurrection in opposition to their decisions can in future prevent the regular and usual course of justice."

Speaking of the increasing strength of the federal government, Hamilton asserted: "At this time we are capable of making considerable exertions, even maritime ones, if from circumstances it became a measure of government to encourage them. . . . It would be an act of wisdom in the ministers of Great Britain to attach and connect the States upon political as well as commercial considerations." [32]

Contrasted with the import of these confidential

32. Ibid. Beckwith to Grenville, Nov. 3, 1790.

conversations was the attitude of the Secretary of State, who believed that Morris had conducted his negotiation in a praiseworthy manner and who was convinced that the general conduct of Great Britain since the War of Independence was not calculated to arouse kindly dispositions in America. To the author of the Declaration of Independence any political connection with Great Britain was abhorrent. "As to the alliance they propose, it would involve us against France and Spain. And considered even in a moral view, no price could repay such an abandonment of character. . . . we are truly disposed to remain strictly neutral." [33] But in himself as a "political man," wrote Jefferson to a friend, the British would find no passion for or against them. Were they disposed to come halfway, he would meet them, because he thought it would be for the good of the country, but he had no idea they would advance that far.[34]

When Jefferson took up his office in March, 1790, Washington turned over to him the direction of the Morris negotiation. In December the Secretary of State submitted a report on the mission, based on Morris's dispatches as late as September 18. Jefferson's conclusion was that England had absolutely no intention of giving up the posts, that if her suggestions of indemnification for unpaid debts were met the amount would be placed so high as to insure a disagreement, in order to preserve the pretext under which the posts were held. Were the other insurmountable obstacles removed he was of the opinion that the question of deported

33. Quoted from Jefferson Papers by Ford, *U. S. and Spain in 1790*, p. 67.
34. Jefferson to Francis Kinloch, Nov. 26, 1790, *Writings*, V, 249.

Negroes could be settled. As to a commercial treaty the British equivocated on every proposal made them, from which it was concluded "they do not mean to subject their present advantages in commerce to the risk which might attend a discussion of them. . . . Unless indeed we would agree to make it a treaty of *alliance* as well as of *commerce* so as to undermine our obligations with France." He adopted Morris's opinion that differences in the British Cabinet prevented the Secretary for Foreign Affairs from carrying out his own inclination to send a minister. It would be dishonorable and even injurious, decided Jefferson, to renew overtures or an exchange of ministers until proposals should be brought forward earnestly on the other side: the demand for the posts and for indemnification for the deported slaves ought not to be made again until the country should be in readiness to do itself the justice which might be refused.[35]

Though Congress was then in session, Jefferson's report lay on the President's desk two months before it was transmitted to that body by Washington. Even before any official information was received of the Morris mission and its failure, anti-British sentiment had been rising in the House of Representatives. It seemed quite likely that national navigation laws similar to those of England would pass during the session, Hamilton informed Beckwith, January 19, 1791. The Secretary deprecated the effect which such legislation would have on British shipping. Nevertheless he was using all his tremendous influence to prevent enactment of the laws. That very night an English packet arrived with private letters that repeated the rumor, which

35. *Writings*, V, 262, Dec. 15, 1790.

Morris had heard in London, that a British Minister, one Elliot, was to be sent to the United States. In the morning Beckwith asked Hamilton if the arrival of the packet had changed his ideas of the day before. Hamilton replied that it had: the intention of the British Government to send a minister would "put an end to the suggestions of that party with us, who wishing well to a French interest, take every occasion to insist that we are held in no consideration by the English Government.

"Upon the subject of commerce and navigation, which I mentioned to you yesterday, I think I can assure you that nothing will take place during the present session to the injury of your trade." [36]

The rumors of a British Minister were by no means official notice. Congress grew increasingly hostile. Several communications from the executive proved well timed, as at least the Secretary of State must have realized, to increase that hostility. The first of these was a report by Jefferson on the state of the whale and cod fisheries, transmitted February 4, 1791, showing how British protective legislation was injuring the markets of the New England fisheries. He recommended bounties for American fishermen and reprisals against British commerce. For the last century, Jefferson ingeniously pointed out, England had controlled the Anglo-American carrying trade and during that time had experienced three years of war to five years of peace. If she were to retain that control American citizens would continue to pay not only the ordinary profitable freightage to English carriers but nearly half

36. Beckwith to Grenville, N. Y., Jan. 23, 1791, Rec'd Mar. 17, P.R.O.,F.O., 12.

the time would be compelled to pay also a freight rate
fifty-five per cent higher because Great Britain happened to be at war.[37] Two days before this report
Jefferson sent to the Senate a report of a committee of
the French National Assembly recommending a new
commercial treaty, which that Government desired in
order to avoid some of the consequences of the American tariff and tonnage laws. This request emphasized
the persuasive power of such legislation and brought
into contrast the disinclination of England to negotiate
a treaty of commerce.[38] Finally on February 14, the
President sent in to Congress Jefferson's strongly
worded report on the Morris mission.

The cumulative effect on the House of Representatives of these reports was to bring quickly to the front
in a stronger form than ever the discriminatory legislation which had been voted down in the summer of 1789.
The strong but vigorous minority that had championed
Madison's old proposals was now able to assert that
forbearance had done nothing to alter the situation and
that England had spurned our honest overtures for a
commercial treaty. The committee to which Jefferson's
reports had been referred now brought forward a bill
which was an exact imitation of the British Navigation
Laws in that it prohibited the importation into the
United States of goods not the growth, product, or
manufacture of the country under whose flag they were
shipped, when such country refused to allow the importation of American products in American vessels

37. *A.S.P.*, *Commerce and Navigation*, I, 8. See also *A.S.P.,F.R.*,
I, 121.
38. F. J. Turner, ed., *Correspondence of the French Ministers to the
United States, 1791–1797*, A.H.A., *Ann. Rept. 1903*, II, introduction.

(as Great Britain refused to do in the case of the West Indies).[39] Such a law would strike at the heart of the British carrying trade. It threatened the stability of England's best foreign market. The bill reached a second reading (February 22, 1791). On that day a motion to refer it to the Committee of the Whole produced a warm debate from which the House adjourned without decision. During the night heads were put together, for the next morning the bill mysteriously "vanished"[40] in a vote to refer the message of the President to the Secretary of State for report to the next session of Congress.[41]

Despite this proven influence of Hamilton the strength of the discrimination movement appeared most ominous to Beckwith. In it he saw danger of the ascendancy of Jefferson and the francophiles. While the bill was before Congress he had unloaded his apprehensions to Hamilton, who assured him that little would come of the movement and declared that, whatever might have been the idea of certain "others," the President had no thought of timing the reports to play into the hands of a French party. The bill had been defeated, wrote Beckwith, only in expectation of an amicable settlement during the summer recess of commercial difficulties with England. If this were not undertaken immediately he was persuaded that British commerce would not remain in the existing favorable condition after the reassembling of Congress in October. A treaty of commerce might even lead to a treaty of

39. Beckwith learned that the bill was carried through the committee by a majority of only one. Beckwith to Grenville, Mar. 3, 1791, P.R.O.,F.O., 4, 12.

40. Jefferson to Rutledge, Aug. 29, 1791, *Writings*, V, 375.

41. *Journal of the House of Representatives*, Feb. 14–23, 1791.

alliance, if desired, but if no negotiations with the
United States should take place within the next few
months the "French interest" would triumph. Jefferson and his following, chiefly from the southern states,
would go to any length during the summer to attain
their objects at the next session, though the party of the
"British interest" was equally determined.[42]

"Our treasurer [i.e. Hamilton]," the Secretary of
State wrote privately to James Monroe, "still thinks
that these encroachments on our carrying trade must
be met by passive obedience and non-resistance, lest any
misunderstanding with them should affect our credit or
the prices of our public paper. New schemes are on foot
for bringing more paper to market by encouraging
great manufacturing companies to form, and their actions, or paper shares, to be transferable as bank-stock.
We are ruined, Sir, if we do not overrule the principle
that 'the more we owe, the more prosperous we shall
be' . . ."[43]

Jefferson's official correspondence in the spring of
1791 shows that he expected the discrimination bills to
be passed at the next session, and his private letters
indicate that the collapse of these measures during the
following summer meant a personal defeat to him. He
wrote the American *chargés* in France, Spain, and Portugal of the anticipated legislation and instructed them
at the proper time to intimate that the adoption of similar laws by those nations would be all that was necessary to make the system tight against England.[44] In

42. Beckwith to Grenville, Mar. 3, 1791, Rec'd May 1, P.R.O.,F.O.,
4, 12.
43. *Writings,* V, 318, Philadelphia, April 17, 1791.
44. *Writings,* V, 302, 303.

May and June he and his lieutenant Madison made a
vacation tour through New England. It is unreasonable
to suppose that they neglected opportunities to advance
their political ideas. Beckwith believed this trip to be
for the purpose of agitating an anti-British policy and
he imagined that his own personal exertions in a tour
which he made ahead of the Virginians had been successful in frustrating their object.[45] Nevertheless, the
anti-British party increased in strength during the summer.[46] There was good reason to anticipate vigorous

45. Jefferson, *Writings*, V, 336–42; See P. L. Ford's introduction to
this volume. Beckwith to Grenville, June 14, 1791, P.R.O.,F.O., 4, 12.

46. "I am sorry to inform Your Grace that the Secretary of State's
Party and Politicks gains ground here, and I fear will have influence
enough to cause acts and resolves which may be unfriendly to Great
Britain, to be passed early in the next session of Congress. The Secretary of State, together with Mr. Madison . . . are now . . . gone to
the Eastern States, there to proselyte as far as they are able to a
commercial war with Great Britain. . . .

"Lord Dorchester has had one of his aides de camp here and at
Philadelphia for the year Past! The stationing of this person about
Congress hath indeed disgusted not a few who leaned toward Great
Britain. 'An Envoy,' say they, 'from a Colony Governor, to a sovereign
power is a business heretofore unheard of! he can be considered in no
other light than as a petty spy.'

"What the purposes of Major Beckwith's being sent here, By what
authority he is here,—or, of what his Powers may be (if he has any in
the Diplomatic line), I am totally ignorant! I have, however, shown
him all the countenance and respect, due from me to an officer of His
Majesty's army, and heartily wish that his mission, if he has any from
Authority, may not turn out fruitless, or Detrimental to His Majesty's
General Service in the States." Sir John Temple (Consul at N. Y.)
to the Duke of Leeds, May 23, 1791, rec'd July 23. The consular correspondence for this year, especially that of Phineas Bond (at Philadelphia), and Temple, is a valuable source; but since its general information duplicates Beckwith's, the latter and other sources closer in touch
with American politics have been more generally cited. See P.R.O.,F.O.,
4, 10 and 12.

action when the report requested from the Secretary of State should be duly submitted to Congress in the autumn.

Turning now to note the development of Pitt's American policy after the departure of Morris and the termination of the Nootka controversy, it will be remembered that in December, 1789, Lord Grenville had referred the American tariff and tonnage acts to the Committee of the Privy Council for Trade, for study and report. At his request, the Committee presented, January 28, 1791, a report on those laws and their effect on British commerce. The purpose of submitting the report at this time was, as explained therein, in order that the information and advice of the committee might be utilized *for the instruction of the Minister who was about to depart for America.* Since Grenville himself was the ablest member of the Committee, it is likely that he caused the report to be made immediately after the Ministry had reached a decision to send a minister. At any rate, this is the first evidence of such a decision that the present investigation has revealed. The industry of the Committee and the vast amount of material which it had sorted and arranged make this report one of the best of all sources for the student of early American economic history. After examining the whole field of Anglo-American trade and establishing its conclusions with many tables of statistics, the Committee declared that nine-tenths of the exports of Great Britain to the United States paid the same duties as similar exports of other nations, the American duties were less than charged by any other government, and there was no fear of competition in the supply of these goods as long as Congress made no discrimination among different foreign nations. American manufactures would receive little impetus from legislative encouragement, and no objection could be made to the existing tariff and tonnage acts, constituting as they did an act of administration universally the custom of independent nations. The Committee held that the condition of Anglo-American trade, as it stood in 1790, untouched by any discrimination against England, was eminently satisfactory.

As advice for commercial policy, to be the guide of any negotiations with the United States, the Committee recommended the Government should seek a pledge by that nation not to raise any higher the duties on British manufactures, or at least to make them no higher than the same goods from other foreign nations, and this privilege *should be guaranteed against all future domestic legislation.* In return England might make the concession that imports from the United States would never be taxed more heavily than those of the most-favored nation. The West Indian Islands question should be avoided. The present footing should be continued for a term of years: under no consideration should that commerce be opened to American ships. Finally, if demanded, American vessels might be exempted from the payment of light, port, and Trinity dues in the British Isles.[47]

47. Report of the Privy Council on American Trade, Jan. 28, 1791, in *Collection of Interesting and Important Reports and Papers on Navigation and Trade,* p. 45. The peculiar nature of the port, light, and Trinity dues was that, according to the computations of the Committee itself, the sums which American ships had to pay on their arrival in British ports for such taxes more than balanced the additional tonnage duties demanded in the United States on foreign ships. A committee of London merchants prepared for the Privy Council an illuminating

Grenville lost no time in getting news to proper persons in America of the decision to send a British Minister to the United States.[48] The Foreign Secretary invited to his office at Whitehall Colonel William S. Smith, former secretary of John Adams's American legation at London. Smith, who was Adams's son-in-law, had been sojourning in the British capital in pursuit of personal affairs and was about to return home. He was then esteemed to be one of the "moderate party" in America. To him Grenville emphasized a strong desire for a settlement of existing difficulties with the United States and for a "commercial arrangement." For these purposes, the Secretary declared, a British Minister would be sent within three months. He added that His Majesty wished that some means might be taken to end the unfortunate hostilities in the Indian country and requested Smith to convey this information to persons of authority. The April packet for New York was held by Government's orders at Falmouth until Smith could board it.[49]

Smith reached New York on June 5, 1791, and im-

comparison. It showed that an American ship of 160 tons paid in England nine pounds sterling more than a British ship of equal weight would be charged in American harbors for tonnage dues above those levied on domestic vessels. At this time American ships enjoyed exemption from certain alien duties levied on other foreign shipping: this boon ought to cease, declared the report, in the face of the American tariff and tonnage acts.

48. Beckwith's dispatch of January 23, 1791, reached London March 17; that of March 3, written after the appearance of Jefferson's reports and the House Committee's navigation bills of February, did not reach London until May 1, although Grenville may have had unofficial news before that date of resurrection of the discrimination bills in Congress.

49. P. Colquhoun to Grenville, July 29, Aug. 15, 1791, *Dropmore Papers*, II, 145, 157, 160; Beckwith to Grenville, July 31, 1791, P.R.O.,F.O., 4, 12; C.A., *Rept. 1890, 172.* The interview was on April 9.

mediately communicated Grenville's assurances to the
persons for whom they were intended. His information
gave weight to the arguments of the Federalists against
discrimination. During the summer private letters arrived from other official sources, corroborating Smith's
report. The satisfaction of Hamilton and his followers
of the "moderate party" was expressed to Beckwith.
The only detail which continued unsatisfactory, said
Hamilton, was Lord Grenville's remark to Smith concerning the termination of Indian hostilities; this might
be so construed as to indicate a desire of the British
Government to take some step to that end, and it would
be unfortunate if anything of so trivial a nature should
prevent a happy adjustment.

Expectation of arrival of a minister soon shattered
the plans of the followers of Jefferson and Madison,
whose hopes for the passage of the drastic navigation
laws at the next session of Congress had appeared so
well grounded. "I have little hope," wrote Jefferson to
a friend, in August, "that the result will be anything
more than to turn the left cheek to him who has smitten
the right; we have to encounter not only the prejudices
in favor of England, but those of the Eastern states,
whose ships in the opinion of some will over run our
land." [50]

A careful study of the dates of Beckwith's dispatches, both of departure from America and reception at Whitehall, shows conclusively that the British
Government had come to a decision to send a minister
to the United States (in January, 1791) before revival
of the movement in Congress for navigation laws which
in effect would discriminate against the commerce of

50. Jefferson to Rutledge, Aug. 29, 1791, *Writings,* V, 375.

England. When this news did reach England in April
or May it undoubtedly accelerated[51] a move which had
already been decided some weeks previously. Apparently a decision made in the autumn of 1790, rumors
of which reached America in January, 1791, was later
suspended upon the settlement of the Nootka crisis,
after which little disposition was manifested to treat
seriously with the unpleasing Morris.[52]

51. A letter to Grenville from the Lords of the Committee of the
Privy Council for Trade, dated Whitehall, May 26, 1791, transmits
letters from the Consuls in the United States (from Bond [Phila., 3
Jan., 1791], from Miller [Charleston, 8 Feb., 1791], from Bond [Phila.,
14 March, 1791]). Bond's last letter explains fully the probability of
the session of Congress placing duties on British produce and manufactures. The Committee comments, "The Lords of the Privy Council
are therefore of the opinion that as little time as possible should be
lost in making proper plans for counteracting the Intention of those
Members of Congress, whose Interest or Inclination it may be to support any Propositions which may be unfriendly to the commerce and
navigation of this country." P.R.O.,F.O., 4, 10.

52. In 1795 Gouverneur Morris, disgusted at the lengths to which
the French Revolution had gone, arrived in England after travels in
Germany and offered his services, as regarded his information of European affairs and his personal connections, to Grenville, then Foreign
Secretary, believing that it was essential for the welfare of Europe
and America that Britain should triumph in the war with France. He
then told the Undersecretary for Foreign Affairs, Burges, that whatever the impression on his mind might have been when he went to
France in 1790, the experience he had gained there had satisfied him
that no connection could be so advantageous to America as one with
England. He said to Burges that he believed when last in England
(1790) he had been looked on with doubt and suspicion, that he had
abstained from appearing at Court; but that he now felt a great desire to be presented, "as, from the signature of the late treaty [Jay's
Treaty] and from the sentiments he entertained towards His Majesty
and this country [England], he conceived that such a step on his part
would not be unacceptable." Burges to Grenville, *Dropmore Papers*,
III, 87. Morris's offer to supply political information was accepted. For
his letters to Grenville, mostly from Berlin, see *Dropmore Papers*, III,
index.

The establishment of a legation at Philadelphia followed directly the informal conferences between Hamilton and Beckwith of the last months of 1790 and the arguments for an Anglo-American understanding which the Federalist leader advanced therein. Pitt's Government had to choose between beginning diplomatic relations with a country in whose administration an influential party with an amenable leader favored more cordial relations with England on the one hand, or, on the other hand, prolonging a situation which could only play into the hands of the anti-British and anti-Federalist party now crystallizing under the leadership of Thomas Jefferson, the friend of France. The latter choice could lead but to the injury of British commerce. The Report of the Privy Council of 1791 had given an economic as well as a political recognition of that American independence which the treaty of peace had legally acknowledged.

# CHAPTER 5

# Jefferson, Hammond, and Hamilton

THE person selected for the appointment to America was George Hammond, a young diplomat of twenty-seven years, who was possessed of some experience in minor positions at several of the European courts. At Paris in 1783 when secretary to David Hartley during the peace negotiations he had made the acquaintance of Jefferson. Endowed with a fairly keen mind and a fluent pen, Hammond was an assiduous worker who devoted himself unflaggingly to his duty during his stay in the United States and followed his instructions with a diligence which uniformly met the approbation of his superiors. Upon his return to England in 1795 he was made Undersecretary for Foreign Affairs, a post at which he spent a life which was long and serviceable but never brilliant.[1]

Hammond's instructions underwent an interesting evolution. The first draft was written by Lord Hawkesbury,[2] who as Charles Jenkinson had been Lord North's

1. While residing in Philadelphia he married the daughter of Andrew Allen, by whom he was father to Edmund, Lord Hammond. For details of his life see *Dictionary of National Biography*.

2. Charles Jenkinson, Lord Hawkesbury, 1727–1808; Undersecretary of State, 1761; House of Commons, 1761–1786; created Baron Hawkesbury, 1786; Earl of Liverpool, 1796; served as a Lord of the Admiralty

Secretary at War during the latter years of the American Revolution and who at this time was President of the Committee of the Privy Council for Trade and Plantations. In this capacity he was one of the Government's principal advisers on American affairs. Hawkesbury recommended to Grenville that the minister to be sent to the United States be empowered to negotiate a treaty of commerce on the basis of the proposals suggested by the Report of the Privy Council Committee for Trade[3]—proposals which would concede practically nothing and in return would require a guaranty of no future discrimination by Congress against British goods, and if possible an agreement never to raise any higher the existing tariff on British manufactures. As to the differences which had arisen over the execution of the treaty of peace, the minister should be authorized merely to *discuss* those points *ad refendum* and should be given no power to conclude any definite settlement. Hawkesbury's experience had convinced him that the posts were still indispensable to the control of the navigation of the Great Lakes and monopoly of the fur trade as well as being security for fidelity of the Indians. His recommendations betray a strong disinclination to abandon an excuse for continuing to occupy these strategic positions. In case of a movement in the American Congress for discrimination it was Hawkesbury's opinion (perhaps based on the success of Beckwith)

---

and of the Treasury under the Duke of Grafton, 1767–1772; leader of the King's Friends under Lord Bute, 1763; Privy Council, 1773–1808; Secretary at War under Lord North, 1778–1783; President of the Committee of the Privy Council for Trade and Plantations, 1786, and Chancellor of the Duchy of Lancaster; active in the Lords until the failure of his health in 1805.

3. See above, p. 117.

that the minister might cultivate the aquaintance of
members of Congress and argue them out of it, either
by demonstration of greater benefits of the existing
commercial status or by threats of counter-discrimina-
tion by Parliament. Under no circumstances, declared
Hawkesbury, should monopoly of the West Indian
navigation be broken into in favor of the United
States.[4]

Grenville's final instructions to Hammond embodied
certain modifications of Hawkesbury's draft. Gren-

4. "I have only to observe that as these posts are of great Service in
securing the Fidelity and Attachment of the Indians, and as they afford
to Great Britain the means of commanding the Navigation of the
great Lakes and the communication of the said Lakes with the River
St. Lawrence, they are certainly of great importance to the Security of
Canada, and to the Interests of this Country, both in a commercial and
political view. It is to be wished therefore that they should remain in
His Majesty's possession, if the Conduct of the United States should
continue to justify this measure on the part of Great Britain." Draft
by Lord Hawkesbury of the Formal Instructions to be given to H. M.
Minister to the United States, P.R.O.,F.O., 4, 10. See also Bernard
Mayo, ed., *Instructions to the British Ministers to the United States,
1791–1812*, A.H.A., *Ann. Rept. 1936*, III (Washington, 1941), pp. 5–8.

On February 22, 1782, General Conway introduced his motion in the
House of Commons for an address praying His Majesty that the war
on the continent of North America might no longer be pursued for the
impractical purpose of reducing the inhabitants of the country to
obedience by force. The motion was lost by one vote. Defending Lord
North's tottering Government, Jenkinson, then Secretary at War, made
a remark which is highly significant of his consistent policy in regard
to the frontier posts and altogether on all fours with the recommendations he was giving to Pitt's Government in 1791. He stated that it was
the intention of the Government to convert the war in America into a
*"war of posts."* " 'His idea was that we were to keep no regular army
in the field; but, in keeping those posts we had, we might add others
to them whenever they should be found advantageous to us: thus
affording us the means of attacking the enemy if an opportunity served
of doing it with success.' " G. O. Trevelyan, *George the Third and
Charles Fox* (2 vols. London, 1912–14), II, 436.

ville's policy was to withhold powers to conclude a commercial treaty but to emphasize settlement of the frontier question. His Majesty would be justified, the instructions read, in holding the posts at this time, even did the United States comply in full with the terms of the treaty of 1783, because when a party refuses for an indefinite time to comply with a treaty it cannot after so long a refusal and the resulting damage suddenly fulfill the stipulations and claim all advantages originally reserved for it in the treaty. Nevertheless the Minister might enter into a negotiation on these heads.

> In all your conversations upon the Subject, you will be careful to let it be clearly understood that it must be an essential and sine qua non condition of any such Arrangement that every practicable measure should be adopted by the States for the execution of the Fourth, Fifth, and Sixth Articles of the Treaty of Peace[5] as far as the circumstances of the length of time which has elapsed, render it possible that effect should now be given to those stipulations. You are to consider this as the first and leading Object of your Mission.

Hammond was directed upon his arrival in America to secure specific information as to the instances wherein the treaty of peace had been violated by the United States.

> You will lose no time in stating these Particulars to those with whom you may treat in America, *and to the Persons of distinction and weight in the American Government,* in order to learn how far they are disposed and by what means, to supply

5. For literal text of the treaty, see Appendix VI.

such deficiencies as may still be found to exist. I am
not without hopes, *from the circumstances of the
late Communications which have passed on this
Subject, that there exists among those who have
the greatest Influence in the Government of America, a real disposition to meet the just Expectations
of this Country in that respect.* And if you should
find this Opinion confirmed by the nature of the
conversations which you will hold with these Persons on your arrival in America, you may assure
them of His Majesty's disposition to contribute
on His part towards removing the Grounds of
future difficulties by some practicable and reasonable Arrangement on the Subject of the Posts.

On this point more definite instructions were promised after a conference should have been held with Lord
Dorchester, whose arrival in England was expected
soon; but in general Hammond was directed to propose
mediation of the British Government for the ending of
hostilities between the United States and the hostile
western Indians.

The Circumstances of the War, as far as they are
yet known here, have been such as will probably
render the Americans sincerely desirous of Peace,
and if any opportunity should occur, in which it
should appear to you that your interposition, or
that of the Government of Canada could conduce
to that Object, in a manner not inconsistent with
the security of the Indians, you are authorized to
exert yourself for that purpose, taking care always
to adopt no measures respecting it, except in concert with His Majesty's Government in America,

under whose direction the superintendance of Indian Affairs has been placed by His Majesty.

In case of any hostilities between the United States and Spain, Hammond was to be careful not to commit England in such complications, but to preserve a strictly neutral attitude.

In carrying out his instructions he was to express a readiness to discuss the different points necessary to a fulfillment of the treaty and was to receive and transmit any reasonable proposal for the same; pending such negotiation the *status quo* to be preserved by the American Government, and every degree of discouragement to be given by that Government as well as by His Majesty's officers to any Americans who might attempt to settle "within the limits of the Country now occupied by the British."

A separate paper set forth instructions as to commercial questions. In case of another attempt by Congress to pass discriminatory legislation he was to assure the "Members of the Government" that Great Britain was desirous of a "reciprocal advantage" and that he was empowered to enter into negotiations for a commercial treaty on the most-favored-nation principle, both as to British colonies and home dominions. He was to point out that some duties on American goods imported in American ships into England were lower than duties on similar goods from other nations; these favorable distinctions could not continue without equivalents rendered by the United States. In case of a tendency in Congress to increase discrimination in favor of American shipping he was to let it be understood that plans for similar measures were dormant in Parliament. Any proposals whatsoever for a commercial treaty were to be received *ad referendum* only. For his confidential information Hammond was furnished with a copy of the Report of the Privy Council for Trade on American commerce.[6]

The nature of these instructions makes it obvious that the primary purpose of Hammond's mission was to prevent, by presence of a British Minister and procrastinated negotiation, a revival of the discrimination movement. He was not empowered to conclude any definite settlement either as to the frontier or as to commerce. The necessity of referring any proposal back to London for further consideration made it possible to resort to infinite delay as long as British commerce continued on the existing favorable footing. Relinquishment of the frontier posts, which we remember Grenville in 1790 had decided to be practicable and which he must have realized from Hamilton's communications to be necessary to any adjustment with the United States, was now apparently coupled with a proposal to mediate between the American Government and its own hostile Indians. Under cover of this mediation it would be possible to shift the garrisons to equally strong positions just across the boundary and to keep the American Indian country in the possession of the natives who would continue to be under the influence of the Indian Department of British North America. In such circumstances an evacuation of the posts need be attended by little inconvenience to English interests. This project is of such importance to the history of the American West that it is reserved for special study in a separate chapter.

6. Grenville to Hammond, Nos. 1 and 2, Sept. 1, 1791, P.R.O.,F.O., 4, 11. Italics inserted. Printed in Mayo, *Instructions,* pp. 13–19.

The British Minister's presence was officially communicated to Jefferson by the consul at Philadelphia, who declared that Mr. Hammond would be ready to present his credentials as soon as he was informed of the appointment of an American Minister to London. Jefferson later assured Hammond that a minister would be appointed and asked if such assurance were sufficient authority for him to assume his functions. Hammond would not present his credentials until a nomination should be made. This was made on November 9, 1791, and though it could not be certain for a few weeks whether the nominee would accept, the Englishman deemed the nomination in itself sufficient authorization for him to begin his official duties.[7] He was soon able to report that Thomas Pinckney of South Carolina had been appointed as Minister to the Court of St. James's.[8] Thus was Jefferson's determination requited—that another American Minister should never be sent to England until a duly authorized representative of Great Britain had arrived in the United States.

Hammond informed Jefferson—who speedily reminded him of nonexecution of Article VII of the treaty[9]—that he was empowered to discuss reasonable means of fulfilling this article as well as Articles IV, V,

7. Hammond to Grenville, Oct. 23, Nov. 1, 16, 1791, P.R.O.,F.O., 4, 11.

8. "Those persons of this country who are desirous of promoting and preserving a good understanding and harmony with Great Britain are extremely well satisfied with Mr. Pinckney's appointment, as they consider the circumstance of his education at Westminster School, and of his having passed a great part of his life in England, as having a natural tendency to inspire him with a predilection for the country, and a desire of rendering his conduct satisfactory." Hammond to Grenville, private, Jan. 9, 1792, *Dropmore Papers,* II, 250.

9. For literal text of the treaty, see Appendix VI.

and VI, which, he asserted, had not been executed by
the Government of the United States. He took care to
have it understood that the King was ready to promote
and facilitate commercial intercourse on "principles of
reciprocal benefit." Jefferson with adequate precision
assumed that such words meant in reality no powers
to negotiate a commercial treaty or to make any
specific provisions for one, but merely a readiness to
concur in appointing persons, times, and places for
commencing such a negotiation. By this proper caution
he at the start forced Hammond to admit that he had
no powers to conclude anything definite.[10] Hammond
believed that this "preciseness" was caused by the
Secretary's set hypothesis that Great Britain had no
inclination for a definite commercial treaty and by his
desire to incorporate in his forthcoming report to
Congress a corresponding statement. Hence the British
Minister deemed it consistent with his instructions to
answer him in such a way as to leave no doubt of a
*disposition* to suffer the question to be discussed candidly.

Jefferson's hypothesis certainly was correct. The
evidence adduced in this and previous chapters shows
that there was no desire in England to initiate any
commercial treaty. Whether Hammond's conjecture
about the report in preparation was accurate cannot be
said; at any rate Jefferson postponed the report and
entered on a discussion of infractions of the treaty of
peace. He formally enumerated the American heads of
complaint: retention of the posts; carrying off of Negro
slaves; the necessity of settling the disputed boundary

10. *A.S.P.,F.R.*, I, 189.

on the northeastern frontier.[11] In an appendix to the
note he summarized the correspondence with General
Sir Guy Carleton, the British military commander in
1783, over the Negro question. Jefferson took the
view that the treaty in forbidding "the carrying away
of negroes or other property" prohibited embarkation
of any Negroes whatsoever after the proclamation
of cessation of hostilities. This was contrary to the
idea of the British commander-in-chief, who had maintained that such former slaves as had taken advantage
of army proclamations manumitting them upon their
entrance within British lines continued upon the descent
of peace to be free men; hence they were not included
in the meaning of the treaty clause, which stipulated
property.[12] Presentation of these formal charges by the

11. The famous northeastern boundary dispute, arising over the
doubtful identity of the River St. Croix—stipulated as the boundary
between the United States and New Brunswick, and from the source
of which the line was to run north to the "highlands of Nova Scotia"
—arose soon after the treaty had been ratified. The river is indicated
on Mitchell's Map, used by the negotiators, but there proved to be no
stream in that vicinity commonly called the St. Croix. The United
States maintained that the Magaguadavic was the river really meant
by the treaty. Great Britain asserted that it was the Schoodiac, nine
miles west of the Magaguadavic. The disputed area at this time
comprised between 7,000 and 8,000 square miles. For details see J. B.
Moore, *History and Digest of the International Arbitrations to which
the United States Has Been a Party* (6 vols. Washington, 1898), I, 5;
*A.S.P.,F.R.,* I, 90–100.

12. F. A. Ogg, "Jay's Treaty and the Slavery Interests," A.H.A.,
*Ann. Rept. 1901,* I. Material not available to Professor Ogg but containing little essentially new information is the correspondence of
the Foreign Office, especially Hammond's dispatches to Grenville and
Dorchester. Also relevant is an abstract of the Negro controversy in
the Chatham MSS, Bdl. 344; and letters between the historian
George Bancroft and Mr. John Jay, descendant of the Chief Justice,
in 1882, of which the originals are preserved in the N. Y. Public
Library.

Secretary of State opened a one-sided diplomatic duel which constitutes the chief feature of Anglo-American diplomacy in the year 1792.

With the help of the British consuls, especially the industrious Phineas Bond of Philadelphia, Hammond proceeded to gather a mass of material in the shape of acts of law and judicial decisions which he believed would establish American violations of the treaty. On this basis he drew up a formal abstract and presented it to Jefferson, in March, 1792. At the end of the document, which Hammond believed to be really formidable,[13] he grouped the titles of acts and decisions substantiating statements made in the text. In no case was the matter in the appendix specifically cited. This note and Jefferson's reply to it go to the root of the controversy as to who was to be blamed for the nonfulfillment of the treaty.

By recrimination Hammond quickly disposed of American complaints as to retention of the posts. He simply asserted that the stipulations of Article VII had been "suspended" because of previous American infractions of the treaty. He then set forth the instances wherein British subjects had suffered and were suffering as a result of such infractions, classifying the cases under the heads of those relating to Loyalists, and confiscations of their property; and of those concerning legal obstacles placed by the states in the way of recovery of debts by British creditors.

As to Loyalists and confiscations, Hammond maintained that the recommendations agreed on by Article

13. "A body of proof so complete and substantial as to preclude the probability of cavil and contradiction on the part of this government." Hammond to Grenville, Mar. 6, 1792, P.R.O.,F.O., 4, 14.

V of the treaty (i.e., "recommendations" by Congress to the several states for restitution of property confiscated from British subjects during the war) had not been carried out consistently with justice and the spirit of conciliation. On the contrary, state laws enacted during the war for confiscation of Loyalist estates remained unrepealed, as did acts of proscription, banishment, and attainder: further, he averred that acts of confiscation had been passed since the peace in violation of Article VI. Thus one state had laws giving damage for trespass on property occupied by British military forces; in another British subjects had been indicted for murder committed within the royal lines before cessation of hostilities. As to debts, the statement claimed that, despite the provision of Article IV that there should be no impediment in the way of recovery of the full value of debts contracted before the war, legal obstacles did exist. Such were acts to prohibit suits for recovery, personal disability acts, acts suspending recovery or compelling creditors to take payment in lands at appraised values, often arbitrary. All this legislation of individual states during the war remained unrepealed after the peace. Laws obstructing recovery of debts actually had been passed since ratification of the treaty, new tender and valuation laws, and laws allowing payments in depreciated paper currency and in installments over a lengthy period. Decisions of state courts had been contrary to Article IV, in that interest on debts during wartime had not been allowed; the treaty phrase providing for the recovery of "full value" of debts in "sterling money" ought to include interest. Moreover, decisions on questions of recovery had been postponed. Again, while British creditors underwent these hard-

ships they were made to give security for all debts owed
by them before they could institute a suit. Finally, Hammond contrasted the righteous and even-handed justice
of British law courts, where American citizens were
concerned, with the faulty procedure of the American
judiciary. He expressed the desire of his Government to
remove every cause of misunderstanding that had led
to the present negotiations.[14]

In the way he fashioned his case Hammond invited
attack. He had contented himself with many general
statements and accusations not specifically documented
in his neat appendix. His more experienced and able opponent was quick to take the obvious advantage offered
by such faulty technique and proceeded with infinite
industry and ingenuity bit by bit to demolish the abstract.

First Jefferson considered Hammond's allegations
as to exiles and confiscations. Premising that all laws
passed during hostilities were lawful acts of war, he
turned to examine in detail every act included among
those the titles of which were listed in Hammond's appendix. He discovered that in no case had an act been
passed since the peace that had concerned property not
already divested of title as an act of war. Subsequent
legislation was therefore simply an act of administration of property already confiscated during war. As to
insufficiency of the Congressional recommendations
complained of by Hammond he declared that the word
"recommend" as used in the treaty had no other meaning than its plain ordinary sense. It had been beyond the
power of the American peace commissioners to stipulate
and of Congress to enforce upon the states other than

14. *A.S.P.,F.R.,* I, 193–200.

recommendatory measures. Jefferson easily produced abundant testimony to show that at the time it had been so understood not only by the negotiators on both sides but also by both Houses of Parliament. The recommendation had been made in good faith by Congress to the individual states; some of the states had refused and some had complied; in fact, more had complied than expected. Compensation by the British treasury, which had been granted to Loyalists by Parliament, had been the alternative of that Government's own choice.

Disposing of these objections, Jefferson excused manifest inconsistencies between the action of different states and the provisions of Articles IV, V, and VI, by laying the onus of original infraction at the door of the British Government. Here Hammond found his weapon of recrimination to be a boomerang. Negroes had been carried off as late as May 8, 1783, Jefferson noted, while official notification of ratification of preliminaries of peace had been received by British commanders April 15. Correspondence of the Canadian Government with American officials showed, as late as July 13, 1784, that no orders for evacuation of the posts had been received; hence it was natural to suppose that none had been given or intended. If none had been intended the infraction dated from the going into force of the treaty; but using the criterion "all convenient speed," it dated from April, 1783, when New York had been evacuated. As these infractions had preceded so they had provoked the acts of the individual states of which complaint was made; when one party breaks a stipulation the other party is entitled to break the treaty either in whole or in part. Congress having made no election to do such, four states only, according to the

laws cited in Hammond's paper, after these previous
infractions on the part of Great Britain, had passed
laws to "modify" the recovery of debts. This was
effected by granting citizens longer and more practicable terms of payment, by liberating their bodies on
delivery of property to the creditor and to the full
amount of his demand after fair appraisal, and by
admitting payment in paper money. Congress at length,
induced by assurances from the British Court that it
would concur in a fulfillment of the treaty, had declared its will to the states that even the appearance
of obstacles should be removed. At present the federal
courts were open to take cognizance of all cases
where the interests of British subjects were involved
under the treaty, which by the Constitution had become the law of the land. Resort to these courts had
been frequently availed of, and the debts remaining
unsettled were small in proportion to the original sums.
Moreover, any obstacle encountered in an inferior court
was subject to appellate jurisdiction of the Supreme
Court.

Jefferson could not pass by Hammond's allusion to
the excellence of the British courts without citing a few
American cases in those tribunals where much delay
had been encountered, especially the famous case of the
Bank Stock of the State of Maryland, which had already dragged through nine years of inconclusive litiga-
tion. The trivial points raised by Hammond as to the
trespass laws and the murder case were easily and
satisfactorily disposed of.[15]

As to suspension of interest on debts during war,

15. Sections 41 and 42, Jefferson's reply. The reply is printed in
*A.S.P.,F.R.*, I, 201–37.

allowed by state court decisions, Jefferson held that no interest was stipulated in the treaty and that the reasons given by the courts were so weighty (such as absence of the British creditor from the country, the laws of Great Britain which had cut off all communication between the belligerents, and the great national calamity that had rendered all lands unproductive) as to absolve the charge of palpable wrong sufficient to justify diplomatic complaint. It was at least a disputable point which could best be determined by the federal judiciary under the provisions of the Constitution.

Having to the most minute degree answered the complaints and contentions of the British case, Jefferson professed to consider all objections explained away and requested execution forthwith by Great Britain of Article VII.

To one who reads even casually the documents of this controversy there can be no doubt that there had been infractions of the treaty by individual states. Jay's report to Congress in 1786 on British complaints, and the circular admonition of Congress to the several states in the next year admitting that violations of the treaty had occurred in many cases and requesting adherence to that instrument, establish this sufficiently.[16] It is difficult for the candid student to assume, as Jefferson did, that these violations of national faith would not have happened if earlier breaches of obligation had not occurred on the part of the English. Under the weak and divided government of the Confederation infractions undoubtedly would have been experienced

16. *Secret Journals of the Acts and Proceedings of Congress,* 1775–1788 (4 vols. Boston, 1820), IV, 135, 294, 329. Jay's report is dated Oct. 13, 1786; the circular letter was adopted on April 13, 1787.

even had the other side held scrupulously to the treaty.
Nevertheless the argument of Hammond, that prior
American infractions caused Great Britain to hold the
posts as security for the fulfillment of the treaty by the
United States, would appear sounder had it been presented at the time of the commission of the first infraction by the United States instead of having been discovered conveniently some months after orders had
actually been given, before ratification by Great Britain,
to hold the frontier forts. If one grants—and it cannot
really be granted—that violations were committed first
by the Americans, then there was great weight in the
argument developed by Grenville in Hammond's instructions that one party could not withhold fulfillment
of a treaty for a term of years, and then, by suddenly
asserting its readiness and ability to carry out its obligations wholly and faithfully, demand the entire observance by the other party of its part of the contract. But Jefferson had sawed away the scaffolding of
any such argument by demonstrating that the United
States could not be proven to have violated any portion
of the treaty *before* Great Britain did. The correspondence of the home government with the Governor
General, which has been set forth at the beginning of
this essay—evidence which Jefferson only guessed at—
shows conclusively the validity of the contention of the
Secretary of State. Jefferson was well justified, too,
as good diplomatic sparring, in making the most of
the Negro question. Technically the American argument as to the deported Negroes was strong, though
the modern mind must acknowledge the superior moral
persuasion of the British point of view. As to interest
during the war on prewar debts, Jefferson's point that

this was a matter for the judiciary was unexceptionable. Comparing the two arguments one is impressed by the mediocrity of Hammond's case. Its loose arrangement enabled Jefferson to attack it damagingly on the ground of fact by showing that the evidence cited by his adversary did not support the very general allegations made. In assuming that the burden of original infraction lay on the United States Hammond took a difficult position. It might be comparatively easy for him to have been convincing on the question of Negro deportations and possibly on the point of American prior infraction of the treaty—for he probably knew nothing of the correspondence of the Home Office with Quebec in 1784. But at the very moment when he was submitting his abstract to the Secretary of State, Hammond was acknowledging to Grenville that the federal courts and most of the state courts were able and competent, that in every instance where judgments of the former had been rendered involving recovery of debts the stipulations of the treaty had been validated. Aside from the frequent abatement of interest during the war, there was, Hammond privately admitted, but one cause for complaint, the repeated postponement of a test case in Virginia.[17] Even in that instance he himself anticipated ultimately a favorable decision. He also declared to his chief, on receiving a copy of an *ex parte* statement of the amount of debts owed in America to British creditors, that the figures had been grossly exaggerated.[18] Thus, in addition to the

17. Hammond to Grenville, Mar. 6, 1792, P.R.O.,F.O., 4, 14.

18. The statement was submitted to the Ministry, Feb. 5, 1791, together with a memorial for relief which repeats the substance of a similar one made in 1783, to the effect that the fourth article of the

fault of loose construction, Hammond's indictment did not altogether possess the sincere respect of the author himself.

If Jefferson's reply to the abstract of the British Minister was in itself a document of uncommon power, admirably strengthening the position of the United States at the outset of the discussion, its intrinsic force was undermined by an influence of which Jefferson was to a degree aware but which he could not prevent. It was an influence which with other differences was rapidly leading him to a decisive break with his colleague. For Hamilton continued with the officially accredited British Minister the same relations which he had held

---

treaty did not give the satisfaction and security that had been depended on from the assurances given the creditors by the Government since they had found themselves left at the mercy of the law courts and juries of America. The sum total is as follows:

| State | Amount of Debt | | |
|-------|------|------|------|
| Virginia | 2,305,408 | 19 | 2 |
| Maryland | 517,455 | 7 | 4 |
| S. Carolina | 687,953 | 18 | 4 |
| N. Carolina | 379,344 | 7 | 9 |
| Georgia | 247,781 | 14 | 9 |
| Pennsylvania | 229,452 | 4 | 4 |
| New York | 175,095 | 11 | 8 |
| Rhode Island | 49,208 | 9 | 6 |
| Massachusetts | 287,982 | 13 | 3 |
| Connecticut | 28,653 | 14 | 6 |
| New Hampshire | 21,795 | 14 | 0 |
| New Jersey | 524 | 8 | 6 |
| Total | 4,930,656 pounds | 13 shillings | 1 pence |

"In the above sum is included fourteen years' interest, which as near as at present can be computed amounts to two million and upwards." That is, the committee of creditors included interest during the seven and one-half years of war. Chatham MSS, Bdl. 343, also P.R.O.,F.O., 4, 14. Totals corrected.

with the informal agent Beckwith. Hammond, too, fully aware of the opposite policies of the two American Secretaries and of the different political and economic systems with which they were identified, zealously cultivated Hamilton. The Englishman divined with considerable accuracy Hamilton's motive for not wishing to upset good relations with Great Britain. "Of this gentleman's sincerity," he wrote, "I have the surest pledge in the knowledge that any event which might endanger the tranquillity of the United States would be as fatal to the systems he has formed for the benefit of his country as to his present personal reputation and to his future projects of ambition." In 1793 Hammond stated that he preferred to make most of his communications privately to Hamilton and to have relations with Jefferson only when absolutely necessary.[19]

Hammond's first "long and confidential conversation" with Hamilton, which confirmed his previous impressions of "that Gentleman's just and liberal way of thinking," had been on the subject of Indian hostilities and foreign relations of the United States in general. Hamilton then had hinted that the affairs of the country were in an important crisis from which would issue the complexion of its political as well as of its foreign relations, and he allowed it to be understood that France in a proposed treaty had offered additional advantages to American navigation. This, he said, had led him to prepare a report on the actual state of the navigation and commerce of the United States to show that French laws were more favorable to American shipping than British, but that England presented the better opportunities for American commerce generally;

19. Hammond to Grenville, April 2, Nov. 7, 1793, P.R.O.,F.O., 5, 1.

balancing the two systems the scales would incline decidedly in favor of the commercial advantages of Great Britain.[20]

This intimacy between the two men existed throughout Hammond's stay in the United States. During all of his official negotiation with Jefferson he was in constant communication with the Federalist leader. When the Secretary of State began the negotiation with an enumeration of American charges against Great Britain, which led to the preparation of Hammond's abstract, the British Minister discussed confidentially with Hamilton the actual weight of those charges. Hamilton at once admitted that there had been contraventions of the treaty in the United States, some of them of great magnitude, which were not to be excused on any other principle than the inefficiency of the former Congress to enforce respect for its own regulations; but he stated the federal courts could now do full justice. If the posts should be evacuated he thought some arrangement might be made to secure the interests of British fur traders. He believed some settlement could be effected for other infractions by the United States and that the Government would consent to any reasonable and practicable means of doing so. British trade was important to the United States: he hoped that commercial questions could be adjusted amicably and that the West Indian Islands could be opened to American vessels of limited tonnage. Hammond listened attentively, letting fall no hint that Great Britain would retreat from her system in the West Indies. He then asked when Jefferson's anticipated report on commercial restrictions might be expected. Hamilton be-

20. Same to same, Dec. 19, 1791, P.R.O.,F.O., 4, 11.

lieved that the report had been abandoned now that a British Minister had arrived and negotiations had been started.[21]

Before Jefferson delivered his reply to Hammond's abstract he had submitted it to the Secretary of the Treasury with a request for advice, something which a man of the Virginian's acumen certainly never would have done had he known that practically every argument so strongly made therein had already been neutralized by his colleague in confidential oral negotations with the British Minister. Upon reading the document Hamilton concluded that much strong ground had been taken and strongly held, especially as to the recommendatory clauses of the treaty and the lodging of the burden of prior infraction with Great Britain. He thought that the question of interest, and the suggestions of the British Minister touching particular acts and adjudications, were met satisfactorily but doubted strongly the expediency of the argument of retaliation and the soundness of the doctrine that all acts prior to proclamation of the preliminary articles of peace were cut off from discussion. He considered it better to extenuate than to vindicate the action of the states. He added a few minor and technical and rhetorical suggestions. Jefferson accepted the latter but left unaltered the main principles of his case. He submitted a copy of

21. Hamilton, in anticipation of Jefferson's report, had been assembling statistics to counteract the severity of the Secretary of State's opinion. He took care to let Jefferson know of his activity in this respect. Though thoroughly prepared by Hamilton the material was held in abeyance because of the immediate developments which caused Jefferson's report to be postponed. In 1794 it was put into the mouth of a Federalist member of Congress in a speech to neutralize hostility aroused against England.

Hamilton's criticism to Washington together with a summary of his own views. The President sanctioned Jefferson's statement as it stood, being especially convinced that the charges as to recovery of debts should be vindicated rather than extenuated.[22]

Upon delivery of Jefferson's stunning reply the British Minister, greatly aroused by what he termed an "extraordinary performance," immediately went to Hamilton. On being told in astonished tones of the note, the latter lamented the "intemperate violence of his colleague," saying that it was far from a faithful exposition of the true sentiments of the United States Government, that the President had had no opportunity of reading it and had relied on Jefferson's assurances that it was conformable to the opinions of the other members of the Cabinet. "Notwithstanding this explanation," writes Hammond, "which in reality I could esteem only a decided proof of personal confidence, I thought it my duty to take some immediate notice of this paper to Mr. Jefferson himself."

An interview with the Secretary of State followed, from which Hammond gathered that there was a total disagreement as to the facts of his case, since the accuracy was questioned of his statements made on the basis of evidence collected by the consuls.

> Though I presumed there might exist some errors in my statement, I still imagined that the general evidence of the infractions imputed to this country [i.e., the United States] was not materially invalidated by his counter-representation. . . . But that even admitting for an instant the whole force

22. Jefferson to Madison, June 1, 1792, Jefferson, *Writings,* VI, 69.

of his argument, there were other matters to be settled exclusive of an arrangement on the subject of the posts and the satisfaction of the claims of the Loyalists and the British creditors.

He therefore determined to refer the whole matter to his superiors for consideration.[23]

Jefferson retired from the same interview strengthened in his set conviction that Great Britain had no intention whatsoever to give up the posts, and that, from mention Hammond had made about the disputed source of the Mississippi (a question which now for the first time had been brought forth as one of the "other matters" which were to be adjusted), there was not only a disinclination to evacuate the parts of American soil already held but a desire to slice off a part of our Northwest Territory.[24] We shall allude to this last point in another connection.

Jefferson's "extraordinary performance," its real force quite destroyed, was sent to London. With it went Phineas Bond, the Philadelphia consul, whose

23. Hammond to Grenville, June 8, 1792, P.R.O.,F.O., 4, 15.

24. Jefferson to Madison, July 4, 1792, *Writings,* VI, 71. Hammond had discovered that, the upper reaches of the Mississippi being still doubtfully explored, there was no certainty whether the treaty line due west from the Lake of the Woods to the Mississippi would ever strike that river. The indications were that it would not, since the source by latest information was supposed to be considerably south of the Lake of the Woods. Recollecting that the treaty had given to each party the free navigation of the river, he thought that in a new adjustment of the doubtful boundary there would be an opportunity to get for British territories a practical outlet to the "navigable waters" of the upper Mississippi, without which he professed to believe the free navigation of the river would be rendered nugatory. Hammond to Grenville, private, Feb. 2, 1792, *Dropmore Papers,* II, 254; P.R.O.,F.O., 4, 14.

industry had contributed largely to the material presented in Hammond's abstract, deputed to furnish the
Ministry with any additional technical information that
might be needed. At Grenville's request he spent not a
small part of his vacation in England composing a
memorandum on Jefferson's note.[25] But by the time this
statement was ready the Foreign Office was devoting
all its energies to the far more pressing, more difficult,
and more important question of relations with France.
The subject of additional instructions to Hammond
was lost sight of when the war with France broke out
on February 1, 1793. After the declaration of war the
legation at Philadelphia devoted all its attention to
counteracting the new French Minister, the Citizen
Genet. It then proved well for Britain that a resident
minister had been established in the United States.

25. "Letters of Phineas Bond, British Consul at Philadelphia,"
A.H.A., *Ann. Rept. 1897*, pp. 500–23.

# CHAPTER 6

# The Neutral Indian Barrier State Project

THE favorite project of British frontier diplomacy from 1791 to 1795 and at times thereafter until 1815 was to create a neutral Indian barrier state inside the recognized boundaries of the United States. It was designed to undo the American territorial triumph of 1783. Its purpose was to separate from the jurisdiction of the United States a wide area along the whole line of the Canadian frontier by constructing a nominally independent and neutral state from which both British and American troops were to be excluded. Under cover of such a stratagem the posts could be evacuated greatly to the profit of British colonial expansion; for, while the territory in question would be completely severed from American sovereignty, British traders and the agents of the Canadian Indian Department would continue to have free play for their activities. The resulting buffer zone would shut off the United States from all contact with the Great Lakes and the St. Lawrence and would secure the strategic approaches to Canada.

This ambitious scheme would have cut the very heart out of the future American Middle West. Nowhere would the territory of the United States have reached north of the Ohio River. The plan in its fullest

conception included an extension of the buffer state eastward across the newly settled areas of western and
northern New York. Had the old Northwest Territory
thus been separated and placed under nominal Indian
control with actual British tutelage it would have been
only a few years—unless the process were blocked by
war—until tutelage over a vanishing race would have
been replaced by an undisguised protectorate. White
settlement then would have spread westward under the
British flag. Chicago would have arisen the metropolis
of a British state in the upper Mississippi Valley. The
great stretch of territory to the west of the Mississippi
and north of a line from the mouth of the Ohio to San
Francisco might easily have become a sphere of influence, eventually a possession, of the British Empire rather than one of the most essential parts of the
United States. The results of the American Revolution
would have been brought within bounds. Such is one
of the might-have-beens of history which threatened
to be a tremendous reality.

To place this chapter of border diplomacy in its
proper setting let us recapitulate the relations of the
United States Government with the Indians of the
Northwest Territory.

When Great Britain transferred sovereignty over
all the territory within the stipulated boundaries the
precise relationship between civilized governments and
uncivilized peoples dwelling under their jurisdiction
had not been defined. European nations had followed
the practice of securing against each other rights of
pre-emption over native lands within their respective
dominions. In the United States the status of Indian
tribes was not defined judicially as that of "domestic

dependent nations" until 1831,[1] but from the beginning the Government had followed in practice what corresponded to such a definition. In 1783 Congress, acting on the assumption that by hostilities during the recent war the western tribes had forfeited title to their lands, proceeded to dictate boundaries for them. Settlers were excluded from the Indian country while peace commissioners were dispatched to effect a settlement by which the natives were to retain all lands north of the Ohio and west of a line, in terms of present-day geography, from the southwestern corner of the state of Ohio to the city of Dayton and thence to Lake Erie near where Toledo now stands.[2] These terms were to be embodied in a single peace treaty with all the hostile tribes. After extinction in this way of Indian title the lands were to be sold by the Government for settlement, the proceeds being regarded as pledged for payment of the national debt.[3]

Efforts to treat with all the western tribes as a unit proved unsuccessful. The commissioners' instructions were therefore modified in 1784 to allow conventions with separate tribes, and the desired boundary line was marked farther to the west, at the meridian of the Falls of Ohio, from that point north to the northern boundary of the United States.[4] Between 1784 and

1. Case of the Cherokee Nation, James Kent, *Commentaries on American Law* (4 vols. 12th ed. Boston, 1873), III, 382.

2. From the mouth of the Great Miami to the Mad River, thence to Fort Miamis on the Maumee and down that river to Lake Erie. *Journals of the American Congress* (4 vols. 2nd ed. Washington, 1823), IV, 275; *Secret Journals*, I, 243.

3. O. E. Leavitt, "British Policy on the Canadian Frontier, 1782–92," *Wisc. State Hist. Soc. Proc. 1915,* 154.

4. J. H. Perkins, *Annals of the West* (Cincinnati, 1846), p. 260.

1789 a number of treaties[5] were concluded with different tribes and groups of tribes in which they ceded lands and recognized American sovereignty, but these treaties were not satisfactory because they lacked the unanimous sanction of all the western tribes. In truth, the absence of definite constitutional or political organization among loose Indian tribes and still looser confederacies has always made treaty-making at best impractical. Such was the case here. As a result of these treaties, the last of which was that signed at Fort Harmar in 1789, the Government maintained that Indian title had been extinguished over a region comprising roughly the eastern third and southern two-thirds of what is the present state of Ohio. The majority of the western Indians denied this. They insisted that their lands extended south to the Ohio River and east to the line of the old colonial treaty of Fort Stanwix negotiated by Sir William Johnson in 1768.[6]

As already narrated, the dissatisfied natives north of the Ohio organized under a few powerful chiefs, with the help of the agents of the Canadian Indian Depart-

5. Treaties of Ft. Stanwix (1784), with the Six Nations; Ft. McIntosh (1785), Ft. Finney (1786), and Ft. Harmar (1789). For these treaties, and negotiations, see *A.S.P.,I.A.*, I; Perkins, *Annals of the West;* for various Indian tribes (Wyandots, Delawares, Chippewas, Ottawas, Pottawatomies, Sacs, as well as Six Nations) see F. W. Hodge, *Handbook of American Indians North of Mexico* (2 vols. 1907–10); Justin Winsor, *The Westward Movement* (New York, 1897).

6. M. Farrand, "The Indian Boundary Line," *A.H.R.*, X, 789. The line ran up the Allegheny and northeast to Ft. Stanwix in central New York, but the Six Nations did not contest American titles beyond the line of 1768. See map, p. 152. For facsimile of Sir Guy Johnson's map illustrating treaty of Ft. Stanwix, see Winsor, *Westward Movement,* p. 19.

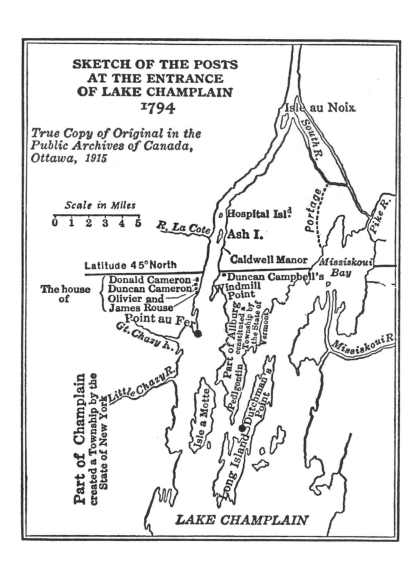

SKETCH OF THE POSTS
AT THE ENTRANCE
OF LAKE CHAMPLAIN
1794

*True Copy of Original in the
Public Archives of Canada,
Ottawa, 1915*

Scale in Miles

0 1 2 3 4 5

R. La Cote

Latitude 45° North

The house
of

Donald Cameron
Duncan Cameron
Olivier and
James Rouse

Point au Fer

Gt. Chazy h.

Little Chazy R.

Part of Champlain
created a Township by the
State of New York

Isle a Motte

Long Island

Isle au Noix

South R.

Portage

Pike R.

Hospital Isl.

Ash I.

Caldwell Manor

Missiskoui Bay

Duncan Campbell's

Windmill Point

Part of Alburg constituted a Township by the State of Vermont

Pedlgontin

Dutchman's Point

Missiskoui R.

LAKE CHAMPLAIN

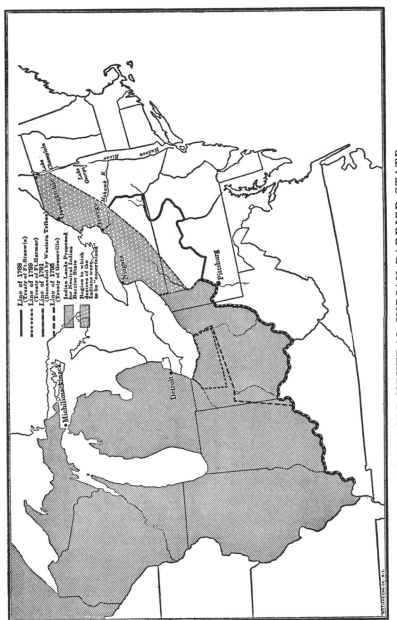

PROPOSED NEUTRAL INDIAN BARRIER STATE

Line of 1768
(Treaty of Ft. Stanwix)
Line of 1789
(Treaty of Ft. Harmar)
Line of 1791
(Demanded by Western Tribes)
Line of 1795
(Treaty of Greenville)

Indian Lands Proposed
for Neutral Indian
Barrier State

Region in which
desires of the
Indians were
to be "ascertained"

ment. The confederacy, under the leadership of the able Mohawk war chief, Joseph Brant, disavowed all treaties subsequent to the colonial treaty of Fort Stanwix (1768) as not possessing the consent of the now united tribes. Though he failed in his mission to England to secure open assistance in resisting the claims of Congress, the astute Brant easily obtained the active sympathy and covert assistance of the British Government and its Canadian officials, who encouraged the Indians to resist the "encroachments" of the Americans and to present a united front to their enemies.[7]

After the failure of the old Congress to secure a general peace on its own terms with the western Indians, the administration of President Washington determined to demonstrate the force of the new Government by a vigorous military offensive. An irresolute and abortive campaign of the national army under Colonel Harmar in 1790 was followed by more elaborate preparations the next spring. Governor St. Clair of the Northwest Territory was given command of the small regular army, with levies of raw and shamefully inefficient militia, and was ordered to advance from the frontier at Fort Washington (near the present Cincinnati) northward to the Indian towns on the Maumee River. By basing his forces here it was hoped that he could subjugate the various hostiles and dictate an Indian boundary from the Mississippi to Lake Erie on the line of the Wabash and Maumee Rivers.

In anticipating the execution of St. Clair's orders, possible friction with British forces at Detroit was foreseen, and, as already noted, General St. Clair was

7. See above, Ch. 1.

instructed to avoid all trouble and to give formal notice
to the British commander that his operations meant no
hostility to the garrisons of the posts. In another letter
to him, which fell into the hands of the Canadian
Indian Department's agents, the Secretary of War
stated: "We must, by all means, avoid involving the
United States with Great Britain, *until events arise of
the quality and magnitude as to impress the people of
the United States and the world at large of the rank injustice and unfairness of their procedure,*" [8] a sentence
later accepted in a hostile sense by the first governor
of Upper Canada.

General St. Clair never got near enough to the
Maumee to annoy Detroit. His desultory campaign, ill
supported as to supplies and communications and exhibiting no professional skill, collapsed in a disaster that
sent a shudder through every pioneer home in the western country. Some ninety miles north of Fort Washington the Indians fell on the poorly equipped and badly
officered army and inflicted a veritable second Brad-
dock's defeat, November 4, 1791. The catastrophe
paralyzed American military operations for nearly a
year.

These American campaigns in the western country
threatened eventually to destroy British economic and
political control over the Indians south of the international boundary line and to bring the troops of the
United States dangerously close to the occupied posts.
The possibility of putting an end to them by means of a
mediation between the Indian tribes and the United

8. Knox to St. Clair, July 14, 1791 (italics inserted), *M.P.C.*, XXIV,
288. The St. Clair military correspondence, captured by the Indians
and turned over to British officers, is calendared in C.A., *Rept. 1890*.

States Government occurred to Lord Dorchester in February, 1791, as the result of one of Beckwith's interviews with Alexander Hamilton. During the Nootka crisis Beckwith had taken great pains to set forth his chief's disapproval of Indian depredations on the Ohio. This did not deter President Washington from causing it to be intimated that the Government strongly objected to activities at the posts which resulted in furnishing the Indians with war equipment.[9] Beckwith then argued to Hamilton that the frontier warfare was ruining the fur trade[10] and that if only for this reason the traders really wished to see it ended. He had even brought one of the Detroit traders, who chanced to be passing through New York, to Hamilton to testify to that fact.[11] Hamilton in return intimated that Lord Dorchester might win the appreciation of the United States Government as well as that of the fur traders by using his influence with the Indians to induce them to make peace. The Governor General professed to interpret this observation as a request for his good offices. Through Beckwith he immediately expressed his happiness to be instrumental in effecting a peace, should he be formally requested by either party to mediate, but declared he would have to be informed specifically of

9. Washington to Jefferson, April 3, 1791, *Writings*, XII, 31; Jefferson to Washington, April 17, 24, 1791, Jefferson, *Writings*, V, 321, 324.

10. A memorial was presented by the North West traders in 1790 to Sir John Johnson, Superintendent of Indian Affairs, requesting the Government to put an end to the Indian troubles because of their injury to the fur trade. See C.A.,Q, 52, 272. This memorial was later sent to Hammond at Philadelphia, and by him considered of great use to exhibit practical evidence why the British Government wished to end the warfare between the Indians and the United States.

11. C.A., *Rept. 1890*, 166–68. Conversation between Hamilton, Hammond, and Wm. Macomb of Detroit, Phila., Jan. 31, 1791.

acceptable peace terms.[12] He straightway directed the Superintendent of Indian Affairs, Sir John Johnson, to get a statement from the natives of their terms of peace, based on "equity, justice, *and policy*." [13]

When Dorchester's proposal was brought before Hamilton he declared that his earlier suggestion which "as an individual" he had made for the prosperity of the British trading interests on the frontier, was not to be regarded as any request for mediation.

> If the United States were at war with a great or respectable nation the case would be different, a foreign mediation under certain circumstances might be desirable, in that case the manner of the application would be official and of course not to any public officer of that country abroad, but to the administration at home. On the present occasion the thing in its existing shape is inadmissible, and *I could not submit such a paper to the President's consideration*. The objects of warfare are certain vagrant Indian Tribes who cannot be considered to be on the footing on which such a system as this would place them.

Peace negotiations with the western tribes would be initiated during the summer, Hamilton explained, and if Lord Dorchester would "suggest that a friendly accommodation and settlement would be pleasing to his Government, it might have a tendency to promote it." [14]

It was from a study of this correspondence between Dorchester and Beckwith that the idea of exploiting

12. Motz to Beckwith, Feb. 10, 1791, C.A., *Rept. 1890,* 168.

13. Dorchester to Sir J. Johnson, Feb. 10, 1791, C.A., *Rept. 1890,* 169. Italics inserted.

14. C.A., *Rept. 1890,* 171. Italics inserted.

the American hostilities with the western Indians by means of a mediation appears to have developed at the Foreign Office. Hammond's first written instructions directed him to make proposals to this end at the opportune time, and Dorchester simultaneously was bidden to cooperate. The Governor General, after the passing of the Nootka crisis and the failure of his own mediation efforts, had given orders to discountenance all attempts on the part of citizens of the United States to press forward to the treaty line.[15] Now he was carefully enjoined to hold himself in a neutral position between the two belligerent parties. The guiding policy of the proposed mediation, he was told, would be to secure the Indians in the quiet possession of their lands, for if they should be "either extirpated from their countries, or rendered insecure in the possession of them, our trade in that quarter, and much which Your Lordship and the merchants of Montreal state to be so valuable, must be injured, and the enjoyment of it rendered altogether precarious."[16]

Dorchester was already at sea on his way to England when this dispatch arrived at Quebec. He took to England the terms of peace which had been found acceptable to the Indian confederation. Under the direction of Alexander McKee, the Deputy Indian Superintendent at Detroit, whose influence over the savages was unsurpassed, the demands of the tribes had been formulated in writing. A delegation of chieftains conveyed them to Quebec in August shortly before Dorchester's departure. They requested him to help them to secure a boundary which would follow the Ohio River as far

15. Dorchester to Grenville, Quebec, June 14, 1791, C.A.,Q, 50–1, 82.
16. Dundas to Dorchester, Sept. 16, 1791, C.A., *Rept. 1890,* 172–73.

east as the mouth of the Muskingum, thence up the
Muskingum as far as the portage into the Cuyahoga
and from that portage east to Venango, from which
place the line to be that agreed on in 1768 as far as
the purchase made by Pennsylvania in 1784.[17]

To the Indians' request for his help Dorchester replied that because he was at peace with the United
States he could not join in any hostilities, but that he
would be glad to mediate between them and their
enemies. He explained the British attitude as follows:

> When the King made peace and gave indepen-
> dance to the United States, he made a treaty in
> which he marked out a line between him and them;
> this implies no more, than that Beyond this line he
> would not extend his interference.
>
> The posts would have been given up long since,
> according to the Treaty, had the terms of it been
> complied with on the part of the states; but they
> were not: the King therefore remains in possession
> of the Posts and will continue to hold them untill
> the differences between him and the States shall
> be settled. But Brothers, this line, which the King
> then marked out between him and the States, even
> supposing the treaty had taken effect, could never
> have prejudiced your rights. Brothers, the King's
> rights with respect to your territory were against
> the nations of Europe; these he resigned to the
> States. But the King never had any rights against
> you, but to such parts of the country as had been
> fairly ceded by yourselves with your own free

17. See "Line of 1791" on map, p. 152.

consent, by public convention and sale. How then can it be said that he gave away your Lands?

Dorchester's reply to the natives, together with a map describing their boundary claims, was forwarded to Whitehall shortly before he himself embarked.[18] Dorchester's presence in England during the winter of 1791–1792, and the abundant information which was available through him, made possible a thorough discussion of the whole frontier question. The neutral

18. Dorchester's Speech to a Deputation of the Confederated Indian Nations, Quebec, Aug. 15, 1791, printed in *M.P.C.*, XXIV, 309–13. For representations of the Indian deputies see ibid., 318–21. For the Indian council at the Maumee Rapids, see McKee's Correspondence from Miamis Rapids, April 1 to July 5, 1791, in C.A.,Q, 50–1, 150, 230; Q, 51–2, 734, 785; Q, 52, 234 ff.

The map representing the Indian boundary claim is now in the Colonial Office at Whitehall where it was shown to the writer through the courtesy of the Librarian, Sir Walter Langley. A line drawn in red runs from the mouth of the Muskingum up that river to the portage to the Cuyahoga, thence in a line east to Venango, thence up the Allegheny River, stopping at a point on the meridian of the western boundary line of New York. Attached to the map with an official seal is the following legend: "Joseph Brant, on behalf of the deputies declared their nations were disposed to make peace with the United States upon the basis of the following boundary line being established between them, that is to say, a line running up from the confluence of the Cherokee [i.e., Tennessee] River with the Ohio to the mouth of the Muskingum thence to the portage which crosses to the Cuyahoga, from there in a direct line across the country to Venango, where it joins the line agreed upon in 1768, from thence along the said line until it strikes the line of purchase made by Pennsylvania in the year 1784." This last phrase appears to indicate that the Indian line ended where it met the meridian of the north and south boundary between Pennsylvania and New York.

Dorchester's theory above quoted of course champions the claim of the Indians that none of the treaties with the United States from 1784 to 1789 possessed the sanction of the Indian confederacy which had been organized since the treaty of peace with Great Britain.

Indian barrier state project was now fully elaborated
and embodied in additional instructions to Hammond,
March 17, 1792. It was proposed to couple the settlement of Article VII of the treaty of peace, the article
stipulating evacuation of American territory, with a
mediation by the Canadian Government which should
secure to the Indians their lands as they had recently
defined them. This territory was to be guaranteed as a
neutral, independent state, safe from the "encroachments" of both the United States and Great Britain.
It was to constitute "an effectual and lasting barrier"
between the possessions of the two countries.

Nor was this all. The boundary actually requested
by the Indians was calculated to fulfill the purpose of
the barrier state project to a certain extent, but the
project was by no means limited to that line. An expansive solicitude for the savages in the quiet possession
of their lands induced the Secretaries for Home and
Foreign Affairs to attempt to secure a liberal strip
along the whole length of the British-American boundary of 1783 "within which both parties should stipulate not to suffer their subjects to retain or acquire any
land whatsoever." The zone in question was to be
reserved for the undisturbed and independent possession of the natives.

"By placing the natives in such a possession," explained Dundas,[19] the new Secretary for Home Affairs,

19. Henry Dundas, 1742–1811; member of the House of Commons,
1774–1790; Lord Advocate, 1775–1783, and staunch opponent of
conciliation with America; Privy Council, 1782; committee of the
Privy Council for Trade and Plantations and member of the Indian
Board of Control, 1784–1801; Secretary for Home Affairs, 1791–1794;
Secretary of State for War, 1794–1801; First Lord of the Admiralty,
1804–1805; removed from Privy Council, 1805; impeached by Lords

they will become a natural barrier against mutual encroachments, and at the same time hold a situation in which their attachments and friendly dispositions to His Majesty's subjects may be capable of the most serviceable because of the most amicable operations. . . .

I shall not add that in ascertaining the territory to be granted to the Indians, three points I conceive to be attended to. One, to secure, as much as possible, our Intercourse and trade with the Indians; the second is that the interposed country to serve as a barrier should extend along the whole line of His Majesty's Dominions, and that of the United States of America; and lastly to take care that their intervention, and the space allotted to them shall be most considerable in such points of His Majesty's frontier as from their situation are most obvious to attack or interruption from any Quarter belonging to the American States.[20]

In the project as thus outlined was no mention of withdrawal of British agents from the proposed independent neutral territory. British subjects were forbidden to acquire land there, a privilege which since the peace had been technically subject to American, not British, permission, but there was nothing to prevent perpetuation of the ascendancy already established over the natives by traders and by agents of the Indian De-

---

for misuse of public funds, 1806; restored to Privy Council, 1807. A friend and trusted lieutenant of William Pitt, he was created first Baron Melville, 1802.

20. Dundas to Dorchester, Mar. 15, 1792, C.A.,Q, 58–1, 59; Grenville to Hammond, Mar. 17, 1792, P.R.O.,F.O., 4, 14. Printed in Mayo, *Instructions*, pp. 25–27.

partment. As the Governor of Upper Canada later had
occasion to remark: "The Indians know no such thing
as neutrality." American citizens, it is to be observed,
were neither to acquire nor to *retain* land within the
limits of the barrier state thus to be erected out of their
own sovereign territory.[21]

Such was the nature of the proposal which Hammond was now to make the United States. Copies of the
correspondence with Dorchester and of the map describing the boundary demanded by the western tribes
accompanied these latest instructions. The Minister
was directed to couple the mediation proposal with the
question of evacuation of the posts, the time and manner of making such a proposal being left to his own
discretion to be governed by circumstances on the
spot. A special messenger carried dispatches for the
Canadian authorities directing them to cooperate in
every way and to send to Hammond an expert adviser
on Indian affairs, such as McKee.[22]

21. Gouverneur Morris's extraordinary contact with good sources
of information is illustrated by the fact that he had information of
the mediation project the very day it was outlined to Dorchester.
Morris was in London on a visit at the time. He wrote Washington
that he learned from a confidential quarter that Pitt "means to offer
his mediation for a peace with the Indians. If all this be true, his
game is evident. The mediation is to be with *us* a price for adopting
his plans, and with the *Indian tribes* a means of constituting himself
their patron and protector. It may be proper to combine all this with
the late division of Canada [i.e., the creation of the province of Upper
Canada], and the present measures for military colonization of the
upper country, and, above all, with what may come from Mr. Hammond." Morris to Washington, London, Mar. 17, 1792, *A.S.P.,F.R.*, I,
392.

22. Dundas to Clarke (Lieutenant Governor in Dorchester's absence), Mar. 16, 1792, C.A.,Q, 58–1, 63, printed in *M.P.C.*, XXIV, 384;
Dundas to Simcoe, Mar. 16, 1792, C.A.,Q, 278, 36.

Hammond, following out his earliest instructions, had already broached the subject of mediation informally to Hamilton. He was informed that the Administration was determined, if necessary for a proper peace, to prosecute the war to a final conclusion. If the voluntary interposition of the King's Government in Canada could help toward peace, such would be received with gratitude, but as to a British mediation Hamilton displayed no enthusiasm. He would do no more than intimate that if the posts should be surrendered the United States would be willing to grant special privileges and immunities to British subjects engaged in the fur trade. Hammond reported that he heard from "pretty good authority" that the Government was determined not to admit of any mediation while the posts were still retained.[23] His dispatches arrived in London the day after his instructions, described in the preceding paragraphs, had been prepared. Nevertheless Grenville allowed the last instructions to stand as they had been written and followed them with further suggestions, recently formulated by Dorchester, for a rectification of the boundary line in the region of Lake Champlain in such a way as to include within British territory Grand Isle and Isle La Motte, "indispensable to the security of His Majesty's Dominions in that Quarter, where they are indeed more vulnerable than in any other."

Though Dorchester acknowledged that there were no Indian claims in the strip along the shores of Lake

23. Hammond to Grenville, Jan. 9, Feb 2, 1792, P.R.O.,F.O., 4, 14. See also Hammond to Jefferson, Jan. 30, and Jefferson to Hammond, Feb. 2, enclosed with Hammond's to Grenville of Feb. 2. Hammond's dispatches of Feb. 2 were received March 13.

Ontario and the St. Lawrence River, it was suggested that the desires of the natives in that region be "ascertained." In the Champlain country there were no Indians with claims which could be used to devise a barrier; hence a boundary rectification would be necessary to secure British interests there.[24] Grenville suggested that this might be brought forward in lieu of a "more invidious" money compensation for American infractions of the treaty of peace and that doubtless on this point Hammond's abstract (to which Jefferson's effective rejoinder had not yet been received) would prove a strong persuader. Arguments for the rectification would readily occur to the Minister. "The Sacrifice on the Part of the Americans must be allowed to be extremely small, when compared with the private Losses and public expense . . . incurred by this Country, in consequence of the Infractions of Treaty by the States." [25]

Hammond was directed to continue to press the mediation-rectification project notwithstanding the apparent disinclination of the United States Government to accept it, because it was believed that the recent reverses in the Indian country would make that Government more receptive.[26] News had arrived in London of the defeat of St. Clair.

"Humanity shudders at the number of poor Wretches who have fallen in this Business," read a graphic letter inclosed in the official pouch. Yet some good might come out of that bloody horror, thought the

24. Dorchester to Dundas, London, Mar. 23, 1792, *M.P.C.*, XXIV, 386–89.

25. Grenville to Hammond, April 25, 1792, Mayo, *Instructions*, pp. 27–29.

26. Ibid.

anonymous writer. "I wish our peace makers of '83 had known a little more of this country," he added. "I wish our present Ministry were informed of its actual situation: perhaps this is the important moment in which the unfortunate Terms of that Peace may be altered: perhaps this Moment will never return." [27]

A perusal of these latest instructions convinced Hammond that the mediation proposal was so impractical as to cripple the whole American negotiation. Even the influential Hamilton had asserted that the Indians within American territory were "in some sort the subjects of the United States," in regard to whom no mediation could be accepted, that if the peaceful policy of adjusting Indian troubles by treaties (which had been reverted to after St. Clair's defeat) should fail, the tribes would have to be subjugated by war. The Government, Hammond noted, had consistently claimed lands beyond the Muskingum-Venango line which the Indians were now demanding through Lord Dorchester, and the tide of western settlement already had flowed around the territories of the Six Nations in western New York and Pennsylvania, between them and the western Indians, and had reached the shores of Lake Ontario. The Six Nations had transferred land in unquestioned title to settlers and to the Government in western New York and Pennsylvania. Hammond indicated to the Foreign Office that in accepting such a mediation the United States would not only have to abandon lands ceded by undisputed treaties, but would have to "repurchase the territory acquired by contract of bargain and sale, as well by the separate States as by individuals." The district in question, in-

27. P.R.O.,F.O., 7, 11.

creasing daily in population, had been parceled out in
small lots, and its repurchase would be attended with
insurmountable difficulties.[28]

Somewhat reluctantly the Minister determined to
make liberal use of the discretion which his instructions allowed and not to propose the mediation formally. To Hamilton he loosely sketched the British
offer. Hamilton listened attentively but would not
discuss the project beyond replying "briefly and coldly
. . . that any . . . cession of territory or right or
the allowance of any other Power to interfere in the
disputes with the Indians would be considered . . . as
absolutely impracticable and inadmissible." [29] In conversations with Jefferson and General Knox, Hammond ventured to throw out suggestions that the Indian
disputes might be ended by the interposition of a native
territory. Both declared that any terms which would involve cession of lands were impossible. Like Hamilton,
these two Cabinet members asserted the readiness of
the Government to adjust political or commercial inconveniences which might result to Great Britain from
evacuation of the posts, even to the extent of limiting
the size of American garrisons in those forts and a mutual limitation of armaments on the Great Lakes, and to
consent to any measures which the Government of Canada might think necessary to the security and protection
of the persons and property of British subjects engaged
in the fur trade on the lakes and on the communications between the different lakes.

So anxious were the Americans for the evacuation
of the posts, reported Hammond, that they would

28. Hammond to Grenville, June 8, 1792, P.R.O.,F.O., 4, 15.
29. Ibid.

probably consent to raze them and to agree only to have small log forts in the Indian country and declare all communications between the lakes free to the subjects of both nations, also to allow British subjects engaged in the fur trade to maintain factories and depots on those communications, which according to the terms of the treaty were well within American lines. "I am also of opinion," Hammond added, "that this government would admit such a regulation of the north Western boundary as would afford a free and *effectual* communication with the Mississippi by means of some of the rivers falling into Lake Superior," for Hamilton had declared in his last conversation that undoubtedly the United States would allow a free intercourse with the Indians on the American side of the boundary if the British Government would extend similar privileges to American subjects on the Canadian side.[30] As we shall have occasion to notice later, this last was precisely the solution of the frontier question accepted by the United States in Jay's Treaty.

Apropos of the last statement of Hamilton in regard to the entrance of Great Britain into the Mississippi from the north, it should be mentioned that it was during the summer of 1792 that he was seriously advocating in the Cabinet, in opposition to Jefferson, the expediency of offering Great Britain a territorial access to the navigable waters of the Mississippi, an idea which he received from Hammond,[31] as an equivalent for an Anglo-American alliance, one of the advantages of which to the United States would be the joint assertion and maintenance against Spain of the

30. Hammond to Grenville, July 3, 1792, P.R.O.,F.O., 4, 16.
31. Ibid.

free navigation of the Mississippi to the ocean. It is
enough to notice that President Washington promptly
dismissed this proposal with the remark that the
remedy was worse than the disease.[32]

Much to Hammond's relief, Lord Grenville, after
reading the detailed explanations of the impracticability
of any formal proposal for a mediation, approved the
course which his Minister had taken.[33] The neutral
Indian barrier project was suspended, at least for the
time being, by the Foreign Office. Meanwhile there had
arrived on the frontier one of the most extraordinary
personalities in Canadian history, who did not so
readily abandon that project. This was Colonel John
Graves Simcoe, appointed first Lieutenant Governor
of Upper Canada when that province was created by
the Constitutional Act of May 16, 1791. With his
civil office of Lieutenant Governor was united, at his
request, military command of the new province, subordinate to Major General Alured Clarke at Quebec.
Because Simcoe is such an inseparable part of the
frontier question for the next five years, let us pause to
note briefly what abundant documentary records have
to say of his early history and his character.

The son of an English army officer who had followed
the immortal Wolfe to a gallant death on the Plains
of Abraham, Simcoe was a restless youth who focused
all his ambition and energy on a career of empire-
builder in his father's profession of arms. At the beginning of the American Revolution he purchased a

32. Jefferson, *Writings,* I, 207; *A.H.R.,* XXVII, 465.
33. Grenville to Hammond, Aug. 4, 1792, Mayo, *Instructions,* pp.
30–31.

commission with command of a regiment of light horse called the Queen's Rangers. To the perfection of this troop he devoted a very considerable ability and part of his private fortune. He succeeded during the war in raising his command to a creditable state of efficiency, and the memory of the Queen's Rangers and of the devotion of the ranks to their commander is still associated with the lesser annals of American military history.[34]

Simcoe wrote a *Journal of the Operations of the Queen's Rangers,* which is somewhat a reflection of his ambition and thirst for military glory. Written in the third person, obviously in imitation of the style of the *Gallic War,* he records the minute details of the troop's operations, as if for the eyes of a posterity anxious for the preservation of each scrap of the youthful history of a great commander. The smallest skirmishes become affairs of great importance. As Cæsar in his *Commentaries* explains his military notions, so Simcoe scrupulously and fully exposes the strategy and tactics which impelled the commander of the Rangers to adopt and carry out each petty maneuver.[35] One of the more noteworthy episodes in his military career was his connection with the British plans

34. *S.P.,* I, 166; D. B. Read, *The Life and Times of Gen. John Graves Simcoe* (Toronto, 1890); D. C. Scott, *John Graves Simcoe* (Toronto, 1912). There is still no definitive biography of Simcoe, based on a full study of the rich material now made more easily accessible by publication, 1923–31, of five volumes of this correspondence and allied documents herein referred to as *S.P.* (See Key to Abbreviations, p. xviii and Note on Manuscript Sources at end of this volume).

35. Simcoe, *A Journal of the Operations of the Queen's Rangers,* printed for the author, 1787.

which culminated in the treachery of Benedict Arnold; it was Simcoe to whom Sir Henry Clinton had entrusted the operations in northern New York which were interrupted by the capture of Major André. In anticipation of this service Simcoe had taken pains to acquaint himself as thoroughly as possible with the political temper of the people of the Champlain region, an experience which made him acutely conscious of separatist sentiment in that frontier country.[36]

After the independence of the United States the young officer continued an active and inveterately hostile interest in American affairs. He could never be persuaded that the United States was not a crafty, scheming enemy led by unscrupulous and cunning men who were watching for a chance to pounce on the poorly defended province of Quebec. He had a military contempt for George Washington "and such cattle" as well as a unique scorn for the integrity of "Mr. Washington." [37] His imagination surveyed the field of war which he felt certain to come from American aggression against the "British outposts." There he beheld the chance for which he yearned. In his highest flights,

36. Simcoe to Dundas, Aug. 12, 1791, C.A.,Q, 278, 283.

37. For example: "The United States are divided by a set of men, who, divided as they are in parties, and separated in their interests, by their own declarations, find no such bond of union as pretended dread, or real enmity towards Great Britain." Simcoe to Dundas, London, June 2, 1791, C.A.,Q, 278, 228. "To be unprepared is to invite attack: I feel it my duty to say that if agreeable to the expressions of the Americans, in their conversations and writings, they could possibly in one winter seize on Quebec and Canada, no apprehensions of the consequences (politically considered), ought to prevent them." Washington "is by no means averse from such attempts." Same to same, London, Aug. 12, ibid., 283.

he even saw himself personally measuring swords on some American battlefield with the overrated Washington. Awaiting the flood-tide of opportunity, he studied the American frontier difficulties with shrewd concern. When Levi Allen was in London seeking favor for his scheme of a commercial treaty between Vermont and Great Britain as an "opening wedge" to a future political union, Simcoe intrigued for the success of Allen's plans, for his war experience had led him to recognize their value. He had some personal influence with Grenville; we find him suggesting to the latter the bribing of the Vermont legislature to prevent that state from joining the American Union and upsetting the calculations of the separatists. Though perhaps there exists no conclusive documentary evidence (and it is unlikely that such evidence would survive) the sources of this intrigue afford strong suspicion that Allen actually brought British gold back to Vermont and was unsuccessful only because he arrived two days after the legislature of the state had ratified the Constitution of the United States.[38]

Simcoe in 1791 desired the appointment of minister to the United States. Instead of that he received the lieutenant governorship of Upper Canada. Shortly afterward rumors reached him that Andrew Elliot, the first person considered for the Philadelphia station, had declined the office. Simcoe then applied to the Foreign Office to endow the governorship of Upper Canada with the diplomatic duties of a minister near the United States. He was confident that from his capital in the new colony he could attend to all the more important

38. See documents printed in *A.H.R.*, XXI, 547.

political relations with the United States, while the
consuls could manage the routine business.[39] The precedence of Lord Dorchester for such a unique appointment, Simcoe's superior in rank, office, age, and experience, never occurred to him.

Simcoe sailed from England, his fertile mind active
with schemes for establishment of a colonial Utopia on
the Ontario peninsula. In all his plans for empire-
building one element was indispensable: a strong military and naval force for Upper Canada, to be placed
under his immediate command rather than under that
of the Governor General.[40] In order that he might
conduct the mediation between the United States and
the western Indians—from the first the Indian barrier
project had impressed his aggressive imagination—he
also requested, and successfully, that the Superintendent for Indian Affairs be made subordinate to him
rather than to Dorchester, at least within the province
of Upper Canada.[41] He feared that if a peace should
be made between the Indians and the United States
without the mediation or intervention of Great Britain
to give the natives a desirable boundary and to keep
hold of their affections, that the defense of Canada
would be paralyzed before the inevitable American invasion, that the Indians themselves, disappointed at

39. Simcoe to Nepean, London, Mar. 16, 1791, C.A.,Q, 278, 226.

40. For his correspondence in regard to the early history of Ontario, see particularly C.A., Upper Canada State Papers, Ser. Q,
vols. 278–83. A noteworthy declaration for official correspondence in
his day and age in Great Britain was: "There should be neither a
*sinecure* mind nor a *sinecure* body thro' the whole province." Ibid.,
278, 228 f.

41. C.A.,Q, 278, 90–97.

the weakness of their former allies, might be turned against them.[42]

In emphasizing here the prejudices and the excitability of Simcoe's character, we do not wish for a moment to deny the Governor's great services to the founding of the province of Upper Canada and the beginnings of the Canadian West. Simcoe's energy communicated to colonial administration had a beneficent domestic influence, even though his more sanguine expectations for the early upbuilding of the colony were not borne out in actuality largely because of the stresses which Great Britain had to bear in Europe in the wars of the French Revolution.

Simcoe believed preventive war to be preferable to defensive war. Convinced that the weakness of the Canadian provinces invited attack, Simcoe appealed in vain, before leaving London in 1791, for a greater military establishment. He proposed personally to drill a corps in the Indian style of warfare as a supplement to regular European tactics, a combination superior both to the natives and to the "hardy American backwoodsmen, more expert and savage than the Indians themselves." With such a force, strengthened by the presence of his old regiment of Queen's Rangers, he hoped to secure British control over the Great Lakes and to be able to counteract American efforts to establish forts in the Indian country near the international boundary: "Congress must acquire a superior naval force on Lakes Erie and Huron before she can act with any permanent effort against Upper Canada, while the forts, and, above all, the Post of Detroit is in our possession." If

42. To Dundas, June 2, 1791, C.A.,Q, 278, 228.

these preparations should be made, "the active exertions of the American servants of the Crown would in the course of a few years place this colony beyond the reach of its enemies, and as the frontier of an Empire which centuries will hardly compleat." [43]

A Ministry which already during the Spanish crisis had shown itself sparing of re-enforcements for Canada did not adopt this advice. Simcoe threatened to resign, declaring that without these necessary troops the post to which he was destined would not hold forth any inducement to that honorable ambition which he had always preferred to all personal considerations, the ambition of rendering essential and distinguished services to his King and Country.[44] But he received only a small garrison, mostly composed of the remnants of the old Queen's Rangers. He did not resign. Even before he reached his province he had to fall back to the strategy of an "absolutely and entirely defensive war, if war there is to be." [45]

43. Simcoe to Grenville, July 23, 1791, C.A.,Q, 278, 257.

44. "I had entertained sanguine hopes of rendering essential service to my country in endeavoring by unremitting assiduity and exertions to repair the great loss which Great Britain has sustained since the peace from the circumstances which have prevented her from availing herself of the immense emigrations from the United States of subjects now settled beyond the Appalachian Mountains.

"I had hoped that the active exertions of the American servants of the Crown might have placed in the course of a few years this Colony beyond the reach of insult from its enemies, and as the frontier to an Empire which centuries will hardly compleat.

"But if these exertions are cramped or wholly fettered by the want of the only good means which appear to me capable of ensuring the rapid establishments and progress of the Colony beyond the slow, unsympathetic and unconnected gradations by which the British Colonies in America have been usually formed, I feel that I should deceive Your Lordship," etc., etc. Ibid.

45. *S.P.*, I, 166.

In his requisitions for military supplies directed to the Quartermaster General, Simcoe often used phrases which indicate his plans for an active offensive campaign against the United States, once war should have broken out. That country was as vulnerable as Canada, he asserted, and he would fetter no garrison with restrictions to prevent its being used outside the colony: "Upper Canada . . . is not to be defended by remaining inside." He asked for the heaviest guns obtainable, of the type of mortar howitzers, before which the feeble log forts of the Americans could not stand.[46] Before his departure for Canada he left at the Home Office a long memorandum emphasizing the absolute necessity of holding the posts—the "barrier forts," he began to call them—for the security and welfare of Canada.[47] In short, although Simcoe's personal preference would have been to conquer the Americans first and reach an understanding with them later, he had to bow to the orders of superiors, whom he could not convert, not to start any hostilities.

Passing by the great mass of material which relates to the vigorous colonial administration of this virile official in the wilds of Upper Canada, let us turn back to the neutral Indian barrier project. It will be remembered that when the idea had been completely developed by Dorchester and Grenville and final instructions had been dispatched to Hammond, in March, 1792, that complementary instructions had been sent at the same time to Quebec to Major General Alured Clarke, Lieutenant Governor of Canada in Dorches-

46. Simcoe to the Duke of Richmond, London, Sept. 12, 1791, ibid., 327.
47. "Observations on the Posts on the Lakes," *M.P.C.*, XXIV, 324–26.

ter's absence, and to Colonel Simcoe, Lieutenant Governor of Upper Canada, directing the Canadian officials to cooperate with Hammond in Philadelphia and particularly to send to him some person qualified to furnish expert advice on Indian affairs. Simcoe was at Quebec when these dispatches arrived. So were Sir John Johnson and his Deputy Superintendent for Detroit, Alexander McKee, a veteran Indian hand. The three conferred as to the best means of carrying out the new instructions. McKee's notorious services for some years past among the Indians made it dangerous for him to go to Philadelphia. Sir John was proscribed in the United States by an act of attainder. He himself advised sounding again the temper of the Indians before sending any one to assist Hammond.

Meanwhile Simcoe and McKee collected all the documents they could find in support of the claims of the natives, for the use of Hammond. They then put their heads together and devised a program to "perpetuate peace between the different nations." This included a proposal even more impractical than the neutral Indian barrier project as evolved by Dorchester and Grenville. In addition to the creation of the barrier out of American territory Simcoe and McKee proposed, as an offset and compensation for allowing the United States to continue in possession of the Genesee country in western New York, that Detroit, including a strip two leagues in depth south of Lake Erie as far east as the Rapids of the Maumee River, should be made over to Great Britain. This obtained, Great Britain should evacuate Michilimackinack and guarantee to demolish the forts of Detroit,

Oswego, and Niagara.[48] Together with documentary material relating to Indian claims this plan was rushed by special messenger (Captain Stevenson, of whom more will be said later) to Hammond. The machinery of the Indian Department was then set in motion for assembling the Indians, to tutor them in resolution, and to learn again their final decision as to a desirable boundary.

Ordinarily the technique of ascertaining the desires of the confederated Indian tribes required much hard work and infinite patience. They had to be assembled from out of the wilderness for hundreds of miles; they had to be entertained; they had to be fed; they had to be harangued in the manner of their native oratory; all the proprieties of savage politics must be carefully observed. McKee's task this time was lightened by the fact that the tribes already were assembling at the Rapids of the Maumee (near the present city of Toledo) to deliberate on peace offers from the United States. The President and Secretary of War had received at Philadelphia a deputation of chieftains from the Six Nations and through them and by means of other native emissaries the pipe of peace was being conveyed to the western tribes. Brant himself had been induced to visit the capital and to talk with Washington, and had agreed to take back to the hostile tribes the peace terms of the United States—an offer of the boundary of 1789 and additional money annuities.[49]

48. Simcoe and McKee to Hammond, Montreal, June 21, 1792, C.A., Q, 278, 191.

49. *A.S.P.,I.A.,* I, 228–38; Stone, *Brant,* II, 328. Brant told Hammond everything that had passed between him and the United States Government. He said he had agreed to convey the terms to the

As McKee was preparing to set out for the Maumee council, letters arrived from Hammond announcing his decision not to make any formal offer of mediation and telling of appointment of the "excitable" General Anthony Wayne to command the American army in the west. Hammond stated that only a decisive defeat of the United States troops by the Indians, or the *voluntary solicitation* by the latter of the good offices of the King, would now favor any chance of successful mediation. If the tribes should ask for such a mediation the request *ought to appear uninvited,* for any suspicion of collusion might defeat the whole plan.[50]

Simcoe, who had proceeded to Niagara to set up temporary headquarters for his new government, immediately set about producing with proper discretion the desired spontaneous and voluntary solicitation by the Indians for his mediation. Though the attitude of the United States had persuaded him that any amicable negotiations about the posts would be impossible as long as Washington, Jefferson, and Hamilton continued at the head of affairs; and though he believed the proper way to get rid of those gentlemen was "by aiming at once to dissolve the Confederacy," he conceded it would be expedient to bring forward a boundary line, without the appearance of mediation on the part of England, before General Wayne could get his army well equipped and drilled.[51] He wrote McKee, who

---

Indians, but that he did not favor them himself. Thus the Canadian officials knew the nature of the American proposals by this means, from Hammond, even before they were made to the natives. See Hammond to Grenville, July 3, 1792, P.R.O.,F.O., 4, 10.

50. Hammond to Simcoe and Clarke, July 11, 1792; Hammond to Simcoe, April 21, 1792, C.A.,Q, 278, 187; *M.P.C.,* XXIV, 478.

51. *M.P.C.,* XXIV, 459–66; Simcoe to Clarke, Niagara, Aug. 20,

had now reached the seat of the native council, that "consolidation of the Indian Territorial Claims, and Rights, is requisite to the formation of such an extensive Barrier as we have in contemplation," but that the tribes should receive no expectation of any actual offensive aid from the British Government; with peculiar propriety they might apply for documents, such as copies of deeds and treaties, to substantiate their claims against the Americans. He enclosed such material of this nature as was available.[52]

The result of the Indian council, at which were present representatives of seventeen native tribes, exclusive of the Six Nations who acted as go-betweens, was a decision to meet American commissioners early the next year at a peace conference at Sandusky on the shore of Lake Erie. The confederated tribes addressed a formal invitation, couched in perfect English, to Simcoe, the person vested by the "Great King our Father" with authority to take care of all his children in this country, requesting his presence as mediator at the conference and asking him to bring all useful documents. Full details of this decision were hastened to Hammond.[53]

The spontaneous and voluntary solicitation had been produced. What would be the American attitude? Hammond was at loss how to bring forward once more

---

1792. C.A.,Q, 61–1, 169. Hammond considered Wayne "the most active, vigilant and enterprising officer in the American Army." Hammond to Simcoe, April 21, 1792, C.A.,Q, 278, 187.

52. Simcoe to McKee. Navy Hall, Niagara, Aug. 30, 1792, C.A.,Q, 279–1, 13, 169.

53. Proceedings of a General Council of Indian Nations, Sept. 30 to Oct. 9, 1792, M.P.C., XXIV, 483–501; Hammond to Grenville, Dec. 4, 1792, P.R.O.,F.O., 4, 16.

the old proposal, already twice repulsed. Ultimately he determined again to talk to Hamilton, a procedure which would protect him from the imputation of being too officious and at the same time would have all the advantages of a formal communication. Hamilton, after listening to Hammond's "personal convictions," assured him that the Government would never accept the Indian proposal for mediation. An interview followed with Jefferson as "the more regular channel of communication." Jefferson agreed to consider the conference informal but to lay the matter before the President.[54]

Before Hammond heard of the President's opinion, which was equally positive with that of his advisers, three weeks intervened. Meanwhile the Six Nations delegates to the Maumee council had returned to Buffalo, where they held another council in the presence of the Deputy Indian Superintendent for Niagara. Here the proceedings of the Maumee council were rehearsed and the reply of the confederacy to the American peace offer was relayed to Philadelphia: namely, that the confederated tribes would insist in any peace negotiation on the Ohio River as their boundary.[55] Hammond utilized the occasion of communicating to Jefferson news of this Buffalo council, which he had received from Simcoe, to put out more feelers. Jefferson replied that mediation by the Canadian Government would form a precedent for mediation by the United States in any dispute between the British authorities and Indians within their jurisdiction, and this would be only a source of never-ending em-

54. Ibid.
55. *A.S.P.,I.A.*, I, 323.

barrassment to both Governments, who had best regard their respective Indians as not possessed of independent sovereignty admitting the mediation of a third party. If Simcoe were to be present at the coming council between the natives and the American peace commissioners he would be regarded by the United States Government not otherwise than as a spectator. Jefferson, however, agreed that the British might have their agents present to explain to the natives the "nature and tendency of the American offers."

Hammond believed that this was some gain, at least, for it would remove these officials from the imputation of improper motives; they could "observe the conduct of the American commissioners, and would be ready to extend their ascendancy over the Indians" in inclining them to reject or to accede to the American offers. If the Americans would recede a little from their demands, Hammond thought, it was probable that the Indians also might relax as to the Ohio boundary.[56]

These informal conferences of December, 1792, mark Hammond's final abandonment of the mediation project. He was convinced, as any sane man must have been, that no such proposal would ever be admitted by the United States as long as it remained an independent nation. Whatever the differences of opinion in the American Administration there was no division on this head, though the rift between Hamilton and Jefferson had assumed the dimensions of an abyss. It is

56. In answer to a request Hammond told Jefferson, and later Hamilton, that the Canadian authorities would have no objection to allowing the United States to contract in Canada for supplies for feeding the Indians at the peace conference. Hammond to Grenville, Jan. 1, 1793, P.R.O.,F.O., 5, 1. This privilege was later denied by Simcoe, notwithstanding Hammond's assurance.

difficult to conceive that Washington would have tolerated the presence in his Cabinet of anyone, no matter how great his genius, who favored the mediation. The only hope of an Indian buffer state now lay in inducing the Indians to insist on terms of peace which, despite some concessions, would secure to them as much territory as possible before they should be conquered and lose all. Henceforth this was the object of the Canadian officials. If such a peace could not be had then it were better that the Indians take the chance of war.

Before we conclude the history of frontier affairs it will be necessary to turn to the European situation which in 1793 became the governing factor of Anglo-American relations.

# CHAPTER 7

# The War of the French Revolution and Anglo-American Relations

WHEN in September, 1791, the first British Minister was sent to the United States, no British statesman dreamed of the great struggle with France which was so close at hand and which for the next twenty years was to tax to the utmost the resources of the Empire. The private correspondence of Lord Grenville shows that near possibility of war with France escaped the prescience of the British Ministry and its representatives abroad up to the very eve of the formation of the Austro-Prussian coalition against France.[1] When Hammond left for Philadelphia it was with the sole intention of *discussing* a settlement of the vexing questions arising from the nonexecution of the treaty of peace, in order to forestall the dangerous possibility of discrimination against British trade by the national commercial laws of the newly established federal Government. There is nothing to indicate that either

1. This statement is confirmed by a perusal of the private correspondence of Lord Grenville as published in the *Dropmore Papers*. In fact, not until November, 1792, did the probability of war with France loom seriously into view; it was rather the fear of revolution that caused apprehension. The possibility of France's "forcing" Great Britain into war is not discussed until that month. Auckland to Grenville, Nov. 26, 1792, ibid., II, 341.

Pitt or Grenville in 1791 had the slightest idea of the
upheaval which Europe was about to experience. As
Lord Bryce has said: "Men stood on the edge of
stupendous changes, and had not a glimpse of even
the outlines of those changes, not discerning the causes
that were already in embryo beneath their feet, like
seeds hidden under the snow of winter, which will
shoot up under the April sunlight." [2] On February 1,
1793, the sudden storm of the war with France broke
and engulfed the Foreign Office with a mass of vital
and complicated business. American affairs fell temporarily into the background. That they should do so
was not unwelcome to Grenville. His wish was for
delay until it might be possible to put forward the
neutral Indian barrier project with some chance of
success.

If war with France had been comparatively unex-
pected in England, it was a complete surprise in
America. There the outbreak of hostilities on the continent of Europe in 1792 had attracted no more than
passive attention. Beyond lively discussion of the successes of the tricolor at Valmy and Jemappes and de-
light at the defeat of troops that were to have marched
into France under the Manifesto of the Duke of
Brunswick, the advance of the Austrians and Prussians
produced no political interest and was regarded as a
purely European affair. When Great Britain entered
the war its aspect changed. It now became a contest of
sea power. The echoes of battles on French frontiers,
which had reached the American public with the belated
arrival of European packets, were replaced by the

2. James Bryce, *Modern Democracies* (2 vols. New York, 1921),
II, 598.

sound of real cannon off the country's very coasts. Commerce and shipping were matters of vital concern. The nation's position as a neutral now had more than academic interest.

The French declaration of war on England found the United States Government wholly without precedent of its own as a guide of conduct and with little information as to specific practice by European nations in previous wars. There were no scholarly digests of international law to which a perplexed official might turn with assurance, no long-standing files of the Department of State to consult, no neutrality laws to declare in force. International maritime law itself was in a state of flux. Questions of contraband, badge of enemy property, reception of belligerent fleets, fitting out of privateers within neutral jurisdiction by subjects of belligerent powers, augmentation of force in neutral harbors, prize jurisdiction in neutral territory, the twenty-four-hour rule, all these were unanticipated problems. The only sources of authority were the dusty tomes of Grotius, Wolf, Puffendorf, the more recent work of Vattel, and the existing treaties. A clever diplomatist could extract from somewhere among the stately periods of these writers a quotation to re-enforce nearly any legal argument he cared to make; and the almost biblical elasticity of the same publicists would permit his adversary to find a text of equally firm support for an opposite exegesis. Treaties, too, varied. Great Britain long had followed the narrowest rules as to the exercise of sea power, but with Holland and Denmark had made special concessions from her usual practice. The Armed Neutrality of 1780 had shown the Baltic powers, France, and Holland, as well as the revolted American Colonies, to be upholders of more liberal measures later adopted in the nineteenth century by the Declaration of Paris. Despite the novelty of the international situation, the American Government met it resolutely and satisfactorily. Some of the precedents created in 1793 have since become long-established principles of international law.

It was not the unprecedented international position of the new republic that caused the greatest difficulty at the outbreak of this world war. The minds of Washington's Cabinet were large enough and able enough to improvise salutary neutrality regulations, but they were not wholly unswayed by the passions that rose in the breasts of the multitude.

Widespread sympathy for France was natural. The doctrines of the French Revolution had met with genial and general approval in America, shared at first as well by the Federalists as by the party which by the Second Congress had come to be designated as Republican. The successes of the French armies in the autumn of 1792 won enthusiastic popular acclaim in the United States, and the church bells pealed only the louder when the French Republic was proclaimed. But the September massacres and the increasing barbarity of French revolutionary methods soon alienated the Federalists, who after the execution of Louis XVI and the entrance of Great Britain into the war commenced to sympathize with the "cause of law and order." [3]

3. C. D. Hazen, *Contemporary American Opinion of the French Revolution* (Baltimore, 1897), pp. 253–78; J. T. Morse, *The Life of Alexander Hamilton* (2 vols. Boston, 1876), II, 81; A. Bertrand, "Les États-Unis et la Révolution Française," *Revue des Deux Mondes* (1906), XXXIII, 392–430. A. J. Beveridge, *Life of John Marshall* (4 vols. Boston and New York, 1919), II, ch. 1, and J. A. Carroll and

Despite the disapproval of the Federalists, enthusiasm for France increased among the general public. France was regarded widely and affectionately as the saving angel of the United States. Frenchmen had spilled their blood on American soil in defense of American liberty. France was the only nation that had opened her island commerce liberally to American vessels. France had shown herself willing to negotiate a commercial treaty. Above all, the United States stood bound to her by the ties of formal alliance. In the treaty of alliance of 1778 it was undertaken to guarantee the French island possessions in North America, and France had pledged herself to guarantee the territory of the United States as it should be defined in the treaty of peace. By the seventeenth and twenty-second articles of the simultaneous commercial treaty of 1778 French privateers, and prizes taken by French war vessels, public and private, were to enjoy the exclusive privilege of reception into American ports in time of war, and enemies of France were to be prohibited from fitting out privateers in those ports.

Those who dwelt fondly on the past services of France could hold up the attitude of Great Britain in deprecatory comparison. Notwithstanding the treaty of peace British garrisons still occupied American territory. To thousands of American settlers in the Ohio Valley the horrors of Indian warfare had struck savagely home. These atrocities were partly ascribed, and correctly so, to British activity at the posts. The busi-

---

M. W. Ashworth (continuing Douglas Freeman's work), *George Washington*, VII, ch. 3, present the latest and most brilliant chapters on this subject. See also Bernard Faÿ, *The Revolutionary Spirit in France and America* (New York, 1927), pp. 305–51.

ness interests, by custom and trade so closely attached
to Britain, had the long-standing grievance of exclusion by the Navigation Laws from the British West
Indies, despite the fact that no legislation obstructed
British ships in the United States. A Yankee schooner
might sail from any foreign port to France but not
similarly to England; only purely American produce
could be transported there in American bottoms. Again,
there were the American debtors, naturally not bitterly
adverse to a rupture with their creditors. In the background was the vision of another new republic strug-
gling against the tyrant from whose dominion the
American nation had wrenched itself with the help of
the very people now embattled.

During the controversy between the United States
and Great Britain over British occupation of the posts,
France had made no move to implement or execute her
territorial guaranty, and the United States had not
invoked it. Secretary of State Jefferson studiously refrained from doing so lest it should inspire France to
invoke the American guaranty of her West Indian islands in some future war with Great Britain and thus
jeopardize the neutrality of the United States. When
France did declare war on Great Britain in 1793, both
Jefferson and Hamilton agreed that neutrality was the
proper policy for the United States. Jefferson's pro-
clivities for France were well known, and his properly stiff attitude during the Hammond negotiations
had shown him to be entirely untouched by the "British
interest." His European experience had been almost
wholly French. His sympathies instinctively went out to
the revolutionary party. A man who professed to believe
a revolution every thirty years was a purgative greatly

to be desired in the life of any nation, he looked with complacence on the decentralizing tendencies of the French Revolutionary Government. With the agility of the doctrinaire his philosophy leaped over the bloody actualities of revolution to the Utopian democracy he thought he saw beyond. Feeling toward those unfortunate human beings who perished in the upheaval the same resigned grief which he had for men fallen in battle, he declared: "My own affections have been deeply wounded by some of the martyrs to this cause, but rather than it should have failed, I would have seen half the earth desolated. Were there but an Adam and an Eve left in every country, and left free, it would be better than as it now is." [4]

There slept fitfully in Jefferson's mind a dread of monarchy and "monocrats," and he believed the Hamiltonian policy was directed toward these monsters. He had little use and less trust for the genius of his colleague. He had but a feeble comprehension of that sound financial policy which had made a reality of independence by supporting the Government with the strong arm of national credit. The very force of the new Government which Jefferson had been applying to claim execution of the treaty was, really, the fresh product of Hamilton's genius. If one cannot wholeheartedly commend the policy of Hamilton in reaching out of his own department to tamper with the Secretary of State's diplomacy, none the more can one excuse the conduct of Jefferson, who was now secretly engineering the notorious attack in Congress on Hamilton's financial administration, one of the gravest charges of which was the absurd accusation that two

4. Jefferson to Short, Jan. 3, 1793, *Writings,* VI, 154.

specific foreign loans for more efficient stewardship
had been lumped into one, that sums had been taken
from the lump to pay creditors abroad instead of making those payments from one specific loan allocated
strictly to those particular creditors.[5] Politically and
personally the two men had come to distrust each other.

Despite his stiff attitude toward Great Britain, Jefferson never desired war with any nation under any
circumstances. He often spoke loudly of it, but his real
pull was for peace. He had inveterate confidence in his
ability to play upon the commercial fears of Great
Britain and upon the embarrassments of that country
in the face of European upheaval. Possessed in 1793,
as later when President, with a passion for peace, Jefferson meant in the last extremities to go no further
than an embargo.[6] He never prepared for war, and this
ought to be conclusive proof that he never expected to
encounter it. He trusted rather to his political ingenuity
and to the chances of the unknown future.

The sympathies of Hamilton were wholly with Great
Britain but for no sentimental or even philosophical
reason. He admired the working of the British Constitution and a strong central government conductive to
"law and order." He had little sympathy for democratic movements and abhorred reform by violence.
The excesses of the French excited profound disgust
in his mind. His was an intellect of realism. He had no
philosophic bent that helped him to see a silver lining
in the clouds beyond the horizon so darkly shadowing

5. Jefferson, *Writings,* VI, 165–79; Morse, *Life of Hamilton,* II,
1–66; Hamilton, *Works,* III, Reports.

6. Henry Adams, *History of the United States* (9 vols. New York,
1889–91), III, chs. 2–6.

the French National Convention. "It cannot be without danger and inconvenience to our interests," he wrote, "to impress on the nations of Europe an idea that we are actuated by the *same spirit* which has for some time past fatally misguided the measures of those who conduct the affairs of France, and sullied a cause once glorious, and that might have been triumphant." [7] To Hamilton, too, the most important fact of American foreign policy was the certain prostration of the new national government which would follow a break with England.

The three most eminent figures in American public life were for peace when in March, 1793, news of the critical relations between France and Great Britain reached the United States. Washington ardently hoped that nothing would force his country into war. With great satisfaction he viewed the recent progress of the nation and foresaw that all which was necessary to "be ranked, not only among the most respectable, but among the happiest people on this globe" was to enjoy uninterrupted for a few years the great natural advantages at hand.[8] Early in April he received letters from Hamilton and Jefferson transmitting unofficial reports of the outbreak of the war, and he hurried from Mount Vernon to Philadelphia to take immediate steps for strict neutrality. A long list of questions, thirteen in number, he submitted to the two Secretaries and to the other members[9] of the Cabinet as to proper attitude toward the belligerents. Everybody in the Administration favored neutrality. Jefferson, who on

7. Hamilton to ——, 1793, *Works*, V, 566.
8. Washington to Humphreys, Mar. 23, 1793, *Writings*, XII, 276.
9. Hamilton, *Works*, IV, 359.

April 7 had written Washington that every justifiable
means should be taken for preserving neutrality and
who had doubted the authority of the executive to pro-
claim it, now assented to a proclamation in which the
word neutrality as applying to the *attitude* of the
Government would be studiously avoided in order that
its absence might lead Great Britain to offer broad concessions for satisfactory assurance as to the ultimate
action of the United States. The wording was changed
in accordance with this opinion, but no bid was afterward made by Great Britain, which power much to Jefferson's disappointment[10] considered the form of the
proclamation satisfactory. The official correspondence
soon began to refer to the "proclamation of neutrality."
Jefferson himself quickly lapsed into use of the term.[11]

The famous proclamation, drafted by Attorney
General Edmund Randolph, was brief. It admonished
Americans to refrain from all acts inconsistent with
friendly and impartial conduct. Those who committed
or abetted hostilities against any of the belligerent
powers would be "liable to punishment or forfeiture
under the laws of nations," and American citizens were
warned of the danger of carrying "articles which are
deemed contraband by the *modern*[12] usage of nations."

10. Jefferson to Monroe, June 4, 1794, *Writings,* VI, 281.

11. Same to same, July 14, 1793, *Writings,* VI, 346; to Madison,
Sept. 8. Ibid., 417; Hamilton, *Works,* V, 552.

12. The word "modern" was used at Jefferson's request. He hoped
under cover of that adjective to sanction a definition of contraband
that would not include foodstuffs. *Writings,* VI, 485. In instructions to
Pinckney, however, Jefferson used the word "neutrality": "You may
on every occasion give assurances which cannot go beyond the real
desires of this country to preserve a fair neutrality in the present
war, on condition that the rights of neutral nations are respected in

The public was informed that instructions had been given to the proper officials to prosecute all persons committing with respect to the powers at war "offenses against the laws of nations, within the cognizance of the courts of the United States." Thus the law of nations, all too vaguely defined, was by executive proclamation made to supply the deficiency of the domestic law. The Foreign Enlistment Act was not passed until the spring of the following year.

The proclamation itself disposed of the first three questions which the President had directed to the Cabinet. The others concerned the official attitude to be taken toward the new French Government and the new French plenipotentiary, who had landed at Charleston coincidentally with the news of war; and the question of what force the American treaties with the former King of France should have with the National Convention. A lively discussion, supplemented by long written papers, ensued in the Cabinet.

Hamilton saw danger in the guaranty of the French West Indian Islands. He believed that circumstances had become favorable for getting rid of this and other embarrassing stipulations. The treaties of 1778 had been made with Louis Capet, he stated, a monarch who had been illegally executed by a body of persons who could in no way claim the political heritage of the Bourbon King. Hence the obligations of those treaties

us, as they have been settled in *modern* times . . ." Jefferson to Pinckney, April 20, 1793, State Dept., Instructions, England, Vol. I, 272–74.

For technical treatment of the neutrality proclamation, see the thorough studies by C. M. Thomas, *American Neutrality in 1793; a Study in Cabinet Government* (New York, 1931), and C. S. Hyneman, *The First American Neutrality* (Urbana, Ill., 1934).

should be regarded as having ceased, just as the National Convention had considered the Family Compact with Spain to have lapsed after the death of Louis XVI. He feared that to receive the French Minister without qualifying his reception would be to recognize the continuance of the embarrassing clauses.[13] But the filaments which Hamilton spun from Vattel, Grotius, and Puffendorf to support this legal opinion were very weak.

Jefferson contended that the treaties continued binding notwithstanding the change in the French Government, the means of effecting which no outsider had a right to criticize. He argued that there had been no question as to continuing force of the treaties when a change had been made in the American Government in 1788, that none the more should such a question arise at this time, that reception of the new French Minister should not be qualified, that nothing should be said about treaties or guaranties, that reception of a minister did not concern the matter of a treaty, which could be reserved for consideration; that there had been as yet no demand from France to execute that guaranty.[14] Jefferson's view was adopted. Citizen Genet was received as the Minister Plenipotentiary of the French Republic on May 17, 1793.

This energetic and imaginative young Frenchman, who had specialized so demonstratively in the principles of democracy and liberty as to remove from himself the taint of first having come into official favor through an experienced diplomatic career under the old régime, was appointed in December, 1792, as the republican

13. Hamilton, *Works,* IV, 362.
14. Jefferson, *Writings,* VI, 217–31.

successor at Philadelphia of the Bourbon Minister, Ternant. His instructions anticipated war with Great Britain. Those to be exhibited to Washington denounced the selfish Machievellianism of Vergennes, exponent of the old régime's foreign policy, condemned secret diplomacy, grandiloquently extolled the bonds of liberty which drew the two republics together, bade him endeavor to strengthen those bonds on principles of eternal truth. To achieve this Genet was to proceed with negotiations already begun by Ternant [15] for a more liberal commercial treaty which was to mingle the commercial and political interests of the two nations "by establishing an intimate concert to foster in every way the extension of the Empire of Liberty, to guarantee the sovereignty of peoples, and to punish those powers with exclusive colonial and commercial systems by declaring that their vessels should not be received within the ports of the two contracting nations."

While waiting until the American Government should thus determine to make common cause against Britain, he was "to take all measures comportable with his position to plant the principles of liberty and independence in Louisiana and the other provinces adjacent to the United States." It was thought the Kentuckians might second his efforts without compromising the federal Government. Expenses of agents to be sent into those districts would be borne by the French

15. Ternant's mission had followed a resolution of the National Assembly advising the King to make a new commercial treaty with the United States. It had at first met with response from Jefferson, but failed because the latter suspected Hamilton was trying to trick him into a similar treaty with England. Turner, *Corres. Fr. Ministers*, p. 9. It was of considerable anxiety to Beckwith.

Executive Council.[16] Supplementary instructions ordered Genet to use vigilance to secure the execution "of
those articles [the treaty of commerce of 1778] which
are favorable to the commerce and navigation of the
Republic"; that is, he was to see that the American
Government prevented *"all fitting out of privateers,
unless for the forces of the French Nation, and the
admission of prizes other than those taken by the vessels of war of the French Republic."* The Minister of
Marine furnished him with blank commissions to be
used to fit out French privateers in American ports.
The Minister of War gave him a quantity of blank
captain's commissions to be distributed among Indian
chieftains to be used against the Canadian frontier,
much reliance being placed on admiration of the natives
for such honors. The guaranty of the West India Islands by Article XI of the treaty of alliance was not to
be demanded *until after it should have been incorporated in the new treaty to be proposed.*[17] Finally, he was
ordered "to observe scrupulously the established forms
of communication between the Government and foreign
agents and to take no step nor make any proposal that
might give umbrage to the free Americans in regard
to the Constitution they have established for themselves." [18]

A representative of the French Convention might be

16. "De prendre toutes les mesures que sa position comportera pour
faire germer dans la Louisiane et dans les autres provinces de
l'Amérique voisins des Etats Unis, les principes de la liberté et de
l'indépendance." Instructions of the Executive Council to Genet, ibid.,
p. 205.

17. A feature of the instructions which frequently escapes the em-
phasis of writers on the period.

18. Supplementary instructions to Genet, Dec. 23, 1793, Turner,
*Corres. Fr. Ministers,* p. 211.

expected to be censored more for lack of fervor in
promoting the principles of liberty than for excess of
zeal in their pursuit. The performance of Genet, however, went even beyond the liberal instructions of the
Executive Council. With the tacit consent of Governor
Moultrie of South Carolina, whom he designated as a
"grand patriot," Genet immediately equipped, commissioned, and sent cruising two French privateers,
and arranged for more. Under Mangourit, consul at
that port, he established prize courts for the judgment
of prizes to be brought in by these privateers. Steps
were taken to set up similar tribunals elsewhere in the
United States. To Canada, Nova Scotia, and Louisiana he dispatched colorful proclamations inviting the
inhabitants of those colonies to throw off the British
and Spanish yokes and promising to aid them.[19] Plans
for an expedition of American frontiersmen from Tennessee against Louisiana, to receive its original impulse
from Georgia and South Carolina, he left to the execution of Mangourit at Charleston. Genet personally
interested himself in the details of a similar movement
from Kentucky with which Mangourit's corps was
eventually to unite. It was to be commanded by George
Rogers Clark, the Revolutionary back-country hero,
who accepted a French commission to lead a legion
of restless frontiersmen down the Mississippi against
New Orleans. Genet had other plans for organizing
a naval force to block New Orleans from the sea while
the western citizens were attacking it in the rear.

Having prepared these stratagems, the new minister
after a "triumphant" journey overland arrived at

19. Dorchester to Dundas, April 26, 1794, C.A.,Q, 67, 191. For
French influence in Nova Scotia see P.R.O.,C.O., 22, 362, 398.

Philadelphia amidst a furor of popular welcome.[20] He
quickly made friends with Jefferson, who, though knowing that one of the Frenchman's agents had plans
against Louisiana, introduced that person to the Governor of Kentucky as a man of science exploring the West
(a character which the agent in reality also possessed)
and enjoying the particular confidence of Mr. Genet.[21]
Of all this plotting the Secretary of State said nothing
to President Washington.[22] Jefferson, who was then
privately condemning the neutrality proclamation as a
milk-and-water instrument and premature since it did
not compel Hammond to offer the United States the
broadest neutral privileges,[23] at first bade fair to become as intimate with Genet as Hamilton was with
Hammond. The Secretary of State even gave Genet
private tutelage as to how the political winds blew
among the different personalities of the American
Administration.[24] But the excitability of the French
envoy, which Jefferson mistrusted from the first, in a
few days convinced him that Genet's appointment had
been "calamitous" for good relations between the
United States and France.[25]

20. J. B. McMaster, *History of the People of the United States*
(8 vols. New York, 1883–1913), II, ch. 8, gives vivid description of
Genet's early popularity culled from newspaper sources, the basis
of his earlier volumes.

21. F J. Turner, A.H.A., *Ann. Rept. 1896*, 984–93.

22. Carroll and Ashworth brand Jefferson's conduct in this instance as "almost indefensible." *George Washington*, VII, 102 n.

23. Jefferson, *Writings*, VI, 328.

24. Genet to Minister of Foreign Affairs, Oct. 7, 1794. "Il m'a
donné des notions utiles sur les hommes en place et ne m'a point
caché que le Sénateur Morris et le Secrétaire de la Trésorerie Hamilton attachés aux intérêts de l'Angleterre avoient la plus grande
influence sur l'esprit du Président et que ce r'étoit qu'avec peine qu'il
contrebalançait leurs efforts." Turner, *Corres. Fr. Ministers*, p. 245.

25. Jefferson, *Writings*, VI, 261, 323, 338, 348.

The proclamation of neutrality antedated Genet's arrival at Philadelphia by several weeks. He soon began to note with Gallic indignation that the cold neutrality of the President was far less encouraging to his schemes than had been the warm welcome of the Philadelphia francophiles.[26] Before he could proceed with his treaty negotiations he encountered a series of formal protests and warnings from the United States Government against the fitting out of French privateers in American ports, the setting up of consular prize courts, captures within American waters, and enlistment of American citizens. These protests he proceeded to answer in such an intemperate and violent manner as to bring a stinging rebuke from his superiors as soon as his first dispatches reached home. Finding his designs thwarted by the neutrality proclamation, he threatened openly to appeal to the people over the head of the Government. This brought disaster. Genet's fate is a classical example of the danger a diplomat runs in appealing not to the Government of the people but to the mob of the people. After enduring his insulting language for three months Washington's Cabinet decided, August 12, 1793, to send to Paris a special courier to demand his recall, though Genet was permitted to exercise his functions until the arrival of his successor. The French Executive Council already had refused to sanction his acts at Charleston and his agitation in Kentucky and had scathingly informed him that he had been instructed "to treat with the Government of the United States, not with a portion of the people; to be an organ of the French Republic near Congress, and not the head of an American party. . . . We can not rec-

26. Turner, ibid., p. 217.

ognize any authority in the United States beyond that
of the President and Congress."

Genet continued on none the less audaciously and
energetically until his successor arrived early in 1794.
His project against Louisiana, long wobbling from lack
of financial support, collapsed utterly upon his recall.

Grenville had soon gotten wind of the decision to
send Genet [27] to the United States. He also had information—inaccurate[28] it now seems—which gave him to
understand that the American Government had intimated to Spain that it would support France in case
of aggression against England. Hammond was warned
early in January, 1793, of the danger of Genet's attempting to cultivate a connection with democratic
sentiment in America and was bidden to use every
effort to counteract it.[29] Immediately France should declare war, Hammond was instructed to make all efforts
to prevent any American assistance: the United States
Government should see that this was not called for by
the treaty of alliance and that it would surely lead to
serious misunderstandings with Great Britain. Suppos-
ing American neutrality clearly to be ascertained, the
Minister must exercise all vigilance to prevent violation
of it by individuals.[30] Later Grenville wrote that one of
the purposes of Genet was to secure shipments of grain
as payment of the American debt to France before it

27. Grenville to Hammond, No. 1, Whitehall, Jan. 4, 1793; Mayo,
*Instructions,* p. 33.

28. Jan. 4, 1793, cipher, ibid., pp. 33–34. Cf. Short and Carmichael
to Jefferson, Apr. 18, 1793, in *A.S.P.,F.R.,* I, and *Dropmore Papers,*
II, 257, 268, also Grenville to Hammond, Jan. 5, 1792, Mayo, *Instructions,* p. 22.

29. Grenville to Hammond, No. 1, Jan. 4, 1793, *supra.*

30. Same to same, Nos. 2 and 3, Feb. 8, 1793, ibid., pp. 34–35.

actually should fall due. Hammond was instructed to
make strong representations against any such arrangement and to send home lists of any vessels loaded with
such shipments.[31]

Hammond received first news of the probability of
war early in March, 1793. With exaggerated suspicions
that Jefferson would not scruple to use any means to
bring the United States into the conflict on the side of
France, he went to the Treasury Department to confer
with Hamilton. Hamilton declared that he would use
all his influence to defeat any French attempt to break
American neutrality and that in this he expected the
support of the country at large.[32] Later in the month,
even before Hamilton had apprised Washington, then
at Mount Vernon, of the possibility of war, he again
avouched to the British Minister that he would work
for neutrality and that the President was of the same
sentiment. He further confidentially divulged the failure of the recent *démarche* of the French Government,
to anticipate the payment of the American debt, the
proceeds to be devoted to the purchase of flour and
wheat in America on French account.[33] Hamilton said
that the Cabinet had discussed this proposal at length

31. Same to same, No. 6, Whitehall, Mar. 12, also No. 7 of May 2,
1793, ibid., pp. 36–40.

32. Hammond to Grenville, Mar. 7, 1793, P.R.O.,F.O., 5, 1.

33. The agent of France in this affair was Col. William S. Smith,
who after arriving home from his conference with Grenville in
1791, had become piqued at what he had considered a lack of attention to him by the American Government. He resigned a position
of minor importance and left for England. In 1792, however, he was
in France. Early the next year, in addition to his character of financial
agent of the French Government, Hammond reported him to be
buying secretly large quantities of munitions and provisions for
France. Hammond to Grenville, Apr. 2, 1793, P.R.O.,F.O., 5, 1.

and had decided to make no change in the previously arranged method of meeting installments as they fell due to the *de facto* Government of France.[34]

Anglo-American relations during the summer of 1793, aside from the frontier situation which we shall have to consider presently, hinged principally on the various questions of neutrality that arose, in most cases, from the activities of Genet. Hammond was indefatigable in his vigilance. Remonstrance after remonstrance went in to Jefferson's office, all couched in temperate and friendly language but all holding the Government to meticulous observance of its neutrality proclamation and the interpretations of international law which it had vouchsafed in other ways. The dispatches of Hammond on these questions have only minor interest for the main topic of this study. They nevertheless show how faithfully the United States adhered to the principles of neutrality despite the strong wave of feeling for France. They also indicate the satisfaction of the British Government with that neutrality.

The blundering impetuosity of Genet as contrasted with the proper conduct of the British Minister, the widespread indignation at the Frenchman's insults to the executive authority, the latent commercial interest for Great Britain, together had placed the cause of Great Britain by autumn of 1793 in a more favorable light than it had experienced during the tumultuous days of the summer. The Frenchman's defiance of the Government and his threats to appeal to the people, which Jefferson had endeavored to withhold from the public, were allowed by Hamilton to leak out indirectly

34. Hammond to Grenville, July 7, 1794, P.R.O.,F.O., 5, 11.

through Senator Rufus King and Chief Justice Jay.[35] The French cause was ruined—as far as that cause aimed at a departure from American neutrality—and the pendulum of public sentiment swung back, for the time being, nearer plumb. The diplomatic situation eased up considerably. Hammond repeatedly expressed his appreciation of the spirit in which the Government had adhered to neutrality. Both in his communications to Jefferson and in his private letters home he testified to his sense of the care with which that neutrality had been enforced and the justice with which his remonstrances had been treated. Grenville wrote Hammond early in 1794 that the Foreign Office was satisfied that in general neutrality was being properly observed by the United States. He expressed himself in similar terms to Pinckney in London.[36]

On the surface, relations between the two Governments were proceeding very promisingly, but there were two troublesome factors merely slumbering. One was the issues arising from the treaty of peace. The other was developing from the maritime measures that Great Britain was determined to use in employing against her enemy the full force of her sea power.

As soon as the more critical points of the question of neutrality had been fairly well settled, Jefferson at the request of the President[37] had addressed a note to Hammond inquiring whether he had received any further instructions regarding the unexecuted articles of

35. Hamilton to King, Aug. 13, 1793, Hamilton, *Works*, V, 574; King to Hamilton, Nov. 16, 1793, ibid., 589.

36. Grenville to Hammond, Jan. 10, 1794, Mayo, *Instructions*, pp. 44–49.

37. Washington, *Writings*, XII, 291.

the treaty of peace. The period since the delivery of Jefferson's note of May 29, 1792, had been sufficient, the Secretary of State stated, to allow for all necessary delay on the subject of its contents. "The interest we have in the Western posts, the blood and treasure which their detention costs us daily" could not but produce great anxiety as to when a reply on that subject was to be expected.[38]

Hammond suggested that pressure of business on the Foreign Office, due to the war, had caused the matter to be postponed for a short time. He said that he was awaiting additional instructions daily. He caught up with considerable asperity the remark about blood and treasure, which he took as insinuating that aid was being furnished from Canada to the Indians. This he fervently denied. Jefferson politely retorted that his reference to the expenditure of blood and treasure had accompanied the thought that, were the United States in possession of the forts, the Indian troubles would long ago have been ended.[39] Again in November, 1793, Hammond was questioned by the Secretary of State, with the unanimous agreement of the Cabinet.[40] Again the British Minister had to reply that he had no instructions such as to enable him "immediately" to renew negotiations.[41]

Nor was his chief, Lord Grenville, any more reassuring when approached on the other side of the water by the United States Minister at London. Despite the rejection of the mediation proposal, Grenville had not

38. *A.S.P.,F.R.,* I, 238.

39. Hammond to Jefferson, June 20, 1793, ibid.; Jefferson, *Writings,* VI, 321.

40. Hamilton, *Works,* IV, 480.

41. *A.S.P.,F.R.,* I, 238.

given up hope for his neutral Indian barrier project,
as will be seen later from his instructions to Hammond
after Jay's Treaty had been signed. To Pinckney he
now assumed what seemed to be an uncompromising
tone on the subject of the posts: that matter was proceeding in another place where it were best to continue
it; to give up the posts would expose the Canadian
settlements to the ravages of the Indians and to "inconveniences and disadvantages," similar to those, as
Pinckney added in his dispatch home, that were being
experienced by the American Government on the frontier. For these reasons, Grenville stated that his Government would not be justified in evacuating the posts
at this time. He regretted particularly that Hammond
had not been permitted to enter into arrangements relating to the posts and Indian affairs. Pinckney asked
him specifically whether, in case the American Government should comply with what was deemed a full execution of the treaty, the posts would be relinquished.
Grenville expressed a willingness to give up the forts,
providing the matter of debts were adjusted, but stated
that when one party had deferred fulfillment of an
obligation for nine years, whereby complete execution
could not be afterward had, a strict compliance from
the other party could not be expected.[42]

This tone may have been fostered by confidence in a
continuation of American neutrality or it may have been
an effort to sound out the United States as to how far
it would press for the posts under circumstances of the
European war. Whatever the motive, it startled Pinckney, who was an impressionable man. The disclosure
of an intention not to cede the posts, he reported in a

42. Ibid., 327.

private letter to Jefferson, "seems to render our taking
a part in the war inevitable, as it will now be . . .
politic and proper." He began to contemplate his departure from England.[43]

The student of today, with more information at his
disposal, would not interpret the interview as did Pinckney. It is quite certain that Grenville's reference to disadvantages to accompany the evacuation of the posts
was made in the light of Hammond's reports that the
United States would consent to particular conditions on
the frontier for the regulation of the fur trade.[44] We
find that only a few weeks later Grenville's colleague
in the Home Office was directing Dorchester to go
carefully on the frontier as it was hoped to adjust the
whole matter of the posts presently.[45]

The reaction most keenly felt in America of the war
of the French Revolution was the application by Great
Britain of a naval policy directly in conflict with neutral
rights. This added another and a heavy issue to the
load of unadjusted disputes already accumulated. The
violence and arbitrariness which were a part of these
British maritime measures brought the whole series
of unsettled questions, including those of the frontier,

43. Pinckney to Jefferson (private), Nov. 27, 1793, State Dept., Dispatches, England, Vol. III. "When I retire from hence I wish to
spend 6 or 8 months in France for the benefit of my children, as it is
not probable that the war will be carried on within our country. I
request your friendly information whether circumstances to which I
may be a stranger will render that step improper." For detailed
discussion of Pinckney's mission in England, 1792–1796, see author's
article in *A.H.R.*, XXVIII, 228–47.

44. Pinckney was informed of only the general condition of the
negotiations with Hammond in Philadelphia. Few details were sent
him, as a perusal of his instructions by Jefferson shows. See State
Dept., Instructions, Vols. I and II.

45. Dundas to Dorchester, Whitehall, Jan. 8, 1794, C.A.,Q, 67, 1.

to an angry head. Let us briefly examine the operation of this naval policy.

When the use of sea power had been concerned Great Britain traditionally had been unwilling to recognize principles that would sap away the might of the strongest navy in the world. By 1793 the principle of "free ships free goods," by virtue of numerous treaties among European nations, had reached the point of becoming equally well established, if not even more strongly fixed, than the ancient principle of the *consolato del mare,* the right to take enemy goods from neutral ships. To the latter practice Great Britain had always adhered. Though she had entered into several treaties sanctioning the former, she held that these modern treaties were merely particular innovations as regarded the general rule of international law which allowed enemy goods to be taken from neutral decks.[46]

International law is made by consensus of treaties as well as by long-standing practice; such is the means by which archaic principles are relegated to desuetude. The point at which the consensus of modern treaties balances against long-followed practice is difficult to determine. Generally the force of arms tips the beam. In 1793 there were precedents of numerous treaties

46. W. E. Hall, *International Law* (8th ed. Oxford, 1924), Part IV, Ch. 7; A. T. Mahan, *Sea Power and the War of 1812,* I, 92; and *The Influence of Sea Power upon the French Revolution and Empire* (2 vols. Boston, 1892), II; Paul Einicke, *Rechte und Pflichten der Neutralen Mächte im Seekrieg* (Tübingen, 1912), chs. 1, 2; L. Oppenheim, *International Law* (2 vols. 4th ed. London and New York, 1926), II, 456–57. The matter of the Armed Neutralities of 1780 and 1800 is set forth in *Armed Neutralities of 1780 and 1800* (New York, 1918), edited by J. B. Scott; and Sir Francis Piggott and G. W. T. Omond, *Documentary History of the Armed Neutralities, 1780–1800* (London, 1919).

over a stretch of one hundred and fifty years and the contentions of the Armed Neutrality of 1780 which set the scale at least evenly against the British policy. Though English jurists and statesmen expressed with nice clarity the opinion that a series of special treaties could not change a general rule from which the treaties made particular departures, the same jurists and statesmen themselves had instituted during the Seven Years' War the famous Rule of the War of 1756 and now claimed for it only thirty-seven years later all the rigor of long-established international law.

Against this British practice the United States had contended in concert with most of the powers of Europe during the War of American Independence. The war beginning in 1793 was the first occasion that the American Republic experienced to assert its position as a neutral. In an issue with Great Britain as to the interpretation of international law, the United States, with practically no maritime force, would have to contest with the greatest naval power in the world regulations the purpose of which was to maintain that power's control of the sea. To do this unaided was impossible without war; to accomplish it by force was equally out of the question.

At the outset of the war with France, Great Britain did not relax her traditional practice of taking enemy property wherever and however it could be found on the high seas. When it became known that France was attempting to secure advance payment of the American debt and to use the money in purchasing arms and provisions in America, Grenville instructed Hammond to impress strongly upon the Government of the United

States that such provisions would be regarded as French property and subject to capture, that the principle of a neutral flag covering enemy property had never been recognized by Great Britain. He added that of course *bona fide* American property on American vessels bound for France would be subject to treatment under the laws of contraband. He defined contraband as including all things "of such a Nature as to enable the Enemies of this Country to carry on the War against Us." [47] In the letter and the latitude of this definition one reads an intention to include foodstuffs. Before this dispatch reached him, Hammond had learned from Hamilton that the advance payments had been refused to the French. He therefore preferred not to open a subject that was bound to be controverted. He restricted his energy to ascertaining what grain ships, French and American, were leaving with provisions for France and, as instructed, regularly sent lists of such vessels for the use of the Admiralty. [48] Privately to Hamilton he explained the views of international law put forward by his chief. Hamilton, he reported, personally agreed as to the justice of such measures, but would not be responsible for the opinion of his colleagues. [49]

The conduct of British naval commanders soon heaped the desk of the Secretary of State high with complaints and bulged the dispatch pouches to and from the American Minister in London. American

---

47. Grenville to Hammond, Mar. 12, 1793, Mayo, *Instructions,* pp. 36–40.

48. Hammond to Grenville, Apr. 2, July 7, 1793, P.R.O.,F.O., 5, 1.

49. Same to same, July 7, 1793, ibid.

ships bearing cargoes of grain and supplies to France were brought into English ports.[50] Soon Jefferson informed Hammond that Pinckney had been instructed to make general representations in London for the security of American commerce and navigation. The British Minister then officially announced the policy of his Government. "Mr. Jefferson's answer . . . was so moderate and lukewarm as to incline me to believe that in reality he coincides with Mr. Hamilton. . . . *Any propositions of a contrary tendency which Mr. Pinckney may be instructed to offer are not meant to be seriously enforced.*" [51]

Great Britain's policy as to neutral rights was announced to the world in the Order-in-Council of June 8, 1793, embodying instructions to naval commanders. France in February had thrown open the ports of her colonies entirely to vessels flying the Stars and Stripes on terms similar to those enjoyed by French shipping.[52] To the extent that this gave privileges not enjoyed before the war it was in direct opposition to the British Rule of the War of 1756. On May 9 the National Convention issued a decree authorizing seizure of neutral vessels loaded with provisions and bound to enemy ports. Enemy merchandise found on such ships was declared to be lawful prize, but foodstuffs which were neutral property were to be allowed the price they would have commanded at the port to which originally consigned. Freight and demurrage were to be granted

50. For instance, the *Sally,* bound from the United States to Havre, Grenville to Hammond, May 2, 1793, ibid.

51. Hammond to Grenville, July 7, 1793, ibid. Italics inserted.

52. Decree of Feb. 19, 1793, J. B. Duvergier, *Collection complète des lois, décrets, ordonnances, règlements, avis du Conseil d'État,* 1788–1830 (30 vols. 2nd ed. Paris 1834–38), V, 112.

the owners of the ship. It was an attempt to turn consignments of grain to England into the bins of France and expressed in words the very regulation which Grenville had been intending to use against France and which he had been explaining to the United States informally through Hammond. The United States was expressly excluded from the operation of the French decree. The action of the French Government in enforcing this exemption, however, seems to have been subject to gross and injurious inconsistencies.[53] This decree for the pre-emption of neutral foodstuffs bound for English consignees was dated two months after a convention had been signed by Great Britain and Russia, in which both agreed to stop all exports of provisions or military supplies to French ports "and to take all other measures in their power for injuring the commerce of France." The two Empires, one professedly neutral and the other belligerent, united their efforts to prevent all other neutral powers "from giving on this occasion of common concern to every civilized State, any protection whatever, directly or indirectly, in consequence of their neutrality, to the commerce or prosperity of the French on the sea, or in the parts of France." [54]

53. *A.S.P.,F.R.*, I, 243. Mahan refers (*Sea Power and the French Revolution,* II, 243) to the fact that this exemption of the United States from the decree of May 9 was repeatedly revoked and reissued, according to the inconsistencies of the ephemeral French parties in power. He cites a statement of Gouverneur Morris, American Minister to France, showing these inconsistencies and their consequences to American shipping. A search through the French compilation, *Collection complète des lois, etc.,* does not detect any published decrees subsequent to the Navigation Act of Sept. 23, 1793, which was to operate from Jan. 1, 1794.

54. *A.S.P.,F.R.*, I, 243. Similar articles were incorporated in the treaties of alliance between Great Britain and Prussia (July 14, 1793),

The British Order-in-Council which we are to consider cannot, therefore, be considered as a measure of retaliation against France, nor was it defended as such by its authors. It was a part of the naval-diplomatic policy of cutting off France from the sea.[55]

The Order-in-Council of June 8, 1793, instructed naval commanders to bring in all neutral ships bound for French ports with cargoes of corn, flour, or meal. Such cargoes were to be "purchased" by the British Government with due allowance made for freight. No exception was made for American ships,[56] as was the case with the French decree. News of the "Provision Order" arrived in the United States August 24 and immediately caused considerable alarm among the merchants and perturbation in the councils of the Government. Hammond, who had just been informed from the usual "confidential quarter" of the request for Genet's recall, was disturbed lest a "wrong conception" of the Order should work to neutralize the advantage thus secured over the French. He sought the usual surcease for his troubles, in a conversation with the "confidential quarter." Hamilton said he regarded the policy of June 8 as harsh and unprecedented and stated that it would be necessary to protest to the Court of London. He wished in the meantime to be furnished with any exposition of the measure that might be received, as a timely explanation might remove the unfavorable impression. Hammond defended the Order as well as he

---

Austria (Aug. 30), Spain (May 25). The treaties with Portugal (Sept. 26) and the Two Sicilies (July 12) had similar articles, except for the stipulations concerning neutrals. *The Parliamentary History of England* (36 vols. London, 1806–1820), XXX, 1053–58.

55. *A.H.R.*, XXIV, 26.
56. *A.S.P.,F.R.*, I, 240.

was able but could see that his defense carried no conviction. A little later came a dispatch from Whitehall bidding the Minister officially to convey the new Order to the United States Government and to submit some remarks which were inclosed in support of it.

An echo of this exposition, which was also used to answer Pinckney's representations on the other side, reached modern ears in the perplexing days of 1914–1917. The conflict was different from all other wars, Grenville asserted. The peculiar conditions pertaining to it, the unusual mode of war employed by the enemy in "having armed almost the whole labouring class of the French Nation for the purpose of commencing and supporting hostilities against all the Governments of Europe," was deemed added justification for applying the law of nations in making provisions contraband. This argument, which is described as "indefensible" by an eminent modern writer on international law who has never been accused of an American bias,[57] was supported by a paragraph from Vattel that was construed to sanction the practice when it offered a prospect of reducing the enemy. Pinckney's answer, that even admitting the force of Vattel there was no good hope to starve the enemy, as grain was cheaper in France than in English ports, was ignored. Pinckney soon became convinced that there was no probability of the British relinquishing the point, which had now become attended with added inconvenience in that the admiralty courts had adjourned without giving decisions as to freight and demurrage.[58] Nor can any modern reader ever imagine that the British Government could have been

57. W. E. Hall, *International Law* (8th ed.), p. 788.
58. *A.S.P.,F.R.,* I, 241.

induced by words alone to give up the strongest weapon
it has ever wielded.

England, of course, had no intention of making such
a relinquishment. A formal protest penned by Jefferson
was delivered by Pinckney in December, 1793. It denied
that corn-meal and flour were contraband, on the
ground that treaties which had enumerated articles of
contraband had omitted provisions, which were to be
considered as not destined for the destruction of mankind. If the United States allowed its exports of food to
be restrained from entering French harbors, argued
Jefferson, it would be unneutral to allow them to be
exported to British ports, just as it had been unneutral
to allow French privateers to fit out in American ports
while Great Britain was excluded from the same privilege. The British practice struck at the very roots of
American agriculture, said the Secretary of State; it
was hoped that in its endeavor to keep neutral the
United States Government would not be reduced to the
dilemma of closing its exports to all European ports
where corn was demanded or of becoming a party to
the war.[59] Grenville directed Hammond to refute this
protest in the same temperate and conciliatory terms in
which he conceived it to be written.[60] Even before
Pinckney's remonstrance on the Order of June 8 had
been delivered, another Order-in-Council of far greater
severity had been issued.

The new Order was dated the sixth of November,
1793, but was not made public until late in December,

59. Ibid., p. 449.
60. Grenville to Hammond, Jan. 1794, Mayo, *Instructions,* pp. 45–47.
*A.S.P.,F.R.,* I, 449; Pinckney to Grenville, July 25, 1794, P.R.O.,F.O.,
5, 7.

thus giving privateers and war vessels time to reach
the cruising grounds and to pick off the fattest prizes
before warning could be given to shipping. British naval
commanders were directed "to stop and detain all ships
laden with goods the produce of any colony belonging
to France, or carrying provisions or other supplies for
the use of any such colony," and to bring in the same
for prize-court adjudication.

This regulation prostrated commerce between the
United States and the West Indies. A great portion of
trade, so far as the French islands were concerned, had
been open to the United States in time of peace. Therefore the Order was unjustified even by the innovative
Rule of the War of 1756, and it was superseded on
January 8, 1794, by a new Order which introduced
relaxations and came back to the standard of the Rule
of 1756. This mandate directed that vessels laden with
French West Indian produce bound for European ports
were to be brought in, as well as all vessels laden with
such produce the property of French subjects no matter
to what port bound. All vessels with military stores
bound to a port in the French islands and all vessels
attempting to break blockade were also to be taken.[61]
But already the mischief had been done under the Order
of November 6.

The November Order reached the Caribbean early
in 1794 when that sea was swarming with American
craft that had hastened to take advantage of the still
more liberal commercial privilege opened up by France
since the beginning of the war.[62] On this busy, unsuspecting merchant marine the British commanders

61. *A.S.P.,F.R.*, I, 430–31.
62. McMaster, *Hist. People U. S.*, II, 166.

swooped down. The Order was executed with the utmost thoroughness and under conditions which imposed great and unnecessary damage and hardship not to speak of gross physical cruelty on American navigators. Hundreds of American ships were soon lying idle in the harbors of the British West Indies awaiting decision of local courts of admiralty, while their crews languished in fever-ridden prison-hulks of those tropical ports.[63] One ship bearing a consul of the United States was captured and his papers together with the captain's seized. Upwards of 250 American merchant ships, most of them taken on direct passage from neutral to neutral ports,[64] were detained by March 1, 1794. One hundred and fifty of these were condemned, leaving the crews stranded and without clothes to cover their backs—wearing apparel was evidently considered good prize, from the accounts of American sailors. The short time allowed for appeal from the island vice-admiralty courts to higher tribunals in England and temporary lack of funds of the ship captains, together with the impossibility because of time and distance to communicate with the owners soon enough to start appeals, seemed to cut off all possibility of ultimate justice.

This indefensible naval policy created a tremendous sensation when the news reached the United States early in the spring of 1794. Congress, which had been

63. Signed protest of forty sea captains, P.R.O.,F.O., 5, 7.

64. Fulwar Skipwith, American Consul at St. Eustatia, to the Secretary of State, Mar. 1, and Mar. 7, 1794, *A.S.P.,F.R.*, I, 429. See also Randolph to Jay, ibid., 475. A list of American ships taken by British cruisers was issued by the Department of State, July 31, 1794, and enumerated 307. Enclosed in Hammond to Grenville, Sept. 5, 1794, P.R.O.,F.O., 5, 1.

in session for several months, had not been discussing pleasant topics. Among other things it had begun to review with a great deal of detail the commercial relations between Great Britain and the United States, comparing them with the situation existing between the United States and France. The old discriminatory proposals choked off in 1791 in anticipation of the coming of a British Minister had arisen again in the House and were resting in postponement for final consideration. The sore boil of the frontier situation had become aggravated. As months wore by the peace negotiations of 1793 with the Indians finally had failed. The posts remained in British occupation. To the frontier, then, we must turn again, if we are to understand fully the war crisis of 1794.

# CHAPTER 8

## The Frontier Crisis

AFTER even the "spontaneous solicitation" of the hostile Indian tribes for a mediation by Lieutenant Governor Simcoe had failed, it was the belief of the British Minister at Philadelphia that a tolerable barrier might be had if the native leaders could be properly coached during the negotiations which were to take place between them and American peace commissioners in the spring of 1793. For this reason, we have noted, Hammond had valued Jefferson's acquiescence in the presence of British officers at these peace parleys because it would enable the agents of the Canadian Indian Department to guide the deliberations of the Indians as the King's interest might dictate. He believed that mutual concessions might yet secure the tribes in practical possession of a fairly extensive country between the Great Lakes and the Ohio River, whereas a failure of the negotiations, followed possibly by a crushing victory of Wayne's reorganized frontier troops, might wipe away all possibilities of even a limited native barrier.

The attitude of Governor Simcoe was less resigned. By his personal mediation he had hoped to be instrumental in the creation of the native barrier state, and up to this time his energetic direction of Indian affairs in preparation for such a step had met the approval of the authorities in England. His plans for a diplomatic if not a military conquest of American territory had now been endangered by the flat rejection of all mediation proposals. He was opposed to any Indian peacemaking which should not secure recognition by the United States of a native territory large enough to serve as a protecting buffer along the whole frontier. He had no confidence that the United States would make any such concession. Rejection of the mediation overtures confirmed his conviction of the general malevolence of the government of that country. Even if the natives should give up all settled lands north of the Ohio he was persuaded that "the Avarice of Mr. Washington would insist upon the full Execution of Treaties which the Indians reject as fraudulent and inadmissible." [1] Simcoe refused to give the permission, which Hammond had assured Hamilton would be forthcoming, to purchase provisions in Upper Canada for the entertainment of native delegations by the American Commissioners at the coming peace council. The request, he feared, was only a cover for plans to set up a chain of magazines to connect American military bases with an intended fortress on the Maumee River which would control the overland approach to Detroit; and he was anxious that the prestige of the Indian Department should not be lowered by the Indians' securing supplies from other than British sources.[2] As British officers to be present at the conference he appointed Colonel Alexander McKee, Dep-

1. Simcoe to Clarke, Jan. 27, 1793, C.A.,Q, 62, 144.
2. Simcoe to Hammond, Jan. 21, Feb. 3, 1793; *S.P.*, I, 277–78, 286–87. Clarke to Dundas, with enclosures, Mar. 2, 1793, C.A.,Q, 62, 142, 148, 170. *S.P.*, I, 297–98.

uty Superintendent of Indian Affairs at Detroit, and
Lieutenant Colonel John Butler, who held a similar
commission at Niagara.[3]

This was the general situation on the frontier in the
spring of 1793 before news had arrived of the approaching war with France. Up to this time, we repeat,
the advice and action of Simcoe and the Canadian officials had the support of the home Government.[4] The
European war changed everything.

Wayne continued his preparations and drilling, but
the movement of the army north from the Ohio was
halted while a last effort was made for peace by negotiation. Despite the unfriendly attitude of Governor
Simcoe, the Peace Commission, consisting of three
prominent Americans, Benjamin Lincoln, Timothy
Pickering, and Beverly Randolph, was appointed and
departed for the western wilderness. These men were
chosen by the President rather to give weight and distinction to the personnel of the Commission than to
include men of wide experience and skill in frontier
problems and managing of the natives. General Knox,
the Secretary of War, had assured Hammond that the
Commissioners would be men "of unexceptionable
character, selected because they do not entertain unfavorable dispositions toward Great Britain."[5] As

3. Simcoe to Hammond, Jan. 21, 1793, C.A.,Q, 62, 148. *S.P.,* I, 280–81.

4. Dundas to Dorchester, Nov. 9, 1793, C.A.,Q, 65, 349; Dundas to
Simcoe, May 2, 1793, C.A.,Q, 279–1, 219. *S.P.,* I, 326–27.

5. "It is necessary that characters be appointed who are known to
our citizens for their talents and integrity." Washington to Charles
Carroll of Carrollton, Jan. 23, 1793; Benjamin Lincoln, "Journal of a
Treaty held in 1793, with the Indian tribes north-west of the Ohio, by
Commissioners of the United States," *Coll. Mass. Hist. Soc.,* 3d Ser., V,
109. Of the three Commissioners only Pickering had any experience

peace envoys to the Indians they had instructions to secure confirmation by all the western tribes of the treaty which had been signed by a portion of them at Fort Harmar in 1789. By that instrument the Indians had been confined in territory on the shore of Lake Erie between the Cuyahoga and Maumee Rivers and extending south to include approximately the north-western third of the present state of Ohio. That treaty was regarded by the United States as binding and in-contestable, and the Government already had sold to individuals parts of the land north of the Ohio which had been thus ceded by the natives. To secure the con-sent of the recalcitrant tribes to these terms the Com-mission was authorized to offer additional money bounties and to agree to relinquish all trading or mili-tary posts beyond the line of the treaty of Fort Har-mar, except the frontier posts actually held by the British.[6] They were to treat individually, if possible, rather than collectively with the tribes, in order not to recognize the native confederation.

Equipped with letters of introduction from Ham-mond to Simcoe, prearranged between the two English-men, the Commissioners proceeded on their journey by way of western New York and Pennsylvania to Ni-agara.[7] That post for the time being was the head-quarters of Simcoe, from which he administered the new British province of Upper Canada. At this place

---

with Indian affairs. He had represented the United States Government at a conference of the Six Nations in Pennsylvania in 1791. See Ham-mond to Grenville, Jan. 1, 1793, P.R.O.,F.O., 5, 1.

6. *A.S.P.,I.A.*, I, 340. For "line of 1789" of treaty of Ft. Harmar see map, p. 152.

7. Hammond to Grenville, May 17, 1793, P.R.O.,F.O., 5, 1.

they arrived on May 17, 1793. They reluctantly accepted the hospitality of Governor Simcoe, who treated them with outward courtesy.[8] They actually applied to him for a safe conduct across their own territory to the west and for an escort of British officers to protect them. With both of these requests the Governor was only too ready to comply. The Commissioners also felt constrained to invite the presence of British officers at their peace council.[9] They were surprised at an extract, exhibited to them, from a letter from McKee, who was then in attendance on the natives, stating that the latter were not yet prepared for the council and would not be ready to treat before the end of June. Not until July 11 did the Commissioners, after having been entertained and beguiled at Niagara for over six weeks, finally embark in a British

8. "In a few days after General Lincoln's arrival [Lincoln had taken the route from Albany to Niagara, whereas the other two Commissioners proceeded across Pennsylvania] with the stores and baggage (without which we could not provide for ourselves), we concluded to remove from Navy Hall [to] Queenstown, and there encamp while we should be obliged to wait for the assembling of the Indian nations at Sandusky. But as soon as the Governor understood our intentions, he again insisted on our staying at his house, and in such terms, that we could not, without rudeness, avoid a compliance with his request." Journal of the Commissioners, *A.S.P.,I.A.,* I, 347. Navy Hall was the name given by Simcoe to his headquarters. "When the Governor was informed of our intentions he barred a removal. His politeness and hospitality, of which he has a large share, prevented our executing the designs we had formed." Jour. of Benj. Lincoln, *Coll. Mass. Hist. Soc.,* 3d Ser., V, 123.

9. "Besides the reasons expressly mentioned in the note [presented to Simcoe], there were other inducements to present it. With respect to the invitation to some British officers to attend the treaties, the Commissioners found they were desirous of attending, and thought a direct invitation more eligible than a mere assent to their wishes." Journal of the Commissioners, ibid., 347.

boat on Lake Erie. They arrived ten days later at the mouth of the Detroit River, accompanied by their escort of British officers. Beyond this point [10] the commander of the Detroit garrison refused to let them advance. Accordingly they disembarked on the north (Canadian) shore of the lake and allowed themselves to be entertained at the home of one of McKee's deputies, Captain Elliott. Here the Commissioners, who had no boats of their own, were obliged to await notice from McKee as to when the Indians would be ready to receive them.[11]

Meanwhile what were the hostile chieftains doing in council assembled?

The peace offer which the American Government was prepared to make was far from meeting the minimum demands of the natives, whose greatest concession at any time had been the line of 1791, which they had been induced to request Dorchester to secure for them through his mediation. At the great native councils held at The Glaize[12] in the summer of 1792 the hostile western tribes had framed an address to the Six Nations, the go-between tribes and also members of the confederation, in which they agreed to discuss conditions of peace with the envoys of the United States but at the same time demanded the Ohio River as their boundary line and insisted on the removal of all Ameri-

10. Eighteen miles from Detroit, according to Lincoln's Journal.

11. The sources for the activities of the Commissioners are their official Journal and Correspondence, published in *A.S.P.,I.A.,* I, 337–61; the private Journal of Benjamin Lincoln, already cited; Stone, *Brant;* and the Upper Canada Correspondence of 1793, particularly letters of Simcoe and McKee (see C.A.,Q, Vols. 65 and 66).

12. Just above the Rapids of the Maumee, where that stream is joined by the Glaize, a small tributary from the east.

can settlers who had located north of that line. In return they were willing to relinquish claims to lands east of the river.[13] This demand, far more expansive than that made by the confederation in 1791, represented a change in attitude undoubtedly due to the defeat of St. Clair's army in the previous November. As the American Peace Commission was proceeding on its way west in the spring of 1793, the confederated Indians arranged to hold a general and preliminary council of all the tribes at the Rapids of the Maumee for the purpose of uniting their views in order to present final and unanimous terms.[14] It was here that the native representatives were deliberating in the presence of McKee and his staff when the Commissioners went into camp at Elliott's farm on the north shore of Lake Erie.[15]

The several tribes found themselves by no means agreed on the terms of peace. Their debates were long and excited if we are to believe the reports of McKee

13. *A.S.P.,I.A.*, I, 322–24.

14. Stone, *Brant*, II, 338.

15. A delegation from this council already had met and interviewed the Commission at Niagara in the presence of Simcoe. They had desired to know whether the Commissioners were empowered to negotiate a new boundary. The latter's instructions did not make it impossible to answer that they were not so empowered, and the chieftains were assured that a new boundary would be agreed on if mutual concessions were made on both sides. The Indians complained of Wayne's presence on the Ohio and the hostile appearance of his army. The Commissioners assured them that the General had positive orders to refrain from all hostilities during the negotiation, and to satisfy the natives a special messenger was sent to Wayne with a supererogatory request to this end. The Commissioners personally were not a little alarmed lest some movement of Wayne's troops might put an end to what was virtually a condition of armistice and cause them to perish at the hands of the savages. See B. Lincoln to Washington, Niagara, July 10, 1793, *Coll. Mass. Hist. Soc.*, 3d Ser., Vol. V, 136.

and Joseph Brant. The western tribes stood for the line of Fort Stanwix of 1768. Brant and the delegates from the Six Nations held out for the line of 1791. In this division McKee and Simcoe saw peril to British interests. Their policy had been to keep the Indians united at all costs, for they were the only barrier between the American forces and the garrisons of the occupied posts.

> Brant seems inclined to give up some cultivated settlements on the north of the Ohio, and intimates the Shawnese to be of that opinion [wrote Simcoe to Clarke while the Indian council was in progress]. . . . Your Excellency will see therefore that there still may be a difference of opinion in the Indian councils. I purpose to write strongly on this subject to Colonel McKee, and have endeavoured more strongly to fix upon Brant's mind the necessity of that Union, which I trust in the result will be the safeguard of the Indian nations and highly beneficial to Great Britain.[16]

"Attempts have not been wanting to divide the Confederacy," McKee reported to Simcoe on July 28, "but these have hitherto been resisted with firmness, and I trust will be continued to crush the monster in its birth." [17]

Describing the final result of the debates at the council at the Maumee Rapids, McKee wrote:

> The Six Nations from below dissented from the other nations on the subject of the boundary, and

16. C.A.,Q, 65, 282, July 10, 1793. *S.P.*, I, 383.
17. C.A.,Q, 65, 347.

wanted the Confederacy to give up the lands to the
United States on the east side of the east branch
of the Muskingum, as far northward as the ponds
near the carrying place to Cuyahoga, and from
thence in an easterly direction to Venango, as had
been formerly offered. But the other nations
would not consent to it. All my endeavours were
directed to accomplish a union on that point: and
I did not expect it would be difficult, as they had
heretofore agreed to make peace on these terms.

But whether from a jealousy of the Six Nations,
who are supposed by the others to be attached to
the United States, or from a conviction that it
would be wrong to make such an offer before the
commissioners agreed to the Ohio generally as a
boundary, I did not know; they however persisted
in demanding that River as the boundary without
any limitation. . . .

The acknowledgment which the United States
have at length made, that the Indian nations possess the property or right of the soil of all Indian
lands, has convinced the nations of the falsities,
long propagated, that Great Britain had given
away their country at the Treaty of Peace, and
left them in a much worse condition than they
were before the war.

Those nations who have not already sold their
possessions will now enjoy without dispute all the
lands belonging to them respectively; and these
lands will form an extensive Barrier between the
British and American territory.[18]

18. McKee to Simcoe, Foot of the Rapids, Aug. 22, 1793, C.A.,Q,
279–2, 540. *S.P.,* II, 34–35.

If with all his skill and influence over the Indians McKee could not maintain the unity of the confederation he was at least able to a great extent to keep the American Commissioners ignorant of the divisions of opinion and to cause the terms of the western nations to be presented as those of the united confederacy. Accompanied by a delegation of twenty chieftains, Captain Elliott appeared at the Commissioners' camp on Lake Erie on July 31. The Indians demanded to know whether the Commission had powers to treat on the basis of the old colonial line of 1768. The Americans could only reply that they had no such powers. The Indians would discuss no other terms. On their ultimatum the whole negotiation collapsed. The long-awaited peace talks, of which so much had been expected, amounted to no more than this short interview.

For two weeks more the Commissioners lingered on the shore of the lake, hoping that the tribes might come to some other decision. Reports presently reached them of division of sentiment among the tribes at the Rapids, but the Commissioners were unable to present themselves at the council grounds where, only a few miles away on the opposite side of the head of the lake, McKee and his subordinates were exhorting the natives to stand united in their claims. Already thwarted by the guile of Lieutenant Governor Simcoe, the dignified gentlemen of the Commission, largely unacquainted with savage life and methods of dealing with the aborigines, were wholly unqualified to cope with the blandishments of the experienced McKee. During the whole of their mission, from the time they arrived at Niagara until they left that post on their way back to Philadelphia, they had been under the constant surveillance and actual control of Simcoe's men. This they must have realized sharply when finally they made an effort to get by boat across the head of the lake from Elliott's farm to the mouth of the Maumee, in order personally to confer with the Indians. The captain of the vessel which Governor Simcoe had placed at their disposal was then discovered to have orders not to put in on the south shore of the lake west of Sandusky unless McKee should instruct him to do so.[19] Finally the Commission departed for home. A renewal of the Indian war was certain.

While Simcoe was amusing the Commissioners at Niagara he received word that France had declared war on Great Britain. He proclaimed the fact May 14, 1793.[20] The effect of this news on a man of his temperament and settled conviction as to the envenomed hostility of the United States can easily be imagined even if there were not extant documentary material to describe it. The contingency which had worried the British Cabinet in 1790 when Pitt was deliberating a war with Spain had now come to pass, so suddenly as not to allow the elaborate preparations which the diplomacy of the Prime Minister had made possible during the previous Nootka controversy. England stood confronted by a European war, but with this material difference from the situation anticipated in 1790, that Spain was the ally not the enemy of England against republican and revolutionary France. This fact relieved Canada from any fear of aggression from Louisiana. But American frontier troops were now being drilled by the ablest

19. *A.S.P.,I.A.*, I, 352–61.
20. Simcoe to Clarke, Navy Hall, May 31, 1793, C.A.,Q, 65, 253. *S.P.*, I, 329, 338.

general left in active service, for a campaign against the
Indians, and it was the fixed habit of Canadian officials
to regard the real object of such an operation as the
forcible dispossession of the occupied posts. The Federal Government of the United States was stronger than
ever. It was the American frontier troops which Canadian officials in 1790 had feared rather than a possible
Spanish incursion from Louisiana. Simcoe was sure that
the American attack was now only a matter of convenience. He began to prepare for inevitable American
occupation of the posts. He pressed upon the Deputy
Governor of Canada at Quebec, Major General Alured
Clarke, and upon Henry Dundas, Secretary of State in
Charge of Home Affairs (War, 1794–1801) his plans
for strengthening the defenses of Upper Canada. War
with the United States, to which he had looked forward for years, now seemed at hand. Perhaps the Indian War which, ever since he had arrived at Niagara,
Simcoe had anticipated in case the King's forces should
be withdrawn from the "barrier posts," was now also at
hand.[21]

One of the first steps that Simcoe had taken after
surveying the frontier situation in his new province
was to send a personal emissary to London to plead
with the Colonial Office for more supplies and military
forces for the defense of Upper Canada. Captain
Charles Stevenson, the person chosen for this mission,
was a mature British regular army officer whom the
Lieutenant Governor had taken along with him from
England to Canada. Stevenson quickly became an intimate of Colonel Simcoe's personal as well as military
family. Promptly upon arriving at Quebec November

21. *S.P.*, I, 137–45, 338.

11, 1791, Simcoe sent Stevenson via Vermont to New
York and Philadelphia with dispatches for Hammond,
the British Minister, with whom he conferred on the
Indian question and the projected neutral Indian barrier state.

"The Indian War must not be allowed to subside,"
Stevenson wrote Simcoe from New York, still hoping
for British mediation and a new boundary.[22] "The
continuance of the Indian war is to be desired," he
repeated when he returned to Montreal, again by Vermont, after picking up what information he could
about the Green Mountain State and its supposed weak
attachment to the Union, together with the uncertain
loyalty of the whole American West beset by Indian
war.[23] "Surely upon the breaking up of this vast
machine," reported Stevenson on the new American
Union, "an able Minister with full powers may from
the wreck collect materials enough to form an Empire.
I should like a little mischief amazingly. It would give
you the opportunity of laying aside the State Robe and
of resuming the Sword. It is a pleasanter duty to act
as a General than to officiate as a Chancellor." [24]

Stevenson was with Simcoe again in the summer of
1792 when the Lieutenant Governor arrived at Niagara and set up his first headquarters "Navy Hall"
just across the river from the occupied post of Niagara,[25] fourteen miles down river from the Falls.
There they must have canvassed the Indian question
in all its various possibilities. "[He] is perfectly

22. S.P., I, 101.
23. S.P., I, 127.
24. Stevenson to Simcoe (in Quebec), Montreal, May 8, 1792. S.P.,
I, 155–56.
25. S.P., I, 184, 210.

capable of communicating any Information you may require," Simcoe had written to Dundas as Stevenson set forth upon his mission.[26] Such was the delegate who appeared in England in the spring of 1793 to be regarded in high quarters as Simcoe's "right hand man." [27]

Stevenson did not get down to Quebec soon enough to depart from the St. Lawrence before the river froze for the winter of 1792–93. By the time he arrived in London, France had declared war on Great Britain and the two nations were at grips on land and sea around the globe, less so in Canada than anywhere else. The problem of the American frontier and the neutral Indian barrier state had dropped into a secondary position in British concerns. So occupied was Dundas, the Colonial Secretary, with the larger business of the world-wide conflict that Stevenson found it difficult to get an audience. At length on July 31, 1793, he got through to this Minister, talked with him at length, and left him a long written statement of requisitions "by desire of Colo. Simcoe." [28]

After setting forth requisitions for liberal re-enforcements of men and supplies to protect Canada, the paper continues at length with memoranda of a political nature. The author first states that if Wayne should be allowed to establish an army at the old Miamis fort, the site of an abandoned and dismantled fortification to the south of Detroit on the banks of the Maumee River about twenty miles south of Lake Erie, there

26. *S.P.*, I, 248.

27. Marquis of Buckingham (brother of Lord Grenville and cousin of William Pitt) to Lord Grenville, July 17, 1793. *Dropmore Papers*, II, 405. *S.P.*, I, 391.

28. *S.P.*, I, 409–13.

would be little hope that the King's forces could keep Detroit. There settlers had made their homes under the supposition that Great Britain would not be so impolitic as to abandon the posts. Even should the Americans agree to raze the forts in the event of the posts being given to them, even should they promise to permit British traders to enter the "Indian country" (Hamilton's suggestion to Hammond which the latter had conveyed to Simcoe), the United States once ensconced in that country would find cause for a conflict with England. Knox's instructions to General St. Clair in 1791 clearly proved that the American leaders longed for a popular excuse for a war with England; perhaps it would be convenient to discover such now that Great Britain was involved in war with France. The writer of the memoranda goes on to state that a new boundary line is indispensable to the colony of Upper Canada, for "by the present one Canada is and ever will be open to invasion and we are not in a situation to repel it." He suggests that during the autumn Government should prepare a plan for definitive settlement of the boundary. The details could be dispatched direct to Mr. Hammond by a messenger who could then proceed overland from Philadelphia to Canada to communicate with Lord Dorchester *and* Lieutenant Governor Simcoe, who could then adopt any necessary measures.

The author then proceeds to balance the chances of war:

> Great Britain need not fear a war if she acts with vigor; the most formidable Indian Confederacy is in her favor, and without striking a blow she may

serve to intimidate. . . . The Indians in their
contest with the Americans have shown of what
vast advantage they can be to Government; they
have for four years kept the American power in
check. A communication with the Ocean by way of
the Mississippi, if the Spanish power would let
you hold Pensacola (which places you between
him and danger) will give you both flanks of
America; two such glorious communications with
the Ocean as the St. Lawrence and the Mississippi,
with the back-country ours, must ever keep the
Americans in subjection. . . . The navigation of
the Mississippi and the occupying of Pensacola
would make the State of Kentucky look up to you
for union and alliance, as commerce cannot tra-
verse the Appalachian Mountains to get to them;
they must therefore experience great disadvantages if they continue an American State; four-
fifths of that state are favorably inclined towards
Great Britain; the fifth part is American soldiers
who are placed on the frontier to watch them.[29]

The warlike tone of these proposals obviously was
not in harmony with the neutrality which since the
Nootka crisis it had been the policy of the British
Ministry to maintain on the American frontier. Though
Dundas had approved Simcoe's recent conduct in regard to the American Commissioners and the peace
councils of the tribes, he saw danger in the action contemplated by the Stevenson requisitions. There was
danger to the now dormant mediation plans of his

29. C.A.,Q, 279–1, 264; *S.P.*, I, 411–12. There is a slight discrepancy
in the wording of the two accounts.

Government, even greater danger of hostilities with the United States while England was weighed down with a French war. Dundas saw that it was folly to furnish French sympathizers in America a means of arousing the public to make war on Great Britain. With the help of Alexander Hamilton's confidential conversations with Hammond the Ministry had measured American opinion with tolerable accuracy and hoped that the Republic would submit to the vitally necessary maritime policy of Britain. To offer gratuitous provocation on the frontier was apt to produce the very difficulties which the Government was anxious to avoid. Indeed, Pitt was willing, as he had been during the Nootka crisis, to give up the posts if necessary to preserve the neutrality of the United States, as our study of the negotiations of 1794 is to show.

To the ambitious Lieutenant Governor of Upper Canada, Dundas dispatched a rebuke in the course of which that official was reminded that it was, "as I have already intimated to you in a separate letter, equally important that you should be on your guard as much as possible against the views of America and at the same time you should studiously avoid whatever may give a pretense for urging on and inflaming the popular prejudices now existing . . . against this country." [30]

In view of Lord Dorchester's later attitude upon his return to Canada in the autumn of 1793, it should here be noted that the Governor General, who was still in London, did not regard the proposals of the Stevenson requisitions seriously. He opined that the 4,000 men demanded in the requisitions were desirable (but, of

---

30. Dundas to Simcoe, Oct. 2, 1793, C.A.,Q, 279–1, 251. *S.P.*, II, 81–82.

course; there were none to spare) to strengthen the defenses of Canada, but he considered any measures hostile to the United States to be "highly inexpedient." [31]

When he received Dundas's reproof Simcoe promptly disavowed the whole document which his friend Stevenson had presented in London. The Colonel attributed the fantastic proposals to the imagination of his aide, an explanation which the Ministry accepted. Nevertheless Stevenson continued to assert that Simcoe had dictated the document to him. He felt that he had been sacrificed when the Ministry's disapproval had made it advantageous to Simcoe to repudiate the requisitions, that as a subaltern he had been a convenient medium through which such proposals could be made and later disavowed if necessary.[32] Significantly enough, Stevenson and Simcoe continued to be intimate friends, and the former soon became Deputy Quartermaster General of Upper Canada.

The fact that the requisitions were not signed or dated might suggest that Stevenson's explanation is the true one. Moreover, it is hardly to be believed that an aide would have presumed to embellish at length with ideas of his own fancy an official paper intrusted to his care. When we compare the requisitions with Simcoe's other dispatches the real authorship of the document becomes unmistakable, though doubtless

---

31. Dorchester's answer to Simcoe's requisitions through Stevenson, Aug. 4, 1793, C.A.Q, 279–2, 276. *S.P.*, II, 2–3.

32. Simcoe to Dundas, Feb. 28, 1794, C.A.,Q, 280, 106; Dundas to Simcoe, July 4, 1794, C.A.,Q, 280–1, 143, 525; Dorchester to Dundas, Quebec, Sept. 4, 1794, ibid., Q, 69–1, 176; Stevenson to King, London, June 17, 1794, ibid., 280–2, 507. Also *S.P.*, II, 66, 300, 277.

Stevenson had embellished it somewhat: for example, he put in a word for Simcoe's promotion to Major General, something he knew the Lieutenant Governor had much at heart. The notions which are set forth and the phraseology in which they are displayed is familiar to the student of Simcoe's official correspondence. At least seven ideas can be picked out of the "Requisitions" and duplicated in Simcoe's former dispatches, sometimes in very nearly the same words: the fear of Wayne's ulterior plans, and the strategic importance of the old Miamis fort; the distrust of American motives in possibly offering to raze the posts, if evacuated, and to permit British traders to operate in the Indian country (information available only from Hammond's highly confidential correspondence); the alleged hostile implication of Knox's instructions to General St. Clair in 1791; the necessity of a new boundary line; the desire to cooperate personally with the British legation at Philadelphia in any settlement of the boundary question; the dependence of the trans-appalachian settlements of the United States upon the Great Lakes–St. Lawrence navigation system; the possibilities of military offensive from Upper Canada with the aid of Indian allies into the American back country. These are familiar topics to be found elaborated in Simcoe's letters, as the reader has doubtless perceived already in the foregoing narrative. They force the conclusion that, whoever may have written down the words, Simcoe was unquestionably the real author of the proposals contained in the Stevenson requisitions.

Lord Dorchester returned to Quebec in September, 1793, after a two years' absence in England. He found

Canadian affairs in a condition much different from that in which he had left them.

The new provincial government had been established in Upper Canada and was in active operation. A young and energetic albeit wildly imaginative lieutenant governor was pouring in correspondence which indicated aggression from the United States as inevitable and immediately to be countered. The protégé Indian nations which in 1791 on the eve of the Governor General's departure had unanimously agreed on the Ohio-Muskingum-Venango line as their boundary with the United States, now, at the cost of the unity of their confederation, had brought forward the old colonial line of 1768, a demand which made peace between them and the American Government impossible. The mediation project had collapsed. A well-equipped and well-drilled American army was advancing under a capable leader into the heart of the country which had been intended for the neutral barrier state. "If there is not a check given to these operations," Beckwith had reported from Philadelphia about the vigor of General Anthony Wayne's preparations for a campaign against the Indians and the united support of the government behind him, "I have no doubt but the intention is to drive the English to the northeast end of the continent." [33] The wild enthusiasm with which the French Minister Genet had been greeted by the American populace and the proclamations which he had dispatched to Quebec and New Brunswick inviting revolution against the British Crown were not without effect on Dorchester, notwithstanding the fact that Ham-

33. Beckwith to Dorchester, Philadelphia, Jan. 14, 1793. *S.P.*, I, 299.

mond had since written to Quebec of the generally
satisfactory character of American neutrality.

However sincerely desirous the Governor General
may have been for peace, soon after his return to
Canada he became convinced that war with the United
States was inevitable. Friction between Canadian wood-
cutters and New York settlers near the boundary and
especially some troublesome incidents in the neighbor,
hood of Lake Champlain, where the local municipal
authorities persisted in attempts to exercise jurisdiction
in districts alleged to be within the lines of the occupied
posts at Pointe-au-Fer and Dutchman's Point, further
exercised Dorchester. He connected these trifles with
the failure of negotiations between the Americans and
the western Indians and with Wayne's advance against
the natives. All along the frontier, he was persuaded,
the United States was pursuing a policy of determined
aggression. When officially questioned a few months
later concerning his conduct in the spring of 1794, he
declared that he believed every advance of the Americans into the Indian country and every purchase by
American citizens of native lands was an infringement
of an alleged agreement between Hammond and Jefferson that pending their negotiations the relations
between the two governments should remain *in statu
quo*.[34]

34. This paragraph is based on: Hammond to Grenville, May 17,
1793, P.R.O.,F.O., 5, 1; Simcoe to Hammond, York (Toronto), Aug.
24, 1793, C.A.,Q, 279–2, 525; Dorchester to Dundas, Quebec, Sept. 4,
1794, ibid., Q, 69–1, 176, C.A., *Rept. 1891*, Introduction, xxxviii; Dorchester to Dundas, Quebec, Feb. 24, 1794, C.A.,Q, 67, 88; for Vermont
episode see C.A.,Q, 66, 226–8; ibid., Q, 67, 105; P.R.O.,F.O., 6, 4;
*A.S.P.,F.R.*, I, 463. The dispatches of Hammond and his conversations
and notes to Jefferson, studied in detail by the writer, and re-checked,

In the late autumn of 1793 General Wayne began his advance. On the site of St. Clair's disaster of 1791 he pitched winter quarters. Deserters from his army carried wild stories to Detroit of plans to fortify the American troops at the Maumee Rapids and from there to push on to Detroit. McKee, who had a summer station at the Rapids, fell in with such rumors and believed them.[35] He had long before recommended to Simcoe fortification of the old Miamis fort at the Rapids of the Maumee. Simcoe had been quick to see the strategic importance of such a position as a means of covering Detroit against any attack overland from the south. He relayed McKee's letter to Quebec and to Whitehall. When Dorchester returned to Canada and realized that Wayne was within easy striking distance of the Maumee, he took a step to meet if not to begin hostilities with the United States. He issued orders to Simcoe to send a garrison from Detroit to occupy and fortify the old abandoned works.[36]

Dorchester's order to establish Fort Miamis, as the position at the Rapids of the Maumee was called, itself a serious aggression on the sovereignty and an invasion of the territory of the United States, was accompanied by an almost equally indefensible act, an inflammatory address to a delegation of western tribes

give no evidence of such an agreement. It must have existed only in Dorchester's imagination.

35. C.A., Indian Affairs, 1792–1850; McKee's Journal, Sept.-Dec., 1793, in C.A.,C, 247, 49; Reports of DeLorimier to Dorchester, Oct. 22, 1793, C.A.,C, 247, 42; Ironsides to R. McDonald, May 3, 1794. C.A., Indian Affairs, 1792–1796.

36. England to Simcoe, Detroit, Dec. 14, 1793, C.A.,Q, 67, 91; Dorchester to Simcoe, Feb. 17, 1794, ibid., 97; McKee to Sir John Johnson, Miami Rapids, June 20, 1791, ibid., Q, 52, 234.

who visited him, February 10, 1794, to request British armed intervention against the United States. According to his promise in 1791, he told them, he had done his utmost to bring about peace, but the Americans had refused all the King's offers of mediation. They had repeatedly violated the treaty which marked the international boundary of 1783. For peace they had no desire. The King and they would soon be at war. Then the Indians together with the King's warriors could draw a line to suit themselves. It was news of this speech,[37] which arrived in the United States contemporaneously with that of the Caribbean captures, recounted in the previous chapter, which made war imminent in the spring of 1794, when neither nation wanted war.

Before we turn to the war cloud of 1794, it is convenient here to follow the campaign by which Anthony Wayne subdued the western Indians and to note its effect on the British officers in command of the occupied posts and on the Canadian colonial authorities.

By April, 1794, Simcoe had completed the Miamis fortifications and had also placed a few guns on Turtle Island at the mouth of the Maumee River. The purpose of the Turtle Island works was to prevent Wayne, in case he should advance on Detroit, from establishing communications on Lake Erie by way of a possible naval base at Presque Isle, where American settlers planned a community at the eastern end of the lake. An advance by Wayne to the neighborhood of Detroit, wrote Simcoe, threatened to encircle that settlement and to sever its communications with the Indians,

37. C.A.,Q, 64, 109. This speech is mentioned in one line in Brymner's calendar, contents not given. For text see *Annual Register,* 1794.

preparatory to turning those people against the British themselves.[38] The Miamis position, he hoped, would enable him to stop Wayne's movement on Detroit, while the control of the water route from that post would admit of a prolonged support of the new fort if invested.

All of Simcoe's plans and preparations rested on his assumption that Wayne's real objective was Detroit. To block that design he summoned such resources as Upper Canada could afford. Thanks to continued British influence over the Indians the native confedera- tion stiffened its resistance against the American ad- vance. Through McKee's diplomacy it secured a prom- ise, illusory as subsequent experience proved, of alliance with the tribes on the southwestern frontier of the American western settlements (the Cherokees and Creeks).[39] By June Simcoe felt some confidence in the safety of Detroit. As to his own ability to cope with Wayne he had no misgivings. After repulsing the first incursions of the Americans, he wrote Dundas, a suc- cessful war waged from Canada would soon separate Kentucky and the other "colonies" of the United States west of the Alleghenies. Vermont, he was certain would remain neutral [40]—perhaps even all New Eng- land would come back into the British fold.

38. Simcoe to Dundas, York, Feb. 28, 1794, C.A.,Q, 280–1, 75.

39. Dorchester to Dundas, Quebec, June 7, 1794, C.A.,Q, 69–1, 31. For McKee's correspondence with the southern Indians, see C.A., Indian Affairs, Miscellaneous, Carton for 1792–1796.

40. Simcoe to Dundas, June 21, 1794, C.A.,Q, 280–1, 178. See also C.A., Rept. 1889, note C. While Simcoe was preparing the defenses of Detroit against the expected attack of Wayne he received a dispatch from the Spanish Governor of Louisiana, Carondolet, who had sent a runner overland from New Orleans. Carondolet, alarmed at Genet's intrigues in Kentucky and the projected descent of Kentucky riflemen

The entirely chimerical quality of Simcoe's night-
mares of American aggression is exposed by Wayne's
actual operations. His army started from Fort Recovery in July, 1794. Marching parallel with the
Glaize, a tributary of the Maumee from the southeast,
Wayne struck the main river near the confluence of the
two streams. Fortifying himself strongly at every
halting place and constantly keeping out screens of
scouts as a further protection against surprise attack,
he penetrated in a few weeks to the principal Indian
settlements. The Indians obstinately refused to treat
for peace. Wayne advanced down the river. A few
miles from the new British fort he met the forces of
the natives. They had strengthened their position by
cunningly taking advantage of a windrow of tornado-
blown trees through which had sprung up a fresh
forest growth, a natural barrier difficult to penetrate.
But a quick movement of mounted riflemen outflanked
the rude works and a spirited charge of well-disciplined
infantry overwhelmed the savage warriors. The battle
of Fallen Timbers, August 20, 1794, brought a definitive settlement of the Indian problem which had em-

---

on his capital, proposed common action of the colonial forces of the
two European allies, Spain and England, in case of any attack on
Louisiana. Simcoe, while expressing a hope that the alliance between
the two countries might be strengthened to afford cooperation in case
the United States should force a war, and stating that it was for the
interest of Great Britain that Louisiana remain Spanish, replied that
he could give no assistance at the moment, as he had his hands full
with Wayne. See C.A.,Q, 69–1, 38, 41. For General Wayne's difficulties
with disaffection in Kentucky, Simcoe's "zeal and timerity [sic]," and
Spanish activities, see Wayne's letters to Secretary of War Henry
Knox, R. C. Knopf, *Anthony Wayne . . . The Wayne-Knox-Pickering-
McHenry Correspondence* (Pittsburgh, 1960).

barrassed the United States ever since the end of the War of Independence.[41]

While Wayne was advancing to the Maumee the British officers at Detroit were using every means in their power, outside of actually joining in the hostilities, to unite the Indians and to strengthen their resistance to the American advance. All the warriors in the vicinity of the post who had not yet left for the Miamis were hurried on to join their brethren.[42] McKee furnished large supplies of provisions and ammunition and lamented the poor quality of the guns sent out for the Indians. Detroit was stripped bare of provisions and munitions. Urged by the natives, who held out the raw scalps of American soldiers as they asked for more ammunition,[43] McKee wrote to headquarters for extra supplies which must be sent "provided His Majesty's Posts are considered by His Excellency as objects of importance."[44] Evidence shows that extra munitions and supplies were sent to Detroit from the Indian Department headquarters at this time; so extensively did the disbursements for 1794 eat into the stores for the next year that a much greater supply of gunpowder

41. *A.S.P.,I.A.*, I, 491; Roosevelt, *Winning of the West,* IV, 91. For review of Indian campaigns, including Wayne's, see L. Esarey, *History of Indiana* (2 vols. Indianapolis, 1915–18), I, ch. 5.

42. "We have done everything in our power to hurry on the Indians to the Rapids. We have sent strings of wampum and speeches to the River la Tranche, the River Huron, Saguman . . . and I understand they are all setting out to see their friends at the Rapids." Duggan (storekeeper of the Indian Department at Detroit) to McKee, Detroit, Aug. 18, 1794, C.A., Indian Affairs, 1792–1796.

43. Indian speech to McKee, The Glaize, May 25, 1794, C.A.,C, 247, 161.

44. McKee to Chew (Secretary of the Indian Dept.), July 7, 1794, C.A.,C, 247, 192.

than usual had to be ordered for that Department in 1795.[45]

Simcoe's fears grew apace as Wayne approached the Maumee. Suppose American settlers under land titles from their own states should begin to occupy the shores of the lower Lakes! At the fine harbor of Sodus Bay (east of present Rochester, N. Y.) a settlement was preparing under the management of Charles Williamson, who had obtained a deed from Robert Morris for some 1,200,000 acres in the Genesee country.[46] Simcoe had always considered that "in the course of events" it might be necessary to "seize" that place,[47] the best harbor on the southern shore of Lake Ontario, where an American naval base could counter Kingston, Ontario, at the outlet of the lake into the St. Lawrence River, or could offset the new British fort and capital at Toronto (York). He dispatched an officer with a petty military escort to demand that Williamson desist from making any such settlement, represented as a violation of the King's right in the "Indian Territory." [48]

Another American movement was on foot to settle

45. Chew to Coffin (Secretary to Lord Dorchester), July 10, 1794, C.A.,C, 247, 194. "With this you will receive a requisition for the deficiencies of 1795 owing to our being obliged to use a number of articles for presents, that were intended for that year; so much powder would not have been required did not the Indian Department owe fifty barrels to the Ordnance. It will take very nearly all the blankets and very nearly all the other articles mentioned to complete the approved requisitions for the present year."

46. *S.P.*, II, 393.

47. Simcoe to Dorchester, March 16, 1794. *S.P.*, II, 190.

48. *S.P.*, II, 318, 364. Helen I. Cowan, *Charles Williamson, Genesee Promoter—Friend of Anglo-American Rapprochement* (Rochester, N. Y., 1941), pp. 128–32.

Presque Isle (Erie, Penna.), the best harbor on the
southern shore of Lake Erie, within a "few hours' sail"
of the British Fort Erie on the Canadian bank of the
Niagara River where it flows out from the lake—this
project with a grant of land from the State of Pennsylvania which significantly reserved a sufficient area
for a United States naval base.[49]

What should Simcoe do to fend off such dangers to
the still exclusive British navigation of the Great
Lakes? He had general orders to repel force with force
in case of an "attack" on the occupied posts. He wrote
to inquire of General Alured Clarke, Deputy Governor
General in Dorchester's absence, and of Dorchester
himself upon the latter's return to Quebec from England, whether these orders allowed the use of force
to prevent American craft sailing by the King's posts.[50]
General Clarke replied that pending the return to
Canada of Lord Dorchester he deferred giving precise
orders on a matter then under the consideration of the
King's Ministers; if such an event should happen
(American navigation past ports on the Lakes) "much
must depend upon discretion guided by the circumstances of the moment." Should anything in the most
distant degree endanger the security of the "King's
Posts" (Niagara, Oswego, or Detroit) "I can have no
hesitation to say that if after being warned to withdraw, they should persevere in a contrary conduct,
compulsory measures should be adopted to force a
compliance."[51] Dorchester when he finally arrived
confirmed Clarke's orders, involving "peace or war,"

49. *S.P.*, I, 327–28.
50. *S.P.*, I, 338.
51. Clarke to Simcoe, Quebec, June 24, 1793, *S.P.*, I, 367.

as "discreet and prudent," but warned Simcoe that in case of war the greater part of forces, however inadequate, at the upper posts, would have to be withdrawn for the defense of Lower Canada.[52]

The Governor General sanctioned the protest to Williamson, and even furnished Simcoe with forms for warning off American settlers on the shores of the Lakes, but withheld positive permission to use force to prevent such settlements, or to interfere with American navigation of the Lakes.[53]

In London, with the European war raging and absorbing the King's armaments elsewhere on land and sea, Pitt's Government had come to consider the posts on the American side of the line as temporary objects, pending final arrangement with the United States leading in all probability to their evacuation.[54] And it no longer was disposed to insist on a neutral Indian barrier state as a condition of their evacuation —such was the advantage to the United States in Anglo-American relations of Great Britain's distress in the wars of the French Revolution. All Simcoe was allowed to do was to build up opposing armaments within the feeble resources at his command on land and lake, and to look to his Indian Department to stir Joseph Brant and the doubtful Six Nations to oppose American settlements at Sodus Bay and Presque Isle.[55] Great Britain was too busy in Europe and in the Indies West and East, and the United States too vital a neutral supply of naval stores, to allow any proconsul

52. Dorchester to Simcoe, Quebec, October 7, 1793, S.P., II, 83.
53. S.P., II, 136, 154, 318.
54. Dundas to Simcoe, Whitehall, July 4, 1794, S.P., II, 300.
55. S.P., II, 116, 137, 182, 189, 268, 272, 296, 412.

in Canada to provoke a war with her best commercial customer at a time when war was closing off markets on the continent of Europe.

"I hold War to be inevitable," wrote Simcoe to McKee, August 6, 1794, "and in that case somehow or other Wayne must be driven back. On the best and most rapid method of effecting this purpose, I wish for your opinion in confidence, more particularly, of what we have to apprehend from your Quarter should War be declared about the end of September from an autumnal or a winter campaign?" [56]

Let the reader now return to what Simcoe regarded as the "extraprovincial Indian Country."

The crisis of the frontier was at hand. After the battle of Fallen Timbers, Wayne advanced within range of the British guns at Fort Miamis. Inside the fort torches hovered above the breeches of loaded cannon trained on the American cavalry.[57] Outside the log walls stood Wayne's frontier troops, flushed with their success and indignant at the recent encroachments of the British and at the aid which they believed had been furnished to the savages; for by Wayne's account the bodies of white irregulars had been found after the battle of Fallen Timbers.[58] In this warlike setting occurred the dramatic incident where only the coolness of both commanders, especially that of the British officer inside the fort, prevented a precipitation of hostilities that might have set the whole back country afire. It might have destroyed the last chance for peace at the very time when John Jay and Lord Grenville, in

56. Simcoe to McKee, August 6, 1794. *S.P.*, V, 99.
57. Simcoe to Portland, Dec. 20, 1794, C.A.,Q, 281-1, 129.
58. *A.S.P.,I.A.*, I, 491.

London, were arriving at a comprehensive settlement of the whole frontier situation.

Colonel Campbell, the British commander, sent out a flag of truce to ask how to construe the approach of an American army to a British fort in time of peace. Wayne replied that his victory over the "hordes of savages in the vicinity of your post" was the answer to that question. Campbell sent back word that a further move threatening the fort would meet with armed opposition—and he meant it.[59] Wayne, with an expression of surprise that there should take place in the absence of war such a hostile act as the erection of a fort among Indians at war with the United States, requested Campbell's withdrawal. Campbell replied that he was under military orders only, that the question of why he was there might be left to the diplomats. He refused to withdraw without orders. Wayne did not attack. For three days more he kept his army on the banks of the Maumee, destroying the cornfields and stores of the Indians, particularly the storehouse and residence of McKee. This done, he fell back to Fort Defiance, which he had erected at the confluence of the Maumee and Glaize, "the grand emporium of the hostile Indians of the West," strengthened his works there and placed himself in a position to extinguish effectively any possible renewal of hostilities by the Indians.[60]

59. "I trust that if he attacks us this night he will not find us unprepared." Campbell to Joseph Bunbery, Fort Miamis, Aug. 22, 1794, *S.P.*, II, 408. A carton of loose papers (C.A., Indian Affairs) contains seven letters of Colonel Campbell to McKee from Aug. 21 to Aug. 30, 1794, which furnish additional light upon this incident, of which the official correspondence between Wayne and Campbell has been published in *A.S.P.,I.A.*, I.

60. *A.S.P.,I.A.*, I, 490–91.

At Detroit anxious hours passed while Wayne was on the Maumee. The defeat of the Indians filled the British officers with dismay and fear that the Americans soon would be at their own gates. "The militia do duty here, and I am just going the rounds, so shall leave this unfinished until my return," wrote Duggan, the storekeeper of the Indian Department, who had been mustered into military service. He was conveying the "sorry news" to Montreal. "Half after twelve— and I am just returned from my rounds . . . all is well at present. God knows how long it will be, as there are a great number of disaffected persons here."[61] The officer in command of the post, Lieutenant Colonel England, who saw the unity of the Indian tribes destroyed, their resistance shattered and their effectiveness as a means of preventing an invasion of Canada ruined, could not understand why Wayne "relinquished" an advance on Detroit, "at a time when it would appear he had effectually accomplished his chief object, and defeated the Indians perfectly, and had the whole country at his command." [62]

The only answer is that the United States Government never had any intention of using the Indian campaign to mask a movement against the occupied posts while England was at war with France, that even the "excitable" Wayne did not care to commit himself on his own responsibility to such an adventure.

The frontier situation continued to be tense for

61. Duggan to Chew, Detroit, Aug. 22, 23, 1794, C.A.,C, 247, 244. *S.P.*, II, 409.

62. England to Simcoe, Aug. 30, 1794, C.A.,Q, 70, 39. Simcoe explained it as due to the possible necessity of using Wayne's forces to put down the Whiskey Insurrection in Pennsylvania. Simcoe to Dundas, Navy Hall, Sept. 5, 1794, C.A.,Q, 70, 39. *S.P.*, III, 21.

some weeks after Wayne's withdrawal from the immediate vicinity of the Maumee. During this time the
Canadian authorities proceeded with active preparations for war.[63] The suspense ended upon the arrival
in Upper Canada in October of news of an agreement
reached between Jay and Grenville to the effect that
everything on the frontier should remain in *statu quo*
pending negotiations then proceeding in England, and
that both parties should continue to hold their existing
possessions, all encroachments by either side to cease.
In Canada the government officers construed this new
understanding to allow them to remain in possession of
the Miamis fort, though Jay and Grenville had this
instance of encroachment specifically in mind and had
made the agreement to include it, after Jay had assured
Grenville that Wayne had no orders to molest the old
posts. Jay was given to understand that orders would
be dispatched directly to Simcoe to relinquish the recent
fortification. The fort was not evacuated until the other
posts were given up in 1796 in execution of the treaty.[64]

A flickering hope of a chance of mediation rose in
Simcoe's breast when he received from Hammond a
copy of a letter of Secretary Randolph, who had succeeded Jefferson as Secretary of State, which described
in strong terms the Miamis aggression and the Sodus
Bay incident as acts of actual hostility. Simcoe, to use
his own words, determined "to throw down the gaunt-
let" to Randolph. He dispatched a long letter defending the act for which he had been responsible under the

63. Simcoe to Dundas, Sept. 12, 1794, C.A.,Q, 70, 57.
64. C.A.,Q, 75, 458. For the *status quo* agreement, H. P. Johnston,
*The Correspondence and Public Papers of John Jay* (4 vols. New York,
1890), IV, 33, and Grenville to Hammond, July 15, 1794, Mayo,
*Instructions,* pp. 59–60.

orders of Dorchester, an epistle calculated to open again the whole Indian question. This was to be published by Hammond in reply to Randolph's letter, which together with a brief reply to it by Hammond the Secretary of State had already given to the press. Simcoe trusted that the published discussion would serve to open up the possibility of mediation. In spite of Wayne's victory he hoped it might be possible for the Indians again to take the field. He overestimated the embarrassment to the federal authorities of the Whiskey Rebellion then in progress in Pennsylvania. It would be impossible for the United States to cope with another Indian war and a domestic insurrection at the same time, he reasoned, and this fact might force acceptance of the mediation project.

The hope was short-lived. The Whiskey Rebellion fizzled out when the militia was set in motion against the insurrectionists. The whole affair was turned by Hamilton into an impressive demonstration of the increasing force of the Federal Government. The Indians never assembled for another campaign. Simcoe's formidable challenge, toned down by Hammond, was published together with the relevant correspondence of Hammond and Randolph, an array of type which filled eight newspaper columns.[65] It failed to produce the desired result. The public rightly regarded Wayne's campaign as the decisive factor in the Indian problem.

Simcoe's initial plans for advancing his military career in a campaign against "Mr. Washington" which

65. Simcoe to Dorchester, Oct. 31, 1794, C.A.,Q, 71–1, 127; Simcoe to Hammond, Oct. 20, 1794, ibid., Q, 280–2, 484; Simcoe to [McKee] Oct. 31, 1794, ibid., M, 109, 253; N. Y. Daily Gazette, Dec. 8, 1794; S.P., III, 132–33, 163–65, V, 121.

might break up the new American Union were frustrated: first, by the value of American commerce to Great Britain both in peace and wartime; second, by the weak defenses of Upper Canada during the European war; and finally, by the caution imposed by his superiors in London. Years after the crisis of the frontier had passed, during what Bradford Perkins calls the "first rapprochement" [66] of Anglo-American relations, the would-be Clive of the Ontario Peninsula claimed credit *and consideration* from the Duke of Portland and from the Prime Minister William Pitt for having been the means of preventing a war between Great Britain and the United States.[67]

66. Bradford Perkins, *The First Rapprochement: England and the United States, 1795–1805* (Philadelphia, 1955).
67. See C. R. King, *The Life and Correspondence of Rufus King* (6 vols. New York, 1894–1900), III, 231.

# CHAPTER 9

# The War Cloud of 1794

THE scrupulous neutrality of the United States had been sufficient evidence of peaceful intentions to convince the British Ministry, if not the Canadian authorities, that there was little danger of the American Government following the lead of the French alliance of 1778 into the war. Genet's impetuous diplomacy reacted against the immense popularity which the French Republic had enjoyed at the outbreak of the European war. As the autumn months of 1793 came on, Anglo-American relations appeared to rest in a comparatively quiet condition, while the public attention became absorbed with the dreadful yellow-fever epidemic that fell on Philadelphia and its vicinity.

In reality an adjustment of the various issues between the United States and Great Britain was as distant as ever. Jefferson's reply to Hammond's indictment of American infractions of the treaty of peace was still unanswered, though it had been delivered many months previous. It was useless for the Foreign Office in such an important matter to plead pressure of other business. The procrastination was only too apparent. England seemed to be either unwilling or at a loss to explain the continued occupation of the posts. The diplomatists of Downing Street were still hugging the hope of a

mediation[1] as the final settlement of the frontier question and awaiting the chance which might make mediation acceptable. Such might come from an unsuccessful
and unpopular campaign of the United States against
the hostile Indians.

This deceptive calm lasted only until the assembling
of the Third Congress on December 2, 1793. Foreign
affairs then received full airing. President Washington
promptly submitted several batches of documents describing the negotiations which the executive had been
conducting, between the sessions of Congress, with
foreign powers and with the western Indians. These
communications and the events which transpired soon
after them produced the Anglo-American crisis of the
spring of 1794. First, the Senate received on December
4 the papers relating to recent negotiations with the
hostile Indians and the failure to reach a peaceable
settlement. The documents thus made public included
instructions to the Commissioners, their correspondence with the War Department, under the direction
of which they had been sent out, and the Journal in

1. In November, 1793, Pinckney, the American Minister in London,
had an interview with Grenville on the subject of the posts. Grenville,
who stated that the negotiation was already "proceeding" in Philadelphia, complained that Mr. Hammond had not been permitted by the
United States to enter into a negotiation "for some arrangements relating particularly to the posts, and (as I apprehended him) Indian
affairs, which, he had no doubt, would have terminated in our common
advantage and mutual satisfaction; but that, when Mr. Hammond
wished to open that business, he was given to understand (though in
the most civil terms) that the less that was said on that subject the
better." Pinckney to the Secretary of State, Nov. 25, 1793, *A.S.P.,F.R.,*
I, 327. On January 8, 1794, Dundas wrote to Dorchester cautioning him
to be very careful on the frontier because a settlement of the whole
question was near. C.A.,Q, 67, 1. See above, Ch. 7, p. 206.

which they related their various peregrinations and conferences and the intimate part which the Canadian officials had played in the same.[2] On December 5 the President called the attention of both houses of Congress to foreign affairs and placed before them the correspondence of the United States as a neutral power with the principal European belligerents, Great Britain and France. Neutral rights and belligerent interpretations of international law were set forth in this voluminous literature, together with the circumstances which led to the dismissal of Genet, and the present state of negotiation with Great Britain over issues arising from the treaty of peace of 1783. Copies were included of the several notes which had passed between Jefferson and Hammond, not omitting Jefferson's periodic requests to be informed whether Hammond had been empowered to continue the negotiations which had by this time been suspended for more than a year and a half.[3]

The published correspondence showed England's disinclination immediately to continue the negotiation or at any time to evacuate the posts. The Commissioners' Journal made it evident that the posts were serving as bases for intrigues of the Canadian Indian Department among enemy Indians. Nothing was apparent in this material to show the real reason for England's delay in negotiating a frontier settlement— the hope of successfully mediating at an opportune moment to set up a neutral Indian barrier state. Naturally Congress and the reading public took the correspondence at its face value; indeed, the revelations of

2. *A.S.P.,I.A.*, I, 340–61.
3. *A.S.P.,F.R.*, I, 141–246.

the true motive of Grenville's frontier diplomacy, which could have been known only from the informal discussions which Hammond had held with Hamilton and Jefferson, would have served only to increase bitterness against England. Indignation rose still higher when on December 16 the two houses received from the President information concerning a truce recently arranged by British diplomacy between Portugal and the Bey of Algiers.[4] In promoting this pact the purpose of England had been to free her ally from harassments that prevented efficient cooperation in the war against France. An incidental consequence of the truce was to remove restraint from the Algerine corsairs and thus to loose a swarm of pirates to prey on American merchant vessels venturing through the Straits of Gibraltar. It was not strange that members of Congress, already in no pleasant mood, should consider only the result and not the purpose of such diplomacy.

It was precisely at this time, December 16, 1793, when the Republican opposition could take advantage of the unsatisfactory trend of Anglo-American affairs to renew their proposals for discrimination against British commerce, that Jefferson submitted to the House of Representatives his long-delayed report on the restrictions and discriminations by foreign nations against the commerce of the United States. We remember that the House resolutions for discriminations provoked in February, 1791, by the failure of the Morris mission had "vanished," following unofficial reports that a British minister resident was to be appointed to Philadelphia; and that a motion had then

4. *A.S.P.,F.R.,* I, 288.

been carried to refer the President's message to the
Secretary of State for consideration and report at the
next session. The arrival of a minister during the recess had resulted in an informal agreement between
Jefferson and a committee of the House by which the
report had been pigeonholed for over two years in the
hope that something might come out of negotiations
with Hammond.[5] To the Republicans—that is, the
Democratic-Republicans of the day—at least, it was
now apparent that two years' forbearance had resulted
only in increasing contempt by Great Britain for the
rights and interests of the United States. Release of the
report was well timed to awaken the slumbering anti-
British commercial proposals.

In strong terms Jefferson set forth the discriminations against American commerce which were a consequence of British tariff and navigation laws. He mentioned discriminations by other European powers—
which, he stated, there was no reason to believe could
not be remedied by negotiation—but he emphasized
those by Great Britain and compared them unfavorably
with the milder regulations of France. In conclusion he
earnestly recommended vigorous retaliation in kind as
the best defense of American interests:

> If particular nations grasp at undue shares [of
> ocean commerce], and, more especially, if they
> seize on the means of the United States, to con-
> vert them into their own aliment for their own
> strength, and withdraw them entirely from the
> support of those to whom they belong, defensive
> and protecting measures become necessary on the

5. Hammond to Grenville, Mar. 7, 1793, P.R.O.,F.O., 5, 1.

port of the Nation whose marine resources are
thus invaded. . . .

Proposals of friendly arrangement have been
made on our part to . . . Great Britain . . . ;
but, being already on as good a footing [with us]
in law, and a better in fact, then the most-favored
nation, they [the British] have not, as yet, discovered any disposition to have it meddled with.[6]

Jefferson's Report, received by the House amid the
circumstances which have been outlined, provoked immediate action. On January 1, 1794, it was considered
by the Committee of the Whole, and on January 3 the
day after Congress had passed a resolution calling for
equipment of a naval force to protect the Mediterranean trade—Madison introduced again his famous
resolutions of 1791.[7] In addition to replying to the

6. *A.S.P.,F.R.,* I, 304.

7. The resolutions provided:

1. Additional duties on manufactured goods imported from European
nations having no commercial treaty with the United States.

2. Additional tonnage duties on vessels belonging to such nations.

3. Reduction of tonnage duty on vessels belonging to nations having
commercial treaties with the United States.

4. When foreign nations refused to recognize as United States vessels, vessels not built within the United States, reciprocal action to be
taken by the United States.

5. When produce or manufactures of the United States are refused
admission except in United States ships; or when admission is refused in United States vessels of produce or manufactures not imported from any place within the United States, reciprocal restrictions
to be levied by the United States.

6. "Where any nation may refuse to the vessels of the United States
a carriage of the produce or manufactures thereof, whilst such produce or manufactures are admitted by it in its own vessels, it would be
just to make the restrictions reciprocal; but inasmuch as such a measure, if suddenly adopted, might be particularly distressing in cases

British Navigation Laws in kind the resolutions now embodied a provision by which the resulting additional tariff revenue would be devoted to liquidating claims of American citizens arising out of damages sustained by the operations of "particular nations in contravention to the law of nations." This referred only to operation of the Order-in-Council of June 8, 1793. News of the more drastic Order of November 6 and captures made under it had not yet arrived in Philadelphia.

The Federalists immediately closed their ranks in opposition to these resolutions. For the same reason as in 1791 they were unwilling to begin a war of trade legislation with Great Britain or to encumber with renewed friction the negotiations over nonexecution of the treaty of peace. This time they succeeded only in postponing debate in order to give time to consider the proposals. The Republicans—that is, the Jeffersonian Republicans—argued that the question already was four years old and that little additional consideration was necessary to ripen opinions already mature. From January 13 to February 3 Madison's resolutions were debated in Committee of the Whole. It was the most detailed and exhaustive debate that up to that time had

---

which merit the benevolent attention of the United States, it is expedient, for the present, that a tonnage duty extraordinary only of —— be imposed on the vessels so employed; and that all distilled spirits imported therein be subject to an additional duty of one —— part of the existing duty." (The effect of this would be to levy an extraordinary tonnage duty on British vessels plying between the British West Indies and the United States, from which commerce American vessels were excluded by the Navigation Laws.)

7. The proceeds of these additional duties to be devoted to the liquidation of claims of American citizens arising out of the operations of particular nations in contravention to the law of nations.—*Annals of Congress,* Jan. 3, 1794.

taken place within the halls of Congress. The minutes
of the House of Representatives for those days give a
full exposition of American opinion on the British
Navigation Laws. They well illustrate the division
which had now developed on strictly party lines. The
Federalists, whose system born of Hamilton depended
on commerce for revenues to stiffen the authority and
power of a resolute national government and to ally
with it the business interests of the country, saw in
interruption to Anglo-American commerce the destruction of American nationality itself. The Republicans,
Madison their spokesman, beheld in the monopolistic
system of Great Britain an attempt to make the commerce of an independent nation subservient to the
shopkeepers and shipowners of a foreign power, a
power still in possession of parts of American territory
and posing as protector of the Indian enemies of the
United States. They were exasperated, too, at the
controlling influence of England over American overseas trade. They were indignant at her insolent disregard of neutral rights of United States citizens to sail
the ocean lanes in pursuit of legitimate enterprise.
In Hammond's unsatisfactory correspondence with Jefferson they saw only pertinacious and unbending determination of the British Government to continue on
its chosen path regardless of American protests. They
believed that not only the interest but also the self-
respect of the United States demanded that Congress
reply in kind to the Navigation Laws.

When back in 1791 Jefferson's report seemed about
to be submitted to Congress, it is remembered, Hamilton had occupied himself with compilation of a state-

ment intended to controvert the conclusions anticipated
from the Secretary of State.[8] As long as Jefferson's
document had been held back Hamilton had kept his
own in his desk. He now gave it to William Smith of
South Carolina, who fashioned from it the leading
speech of the Federalists in opposition to Madison's
resolutions and who, it should be remarked, was burned
in effigy for his pains in the streets of Charleston.[9] By
a table of statistics from the Treasury Office, Smith
attempted to show that the country really did not fare
so badly at the hands of Parliament as had been represented, that there was no discrimination against the
United States specifically nor anything particularly injurious or unfriendly to American tonnage. In regard to
certain commodities the system of Great Britain even
made special concessions to the United States over
other nations. This was true of duties on tobacco, rice,
wood, pot and pearl ash, naval stores, pig and bar
iron, which were lower than those levied by France.
For the year 1792 Smith pointed out that exports to
Great Britain were $8,260,463; to France $5,243,543.
Imports from Great Britain for the same year were
$15,285,426; from France $2,069,348. Thus American commercial interests were far more dependent on
Great Britain than on France. Three-fourths of American trade was carried on with Great Britain, whereas
only one-seventh of all British trade plied back and
forth between that country and the United States. Was

8. Hamilton, *Works,* V, 80.
9. "Letter from a Member of Congress to a Gentleman in London,"
Phila., May 4, 1794, P.R.O.,F.O., 5, 7. The letter is unsigned but the
text indicates that its writer was Smith.

it reasonable, then, to expect that in a legislative war Great Britain was more to be injured than the United States? [10]

Madison opposed this speech in an able argument in which he advanced most of the views previously presented by Jefferson and compared the favorable legislation of Congress with that of Parliament. The Republicans were quick to couple the Navigation Laws with the other grievances against Great Britain.[11] The trifling privileges which were held out to certain American raw materials necessary to British manufactures and to a few other products like rice and tobacco, which Sheffield had pointed out were in danger of deserting the English *entrepôt* for direct carriage in American ships to European consumers, these concessions did not blind people to the mercantilistic policy which was the general purpose of British commercial regulations. With Madison as spokesman of Jefferson, and Smith as the representative of Hamilton, the debate in the House was one between the systems for which these two remarkable men stood. It contributed to the definite crystallization of party politics in congressional history.[12]

In the Committee of the Whole the debate was not favorable to either party. The resolutions were not passed immediately. Nor were they rejected. By a vote

10. *Annals,* Jan. 14, 1794.

11. Hammond to Grenville, Feb. 22, 1794, P.R.O.,F.O., 5, 4.

12. Joseph Charles, *The Origins of the American Party System* (Williamsburg, Va., Institute of Early American History and Culture, 1956), p. 94. For a good account of Madison's effort, see Irving Brant, *James Madison, Father of the Constitution* (Indianapolis and New York, 1950), pp. 388–400.

of 51 to 47 they were postponed for further consideration.

Submission of the diplomatic correspondence to Congress and revival of the discrimination movement immediately awoke the anxiety of the British Minister.
Though a ready student of the political situation in
the United States,[13] Hammond never fully appreciated
the democratic functioning of which American diplomacy was capable. The custom of submitting live correspondence to Congress for public deliberation was an
innovation which neither he nor the Foreign Office
would understand or justify, despite the fact that
negotiation over the issues with England had been suspended for more than a year and a half. He could not
see why his official notes should be handed over to piti-
less publicity in Congress and allowed by that body to
appear in a "common newspaper." He protested to
Randolph on this point. At the same time he was
obliged to answer negatively to another demand from
the Secretary to know whether instruction had yet
been received from London to renew the negotiation.
This, too, was given to Congress and published. The
procedure was defended by Randolph with an asperity
not unequal to that of the British Minister.[14] The latter
saw no reason, either, why Jefferson's report should
have been made at this particular moment. Submis-

13. For an example of this see his analysis of American party development in dispatch to Grenville of Mar. 7, 1793. P.R.O.,F.O., 5, 1.
14. *A.S.P.,F.R.,* I, 328; Grenville to Hammond, Aug. 8, 1794,
P.R.O.,F.O., 5, 5; Jay to Grenville, London, Nov. 22, 1794, *Corres. of
Jay,* IV, 145. Jefferson had retired from the Department of State, Dec.
31, 1793, and was succeeded by the Attorney General Edmund Randolph.

sion of the correspondence, he wrote to his chief, had
been intended merely to prepare for the report by dis-
ingenuously making the public mind receptive for discussion that would come in Congress in that session;
it was Jefferson's effort to offset the opprobrium fallen
on France by calling attention of Congress to the accumulation of injuries from Great Britain.[15]

While Madison's resolutions were thus hanging in
air, news of the Caribbean captures made under the
Order-in-Council of November 6, 1793, arrived in
Philadelphia.[16] This happened shortly after the President had communicated to the House a letter from
Pinckney telling of the interview in November, in
which Grenville betrayed no enthusiasm for resumption
of the suspended negotiations and spoke with disappointment of the unwillingness of the United States
to couple any arrangement for evacuation of the
posts with a settlement (by mediation) of the Indian
troubles.[17] Among Federalists and Republicans alike
the news from the West Indies was greeted with greatest indignation. Hamilton defined the new Order as
"atrocious" and in a letter to Washington advised immediately recruiting and equipping a federal army of
20,000 auxiliary troops and construction at the principal ports of fortifications sufficient to resist anything
short of a regular siege.[18] The public was wild. The
Democratic Republican societies, temporarily prostrated by the downfall of Genet, revived with increased

15. Hammond to Grenville, April 17, 1794, with enclosures,
P.R.O.,F.O., 5, 11.

16. The news from the West Indies had begun to come in February.

17. *A.S.P.,F.R.*, I, 328; *Annals*, Feb. 24, 1794.

18. Hamilton, *Works*, IV, 506, 552.

enthusiasm. Throughout the land meetings were held to denounce the tyrannical action of England.

Though genuinely indignant at insults to the nation and resolute for firm action in case of absolute necessity, the Federalists now marshaled all their efforts and influence to avoid a disastrous war. Sedgwick of Massachusetts brought forward the military measures, announcing in the House that he would make proposals for national defense in view of the existing situation. But on the same day four eastern Federalist Senators —Cabot, King, Ellsworth, and Strong—were conferring to discover some means to prevent hostilities. They decided to recommend a special envoy to the Court of St. James's as a last resort to preserve peace. Meanwhile they would urge measures for vigorous national defense. The four delegated Ellsworth to call upon the President and submit their views. Ellsworth saw Washington on March 12 and proposed the mission, recommending Hamilton as the person best qualified to undertake it. The Federalist group found further reenforcement in Robert Morris, who agreed to use his influence with Washington in support of the plan.[19] At the same time Sedgwick was introducing into the House his resolution calling for a new federal army of 15,000 men and an embargo on all shipping in American harbors. The embargo was designed to shut off the food supply of the British West Indies, from which as a base the royal army was attempting to subdue the French islands. Such were the circumstances when on March 14 the House of Representatives resolved itself into a Committee of the Whole for further consideration of Jefferson's report and Madison's resolutions.

19. King, *Life and Corres. of Rufus King,* I, 517, 518.

The resolutions now found great favor. Smith, mouthpiece of Hamilton, was forced to approach the subject of commercial discrimination against England very cautiously. His previous opposition to the Madison program, he explained, had been due to the conviction of many members of Congress that it would be possible soon to adjust peaceably the troublesome commercial questions and that meantime it were wise not to begin a system of legislation which would embitter rather than better relations between the two countries. The attitude of Great Britain had shown, however, that she did not wish for peace; "aggression had been heaped upon us with tenfold aggression." Still, he hoped that it would be possible to avoid war. He would not confuse the purely commercial question of discrimination with the political issue of peace or war. Rather than to the resolutions before the Committee he would draw the attention of Congress to the necessity of effective fortification of the seaports, to the organization of an army, to the adoption of financial measures to nerve the sinews of war by preparing for the loss of revenue which would inevitably follow a decline in commercial activity.[20] The policy of the Federalists, thus voiced, was to urge preparation for war while making a last stand for peace. On the other hand, the Republicans were for a sharp and quick reply to Great Britain accompanied by measures of commercial discrimination. They believed this procedure would bring results quicker than negotiations of the kind already repeatedly repelled.

Little progress had been made in the discussion of Madison's resolutions when news was received by

20. *Annals,* March 14, 1794.

Congress which indicated not only ruthless disregard by England for American rights on the seas but an intention to begin actual hostilities on land. The President on March 25 submitted two letters from the American Consul at St. Eustatia describing in detail the capture of American ships and the unnecessary hardships suffered by the crews.[21] Next day the Senate agreed to the embargo already passed by the House on all shipping in American ports for the period of one month.[22] This was proclaimed in force by the President two days later. By this time the newspapers were printing reports of Lord Dorchester's inflammatory address on February 10 to the western Indians. Despite the Governor General's caution this indiscreet speech—which seemed final proof of all that Americans had suspected of British intrigue among the natives—had leaked out and reached the American press.[23]

21. *A.S.P.,F.R.*, I, 428.
22. *Annals* (Senate).
23. Dorchester never intended the speech of February 10, 1794, to be made public. It appears that the interpreter who delivered it to the Indians gave it to Colonel Campbell, who was to have copies of it made for the information of officials in Upper Canada, that the copying was done by somebody outside the government service (Chew to Coffin, Montreal, Mar. 6, 1794, C.A.,C, 274, 79), and that the news got out in this way. Several copies were obtained and circulated by private individuals in Montreal, Quebec, St. Johns, Albany, and Boston. Governor Clinton of New York was said to have a correspondent in Montreal (Dr. Kerr to Chew, June 10, 1794, ibid., 143), who supplied him regularly with accurate information. Clinton, at any rate, sent Washington news of the speech on March 20 (Washington, *Writings*, XII, 408). The speech, once made public, created a sensation in Montreal and Quebec where it was construed to indicate that Dorchester had some private information which made him confident war was to break out shortly. An investigation made at Dorchester's orders and continued for over two months, while not disclosing much, points to the explanation here given as to the source of the leak.

Dorchester's hostile speech and his manifest intention to use Indian allies against the settlers on the American frontier was about the last straw. For the moment Madison's resolutions were forgotten in the discussion of much stronger measures.[24] Dayton of New Jersey proposed the sequestration of all debts owned by British creditors, as compensation to American citizens for injuries received from the commanders of British war vessels in violation of international law. A report of a committee on Sedgwick's resolutions, made the same day, advocated an increased federal army and recommended a force not of 15,000 but of 50,000 men to be held in readiness. These resolutions were adopted March 31 by the Committee of the Whole and referred to the House proper.[25] Another resolution, made by Clark of New Jersey while Dayton's sequestration proposal was still pending, advocated suspension of all commercial intercourse with Great Britain until compensation should have been made for the illegal captures, the posts evacuated, and American owners reimbursed for the Negroes carried away in 1782. This was advanced notwithstanding the fact that news already had been received and communicated to the House of the Order-in-Council of January 8, 1794, which superseded the drastic Order of November 6 and allowed noncontraband trade (as defined by the British Admiralty) between the United States and the French colonies. An explanation also had been made in London by Lord Grenville to Pinckney of the Algerine truce.[26]

24. Jefferson, *Writings,* VI, 503, 508; *Annals,* March 27, 1794.
25. *Annals,* March 31, 1794.
26. *A.S.P.,F.R.,* I, 327, 430; Mayo, *Instructions,* pp. 47–50.

Clark's nonintercourse proposal was debated for several days in Committee of the Whole, shaped into a bill,
and passed by the House, April 25, by a vote of 53–44.
By agreement of both houses the embargo was continued for a second month.

Amidst this furor the plan of the Federalist leaders for a special mission to England was gathering
strength. Senator King had an interview with Hammond on April 7, in which the Minister stated that he
did not believe Dorchester had authority to sanction
his speech to the Indians. It was a hopeful indication
to the Federalists. The President conferred with
Robert Morris as to the propriety of a special envoy
to London. Morris supported the plan already
broached to Washington by Ellsworth and urged immediate action on it. He proposed Hamilton as the
plenipotentiary, objecting to John Adams or Jefferson,
who seem to have been in Washington's mind. King
called on Jay shortly afterward to discuss with him
the object of the "friends of peace." King explained
that although Hamilton was the natural choice for such
a mission the circumstances made it impossible to send
him. He declared that Jay ought to undertake the negotiation. The two then considered the resolutions for
sequestration and nonintercourse which were before
the House of Representatives. Jay agreed to the suggestion that such legislation, if enacted, would frustrate
the mission. He promised to say as much to the President. According to King, Secretary Randolph was making every effort to prevent the appointment of Hamilton and was urged to do this by Fauchet, the successor
of Genet at Philadelphia, whose notorious intimacy

with Randolph was subsequently the cause for the latter's downfall.[27]

A letter from Hamilton on April 14 made up Washington's mind. In it the Federalist leader analyzed at length the existing situation. He affirmed that prompt and resolute action was required. The nation ought to be placed upon the best possible footing of defense, meanwhile a special envoy should be sent to London. He abandoned any idea of undertaking the mission himself—the Republican opposition to him was too strong—and recommended Jay.[28] The President proposed the mission to Jay. Jay expressed strong opposition to the nonintercourse and sequestration resolutions, which he said would make any mission by him impossible if they should be enacted. The Federalists were now planning to extinguish this "mischievous" [29] legislation by arranging for the President to propose that such measures remain in abeyance during the negotiations. Hamilton, Cabot, Strong, Ellsworth, and King called on Jay the day following his conference with Washington and urged him not to decline the appointment. He accepted. Washington hurried the nomination to the Senate.[30] It was confirmed within three days by a vote of 18–8. The opposition dwelt on Jay's well-known English predilections as rendering him unfit for such a negotiation.[31] On May 12, 1794, Jay embarked for England.[32]

27. King, *Life and Corres. of R. King,* I, 519, 523. King kept minutes of the various conferences.
28. Hamilton, *Works,* IV, 519.
29. Ibid., 564.
30. Washington, *Writings,* XII, 419.
31. *Life and Corres. of R. King,* I, 521.
32. The following explanation was made by Randolph to Pinckney,

The nonintercourse bill was up for debate in the
House when Washington sent in Jay's nomination to
the Senate. The Federalists opposed the bill on the
ground that an envoy had been nominated by the President, that the adoption of nonintercourse legislation
would embarrass the negotiations and be an indelicacy
toward the executive branch of the government; since
it would necessarily lead to war, other measures should
precede its adoption. The Republicans answered quite
pertinently that the power to regulate commerce was
vested in the legislature and was its constitutional duty,
that the bill already had been proposed and debated
several days before the nomination of Jay; if there
were to be any clashing of the legislative and executive
the indelicacy would be on the part of the executive.
The measure would not lead to war, they stated; any
independent nation had a right to regulate its own commerce. Bitterness for Great Britain was too strong to
allow the bill to be blocked in the House. Even in the
Senate it was thrown out only by the casting vote of
Vice President Adams.[33]

the regular Minister at London: "He [the President] was induced to
take this step for several reasons, among which were an anxiety for
peace, etc., etc. The . . . principal objection to the appointment of an
Envoy arose from a respect for you; it being a maxim with the President to be delicate to every office of the Government. But it was represented to him that you were too well acquainted with the course of
diplomatic business to feel the smallest dissatisfaction with a measure
the solemnity of which so strongly coincides with the crisis hanging
over us." Randolph to Pinckney, May 10, 1794, State Dept., Instructions, England, Vol. II, 76–79. Pinckney, on receipt of this dispatch,
loyally submitted to the extraordinary envoy, but confessed to Randolph an unpleasantness in his situation.˙ Pinckney to the Secretary of
State, June 23, 1794, State Dept., Dispatches, England, Vol. III.

33. *Annals,* April 18–28, 1794. The Senators who voted against the
bill were Potts, Rutherford, Strong, Vining, Cabot, Ellsworth, Foster,

The confirmation of Jay's nomination and the death
in the upper house of the nonintercourse bill marked the
climax of the storm in Congress. Again economic considerations had prevailed and the Federalists had their
way by the scantiest of margins.[34] No more anti-British
legislation made serious headway during the remainder
of the session, which ended in June. Fortunately for
peace the news of construction of the Miamis fort on
American territory did not arrive in Philadelphia until
Jay was already at sea. An effort to continue the embargo, which had expired after two months' operation,
was made in May but failed. Another bill for nonintercourse was introduced after the arrival of news of the
Miamis aggression. What undoubtedly would have
been just sufficient provocation to insure the success of
Dayton's bill in the previous April now failed even to
pass the House.[35]

It was with the greatest uneasiness that Hammond
had seen the discrimination movement of 1791 reviving
with more strength than ever. This time the accumulation of grievances seemed certain to force the nonintercourse, sequestration, and discrimination proposals into

---

Freylinghuysen, Bradford, Henry, Izard, King, Morris, and Vice
President Adams. In its favor were: Bradley, Brown, Burr, Butler,
Edwards, Gunn, Hawkins, Jackson, Langdon, Martin, Monroe, Robin-
son, Taylor.

34. "With great exertion we have at length obtained a cessation of
the national violence until the issue of Mr. Jay's negotiations shall be
ascertained. We hope that your Minister [i.e., the Secretary of State
for Foreign Affairs] will not be disposed to drive us into a war which
will forever alienate the good will of this country and force us to a
closer union with France." Letter from a Member of Congress to a
Gentleman in London, Philadelphia, May 4, 1794, P.R.O.,F.O., 5, 7.
The writer was probably Smith.

35. The vote in the House was 24 to 46. *Annals,* May 23, 1794.

actual enactment and to bring about the very thing which it was his business to prevent, even more, war itself at a time when England was busily engaged with a European enemy. It must have been with great relief that he heard in March that the Federalists were planning a special mission to England.[36] He had just received news from Grenville of the new Order-in-Council of January 8, 1794. Unaware of the excitement in the United States, Grenville had sent along some mollifying observations for Hammond to employ in explaining the Order of November 6.

The Minister took advantage of the opportunity afforded by communication of these remarks to endeavor to get from Hamilton the real purpose of Jay's mission. The interview which followed shows how completely Hamilton now—after the resignation of Jefferson—dominated all matters of greater importance in the Department of State, as well as in the Treasury, and, in fact, in the War Department, as was to be shown shortly in the Whiskey Rebellion. It also shows that Hamilton, speaking for the Administration, though the interview was technically informal, was prepared to accept the principles put forward by the British Orders-in-Council of June 8, 1793, so vigorously controverted by Jefferson, and January 8, 1794; namely, foodstuffs can be contraband, and the neutral flag does not always cover enemy goods. These conceptions dominated the negotiation of Jay's Treaty, as a perusal of that document will show. They did not correspond with the practice of the United States as written into treaties with France, Prussia, The Nether-

36. Hammond heard of it as early as March 23. Hammond to Grenville, Philadelphia, March 23, 1794, P.R.O.,F.O., 5, 4.

lands, and Sweden, and expressed in the official protest of the Secretary of State to the Order of June 8, 1793. As Hammond had already written home, this protest of Jefferson was not to be seriously heeded.

Hammond began by observing the confidence he had shared in conveying in this way the attitude of his Government. He asked in return to be informed with equal candor the purpose of the proposed mission. The Englishman's explanations were not received so cordially as he had anticipated. Hamilton entered into a rather copious recital of the injuries which the commerce of the United States had suffered from British cruisers and defended the view that American citizens had a claim on their government for violation of their rights. He spoke nevertheless in a conciliatory tone, holding that the United States could not regard as binding the decisions of the West Indian vice-admiralty courts that appeals could not be entered save within a limited time. Compensation would be expected from the British Government for any loss sustained by American citizens in consequence of *interpretations* of the instructions of November 6, 1793, *by those courts.*

From Hammond's account of this interview it is apparent that Hamilton did not expressly deny the legality even of what he had denounced as the "atrocious" order of November 6. He condemned only the extreme interpretations of that order by the local vice-admiralty courts of the West Indian colonies. Yet Hammond thought it strange that the Secretary's opinions should be, as he considered them, so similar to those being expressed in the House of Representatives.

> I therefore desired him to inform me expressly whether I was to understand from what he had

advanced that as an indispensable condition of an amicable arrangement, the gentleman who might be employed in the negotiation would be instructed to require from His Majesty's Government compensation for all vessels which might have been captured in the British West Indies and for which recovery could not or might not be instituted. To this he replied that the gentleman who would be despatched to the West Indies[37] [i.e., an agent of the United States] would be directed to abandon all cases of prize, *in which the property of the cargo should be satisfactorily proved to be French*,[38] but that in cases in which the proof should not have been conclusive, or for which appeals could not be instituted, this Government would expect from Great Britain an indemnification for any loss resulting from the two causes last assigned, as an indispensable basis of a friendly adjustment.

Nothing was said of any expectation that the West Indian trade would be opened to the United States, though this latter was made a *sine qua non* of Jay's instructions for a commercial treaty. Hamilton, speaking as the dominant force in the American Administration, thus expressly acquiesced in the Rule of the War of 1756, if he did not formally accept its principle. This conversation was to relieve Grenville from the necessity of considering, during the negotiations with

37. At the same time that Jay was nominated, Washington sent a special agent to the West Indies to enter appeals in prize courts on account of American vessels.

38. Italics inserted.

Jay, any relinquishment of the operation of that innovative rule.

Hammond then dwelt on the extraordinary character
of the war, in language which sounds familiar in the
twentieth century and which was very acceptable to
Hamilton's ideas of the French Revolution.

> In every war powers that are neutral must expect
> to suffer some inconveniences; but that if ever
> those inconveniences should not be too nicely scru-
> tinized they certainly should not be so in a war like
> the present, in which (as he had often agreed with
> me) all the dearest interests of society were in-
> volved, and which was a contest between govern-
> ment and disorder, virtue and vice, and religion
> and impiety, and that in the prosecution of this
> most just of wars the government and people of
> Great Britain, united as they were in a common
> interest beyond the precedent perhaps of any
> former period (as indeed the war itself was with-
> out example) could not be intimidated by any
> menaces from the exercise of any just principles of
> carrying it on which they had found it necessary
> to establish, and though they would certainly not
> violate the rights of neutral powers, they could as
> certainly not suffer those powers to derive from
> the existence of the war and from the distress of
> our enemy a commerce which, however advantage-
> ous it might be to them, would be perhaps more
> beneficial to our enemy. Here Mr. Hamilton inter-
> rupted me with some degree of heat and remarked
> that however the government and people of Great
> Britain might be united against France, he doubted

not that when the wrongs which the American
Commerce had suffered were known in Great
Britain, a very powerful party might be raised in
that nation in favor of this country. In answer to
this insinuation I contented myself with expressing
my astonishment at his indulging a belief, which
however it had been entertained by the dema-
gogues of the house of representatives, and by
the uninformed mass of the American Community,
I should never have ascribed to him, and thus I
dropped the conversation, which thence took another turn, and we parted amicably.[39]

As Jay sailed, the bundle of these dispatches from
Hammond left for Downing Street, telling of the increasing popular bitterness, the various proposals of
inimical legislation—all of them passed through everything but the final stage of enactment—the *sine qua non*
as expressed by Hamilton, the certainty that if the
coming negotiation should fail the legislation would
pass the next session of Congress, the imminent danger
of war itself. It was the situation of 1791 repeated but
this time piled high with new grievances, while the
apparent studied neglect of American complaints and
the daily increasing irritation on the frontier had added
to make the posture of affairs downrightly dangerous.
This was the war cloud which lowered over the American shore as it receded from Jay's vision in the spring
of 1794. In the opinion of the Federalists the failure
of his mission would result in the wrecking of American
nationality as founded on the Constitution of 1787.

The scene of interest now shifts to London, where

39. Hammond to Grenville, April 17, 1794, P.R.O.,F.O., 5, 4.

Jay and Grenville were to sift out the points of dispute
and to the policies and personalities which controlled
his negotiation.[40]

40. News of the occupation of the Miamis fort was at once made the
subject of a sharp note by Randolph to Hammond, which began a long
exchange of acrimonious, almost vituperative, correspondence between
the two men. Fortunately the bad taste of this correspondence on the
part of both men did little harm, because the main negotiations had
now been transferred to London. There is no space here for even a
summary of what may be found scattered through several volumes in
P.R.O.,F.O., 5, Vols. 1, 4, 5, 8, 9. See also *A.S.P.,F.R.*, I, 461–62, 464–66.

# CHAPTER 10

## Policies and Personalities

JOHN JAY, to whom the negotiation was intrusted by the United States, had participated at home and abroad in nearly every phase of American public life. Of French and Dutch ancestry, he was one of the few eminent men who took part in the War of Independence who was not of English descent. In positions of the most responsible and important character from 1775 to 1794, he had been unremittingly devoted to the service of his country. It was when he was rapidly rising as a member of the New York bar that the trouble with England convulsed the colonies. Jay was one of the most conservative of all the Fathers and one of the last to be convinced of the propriety of separation from the Empire, but once the fateful step of independence was taken he threw his whole considerable ability and energy into prosecution of the war. He was a member of the original Committee of Fifty-one, in New York, on British grievances. He was influential in promoting the meeting of the Continental Congress, to which he was a delegate. In 1777 he drafted the constitution of the state of New York. As Chief Justice of the state he soon became interpreter of that constitution. During this time he retained his seat in the Continental Congress and in 1779 was elected President of that body.

Throughout the Revolution he was a colonel in the New York militia and a member of the secret Committee on Military Affairs in the Continental Congress. In 1779 he resigned the chief justiceship, as well as the Presidency of Congress, in order to repair his badly depleted personal finances. It would be difficult to find a more patriotic American or one seemingly less susceptible to British influence.

Jay's intention to return to private life was soon frustrated by his appointment as Minister of the United States to Spain to secure the adhesion of that kingdom to the Franco-American alliance and to obtain a loan of money. This, his first foreign mission, which held him at Madrid until 1782, was not fruitful. Spain, consistently inimical to American independence and dominated by her own peculiar colonial and anti-British policies, never recognized the United States until after the peace. Toward the close of the war Jay's diplomatic services became necessary in another quarter. He left Spain for France to take part in the peace negotiations with England. In this capacity he rendered the most brilliant service of his public career. It was Jay who rightly or wrongly suspected an *arrière-pensée* in Vergennes' American diplomacy and who induced Adams and Franklin to break their instructions and to negotiate with the British agents without the complete confidence of the French Court. If this independent action is responsible for the final treaty, that diplomatic triumph should be attributed to John Jay. On his return home after the peace Jay found himself selected by Congress as its Secretary for Foreign Affairs. He held this position until the organization of the new government under the Constitution, when his office was taken over by Jefferson as Secretary of State. Washington had offered Jay his choice of appointments under the new government. He took that of Chief Justice of the United States, an office which he continued to hold while engaged in the negotiations of 1794.[1] The special plenipotentiary was thus a diplomatist of established reputation and political experience.

Forty-eight years of age, Jay was now in the prime of mental activity and of a life that had been a model of virtue both in private and public affairs. His biographers aptly describe him as one of those epitomes of abstract propriety who existed and prospered in the early history of the United States in such immaculate characters as Washington and the elder and younger Adams. Of profound piety and unbreakable religious faith, unbending in patriotism, endeavoring always to keep an independent and evenly balanced political outlook, fond of good society, and with the strongest and most affectionate attachment for domestic life, Jay was a man on whose personal character the historical student may look back with pleasure.

He was not without his petty faults, if we can trust contemporary character sketches. He gloried in the independence of his politics and his fairness and candor in judiciously examining all sides of a question and deciding it purely on its merits, and he duly appreciated

1. Jay returned from England in 1795 to find himself elected Governor of New York, an office for which he had been a candidate in 1792, when he received a majority of votes but lost the election because votes in three counties were thrown out by electoral technicalities engineered by his Republican opponents. George Pellew, *John Jay* (Boston and New York, 1898), pp. 247, 284; Frank Monaghan, *John Jay* (New York and Indianapolis, 1935), pp. 333–40, 405.

the great value of modest comportment; but in his heart
Jay was none the less appreciative of his own importance in the affairs of the world. In this vanity he did not
suffer from the illusions of spurring ambition—like
others of the Fathers he always had the Cincinnatian
desire to return to private life—but his self-estimation
made him susceptible when played on with finesse. "He
argues closely but is long-winded and self-opinioned.
He can bear any opposition to what he advances provided that regard is shown to his abilities. He may be
attached by good treatment, but will be unforgiving
if he thinks himself neglected . . . almost every man
has a weak and assailable quarter and Mr. Jay's weak
side is *Mr. Jay.*" [2] Such was the advice which reached
Lord Grenville from one who had been associated
closely with the American Chief Justice in legal and
public affairs before the Revolution. Grenville seems to
have made use of it with good results. He shrewdly ma-
nipulated Jay during the negotiations. For example, in
conveying the news of James Monroe's fraternal kiss
received in the French Convention, in September, 1794,
Grenville appealed to Jay as one "whom I know to be
a person of distinguished abilities and character and of
great weight in the government of your country," who
would consequently share a dislike to Monroe's proceedings. A glimpse at Jay's weakness for the allurement of such phrases, which Grenville constantly used
with him, is afforded by a sentence in the self-confident
reply on this occasion: "Indeed, I have been so long
conversant with men and human affairs, that few occur-
rences surprise me." [3]

2. *Dropmore Papers,* II, 578.
3. Grenville to Jay, and Jay to Grenville (private), Sept. 7, 1794,
P.R.O.,F.O., 95, 512. See also private letter of Jay to Randolph, Sept. 13,

Jay was particularly *persona grata* to the British Court. Beckwith during his trip to Philadelphia in 1790 had met the Chief Justice and had written most approvingly of him to the Foreign Office. Jay is reported by Beckwith to have said: "There has been an astonishing change in the condition of your Empire since the peace; your administration is an able one, and Mr. Pitt a very extraordinary man. The wisdom and the liberality of your Government in the exertions that have been made in behalf of the Loyalists, whom we term Refugees, must command the respect of all the world. They have erred greatly in France in not forming their Government more upon the model of yours." Beckwith noted: "In these and similar observations, Mr. —— marked clearly to me, a performance in favour of an English interest, and that he wished to show it." [4] Jay's Federalism had brought him naturally into conflict with the Jeffersonian school. In English eyes this opposition made him one of the upholders of the "cause of law and order" against the theories and excesses of the French Revolution.

What impressed the British Government particularly was the attitude which Jay had taken, while Secretary

---

1794, State Dept., Dispatches, England, I. Among the Jefferson Papers in the MSS. Division of the Library of Congress there is a letterpress abstract and digest, barely legible, of the Jay correspondence as submitted to the Senate. Interior evidence indicates that the abstract was prepared by Jefferson himself in 1796 or thereafter. There is one point of historical interest contained in this otherwise mechanical digest. That is a comment contained in the abstract of Jay's letter of November 19, 1794, to Randolph, enclosing the treaty. This comment reads: "General remark that his lres are full of encomiums on the candour, liberality, good humour, cordiality, conciliatory disposn, friendliness, delicacy, etc., etc., etc. of the govmt of Engld and particularly Ld.G."  .

4. C.A., *Rept. 1890,* 140.

for Foreign Affairs of the Continental Congress, on the questions of frontier posts and British debts. To him Congress had transmitted the answer of the Marquis of Carmarthen (later Duke of Leeds) to John Adams's request in 1785 for the evacuation of American soil. It was the answer in which the British Government refused to give up the posts on the ground that the United States had failed to remove legal impediments in the way of recovery of debts. Jay made a long report on the British note, which was submitted to Congress in secret session. From the facts as he saw them he declared Great Britain wholly justified in retaining the posts. He believed honestly that she could not be blamed for holding them while the United States on its side impeded full execution of the treaty. As to the deported Negroes, he held that technically the treaty clause restored them to their American owners, but since the proclamations of emancipation by the British military commander were inconsistent with the treaty in a strongly humanitarian way he would not insist on strict compliance with the letter of the instrument but would accept compensation in money in lieu of the persons of the deported Negroes.[5]

This report naturally was not made public; but Jay confidentially divulged its nature to Sir John Temple, British consul at New York, who had been instructed by Carmarthen to ascertain the attitude of Congress and who was on intimate social terms with Jay. He declared to Temple that the report was a full acknowledgment that many of the most important contentions of Carmarthen's statement were just, must be admitted

5. *Secret Journals of Congress,* IV, 185, Oct. 13, 1786.

in fact, and consequently must be considered as a violation of the existing treaty; it followed that the British
were in every way justified in holding the western posts
until the states manifested a fair and favorable disposition to fulfill their obligations under the treaty.[6] The
imparting of such confidential information by a man in
Jay's office must have considerable significance in explaining the delay of Great Britain in evacuating the
posts. From that time on Jay, with the exception of
Alexander Hamilton, was the most popular in British
councils of any American in official station. Beckwith
had more confidential conversations with him in 1791.[7]
Hammond without exception spoke in warm terms of
his good sense. In December, 1792, he was chagrined
to learn that Jay's illness prevented him from sitting
as Supreme Court Justice on circuit when the question
of British debts was being argued in the federal court
of the Virginia district.[8] Jay's opinion, that the confiscation of debts to British subjects by the State of Virginia during the war was illegal, was in 1793 overruled
in part by his two associates, though the Supreme Court
three years later agreed with his construction.[9] For

6. Temple to Carmarthen, N. Y., Dec. 7, 1786, P.R.O.,F.O., 4, 4. Jay
told Temple that he did not care to have this information go any
further in America. It was, however, quite well known in Congress.

7. Beckwith to Grenville, Phila., Aug. 16, 1791, P.R.O.,F.O., 4, 12.

8. Hammond to Grenville, Phila., Dec. 4, 1792, P.R.O.,F.O., 4, 16.
"Had he been present, I should from my knowledge of that Gentleman's character and principles have scarcely entertained a doubt of
the result of the actions being favorable to the British creditors."

9. Ware, Administrator of Jones, v. Hylton, A. J. Dallas, *Reports of
Cases Ruled and Adjudged in the Several Courts of the United States
and of Pennsylvania* (4 vols. 1790–1807); cited as III *Dallas*, 199.
A. J. Beveridge, *Life of John Marshall*, II, 189.

Great Britain a more pleasing choice for the special mission could not have been made by the American Federalists.[10]

The person who represented the British Empire in the negotiations with Jay was a man even more highly trained than the American in matters of public life and national administration. Baron Grenville, from 1791–1801 Secretary of State for Foreign Affairs in Pitt's Government, was, like his cousin the Prime Minister, still a young man. He was born in 1759. Elected to Parliament at the age of twenty-three as William Wyndham Grenville, he remained in active public service until his resignation from the office of Prime Minister in 1807.[11] Soon after taking his seat in Parliament he became chief secretary to his brother, the Lord Lieutenant of Ireland. Upon the formation of Pitt's Ministry in 1783, he was appointed Paymaster General and held that office until his appointment as Secretary for Home Affairs in 1789, a portfolio which then included the direction of Colonial Affairs. During these years Grenville was also a member of the Privy Council, Speaker of the House of Commons (1789), and Vice President of the Committee of Trade of the newly created Board of Control. He was later President of this body. He became one of Pitt's peers in 1790. As Lord Grenville he was the able defender of Government measures in the House of Lords. When in 1791 a change in the office of Foreign Affairs was made

10. Several biographies of Jay have been written: by his son, William Jay, by Flanders, by Whitelock, by Pellew, and the most recent and best by Frank Monaghan.

11. Grenville was Prime Minister, after Pitt's death, from Feb., 1806, until March, 1807.

necessary by the Eastern Question, Lord Grenville succeeded the Duke of Leeds. Subsequently for nearly ten years he was engaged in conducting the enormous business of that office during the war with France and in actively defending the Government in the Lords.

The negotiation with Jay in itself was not a little complex and engrossed the American envoy's entire time. But it was only incidental to Grenville's daily work of handling a foreign business the ramifications of which involved affairs of greatest moment in the chancelleries of all Europe during one of the greatest wars in which Great Britain ever was engaged. The man's capacity for work was astonishing. Believing that it was "perfect blindness not to see that in the establishment of the French Government is included the overthrow of all the Governments in Europe," Grenville was ever an advocate of war to the bitter end and a champion of repressive measures against radicalism at home. The key to his foreign policy was to cripple France and her aggressive democracy, a policy which Pitt adopted in its entirety after 1797, as a result of Grenville's influence.[12] It loaded the Foreign Office with a huge volume of business. Only after one has spent months in perusing but a part of the voluminous mass of correspondence that bears Grenville's signature can one begin to realize the enormous and detailed extent of affairs which passed under his attention.[13]

12. E. D. Adams, *The Influence of Grenville on Pitt's Foreign Policy, 1787–1798* (Washington, 1904).

13. No satisfactory biography of Grenville has been written, despite the rich field of material (such as the published and unpublished *Dropmore Papers,* and the Record Office documents) that invites such a study. A short amount of his life is written by G. F. Russell Barker in the *Dictionary of National Biography.* Mr. W. Fitzpatrick in the

As Secretary for Home Affairs from 1789 to 1791 Grenville had become thoroughly acquainted with the situation on the Canadian frontier, because administration of colonies still remained a part of the business of the Home Office. In his functions of Privy Councilor and a member of the Board of Control he had acquired expert knowledge of the commerce of the Empire in all its manifold phases. As Foreign Secretary the exercise of his office during the critical years from 1791 to 1794 had given him a comprehensive grasp of European politics. His parliamentary experience had endowed him with a complete acquaintance with the attitude of Parliament toward Government and with the demands of the mercantile interests then growing to be so powerful in England, whose support was necessary to the permanence of any government. This is why Grenville, though admittedly a believer in the theories of Adam Smith,[14] defended so strenuously and successfully the Navigation Laws in the American negotiations. Of all

introduction to the *Dropmore Papers,* Vol. III, gives illuminating glimpses of Grenville's activities. See also Bradford Perkins, *The First Anglo-American Rapprochement* for an incisive appreciation of Grenville's American policy.

14. Lord Brougham's *Historical Sketches of Statesmen Who Have Flourished in the Time of George III* (2 vols. London, 1839–43), I, 257–58, says of Grenville: "The endowments of this eminent statesman's mind were all of a useful and commanding sort—sound sense, steady memory, vast industry. His acquirements were in the same proportion valuable and lasting—a thorough acquaintance with business in its principles and in its details; a complete mastery of the science of politics, as well theoretical as practical; of late years a perfect familiarity with political economy, and a just appreciation of its importance; an early and most extensive knowledge of classical literature, which he improved, instead of abandoning, down to the close of his life. . . . his firmness was apt to degenerate into obstinacy; his confidence in the principles he held was not unmixed with contempt for those who differed from him."

men in the Government at that time there was probably no one so familiar with American affairs and their relation to fundamental British policy.

Jay's instructions, which for the purpose of this study it is now necessary to consider in some detail, were the result of Federalist opinion voiced by Hamilton in Washington's Cabinet, with minor additions made by Randolph, Jefferson's successor as Secretary of State. To that part of the instructions purely the ideas of Randolph, Jay paid little serious attention. Soon after Jay's reluctant[15] acceptance of the mission, several Federalist Senators and Hamilton met with him to talk over its purpose.[16] The nature of the discussions at this meeting is not precisely known, but Hamilton's letter to Washington of April 23, 1794, entitled "Points to be considered in the instructions to Mr. Jay," is doubtless an accurate reflection of what was considered. In the anticipated negotiations Hamilton would press for indemnification for depredations on commerce according to a rule to be settled on: namely, that only articles by general usage accepted as contraband should be treated as such; that contraband not concealed should not infect other portions of the cargo; that contraband should include only implements of warfare. If such a recognition could not be obtained it would be desirable to consider a qualification of it; either in the principle that provisions might be preempted, or in an acquiescence in the Rule of the War of 1756, or in an admission of the legality of the Order-in-Council of June 8. Indemnification by the United States should be made for captures by all the proscribed

15. Jay to his wife, Phila., Apr. 15, 1794, *Corres. of J. Jay*, IV, 3.
16. *Life and Corres. of Rufus King*, I, 523.

French privateers. As to regulations to apply in the future, Hamilton would consent to the same qualified definition of contraband and to a stipulation against the sale of prizes in American ports, if insisted on by Great Britain. An article requiring each party to refrain from furnishing hostile Indians with supplies ought to be urged, he believed.

Concerning fulfilment of the treaty of peace, Hamilton held that Great Britain should make indemnification for, not restoration of, Negroes carried away, and should surrender the frontier posts. In return the United States should agree to indemnification on account of obstruction to recovery of debts, the amount not to exceed a fixed sum. Both parties should consent to disarmament on the Lakes and to reciprocal free trade with their respective Indian tribes. As to a treaty of commerce, the United States ought to demand the privilege of trading with the British West Indies in vessels of limited tonnage. As an equivalent, most-favored-nation importation privileges might be offered together with an agreement not to lay duties in excess of ten per cent *ad valorem*. Such a commercial treaty should be limited to a term of years. "But if such a treaty cannot be made," he concluded, "it deserves consideration, whether a treaty on the basis of the *status quo* for a short term (say five years) may not be advisable, as an expedient for preserving peace between the two countries." [17]

17. Hamilton, *Works,* IV, 536. Hamilton was instrumental in preparing drafts for some of the subsequent instructions which Randolph penned to Jay, for example: remarks on Grenville's Commercial Treaty Project prepared for Randolph, *Works* (Hamilton ed., V, 29), which were largely incorporated in Randolph's instructions to Jay of Dec. 15, 1794 (after the treaty had been signed). Some rough notes

In short, Hamilton and the Federalists, with scant consideration for the previous attitude of the nation in treaties with European powers, would accede to all the British contentions—detention and pre-emption of foodstuffs, Rule of the War of 1756, capture of enemy property on neutral ships—provided some compensation were made for the extreme *interpretation* and harsh *application* of the Order of November 6. To get admission to the British West Indies they would consent to bind the United States not to raise the tariff on British goods during a term of years beyond a fixed ratio. This last was the very stipulation which the Committee of the Privy Council in its report of 1791 had declared as necessary to be incorporated in any treaty of commerce.[18]

The actual official instructions were drawn up by the Secretary of State, Edmund Randolph, but Hamilton had constructed the scaffolding of them already. Only two absolutely immutable conditions were laid down for Jay. He was not to enter into any treaty contrary to engagements with France. He was to consent to no treaty of commerce that did not allow entrance of American ships into the British West Indies. Perhaps never in the history of the United States has a plenipotentiary been vested with more unfettered discretion than was Jay in the critical negotiations of 1794. All the rest of his instructions were in the shape of recommendations only. The enumeration of them is somewhat lengthy. Nevertheless it is necessary, in order to show

exist in Hamilton's handwriting in the Hamilton Papers in the MSS Division of the Library of Congress, which indicate that Hamilton prepared another note for Randolph. They present little essentially valuable.

18. Above, p. 117.

how thoroughly the ideas of Hamilton dominated the negotiation, even more strongly than they had controlled the early informal diplomacy with England and the official negotiations between Hammond and Jefferson. Hamilton's influence was now practically unlimited.

As to the spoliations by the Orders-in-Council Jay was to "press strongly" for "compensation for all injuries sustained, and captures." If the British Government insisted that its tribunals as a last resort for justice should be exhausted before claims for compensation were made, he might if necessary wait for a test case. But where the error complained of consisted solely in the law itself, not merely in its application, it should be corrected by the lawmaker and the King should make compensation to the United States. The ground for compensation was not defined exactly. The instructions to press for it were made after the Order-in-Council of November 6 had been mentioned and after it had been stated that one of the principles on which indemnification was demanded was that foodstuffs could not be ranked as contraband as they had been considered in the operation of the Order of June 8.

A second function of Jay's mission, not inferior to the first one of demanding compensation for the spoliations, was to conclude a settlement of all points of difference between the two countries over the treaty of 1783. His instructions stated that the debts to British creditors, being a question of a judicial nature, should be settled in the United States courts. If this could not be agreed to, Jay was *"to support the doctrines of Government with arguments proper for the occasion, and with that attention to your former public opinion which self-respect will justify without relaxing the pretensions which have been hitherto maintained."* [19] It was not discreetly possible to present absolute proof that the British agents were guilty of stirring up the Indians, Jay was reminded, but it was a principle "from which the United States will not easily depart" that the Indians dwelling within the territory of one nation should not be interfered with by another. Infractions of the treaty and spoliations were to be treated as distinct matters, neither to influence the other in any settlement.

In case the two preceding points (i.e., spoliations and infractions) should be so accommodated as to guarantee peace, Jay might listen to or even broach the subject of a commercial treaty. In general the objects of such a treaty should be as follows:

1. Reciprocity in navigation, particularly to the West Indies and even to the East Indies.
2. The admission [to British ports] of wheat, fish, salt meat, and other great staples, upon the same footing with the admission of the great British staples in our [American] ports.
3. Free ships to make free goods.
4. Proper security for the safety of neutral commerce in other respects; and particularly,
   By declaring provisions never to be contraband, except in the strongest possible case, as the blockade of a port, or, if attainable, by abolishing contraband altogether:
   By defining a blockade, if contraband must continue in some degree, as it is defined in the Armed Neutrality:

19. Italics inserted.

By restricting the opportunities of vexation in visiting vessels; and

By bringing under stricter management privateers; and expediting recoveries against them for misconduct.[20]

5. Exemption of emigrants, and particularly of manufacturers, from restraint.[21]

6. Free exports of arms and military stores.

7. The exclusion of the term "the most favored nation" as productive of embarrassment.

8. The convoy of merchant ships by the public ships of war, where it shall be necessary, and they be holding the same course.

9. It is anxiously to be desired, that the fishing grounds now engrossed by the British should be opened to the citizens of the United States.[22]

10. That intercourse with England makes it necessary that the disabilities, arising from alienage in

---

20. Designed to prevent such abuses as those of the famous Bermudian privateers, who brought into the Bermuda prize courts every American vessel they met regardless of destination or cargo.

21. Hamilton's Report on Manufactures, which led to the organization of a stock company in New Jersey for manufactures of various kinds, was the subject of much correspondence by Hammond from 1791–1793, who sent Grenville suspicions of American agents in England who were supposed to be engaging English artificers. Steps were taken by the Ministry to watch the seaports to prevent the embarkation of such persons. Hammond to Grenville, Dec. 6, 1791, P.R.O.,F.O., 4, 11; Oct. 3, 1792, ibid. 4, 16; Feb. 2, 1792, ibid., 4, 14; Grenville to Dundas, Jan. 4, 1792, ibid., 4, 11.

22. Probably referring to certain parts of the coastal waters of British North America where American citizens could not cure and dry fish. Otherwise the Canadian fisheries were entirely open by Article III of the treaty of 1783, about which no objection was made until Great Britain declared the article abrogated by the War of 1812.

cases of inheritance, should be put upon a liberal footing, or rather abolished.

11. You may discuss the sale of prizes in our ports while we are neutral; and this perhaps may be added to the considerations which we have to give besides those of reciprocity.

12. Proper shelter, defense and succor, against pirates, shipwrecks, etc.

13. Full security for the retiring of the citizens of the United States from the British dominions, in case a war should break out.

14. No privateering commissions to be taken out by the subjects of the one, or citizens of the other party against each other.

15. Consuls, etc., to be admitted in Europe, the West Indies and East Indies.

16. In case of an Indian war, none but the usual supplies in peace shall be furnished.

17. In peace, no troops to be kept within a limited distance from the Lakes.

18. No stipulation whatsoever is to interfere with our obligations to France.

19. A treaty is not to continue beyond fifteen years.

Such it was "desirable" to include in a treaty of commerce. It was not to be expected that one could be effected with such a great latitude of advantages. No commercial treaty, however, was to be signed which did not allow the entrance of American ships into the British West Indies on the same terms as those enjoyed by British ships plying between the United States and those islands.

Because we shall return to the subject in the next two

chapters, we here quote from the fifth article of Jay's instructions:

> You will have no difficulty in gaining access to the ministers of Russia, Denmark, and Sweden, at the Court of London. The principles of the armed neutrality would abundantly cover our neutral rights. If, therefore, the situation of things with respect to Great Britain should dictate the necessity of taking the precaution of taking foreign coöperation on this head; if no prospect of accommodation should be thwarted by the danger of such a measure being known to the British Court; and if an entire view of all our political relations shall, in your judgment, permit the step, you will sound those ministers upon the probability of an alliance with their nations to support those principles.[23]

The instructions, while they stated any number of desirabilities, when stripped of their embellishments and reduced to their naked body, correspond very closely to the outline suggested by Hamilton to Washington. An important addition was made by Randolph in the article which alluded to a possible concert with the Baltic powers to uphold the principles of the Armed Neutrality of 1780.

Hamilton addressed to Jay a private letter dated the same day as the instructions. It was only a private letter from the Secretary of the Treasury, but it had more influence than the official instructions. Hamilton warned Jay that it would be best, important as peace was, not

23. Instructions to Jay, signed by Randolph, May 6, 1794, *A.S.P.,F.R.,* I, 472.

to do anything that would not stand the severest scrutiny or that might be construed as a relinquishment of a substantial interest or right: hence it would be well to insist on substantial compensation rather than any appearance of it. "I am however still of opinion," he wrote, "that *substantial* indemnification, on the principle of the instruction of January 8, may in the last resort be admissible." In case "solid arrangements" could be effected with regard to the disputes concerning the treaty of 1783, the matter of indemnification might be managed with less vigor and be even more laxly dealt with if a truly beneficial treaty of commerce embracing privileges in the West India Islands could be had. It might then be worth while for the American Government itself to compensate its citizens. This opinion, we note, conflicts with the mandate in Jay's instructions not to let the question of spoliations be connected in the negotiation with that of the old treaty disputes. It would admit, if carried out, of concessions even greater than those eventually made by Jay. Hamilton called attention of the envoy to the fact that the Rule of the War of 1756 did not cover those commercial privileges enjoyed by American citizens in the French West Indies before 1793— which implies that the Rule was admitted by Hamilton to be tolerable international law. A treaty project was enclosed containing the commercial clauses recommended roughly in the notes to Washington of April 23.[24]

From the official instructions and the added opinions of Hamilton, it is seen that Jay was furnished with an abundance of desirabilities but prepared to make great

24. Hamilton, *Works,* IV, 551.

concessions for peace. In this policy he had the support of the now crystallized Federalist Party—for the definite and distinct formation of which one of the great causes was the issue rising in the question of foreign policy from 1790 to 1795. The Federalists, who followed Hamilton implicitly, were prepared to admit the Rule of the War of 1756, to allow provisions to be so dangerously near the definition of contraband as to be susceptible of pre-emption, to let enemy property be taken from neutral decks. In the last resort, to preserve peace and national credit, which depended for its revenues on commerce, they were willing, in the face of British sea power, to acquiesce in a complete reversion or suspension of the liberal principles incorporated in the American treaties with France, Sweden, Holland, and Prussia.

CHAPTER 11

# The Abortive Armed Neutrality of the North

TIME and distance and the precarious schedules of sailing packets are factors by no means to be over- looked in any study of early Anglo-American diplo- macy. Before the change from sail to steam and the advent of transoceanic telegraphy even the most vital overseas news was long delayed. Often a great ac- cumulation of it would arrive in one consignment after a long period during which little information of any kind had been available. This was the case when Jay landed in England on June 12, 1794. The endorsements on the American correspondence in the Foreign Office files show that Grenville had received only one dis- patch[1] from Hammond since the previous December. It was an unimportant note which arrived May 1, saying that the minister had resumed communication after a lapse of two months and would forward dis- patches very soon.[2] This he did two days later, on February 22, but these dispatches, containing the first real official news on American affairs received for several months, did not reach Downing Street until

1. Hammond to Grenville, Feb. 20, 1794, P.R.O.,F.O., 5, 4.
2. Grenville to Hammond, Downing St., May 10, 1794, ibid.

June 10. On that day all of Hammond's communications from February to May, 1794, along with the contemporaneous correspondence of the Canadian governors, arrived together.[3] But news had begun to drift in from private sources of new and serious difficulties impending with the United States. Through a New York newspaper received from Amsterdam Grenville had learned, as Jay was approaching the coast of England,[4] that an embargo had been laid by the United States. He knew nothing of the circumstances which had caused the embargo and was instructing Hammond to seize every opportunity by private or public conveyance to get news to headquarters.[5]

The belated arrival of Hammond's dispatches deluged the Foreign Office with a quantity of surprising information.[6] American indignation over the Order-in-Council of November 6, 1793, and Dorchester's speech to the Indians of February 10, 1794; the news from Canada of Simcoe's occupation of the Miamis fort; the circumstances of embargo, the sequestration and non-intercourse bills; the mission of Jay; the notable interview of Hammond with Alexander Hamilton in regard

3. In Hammond's of April 17, 1794, ibid.; Dorchester to Dundas, Feb. 24, 1794, C.A.,Q, 67, 88.

4. John Harriott, *Struggles Through Life* (2 vols. London, 1808), II, 164–65.

5. Grenville to Hammond, June 5, 1794, P.R.O.,F.O., 115, 3; Mayo, *Instructions,* p. 57.

6. Hammond's dispatches from Feb. 22 to April 17, 1794, comprising numbers 2 to 15 inclusive, are endorsed as received June 10. Nos. 17 and 18, of April 28 and May 8, were received June 12; No. 19 of May 10, June 20; No. 20 of May 25, July 1, P.R.O.,F.O., 5, 4. Letters from Phineas Bond of Feb. 20 and Feb. 23 were received April 8, with some meager notes on Congress. They arrived through private conveyance.

to that mission; the actual imminence of war in America, made up a budget of news that must have given Grenville considerable food for thought as he unsealed a letter from Falmouth bearing the signature of John Jay and announcing that the American held a commission from the President of the United States as special envoy to the King.[7]

There appears to have been up to this time in England little anxiety over the American situation. Grenville had written to Hammond, in January, that England had been well satisfied with the neutrality of the United States. He said as much to Pinckney. Dundas had admonished Dorchester not to provoke hostilities on the frontier, in view of the fact that a general settlement of American difficulties seemed near. The renewal of agitation for Madison's resolutions, concerning which scanty information had reached London in private letters, was not deemed very dangerous.[8] Resting

7. Jay to Grenville, Falmouth, June 8, 1794, *Corres. of J. Jay,* IV, 22.

8. Among the records of the Foreign Office is a draft of secret instructions to the Governors of British Provinces in America saying that late communications had given reason to suspect that the United States might adopt hostile measures and urging strict attention to that quarter, and to the defenses of the Empire. It is impossible to say precisely when this draft was written, as it is not dated. It is followed by an undated note in handwriting which seems to be that of Grenville, as follows: "Their dispatches seem to indicate that there is a French party in America, of which we always understood Jefferson to be the head. I do not therefore imagine they will proceed to extremities, especially when they hear of the events of this summer in Europe. But there can be no harm in the circular, except that perhaps the preamble states the alarm too sharply." A note signed by Lord Hawkesbury reads: "9 p.m. I think that the preamble of the draft states the alarm too sharply." Following this are some papers enclosed by Hawkesbury to Dundas, including two extracts from a letter from Philadelphia of Feb. 7 (before the arrival there of news

on Hammond's well-founded assurance that any protest by the United States over the Order-in-Council of
June 8 would not be followed up seriously, Grenville
in a leisurely manner had directed his minister to refute
the protest delivered in London by Pinckney in the
same polite language in which it had been received.[9]
The Order of November 6, in turn superseded by that
of January 8, 1794, showed how little importance had
been attached to American protest. Grenville was even
holding up the suspended negotiations over the treaty
of peace and its infractions, concerning which Pinckney
had importuned him in November, in hope of a chance
to put through the neutral Indian barrier project in
case an Indian war embarrassing to the Americans

---

of the Caribbean captures and before Dorchester's speech of Feb. 10)
and one from New York of March 5 (also before news of either of
the two provocations). These letters are endorsed on the back of the
sheet on which they are copied: "Intelligence from New York enclosed in Mr. Brickwood's." On a fly-leaf occurs the legend, "April 9,
1794, Mr. Brickwood." This being so near the draft and so relevant
to it, makes it seem likely that the date of the circular draft was
sometime in April. The Philadelphia letter speaks of Madison's resolutions being postponed until March, "as, I presume, with a view of
learning from England the state of negotiations now pending between
your Court and ours. If Great Britain be favorably disposed toward
us, then I am confident the resolutions will not pass." The letter of
March 5 speaks of irritation over the captures of American ships and
the French embargo, but apparently was written before news of the
Caribbean captures had been received, which information reached the
United States two or three days later. The drafted circular was not
sent out; at least there is no record of it in the correspondence of the
Colonial Office with Upper Canada, Lower Canada, Newfoundland,
New Brunswick, Nova Scotia, and Cape Breton, which has been
examined by the writer for the purpose of verification. See P.R.O.,F.O.,
5, 7. That the circular was not sent would indicate that the American
situation had not been regarded as very dangerous.

9. Above, p. 214.

should follow a failure of the peace negotiations between the United States and the Indians.

The news received in June indicated mistaken confidence in American forbearance. It became immediately necessary to make important concessions speedily or to risk war. It was apparent that even the Federalists could be pushed into hostilities. War at this time, though perhaps it would have been fatal to the United States, would have been seriously unprofitable to England. It meant the loss of her greatest foreign customer and the diversion of ships-of-the-line badly needed to control the critical European situation.

For the solidity of the First Coalition against France was beginning to weaken. Secret agents of the Foreign Office had established already the fact that France was seeking to detach Spain from the Coalition by proposals through neutral Denmark.[10] In fact, we know that the Spanish Minister at Copenhagen really had instructions to make peace overtures to France in that capital.[11] Prussia's interest in the Rhine frontier was diminishing in view of the greater allurement of the Polish spoil. Among the Allies "there was far more of disunion than union."[12]

In addition to these tremors in the masonry of the First Coalition there was an immediate and alarming factor that made a disturbing connection in Grenville's mind between European and American affairs. The old Armed Neutrality of the North, encouraged by French

10. Précis of Secret Intelligence from Copenhagen, P.R.O.,F.O., (Holland), 37, 56.

11. Grouvelle Correspondence, Arch. Aff. Étrang., Danemark, Vols. 169 and 170.

12. J. H. Rose, *William Pitt and the Great War* (London, 1911), p. 204.

diplomacy and promises, was again attempting to lift
its head in support of those principles for which the
United States had contended in its mild protest against
the Order-in-Council of June 8 and which had given
such embarrassment to British naval operations during
the War of American Independence. The French Committee of Public Safety ever since the beginning of the
war had been feeling out the Baltic Powers in the hope
of exciting a "counter-coalition" against the British
naval-diplomatic system with which the allied monarchies were strangling the commerce of France. A plan
outlined in a memorandum left among the Committee's
papers aimed to unite all the neutral naval states under
the support of France in resistance to British sea power.
Sweden, Denmark, Turkey, Poland, Venice, Genoa, and
the United States saw themselves powerless singly to
enforce what they deemed the principles of justice for
neutral flags. It was believed that together they might
constitute a force strong enough to modify British
naval policy. A league was to be founded on the "inde-
feasible rights and independence of these nations and
their immediate interests," and as material help for the
success of the armed neutrals[13] France planned to sub-
sidize a Scandinavian naval armament.

Sweden and Denmark actually ratified an armed
neutrality convention, March 27, 1794, before these
instructions to this effect could be issued to French
diplomatists. The correspondence of Philippe de Grouvelle, the Minister of the French Republic, who was un-
officially received by Denmark in 1793 much to the

13. Projet d'Arrêté du Comité de Salut Public," undated, Arch.
Aff. Étrang., Danemark, Vol. 170, p. 85. See also "Rapport au Comité
de Salut Public," ibid., Suède, Vol. 286, p. 225, *verso*.

chagrin of the monarchies of Europe, indicates that the two northern powers agreed to this convention independently of French endeavor. Nevertheless it coincided with the designs of French diplomacy at Copenhagen since Grouvelle's arrival there in September, 1793. The Swedes, who hoped for liberal financial aid from France, made the mistake of closing the treaty door before the French subsidy horse was safely stabled. After the convention had been signed there was little chance to get funds from the notoriously hollow money chest of the French Revolutionary Government. Failure of subsidies to be forthcoming, the threatening presence of the British and Russian naval forces of the Coalition, which were patrolling the Baltic, and finally the independent attitude which the United States adopted toward the new Armed Neutrality eventually rendered it harmless.[14]

British suspicions as to some secret arrangement between Sweden and Denmark had been early aroused by the increasing naval armaments of those nations. The Danish Chancellor, Count Bernstorff, denied strongly the existence of any connections with France, and in Stockholm specific assurances were given to England that no arrangement was contemplated with Denmark.[15] But in April these two Baltic Powers, situated on both sides of the narrow Danish Sounds, announced to the world the text of their Armed Neutrality Convention of March 27, 1794. They agreed to use their joint fleets comprising, on paper, sixteen ships-

14. *A.H.R.,* XXIV, 32.
15. Lord H. Spencer (British Minister to Sweden) to Grenville, Stockholm, March 18, 1794, P.R.O.,F.O. (Sweden), 73, 17; same to same, April 18, 1794, ibid.

of-the-line for the protection of their subjects in the exercise of rights sanctioned by international law to independent nations. The Baltic Sea was declared to be a closed area inaccessible to the warships of the belligerent powers. In case a power "either in violation of treaties, or of the universal law of nations" should molest the neutral commerce of the two countries, the following timorous procedure was provided: after all means of conciliation had failed to bring satisfaction, the Scandinavian fleet would make reprisals "at the latest four months after the rejection of their behests, wherever they shall be judged suitable, the Baltic always excepted." The convention was to last during the war.[16] In no specific way did it define the legal rights of neutral powers. The definition was to be covered by the interpretations of the Baltic Powers as expressed in their treaties. These were really the principles of the Armed Neutrality of 1780.[17]

The Swedish Minister at London gave the American Minister, Thomas Pinckney, a copy of this convention on April 26, saying: "I beg you to communicate it to your sovereigns with the proposition that they accede to it, which I am commanded by the King to request you to suggest to them (*leur insinuer*)." [18] Pinckney's reply in writing was that since he had no instructions on the

16. See Scott, *Armed Neutralities of 1780 and 1800,* and Piggot and Omond, *Documentary History of the Armed Neutralities.*

17. Isabel de Madariaga has just published a sophisticated study of *Britain, Russia, and the Armed Neutrality of 1780* (Yale University Press, 1962).

18. Engeström to Pinckney, April 28, 1794, Swedish Royal Archives, Anglica. I am indebted to Dr. Lydia Wahlstrom, of Stockholm, who judiciously assisted me, at the time of the original preparation of this work (first edition), in securing transcripts from the Swedish Royal Archives. Professor Stith Thompson translated them for me.

subject he could only communicate the convention and accompanying invitation to his Government.[19] In his conversation with Engeström he seems to have been more enthusiastic. Engeström wrote the Swedish Chancellor:

Yesterday I informed the American Minister, Mr. Pinckney, of the convention between Sweden and Denmark, adding that I had been instructed to propose to the United States of North America that it enter this covention. This pleased him very much, and he requested me to write him a few words about it which he could transmit, an opportunity to do which presented itself today. He said that according to intelligence most recently received he believed that the proposals would be received with open arms. I have written him and the matter is now proceeding well. Fortunate indeed that the convention did not contain a provision that the other neutral powers should be consulted, because in that event England would have sought to win the Americans by complaisance. Now they will be treated like the rest of us and forced into union. The correspondence with America is prolonged, but I hope Pinckney will receive instructions as soon as possible.[20]

The Danish Chancellor, Count Bernstorff, was not so willing to invite the United States to accede. He saw that the American navy was helplessly weak. A mo-

19. Pinckney to Engeström, April 30, 1794, ibid.
20. Engeström to the Royal Chancellor, London, April 29, 1794, ibid.

ment that suited the United States to take action
against England might be fatal to the Northern
Powers.

> They play a safer game than we [the Swedish
> Minister at Copenhagen wrote to Engeström,
> after a conversation with the Chancellor] because
> when they point the blade at England they do not
> have, like us, a neighbor behind them holding a
> sword over their heads. It seems at least worthy of
> consideration whether it is the best time to make
> reprisals when a Russian fleet is patrolling the
> Baltic and when the ships against which it is in-
> tended go to and from the same sea. In this respect
> we are in a different position from the Americans:
> what might be the best policy for them would not
> always be the best for us. The uncertainty as to
> Russia's continence was and continues to be the
> main reason for the caution of Count von Bern-
> storff about the American accession.[21]

The Swedish Chancellor subsequently found it necessary to caution Engeström, the most ardent of all pro-
ponents of the American accession,[22] that any reply

21. Ehrenheim to Engeström, Copenhagen, July 8, 1794, ibid.

22. Engeström was captivated with the idea of the American alliance and constantly urged it on the Chancellor (Sparre) and pressed
Ehrenheim (Swedish Minister at Copenhagen) to argue Bernstorff
into taking up negotiations with the Americans. "Our strength consists in the case of making reprisals on the English merchant fleet
coming out of the Baltic Sea. It is, however, an extremity which we
should try to avoid, by so strengthening our alliance that by virtue of
an armed neutrality our ships would be treated otherwise than they
are now. The alliance cannot be strengthened except by the American
States, who could equip thirty frigates in place of eight ships-of-the-

from the United States must be accepted *ad referendum*, "and nothing further agreed until we have reached a wider concert with Denmark. Otherwise the Danish Court might take unbrage at it, whereby perhaps the whole subject of the envisaged alliance would be lost." [23]

The information which the British Foreign Office had received of the new Franco-Scandinavian design and its aims to include the United States added nothing to Grenville's peace of mind. Practically all of Great Britain's naval stores came either from the Baltic or from America. Here was a collusion of neutral and hostile interests to be avoided at all costs. Grenville's spies regularly perused the Copenhagen correspondence of the Committee of Public Safety. They furnished for his use a digest of all the news revealed by Bernstorff to Grouvelle. Thus the Foreign Secretary was able to inform Hammond, May 10, that he had heard that Engeström by order of his court had proposed to Pinckney the United States accession.[24] He instructed Hammond to make the utmost endeavor to prevent acceptance of such an invitation. In confidential communications with the American "ministers" on this

---

line, with which in consideration of their position they could do more harm than we with thrice that strength. We ought to enlighten the Danish Minister. Denmark is hated but by no means feared by England. They will make us good terms the moment we wish to separate from Denmark. As little as they fear Denmark so much they fear the United States of America, who could easily take England's possessions on the continent and starve their West India islands. If Denmark will not admit the Americans, then I wish we might." Engeström to Erenheim, London, May 26, 1794, ibid.

23. The Chancellor of the Kingdom to Engeström, Stockholm, May 16, 1794, ibid.

24. *A.H.R.*, XXIV, 38.

subject he was directed to emphasize the marked difference in circumstances between the position of the
United States and that of the Baltic Powers. The
United States, Grenville observed, until then had remained apparently uninfluenced by the criminal system
of France that had instigated the policy of Sweden. In
return the neutral position of American commerce had
been considered very favorable by Great Britain (the
dispatch was penned before news received, June 10, of
American feeling as to the West Indian captures). The
United States Government must be aware of the risk
of war with Great Britain, particularly when it considered the ineffectiveness of the Scandinavian navy.[25]
Although Grenville had reason to believe, thanks to the
interception of Grouvelle's dispatches, that the Swedes
lacked the sanction of the Danish Court in the proposals made to the United States, he ordered Hammond
to continue to give this matter the greatest attention.[26]
The accumulation of long-delayed official correspondence from the United States and Canada which arrived in London June 10, soon showed that if the
American Government had not been seduced by the
"criminal" tendencies of France it had been exasperated
almost to the point of war by the arbitrary naval policy
of the British Government and the outrageous conduct
of the Canadian officials on the frontier. A fertile field
had developed into which the enemies of England might

25. Grenville to Hammond, May 10, 1794, P.R.O.,F.O., 5, 4, Mayo,
*Instructions*, pp. 54–5.
26. Same to same, June 5, 1794, ibid., 115, 3, Mayo, *Instructions*,
p. 58.

drop the seeds of armed neutrality proposals. Such an assumption would certainly have been strengthened into conviction if Grenville's spies had read the fifth article of Jay's instructions.[27]

On the day of the first conference with Jay, Grenville received from the British *chargé d'affaires* at Berlin a letter, dated June 10, telling of an interview with Count Finckenstein, the notable Prussian Minister of Foreign Affairs, in which he discussed the dubious disposition of the United States at the existing moment. Finckenstein confided to the British *chargé* some information which, in view of Jefferson's resignation and retirement on January 1, was very fantastic. Nevertheless it must have been startling to Grenville. Jefferson, said the Prussian, was expected soon to arrive in Denmark, probably to concert measures as to the lines of conduct to be followed by the neutral nations. A certain Mr. Marshall, he disclosed, had left Berlin, professedly for London, after having endeavored in vain to have the King and Prince Henry receive letters purported to be from President Washington, the contents of which were unknown.[28] It should be noted that Count Bernstorff, in Denmark, also believed Jefferson to be embarking for that country. At least such was the

27. See above, p. 296.
28. G. H. Rose to Grenville, Berlin, June 10, 1794, Rec'd June 20, P.R.O.,F.O. (Prussia), 64, 29. "Mr. Marshall" was James M. Marshall, brother of the famous Chief Justice. Beveridge, *Life of John Marshall,* II, 33. The Pinckney dispatches explain the mission of Marshall. He was acting as the unofficial personal agent of Washington to secure the release of General Lafayette from an Austrian prison. He was unsuccessful.

content of the dispatches to Paris from Grouvelle.[29] A letter from Hammond of May 25 arrived July 1. It told of the increasing hostility of the American public over the Miamis occupation and enclosed the acrimonious correspondence between himself and Secretary Randolph concerning the incident.[30] At the same time came still more news from Grenville's secret agents pointing to the probability of war with the United States.

This last information was from Genoa, of all places. There was dispatched to London on June 24 one of the celebrated bulletins of Francis Drake, who from that city had been transmitting from his paid informant, supposed by him to be one of the secretaries of the Committee of Public Safety, the pretended minutes of the secret meetings of the group of terrorists then managing the destinies of France. These bulletins had been coming from Drake ever since September, 1792. Those dated after March 1, 1794, spoke of proposals by Gouverneur Morris, the American Minister at Paris, for an alliance against England during the period of the war. The alliance was to be in the form of an armed neutrality and to be financed by French subsidies.

29. A précis of the Grouvelle dispatches for 1794 exists in the Public Record Office (F.O., Holland, ser. 37, vol. 36). The writer has examined the original Grouvelle dispatches as preserved in the Archives des Affaires Étrangères at Paris and finds that the précis is absolutely correct and well done.

30. "The general ferment of this country and the spirit of hostility to Great Britain, which for the last three or four months have been perpetually increasing have now risen to a much higher pitch than before." Hammond to Grenville, Phila., May 25, 1794, P.R.O.,F.O., 5, 4.

Modern research has cast grave doubts on the validity of these dispatches, and in so far as the reports concern the United States it is easy to demonstrate their falsity.[31]

Grenville, from November, 1793, to June, 1794, deprived of official information from America, seems to have attached some weight to Drake's information,[32] perhaps for the purpose of checking up with the statements in the Grouvelle correspondence.

This "secret" information of June 24 from Genoa must have arrived in England early in July, guessing at the time of travel from Genoa to London. It stated that there had been read in the Committee of Public Safety letters from the French agents in the United States dated April 1, which indicated a conflict between that country and England as inevitable and asserted that war would be declared immediately a treaty could be concluded with Denmark and Sweden. The French Commissioners in America were purported to have requested power from their Government to conclude preliminaries of a treaty with the United States and to guarantee to Congress that the National Convention would not treat with the Northern Powers without admitting the United States to any treaty made with them. According to the dispatch, the last request was rejected but the French Executive was authorized to negotiate with the American Minister and to report to the Committee. The report also stated that letters from Stockholm of May 11 represented Sweden as ready to sign a treaty with the French Republic and that French

31. *A.H.R.*, XXIV, 40, note 54
32. *Dropmore Papers*, II, 578.

agents in Sweden knew all that was going on between Sweden and Denmark.[33]

Whether or not Grenville trusted the veracity of the Drake dispatches he had absolutely trustworthy secret intelligence from Copenhagen exhibiting Grouvelle, agent at that Court of the unrecognized French Republic, as a man of great influence who aimed at closest connections between Sweden and Denmark.[34]

Despite Bernstorff's denial of French collusion, the British agents at Copenhagen, Christiania, and Stockholm reported that promises of French money were one of the most powerful stimulants of the Scandinavian naval armament.[35]

All this secret information, true and false, arrived in England just as Jay was about to begin his negotiation. It pointed to one fact: the British Government stood confronted with all the dangers of a revival of the old Armed Neutrality at a time when the First Coalition was giving indication of collapse. Two exceptions there were to the situation of 1780, and they were mighty exceptions. Pitt could count on Catherine the Great as a naval ally against the Baltic Powers;[36] and Prussia, now a nominal ally of Great Britain and absorbed in the Polish partition, had no inclination to join the Baltic combination. There can be no doubt that the Baltic

33. Bulletin No. 25, Dispatches of Francis Drake, *Dropmore Papers,* II, 579–82.

34. Précis of Secret Intelligence from Copenhagen, pp. 303, 312 above.

35. Whitworth to Grenville, St. Petersburg, April 15, 23, 1794, P.R.O.,F.O. (Russia), 65, 27.

36. Russia's treaty of alliance with Great Britain of 1793 provided for measures to induce neutral powers to adopt an harassing attitude toward French commerce.

question, as viewed by the Foreign Office in June and
July, 1794, bade fair to have an appreciable effect on
the American negotiation. It would have been folly for
England to have allowed the United States, her greatest foreign customer at a time when commerce and the
*entrepôt* system were providing the revenue for the
French War,[37] to join in a war against her or in a combination of the Northern Powers effected by French
diplomacy. Such a happening would have served to
divide the energies and diminish the supplies of the
British navy and to weaken the financial strength of the
Empire during the fateful conflict with France. Great
Britain wanted war no more than the American Federalists. The time had come for some kind of settlement.

Another factor in impelling the Ministry toward a
peaceable settlement with the United States was the
very considerable pressure which the American embargo had created on the British West India Islands,
especially Jamaica. The plight of the West India
colonies in 1794 presents a singular example of the
efficacy of embargo legislation in creating political
pressure. By proclamation during the war the governors of the West India colonies had allowed the importation of foodstuffs in American vessels. This relaxa-
tion of the Navigation Laws in favor of American
ships was winked at by the home Government, because
the scarcity of tonnage and increased cost of provisions
had made it impossible to get sufficient food for even
normal times. There was difficulty, too, in satisfying

37. Mahan, *Sea Power and the French Revolution,* II, 18.

the increased demand caused by the presence of large numbers of troops employed for the reduction of the French islands. In the dispatches of the Governor of Jamaica one glimpses the rise in the price of flour at Kingston. When first the embargo began to be felt, flour, which was already high because of war risks, stood at eighty-five shillings the barrel. It had advanced by the end of May to two hundred shillings. Little was to be had at any price. A small two-ounce loaf became a great curiosity. When the embargo was lifted and the American schooners came south again the price tumbled to fifty-five shillings. The Governor anxiously entreated the authorities in England to provide for his food supply in case of a break with the United States or a continuance of the embargo. The colonial agent of Jamaica in London eagerly importuned the Ministry for a settlement with Jay.[38]

As Jay arrived in England and prepared to enter upon his negotiations, the diplomatic situation, as it would have been viewed by a shrewd diplomatist who knew all the cards, all the players, all the stakes in the great international game, would have been pronounced favorable for the United States. But Jay knew only a few of the cards. Grenville, on the other hand, knew almost all of them, or at least he succeeded skillfully in

38. This paragraph can be authenticated abundantly by a perusal of the correspondence of the Secretary for Home Affairs with Governor Williamson of Jamaica, P.R.O.,C.O., 137, Vols. 92, 93, 94, 95; especially Williamson to Dundas, Nov. 25, 1793 (Vol. 92), Dundas to Williamson (ibid.), Mar. 6, 1794, Williamson to Dundas, Jan. 18, 1794 (ibid.), and June 11, 1794 (Vol. 93), Fuller to King, Aug. 27, 1794, and King to Fuller, Aug. 29, 1794 (Vol. 93). Statements of prices are to be found scattered through these volumes.

delaying the game long enough to get a glimpse at their faces.

And we now know that the British Foreign Office had the key to Jay's cipher! [39] Let us now observe how the American Chief Justice fared at the hands of the great Foreign Secretary.

39. The late J. Franklin Jameson told me, Nov. 22, 1932, that when he inspected (years after my own researches in the Public Record Office in 1915–16) a group of Grenville's private papers brought to the Public Record Office for that purpose, he saw among them the key to Jay's cipher.

# CHAPTER 12

# The Jay-Grenville Negotiations

GRENVILLE, as we have seen, had decided long since that the evacuation of the frontier posts was a necessary condition of any treaty with the United States. He had also persuaded himself that any such settlement need not injure British prestige with the Indians because posts of equal strategic value could be constructed opposite the old ones on British soil. Hammond's dispatches, too, had conveyed assurances that, providing the posts were relinquished, the United States would be willing to allow trading privileges to British subjects within the Indian country to the south of the line. He was also certain that freedom of travel over portages and internal water communications within American territory would be allowed. The Foreign Office had delayed any adjustment of the frontier question in the hope that a disastrous turn in the Indian campaign might make the American Government listen with more favor to mediation proposals, that such an event might yet make it possible to set up the neutral Indian barrier state. But the frontier situation had steadily grown worse, from the British point of view.

To the frontier grievance of the United States had been added the violation of neutral rights. A real war-cloud had now risen on the other side of the Atlantic.

The old Armed Neutrality of the North, succored by French diplomacy, was attempting to lift its head again. The coalition against France was pulling apart on the continent of Europe. Manifestly it was no longer expedient for Great Britain to procrastinate. The certainty of injurious commercial discrimination, apart from the imminence of actual war, was enough to convince the Ministry of the desirability of an immediate settlement with Jay.[1]

A desire for conciliation was reflected in the affability with which Jay was welcomed at Downing Street and at Court. When Thomas Pinckney had been first received by George III, in December, 1792, he reported to Jefferson that "the only circumstance worth remarking in my conference with the King was that Lord North's rope of sand appeared not to have been entirely effaced from His Majesty's memory, which I inferred from his mentioning the different circumstances of the northern and southern parts of our country as tending to produce disunion." [2] The increased prestige of the new federal Government in 1794

1. The following extract from a précis of Hammond's correspondence, drawn up for Grenville's use during the Jay negotiations, is significant of the English dread of commercial discrimination. Alluding to the attitude of Congress in February, 1794, it states:

"In addition to the other marks of ill will manifested toward Great Britain a member of the House of Representatives gave notice that he intended to move 'that over and above all duties imposed on the importation of foreign commodities into America, ten per cent of extra duty should be laid on all articles the growth or manufacture of Great Britain.' This, if carried into a law, must tend inevitably farther to reduce the number of British vessels, which has been annually and gradually diminishing ever since the imposition of the first discriminating duty." *Dropmore Papers,* III, 527.

2. Pinckney to the Secretary of State, Dec. 13, 1792, State Dept., Dispatches, Eng., III.

may be partly responsible for the warmth with which Jay was now greeted by the King and Queen. So many agreeable amenities were generally put in his way that he refrained from mentioning them in his official correspondence for fear that a false interpretation might be put on them by the anti-British party at home.[3] In fact, throughout his correspondence the envoy did little more than to enumerate to Randolph the more ostensible features of the negotiation. Though officially under the supervision of the Secretary of State the Chief Justice was a man of infinitely more weight than his francophile chief in the United States Government and in the inner councils of the Federalist Party. Jay paid little attention to what he recognized as Randolph's recommendations for the conduct of the negotiation. Occasionally his correspondence with his nominal superior assumed a tone positively patronizing: "You have, in my opinion, managed that matter well," he wrote to Randolph, anent the correspondence with Hammond over the Miamis post; "continue, by all means, to be temperate." [4]

Immediate steps were taken to relieve the tension. Dorchester was given such a sharp reprimand for his hostile speech of February 10 and his orders for the occupation of the Miamis fort that ultimately he felt compelled to resign. Such action as he had taken, he was tersely told, was more likely to provoke than to prevent hostilities. Dundas instructed him to make

3. Jay to Hamilton, July 11, 1794, *Corres. of J. Jay,* IV, 30. Dinners and soirées in his honor, at least by minor personages, are reflected in Jay's private correspondence in the Iselin Collection of Jay family papers—now in Columbia University Library.

4. Jay to Randolph, July 30, 1794, *Corres. of J. Jay,* IV, 37.

every effort to avoid friction with the United States, especially since a general settlement of all differences was hoped for through Jay.[5] Simcoe, the real instigator of the Governor General's bellicose conduct and the one man most responsible for the hostile attitude of the Canadian officials, escaped reproach. Inferior in command to Dorchester, he did not hesitate to lay the whole blame on him. In one of their first conferences Jay and Grenville agreed that, pending their negotiation, everything should remain *in statu quo* on the frontier, that all encroachments and any hostile measures that might have occurred on either side should be disregarded. This agreement, as we have observed before, did not prevent British retention of the Miamis fort until Detroit and the other posts were finally evacuated in 1796.[6]

Efforts to retrieve the American situation did not stop with the reprimand to Dorchester. One of the first matters taken up by Jay was that of the Caribbean captures. He did not attempt to protest a perfectly good seizure involving the Rule of 1756 [7] but waited for some of the spoliations under the Order-in-Council

5. Dundas to Dorchester, July 5, 1794, C.A.,Q, 67, 175; Dorchester to Dundas, Sept. 4, 1794, ibid., 69–1, 176. In this letter Dorchester says that at the time he delivered the speech to the Indians he believed that war was inevitable, that it was impossible to give the Indians hope of peace through mediation, and that he saw no reason for concealing his opinion from them; nor had he seen anything since to change his opinion. He asked leave to resign. For friction between Dorchester and Simcoe, see Dorchester to Portland (Secretary for Home Affairs, succeeding Dundas), Quebec, Nov. 7, 1795, C.A.,Q, 74–2, 307. Dorchester left Canada in July, 1796.

6. Above, p. 250.

7. The case of the *Charlotte,* an American ship carrying a cargo of produce for the French West Indies and bound directly thence for France, the cargo being American property. *A.S.P.,F.R.,* I, 480.

of November 6, 1793. Concerning the injustice of this measure he made strong representations. One of the documents which he laid before Grenville was the signed statement of the forty American sea captains telling of their unnecessary hardships during detention in the British West Indies[8] as a result of that arbitrary order. Grenville, who professed to have heard of these captures for the first time from Jay,[9] promptly declared that the King had decided that all of these cases should be admitted to appeal. If there should be found cases where redress could not be had *from whatever circumstances* in the ordinary course of law, His Majesty had determined that at all events justice should be done and would be willing to discuss measures and principles for that purpose.[10]

These assurances were followed by an Order-in-Council, August 6, admitting the West India cases to appeal.[11] Further, so much of the Order-in-Council of June 8, 1793, as directed the capture and pre-emption of neutral grain ships bound for France was quietly set aside.[12] By such acts the Ministry more than acceded to the conditions outlined by Hamilton as absolutely in-

8. Grenville to Jay, July 28, 1794, P.R.O.,F.O., 95, 12.

9. A copy of the affidavit of the forty American sea captains captured at Martinique had been received, however, at the Foreign Office, as early as June 12, 1794, ibid., 5, 7.

10. Grenville to Jay, Aug. 1, 1794, *A.S.P.,F.R.,* I, 481.

11. *A.S.P.,F.R.,* I, 482.

12. Instructions to Naval Commanders, approved by the Privy Council, Aug. 6, 1794, P.R.O.,F.O., 95, 512. [Orders-in-Council, West Indies and America, 1786–1797]; Privy Council Register, Series 2, Vol. 141, p. 11. Josiah T. Newcomb, "New Light on Jay's Treaty," *Am. Jour. International Law,* XXVIII (1934), 686.

dispensable to an amicable adjustment.[13] At a diplomatic function shortly thereafter George III. asked Jay if he did not believe that *now* his mission would be successful. Jay replied discreetly that he had received information which led him to hope that it might.[14] In early August the general situation was all in favor of the American plenipotentiary. It was particularly so when we consider the European situation outlined in the previous chapter.

Jay and Grenville meanwhile continued their conferences over the disputes relating to the treaty of peace. No protocols appear to exist for these conferences. What was discussed is known only from the general summaries in Jay's public and private letters and a few memoranda left among Grenville's private papers. Jay made only a perfunctory attempt to place the onus of first infraction on Great Britain. Grenville refused to acknowledge the American contentions as to Negroes. He met the argument of Jefferson, that non-evacuation of the posts had preceded and thus caused American legal impediments to recovery of debts, by asserting that no orders for evacuation need have been given until the proclamation of formal ratification of the treaty had been received in Canada, in July, 1784. Therefore, since incontestable violations had occurred on the American side before that time, it was just to refuse to give up the posts. Jay was inclined to accept the justice of the British construction of the clause regarding Negroes.[15] The other contentions of Gren-

13. Grenville to Hammond, Aug. 8, 1794, P.R.O.,F.O., 115, 3.
14. *Corres. of J. Jay,* IV, 45.
15. Jay to Randolph, Sept. 13, 1794, *A.S.P.,F.R.,* I, 486.

ville, as the latter already knew from Temple's reports, simply agreed with the statement that Jay, who naturally had been ignorant of all that had passed between Quebec and London, had made to Congress in 1786. This statement, we remember, demonstrated the blamelessness of Great Britain in refusing to withdraw from American territory. No *self-respecting*[16] envoy in Jay's position could contradict this statement. He readily agreed with Grenville that it would be useless to pursue the question of original infraction, and more desirable to sink all past disputes in a new agreement to regulate the future.[17]

Discussion by August 6 had reached the stage where Jay thought it advisable to submit a draft of a treaty, leaving many of the "common" articles to be settled by later discussion. Among matters not yet considered were all those dealing with the conduct of belligerents toward neutral commerce. That this draft was received as a likely basis of settlement might be indicated by Grenville's dispatch to Hammond on the eighth of that month stating that it was probable that all disputes would be terminated amicably. Grenville replied to Jay with a counter-project consisting of two proposals, one for settlement of the existing points at issue between the two countries, the other for a commercial treaty.[18] "I am glad that your American treaty goes

16. Above, p. 292.

17. "That Britain was not bound to evacuate the posts, nor to give any orders for the purpose, until after the exchange of the ratifications, does appear to me to be a proposition that cannot reasonably be disputed. That certain legislative acts did pass in the United States in the interval aforesaid, which were inconsistent with the treaty of peace, is equally certain." Jay to Randolph, Sept. 13, 1794, *A.S.P., F.R.,* I, 486.

18. *A.S.P.,F.R.,* I, 487.

on to your liking," wrote the Marquis of Buckingham
to his brother-in-law, Lord Grenville, on August 10,
1794. "We have indeed enough upon our hands." [19]
There followed until September 19 exchanges of
notes on the drafts submitted by each side. By a study
of these projects and the notes on them made by each
plenipotentiary it is to be seen that by September 13
the following points had been agreed on:

1. Evacuation of the posts, Jay desiring it to take
   place June 1, 1795, Grenville wishing another year
   to complete arrangements. Each party to have
   leave freely to trade with the Indians in the other's
   dominions.
2. A commission to settle the northeastern boundary,
   by establishing the precise identity of the St. Croix
   River.[20]
3. Compensation to be made for damages suffered by
   American citizens *under color* of His Majesty's
   instructions and commissions, when adequate compensation could not be had in the ordinary course
   of law; such claims to be settled by a mixed commission sitting in London. Compensation by the
   United States for captures by illegal privateers and
   for captures by privateers within American jurisdiction, the claims to be settled by the same commission.

19. *Dropmore Papers,* II, 614.
20. This dispute arose over the doubtful identity of the River St.
Croix, which was stipulated in article II of the treaty of 1783 as the
northeastern boundary of the United States, and from the source of
which the line was to be drawn northwards to the "highlands of
Nova Scotia." See Moore, *International Arbitrations,* I, 1–5 (contains
facsimile of Mitchell's Map); *A.S.P.,F.R.,* I, 89–100. See above, Ch.
5, note 11.

4. Compensation by the United States for debts the recovery of which may have been prevented by legal impediments, where adequate relief was not then afforded to the creditor by due course of law. A mixed commission sitting in the United States to decide on these claims, which the United States was to pay in specie.[21]

5. Neither party to sequestrate or confiscate debts to individuals, or private securities, in case of national differences. In case of war, debts to be only suspended.

6. American ships of limited tonnage to be admitted to the British West Indies on the same terms as British ships trading between those islands and the United States; providing, however, that the United States agree to prohibit from re-exportation all West Indian exports imported in American ships, except rum made from West Indian molasses.[22]

7. Ports within the dominions of each party, aside from the restrictions pertaining to the West India trade, to be open reciprocally and freely to the other's vessels, no tonnage or other duties to be levied by one on the other party's ships more than that paid in such respect by the most favored nation.[23]

21. Grenville in his project stipulated for sterling money but acquiesced in Jay's desire for specie to be stipulated, since sterling money fluctuated. *A.S.P.,F.R.*, I, 488–93.

22. For origin of the idea of limitation of tonnage see above, p. 62. Hamilton early adopted this scheme as a solution to the question of opening the West Indian trade without breaking into the British trans-Atlantic carrying trade.

23. The "most favored nation" was Grenville's expression. Jay avoided the term.

8. In case either party should be neutral while the other was belligerent, no prizes taken from or by the belligerent to be sold in the neutral's ports. This article was not to infringe on the provisions of any treaty which either of the parties might have concluded already with any other power.

9. An article allowing citizens or subjects of each party to own, sell, and devise land under the same regulations as applied to nationals.

10. An article to prevent impressment by either party of the other's citizens or subjects.[24]

11. Prohibition of captures within the jurisdiction of one party of the other's vessels or property.

In addition to these points, on which there seems to have been agreement on September 13, Jay had pro-

24. Impressment had already led to protests by the United States. Some American citizens were taken, while in British harbors, in the Nootka press on May 4, 1790, but were released after representations by Gouverneur Morris. Jefferson foresaw that the British press system would lead to further difficulties as soon as another European war should appear likely to involve England, and he made it one of the principal duties of Pinckney, during his London mission, to arrange some settlement of this vexing question. Though Jefferson refused to admit that American citizens should be required to prove themselves such before the master of a press-gang, such was the basis of a *modus vivendi*, tacitly accepted by the United States, and American sailors were equipped with certificates of citizenship. Impressments did not cease, particularly after the beginning of the war with France, and there are flagrant cases where American sailors were taken from their own ships not only in British ports but also on the high seas, under the pretention that they were really Englishmen. Pinckney protested these cases and generally where citizenship could be proved the impressed sailor was delivered up. Often this was after months of delay and barbarous treatment on the decks of a British man-of-war. See Pinckney's dispatches in State Dept., Dispatches, Eng., Vols. I, II, III, and his correspondence with Grenville in P.R.O.,F.O. This has been reviewed by the writer in *A.H.R.*, XXVIII, 228–47.

posed indemnification for delay in evacuating the posts, a contention which it must have been difficult for a man of his previously expressed views to support with candor. He preferred to drop this proposal, after what he regarded as an equivalent had been presented in the limited admission of American schooners to the British West Indies, a "concession" which he overestimated in value, believing it to be the first stream through the dyke of the Navigation Laws.[25] Several other proposals made by Grenville remained as a basis for further discussion. Among these were prohibition of violence by individuals against either party (aimed, among other things, at preventing Americans enlisting in the French navy) ; most-favored-nation tariff privileges reciprocally; and a guaranty that neither party should levy any new prohibitions on imports of articles the growth, product or manufacture of the other's dominions,[26] designed to remove the danger of anti-British commercial legislation and by one stroke to prevent the erection of any future American tariff walls against English goods.

Several direct issues had been raised.

No agreement on the questions of the definition of contraband, the status of enemy property on neutral ships, and the Rule of 1756 could be reached. Grenville asserted Britain's position uncompromisingly on these points; Jay would not yet relinquish the American definition of the principles that ought to govern neutral rights.[27] Again, Grenville persisted in demanding a

25. Jay to Washington, London, March 6, 1795, *Corres. of J. Jay,* IV, 163.

26. Articles 4th and 5th of Grenville's commercial project, *A.S.P., F.R.,* I, 489.

27. Jay's notes on Grenville's projects, *ibid.,* p. 492.

rectification of the boundary line in the northwest corner of the United States. He contended that because a line due west from the Lake of the Woods probably would not strike the Mississippi it was necessary to make a new boundary to give effect to the provision of the treaty of 1783 which secured to each party the free navigation of the river. He insisted that free navigation implied access *without passing through foreign territory.*

It is worth while to digress for a moment to examine this matter of the northwest boundary. The question had been raised by the discovery by Hammond, ten years after the treaty of peace had been signed, that because of an "accidental geographical error" there probably existed a gap in the boundary. If not remedied, this, he had professed, would make nugatory the stipulation for free navigation of the Mississippi by subjects of both parties from the source of the river to the ocean,[28] since Canadians could not go down the river directly from Canada.

Great Britain was eager to secure an entrance to the Mississippi from her northern province. Great expectations were placed in the rapidly populating western territory of the United States as a future market for British manufactures to be supplied through Canada by the water route of the Great Lakes. Payment might be taken profitably in corn, wheat, hemp, and other raw materials.[29] The chief avenue of trade would be the

28. Hammond to Grenville, Phila., Feb. 2, 1792, *Dropmore Papers,* II, 254; P.R.O.,F.O., 115, 1.

29. A memorandum among the papers of Pitt adopts this point of view completely. It is indorsed "Considerations on the Propriety of Great Britain abandoning the Indian Posts, and coming to a good understanding with America." Catham MSS, Bdl. 344.

Lakes, but the Mississippi, the tortuous upper reaches of which were not known well, was considered by Hammond and Simcoe as an excellent highway for communication in the future between Upper Canada and the Mississippi settlements of the United States.[30] The lines proposed by Grenville to Jay would have brought the boundary of Canada far enough south to reach the navigable portion of the Father of Waters. He suggested either of two lines: one from West Bay, Lake Superior, due west to Red Lake River, the east branch of the Mississippi, the boundary to run thence down that supposed tributary to the main river;[31] or a line to strike due north from the confluence of the River St. Croix[32] and the Mississippi until it should meet the water passage between Lake Superior and the Lake of the Woods. Considering the then existing vagueness of boundary between Canada and Louisiana, either of these rectifications would have given access from the north to the navigable part of the river. If one bears in mind that the probable intention of the negotiators of the treaty had been to draw a line between the Mississippi and the Lake of the Woods, either line, as Jay pointed out, would have involved cession by the United States of between 30,000 and 35,000 square miles.

The success of this rectification maneuver would

30. Hammond to Grenville, Feb. 2, 1792, *Dropmore Papers,* II, 254; Simcoe to Dundas, London, June 2, 1791, C.A.,Q, 278, 228; Report by Simcoe to the Lords of Trade, Sept. 1, 1794, ibid., Q, 280–2, 307.

31. This line would have been impossible. Red Lake River runs into the Red River of the North, not into the Mississippi. Hence it cannot be illustrated by map.

32. This should not be confused with the St. Croix of the north-eastern boundary. The falls of St. Anthony, the present site of Minneapolis, are just north of the confluence of the St. Croix and make the first serious interruption to navigation.

have yielded to Great Britain what since has proved to be one of the most valuable iron and copper mining districts on the continent. If such a line had been granted, it would have placed the starting point of the boundary to be drawn westward in the future to the Pacific much farther to the south, perhaps so as to make over to Canada the greater part of the present states of Minnesota, North Dakota, Montana, Idaho, and Washington, regions of incalculable potential value and economic consequence. Jay, to whom all credit must be given for refusing, as a matter of principle, to yield this "rectification" in a remote and little-thought-of section of the northwestern wilderness, stoutly declined, as one of the American Commissioners who had drawn up the treaty of 1783, to admit that the eighth article inferred a dominion over the lands adjacent to the river of which the navigation was declared free. He refused to agree that, connected with the circumstance that the territories of both parties were to be bounded by a line terminating at the river, the navigation article meant that the line must end at a navigable part. The just way to settle the dispute, he maintained, was a joint survey to ascertain whether a gap really existed. If a gap were found, a joint commission could settle the line.[33] Indeed, the logical conclusion which we draw from Grenville's contention, that the eighth article meant freedom of navigation without passing through the territory of a foreign power, would be the absurdity that the English negotiators in signing the treaty intended that free navigation of the river from its source to the ocean was only, as far as British subjects were concerned, the right to come

33. Jay to Grenville, Sept. 4, 1794, *A.S.P.,F.R.*, I, 490.

down the river from Canada as far as the Spanish closure.[34]

The month of September was devoted chiefly to a discussion of projects and counter-projects without enough progress to permit Jay to be certain that the negotiation would succeed.[35] Nevertheless he persisted. "If I should be able to conclude the business on admissible terms," he wrote privately to Hamilton, "I shall do it and risk the consequences . . . rather than hazard a change in the disposition of this Court." [36] Nor was Grenville, who had hoped, after receiving Jay's first project, to send Hammond news of a treaty by the September mail, so sanguine now of an immediate settlement.[37] News had arrived in London of the enthusiastic reception given by the French Convention to James Monroe, who succeeded Gouverneur Morris as Minister to France when the recall of the latter had been demanded by reason of his lack of enthusiasm for the régime of 1794. Grenville was disturbed at the outburst of republican emotion which took place upon

34. Article VII of treaty of 1783: "The navigation of the River Mississippi from its source to the ocean, shall forever remain free and open to the subjects of Great Britain and the citizens of the United States." See writer's article on "Jay's Treaty and the Northwest Boundary Gap," *A.H.R.*, XXVII, 465.

35. Jay to Randolph, Sept. 18, 1794, *A.S.P.,F.R.*, I, 496. "Although it is uncertain, yet it is not altogether improbable, that Lord Grenville and myself may agree on terms which, in my opinion should not be rejected. In that case, I shall be strongly induced to conclude, rather than by delays risk a change of views, and measures, and ministers, which unforeseen circumstances might occasion." Jay to Washington, Sept. 13, 1794, *Corres. of J. Jay*, IV, 58.

36. Jay to Hamilton, London, Sept. 11, 1794. Iselin Collection of Jay family papers, Columbia University Library.

37. Grenville to Hammond, Sept. 4, 1794, P.R.O.,F.O., 115, 3; Mayo, *Instructions*, p. 67.

the arrival of the new American Minister in Paris. He was especially taken back by the fraternal kiss bestowed on Monroe by the President of the Convention and the democratic felicitations, so warmly written by Randolph, which the United States Senate by formal resolution had conveyed to the French Republic. The Foreign Secretary made these "unneutral" effusions the subject of private protest to Jay. A pious exchange of epistles[38] followed between these two upholders of "law and order, religion and morality." Jay later made Grenville's complaint the subject of private letters to Washington and Hamilton and of a candid communication to Randolph himself.[39]

The month of September having passed without any definite results beyond agreement on certain articles that had been the result of the exchange of projects, Jay submitted a complete detailed draft of a treaty. He tendered this as a final proposal on September 30.[40] This document was never given to the Senate along with the other correspondence of Jay relating to the treaty which he eventually signed. His official dispatches numbered in unbroken serial form do not contain it, though his short letter of October 2 mentions an attempt to incorporate the two projects, previously drafted, into one treaty. One can guess the reason why this draft—far more important than any of the preliminary projects—was not included in Jay's corres-

38. "I do not believe that you personally will envy Mr. Monroe the honor of the fraternal kiss which he received: and if such an exhibition is thought not to degrade an American Minister I know not why it should not become a matter of complaint on the part of the British Government." Grenville to Jay, private, Sept. 7, 1794, ibid., 95, 152.

39. Jay to Randolph, private, September 13, 1794, State Dept., Dispatches, Eng., I.

40. Jay to Grenville, Sept. 30, 1794, *Dropmore Papers*, III, 516–17.

pondence: it shows up so disadvantageously when compared with the treaty finally signed. It indicates a stupendous retreat by the American plenipotentiary. It would have been a most embarrassing document for the Federalists, or for Jay individually, to have had submitted to the Senate. It is doubtful whether any person outside of the Foreign Office, except Jay, ever saw the document. The writer has been unable to discover a copy in any of the published or unpublished papers of Jay which relate to his negotiation.

It was in this paper that Jay tried to incorporate some of the "common" matters which he had omitted in his first project. He presented, instead of separate commercial and political instruments, one treaty of amity, navigation, and commerce. It is highly instructive to note the following points favorable to the United States stipulated in this draft and not included in the actual treaty.

A provision that neither side, in case of war between the two, should resort to the use of Indian allies; in case the natives themselves were engaged with one of the parties all permission to pass and repass across the boundary line should cease to be enjoyed by them.

"Neither of the contracting parties will form political connections, nor hold any treaties with Indians dwelling within the boundaries of the other."

Each party to the treaty was to endeavor to restrain its Indians in case of war and to make common cause in case of one party's being engaged in hostilities with the natives, "so far as to prohibit and prevent any supplies of ammunition or arms being given or sold even by Indian traders to one belligerent tribe or tribes or to any individuals of them."

No armed vessels were to be constructed by either party on the Great Lakes, and the two nations were to enter into arrangements for withdrawal of forces from the common boundary.

Payment by the United States of debts adjudicated by the proposed mixed commission should extend to those "other than insolvency not imputable to the same impediments or delays."

In return for the United States agreeing not to levy a tax on exports to Great Britain (which was prohibited by the United States Constitution!)[41] that country should guarantee the importation of lumber duty-free from the United States in American vessels, should consent to a reduction of impost on rice and whale oil, and should allow salt to be exported free from Turk's Island to the United States in American vessels.

Jay included some "rules for treatment of neutrals by belligerents in time of war." These were taken from the treaty of amity and commerce of 1778 between the United States and France, and represented American definitions of international law as embodied in subsequent treaties with The Netherlands, Prussia, and Sweden. They laid down the principle that free ships make free goods, and protected passengers on neutral ships other than persons embodied in the armed forces of the enemy. Contraband was defined as including warlike implements only and a list of noncontraband was enumerated. It included raw materials, grain, all foodstuffs, cotton, flax, hemp, naval stores, and lumber. The strength of the definition was weakened by the admission that foodstuffs could be contraband where there existed a "well-founded expectation of reducing

41. Grenville was quick to note this on the margin of the draft.

the enemy by the want thereof." In this case they should be pre-empted not confiscated, with a grant of freight and demurrage; that is, Great Britain's policy under the Order-in-Council of June 8, 1793. Neutral property on enemy ships was to be good prize except such as had been laden within stipulated periods before the declaration of war. This would have reversed the principle of the *consolato del mare,* the British practice, by which enemy goods on neutral ships were prize and neutral goods on enemy ships free. Passports and ship's letters were to serve as evidence of ship's cargo to searching parties, and the size of the searching parties was to be strictly limited. Lack of such passports or papers was not to deprive a vessel's owners of the chance of proving its innocence. Naval officers were to be subject to the law of the land in which they found themselves. Finally, an article provided that before the condemnation of a ship by a prize court be carried into execution, due copies of all judicial proceedings should be delivered to the commander of the vessel.[42]

With exception of the British contention as to food-stuffs being contraband in certain circumstances, not a single one of the above proposals contained in Jay's draft of September 30 was included in the final text of the treaty. It is difficult to understand why Jay allowed himself to submit such an avalanche of neutral rights and other American propositions, especially as to the frontier, and then to permit his position rapidly to melt away in the face of Grenville's refusal. Few experienced diplomatists, if it could be avoided, would care to send home such testimony of surrender. Apparently Jay did not. The reader's attention is called

42. Jay's draft of September 30, P.R.O.,F.O., 95, 512.

for further study of this draft to Appendix III of this volume, where a full comparison of the draft and the actual treaty is presented.

Whether Grenville might have accepted ultimately any of these proposals, many of which were very reasonable, will never be known. Ten days previously he had received news from Hammond [43] that made the outlook much brighter for England. As to the United States' joining another Armed Neutrality, Hammond assured Grenville that there was little danger, an assurance which came from Alexander Hamilton himself. Hamilton had said, "with great seriousness and with every demonstration of sincerity . . . that, . . . it was the settled policy of this Government in every contingency, even in that of an open contest with Great Britain, to avoid entangling itself with European connexions, which could only tend to involve this country in disputes wherein it might have no possible interest, and commit it in a common cause with allies, from whom, in the moment of danger, it could derive no succour. In support of this policy, Mr. Hammond urged many of the arguments advanced in your Lordship's despatch, the dissimilitude between the political views, as well as between the general interests of the United States and those of the two Baltic powers, and the inefficiency of the latter, from their enfeebled condition, either to protect the navigation of the former in Europe or to afford it any active assistance, if necessary, in its own territory."

Hammond could not say whether the proposed Swedish propositions had been received from Pinckney.

43. Grenville to Hammond, Oct. 2, 1794, ibid., 115, 3; Mayo, *Instructions,* p. 68.

From Hamilton's decided manner Hammond believed
that the matter had received his attention before and
that what he had stated represented the deliberations of
himself and the American Administration.[44]

Such was the case. The fifth article of Jay's instructions, mentioning the possibility of sounding Russia,
Sweden, or Denmark as to an alliance on the principles
of the Armed Neutrality, must be regarded as wholly
the work of Randolph. The fact that Russia, close
maritime ally of Britain, is represented by Randolph
as a possible armed neutral shows that the Secretary of
State must have had little comprehension of the Baltic
question at the time Jay's instructions were penned. It
is certain that he had no knowledge of the Scandinavian
convention. Even if he had resources for secret information of the convention before it was made public in
April, it could not have reached the United States in
time to have been of use in drafting Jay's instructions.
Hamilton wrote the Secretary of State a few weeks
before the above-quoted interview with Hammond
that this part of the instructions did not meet the sanction of his opinion.[45]

44. Hammond to Grenville, N. Y., Aug. 3, 1794, Rec'd Sept. 20,
P.R.O.,F.O., 5, 5; Mayo, *Instructions*, p. 54 n.

45. "The United States have peculiar advantages from situation,
which would thereby be thrown into common stock without an
equivalent. Denmark and Sweden are too weak and too remote to
render a coöperation useful; and the entanglements of a treaty with
them might be found very inconvenient. The United States had better
stand upon their own ground.

"If a war, on the question of neutral rights, should take place,
common interest would likely secure all the coöperation which is
practicable, and occasional arrangements may be made. What already
has been done in this respect, appears, therefore, to be sufficient."
Hamilton to Randolph, Phila., July 8, 1794, *Works*, IV, 571.

This amazing revelation by Alexander Hamilton to the British Minister at Philadelphia is a striking example of that evolution of American foreign policy subsequently elaborated in the classic Farewell Address of Washington—which Hamilton drafted.[46] His warning against foreign "entanglements"—the word has been good coinage ever since—was restated later in Monroe's famous message of 1823.[47] Several weeks after the treaty of 1794 had been signed, the event not being then known in the United States, Hamilton told Hammond that the matter of a possible alliance with the Baltic Powers had been discussed in the Cabinet and that it had been agreed that in no circumstances would such a political connection be expedient. Apart from the obvious considerations against such a step, the country was in too unsettled a condition (this was just after the Whiskey Rebellion) to admit of "entangling itself in connexions which might eventually have a tendency to add a participation in the disputes of Europe to the internal causes of agitation." Hammond could not learn whether the cause of the discussion in the Cabinet was the proposal made by Engeström.[48] One thing is certain. There was no danger of the United

46. Washington, *Writings,* XIII, 277.

47. By asserting that here is the true origin of that part of the Monroe Doctrine which avoids foreign entanglements the writer does not mean to state that the idea never before had been mentioned by American statesmen, but that here for the first time it was adopted as a national policy. See the writer's article, "Washington's Farewell Address: A Foreign Policy of Independence," *A.H.R.,* XXXIX 250–68. Felix Gilbert has analyzed the European and American political ideology which lay behind concepts leading *To The Farewell Address* (Princeton, 1961).

48. Hammond to Grenville, Jan. 5, 1795, P.R.O.,F.O., 5, 9; Mayo, *Instructions,* p. 67 n.

States' entering the Baltic combination, as Secretary of State Randolph had continued to suggest.[49] Jay, on the spot in London, had no serious ear open in that direction. On the contrary, he expressed himself against a foreign-entanglement policy as strongly as Hamilton.[50]

Jay did not ignore altogether the Swedes and Danes. Soon after his arrival, Thomas Pinckney, the regular Minister of the United States, asked Engeström for a copy of the Scandinavian convention, "for the purpose, probably, of showing it to Sir [sic] Jay." [51] Later, August 10, Engeström wrote home: "In the beginning Sir Jay avoided me and I let him go his way. When he saw the affair did not go as fast as he expected he looked me up and confided in me. He sees the thing as I do. He is shown all possible courtesy, but as yet has received only promises and no final assurances." [52]

There appears nothing in Jay's correspondence or among the official documents concerning the treaty submitted to the Senate, or among the few unpublished dispatches relating to the negotiation which are now

49. Randolph to Jay, May 27, 1794, *A.S.P.,F.R.*, I, 194; Randolph, Secretary of State, to the Secretaries of the Treasury and of War, and to the Attorney General of the United States, June 30, 1794. State Department Records, Domestic Letters, VII, 5, National Archives.

50. "As to a political connection with any country, I hope it will never be judged necessary, for I very much doubt whether it would ultimately be found useful; it would, in my opinion, introduce foreign influence, which I consider as the worst of political plagues." Jay to Washington, Sept. 13, 1794, *Corres. of J. Jay*, IV, 59. "To cast ourselves into the arms of any other nation would, in my opinion, be degrading and puerile; nor, in my opinion, ought we to form any political connection with any foreign power." Same to same, March 6, 1795, ibid., 168.

51. Engeström to the Chancellor of the Kingdom, July 1, 1794, Swedish Royal Archives, Anglica.

52. Same to same, Aug. 12, 1794, ibid.

preserved in the State Department archives, to show
that Jay had anything to do with the Armed Neutrality
negotiators.[53] He seems to have done no more than to
listen politely to them and possibly to have held in hand
the contingency of cooperation in case he failed to
reach an arrangement with Great Britain. The instructions of the Swedish Chancellor to his London
Minister, November 4, 1794, indicate that the timorous
policy of the professedly armed neutrals would not have
budged from peace even if the United States had been
driven to war:

> When in pursuance of his instructions the
> Minister von Ehrenheim questioned Count von
> Bernstorff about the American accession, the an-
> swer of the latter was that the idea would not be
> blotted out altogether but that for the present it
> could not be accomplished.
>
> According to his ideas the American States are
> no longer neutral, at least it is not certain they can
> continue to be. During such a negotiation the
> American Minister at London might possibly be
> badly treated, which would stop everything, and
> these considerations are so important to him on
> this account that it would not be difficult for him to
> postpone the matter until it could be seen with
> certainty where it leads. But notwithstanding all
> these reasons given by Count von Bernstorff, you
> are to take *ad referendum* the answer which comes
> from America on the first proposition. You are in
> the best position to judge of the situation between

53. The manuscripts of the Jay Papers relating to the negotiation of
1794, now preserved in the collections of the New York Historical
Society, have been examined, with no results.

England and the United States and to how great
an extent that can be so precarious as to make an
opening of negotiations with them contrary to the
neutrality system adopted by Sweden, which must
be maintained however the matter may develop.[54]

The response of the United States to the Swedish
proposal is revealed in a dispatch to the Secretary of
State from Thomas Pinckney, dated London, March 7,
1796, upon his return to England after the negotiation
of the Spanish treaty of 1795:

I transmitted to the Department of State inclosed
in my letter of 5th May, 1794, a proposal from
the Court of Sweden; in a subsequent letter dated
10th December I recalled the attention of Mr.
Randolph to the subject, but I have never heard
a syllable in reply. I was frequently asked for an
answer by the Swedish Minister here before I
went to Spain, and lately again on my return to
this country I received another application on the
subject. It appears to me that respect to a friendly
power requires that some attention should be
paid to a similar proposal, and even if it is directly
declined or taken *ad referendum,* that I should be
authorized to say so.[55]

54. The Chancellor of the Kingdom to Engeström, Nov. 14, 1794,
Swedish Royal Archives, Anglica. Ehrenheim was Swedish Minister
at Copenhagen.

55. Dispatches, Eng., III. "In conversation a few days past with
Baron Stael, ambassador from Sweden, he informed me of a communication formerly made by the court of Sweden to Mr. Pinckney
at London, for our Government, and upon which no answer was
given, although it was much wished. I desired his communication in
writing, that I might forward it to you, and which was accordingly

The treaty finally signed by Jay of course ended all possibility of any accession by the United States to the abortive Armed Neutrality of the North. Judging from the opinion of Hamilton, of the Cabinet, of Jay, and from the above-quoted Pinckney dispatch, there was never any such possibility. "The agreement by which the American agent, Jay, has just terminated the dispute between England and America, breaks absolutely this *liaison*," the French representative at Copenhagen wrote to Paris following an interview with the Danish Chancellor.[56]

If Hamilton in his conversations with the British Minister in the summer of 1794 put into practice what since has become a notable tradition of American foreign policy, he nevertheless released such ideas at a time particularly unpropitious for the success of Jay's ambitious treaty draft of September 30. From Hamilton's astonishingly gratuitous information Grenville now knew that there was no danger of what he most feared, that the United States might enter another armed neutrality. Support by the United States might have given strength at a critical moment to this combination of French diplomacy and the neutral protests of the Baltic Powers. But the two Scandinavian nations could not stand alone against the allied navies of Great

given, and is herewith transmitted. I have no doubt that whatever he says to me is known to the committee [of Public Safety?] as I was informed by some of the members in the beginning of the winter, and before the Baron arrived, that such an application had been made to us from that quarter. It belongs to me only to forward this paper, and which I do, not doubting that I shall receive instructions relative thereto, in the most suitable manner." J. Monroe to the Secretary of State, Paris, July 6, 1795, *A.S.P.,F.R.,* I, 719.

56. Arch. Aff. Étrang., Danemark, Vol. 170, p. 232.

Britain and Russia. The force of the abortive Armed
Neutrality of 1794 expired when the Empress of Russia, in entire accord with Great Britain, on July 30
notified the Swedish and Danish Courts that a Russian
fleet would be stationed in the Baltic Sea to detain all
neutral ships bound or freighted for France.[57]

If there had remained any nervousness on Grenville's
part lest American accession should stiffen the Armed
Neutrality, Alexander Hamilton's assurances to Hammond in Philadelphia had quieted that. He now knew
every one of the cards. No longer was there any reason
why he should even listen to a recital of Jay's propositions for the tender treatment of neutral commerce
and navigation. There was no longer any reason for
haste in the negotiation. Jay, on the other hand, had
grown nervous and timid as the conversations at the
Foreign Office wore on. He could not read his adversary's hand. He feared that in the whirlpool of European polity unforeseen circumstances might rise to de-
range the British Ministry or its attitude toward the
United States and make any adjustment impossible.[58]
The negotiation proceeded leisurely along, on Grenville's part, for six weeks more. Grenville's only further concession was to consent to the principle of a joint

57. The Empress delayed coming to a definite alliance with Great
Britain because of unwillingness to send troops to western Europe,
but by a treaty signed February 18, 1795, Great Britain agreed to
furnish a squadron of 12 ships-of-the-line, including 708 guns and a
crew of 4,560 men, which fleet should remain annually in the Baltic
from May to October. Russia agreed to protect British dominions
(Hanover) with 10,000 infantry and 200 horse. *Parliamentary History,*
XXXII, 212. See also dispatches of the British Minister at St. Petersburg (Charles Whitworth) during the summer of 1794, P.R.O.,F.O.
(Russia), 65, 27; and *Annual Register,* 1795, pp. 274–75.

58. *Corres. of J. Jay,* IV, 58.

survey of the northwest boundary gap, looking to a settlement of the boundary there at some future time. Other new points in Jay's draft of September 30 he declared to be "insurmountable obstacles." [59] He had submitted the later drafts of the treaty to Lord Hawkesbury, President of the Committee of the Council for Trade and Plantations. Hawkesbury opposed the article admitting American ships of limited tonnage to the British West Indies, but went along with the whole Cabinet when it endorsed the final draft.[60]

Convinced that he could get no better terms,[61] that on the whole what he had were satisfactory, the American plenipotentiary affixed his signature, November 19, 1794, to the treaty which since has borne his name.

59. Grenville to Jay, Oct. 7, 1794, *Dropmore Papers,* III, 516.

60. Bradford Perkins, *First Rapproachment,* p. 4. Professor Perkins printed Hawkesbury's memorandum on Grenville's "Heads of Proposals to be made to Mr. Jay," in his article on "Lord Hawkesbury and the Jay-Grenville Negotiations," *Miss. Vall. Hist. Rev.,* XL (1953–54), 291–304.

61. Letters of Jay to Ellsworth, Washington, Hamilton, King, Randolph, Nov. 19, 1794, *Corres. of J. Jay,* IV, 133–144.

# CHAPTER 13

# The Treaty

A GREAT many judgments, widely varying in nature, have been rendered by historical writers on Jay's Treaty, but, so far as the present investigator is aware, none has been based upon an adequate examination of the diplomacy that preceded it. It is hoped that the objective study of Anglo-American diplomatic history between the treaty of peace of 1783 and the treaty of amity and commerce of 1794 which has been presented in these pages may help to form a reasoned opinion as to the advantages or disadvantages of the latter treaty to each party and as to the professional ability of the negotiators. With such a summary we shall conclude this study in commerce and diplomacy.

Let us begin the analysis with a comparison of the position of each Government, at the beginning of the Jay-Grenville negotiations, with the final terms of the treaty. Let us note the minimum and maximum demands of each Government at the outset and the concessions it was prepared ultimately to make. We can then conclude how much more or less than the original minimum each negotiator was able to get; how much ground, if any, was given; how great a surplus of advantages over his *sine qua non* each gained. We may judge how skillfully the respective plenipotentiaries governed themselves by the political circumstances which existed during the negotiation.

Since the negotiation was conducted by the Secretary for Foreign Affairs personally, there are in the Foreign Office no written instructions setting forth definitely the British position at the beginning of the conversations with Jay. But in the private papers of Lord Grenville, preserved at Dropmore, there is an unprinted document entitled, "Project of Heads of Proposals to be made to Mr. Jay." [1] It summarizes with precision the British position and gives a measure of the concessions England had decided to make and the demands she would insist upon. It is divided into four main heads: Posts and Boundary, Debts, Neutral Code, Treaty of Commerce.

As to "Posts and Boundary," the document indicates that evacuation would be agreed to, the actual "cession" not to take place until the summer of 1796, in order to leave time for the traders to remove their effects from American territory. But evacuation was not to be considered to interrupt the "usual course of communication and commerce" between Canada and the Indian nations "to the southward and eastward of the Lakes," and British subjects were to be free to pass and repass with their goods and merchandise over the boundary line and to possess warehouses "in all parts of the territory now possessed or which may hereafter be possessed by the United States." A reciprocal claim if made by the United States might be conceded for freedom of communication and commerce with the Indian nations north of the boundary. Passage over portages and water communications and "roads adjoining thereto" was to be free to British

1. See Appendix II in this volume.

subjects. It was not definitely stipulated just what places this referred to or whether it included reciprocal rights for Americans. There was to be "an unlimited freedom of internal trade and communication between the two Canadas and the United States." The northwest boundary line was "to be carried from Lake Superior to the Lake of the Woods so as to communicate with the navigable part of the said River [Mississippi] at a point to be fixed, and the British shall be free to enter freely into the Bays and Ports and Creeks on the American side, and to land and dwell there, for the purpose of their commerce, in the same manner as in other parts of the United States."

As to debts, their recovery "with interest thereupon from the time of being contracted" was stipulated. A joint commission, to which appeals could be directed from American courts, was to execute this guaranty; and when "strict legal evidence," because of lapse of time or impediments to recovery, did not exist, claimants might petition the commission, presenting any kind of evidence, which the commissioners should "judge equitably and impartially, according to the circumstances." The United States Government was to assume payment of all debts validated by the commission.

As to a "Neutral Code," a treaty embodying most-favored-nation privileges might be signed. "Vessels captured or detained on suspicion of carrying enemy property or Contraband," were to be brought into prize-court without delay. A marginal note here indicates a possibility of discussing a definition of contraband, particularly in connection with the status of provisions. "The present Situation of the West Indies prevents the necessity of any *prospective* regulation as to the neutral commerce in that part of the world." A mixed commission might be established to "inquire into the cases of captures or condemnations when any captures or condemnations shall appear to have been irregular and contrary to the Laws of Nations," and indemnification for established illegal spoliations was to be made by the British Government. The commission might require claimants first to exhaust the resources of the highest admiralty courts. Its adjudications were to be governed by the acceptance in advance of certain stipulated rules: enemy property on neutral ships and "all military and naval stores bound to the Ports of the enemy, or destined for their use" were defined as lawful prize, as were vessels with false papers and cargoes. All products of the French Islands shipped to the United States, or goods shipped from the United States to the islands were to be good prize, subject in effect to the Rule of the War of 1756.

A treaty of commerce might be acceptable, the Project advises, on the following conditions: that no tariff discrimination be levied by either party against the commerce of the other; that no tonnage duties be levied on the ships of one in the ports of the other party higher than on its own ships; that no new prohibitions be levied by either country on the importation of goods of the growth, produce, or manufacture of the other, such agreement to bind Great Britain only in her European dominions. Any *temporary* proposal in regard to American commerce with the British West Indies should be of such a nature as to give the United States an interest in Britain's retaining those colonies. In case of infraction of any of the commercial articles the other commercial articles of the treaty were not to be infringed or suspended, until after "regular application" should have been made and due notice should have been given to the other party. In case of a rupture all just debts were to be secure and all nationals should be at liberty to depart from enemy territory.

Such were Britain's terms. She was willing to give up the posts provided payment of debts was guaranteed, provided the fur trade was secured to her to the south and west of the Great Lakes and provided the American West was opened as a future free-trade market through Canada as a vestibule. To appease the United States she would consent to a commercial treaty. It must needs embody the *status quo,* with possible temporary concessions in the British West Indies. But a reciprocal guaranty would be necessary against future tariff and tonnage discriminations (this reciprocity not to apply to the West Indies) and a mutual protection against sequestration or confiscation of private funds. She would not recognize definitions of international law which condemned the Rule of the War of 1756 or the right to take enemy property or contraband, as defined by English courts, from neutral ships. She also desired certain advantageous boundary rectifications. These were not the immutable British conditions precedent to any treaty. Some of them were indeed abandoned, and we shall see that additional·advantages, not included among these stipulated conditions, were secured. Since the Project is in the nature of a memorandum only, and the British negotiation was governed by Grenville's personal discretion, we can only guess which demands were considered indispensable.

How do the equivalents which Britain secured in the treaty in return for evacuation of the posts and indemnity for spoliations compare with the terms outlined in the Grenville Project? In the first place, the debts article did not stipulate a guaranty of interest *durante bello,* but left to the mixed commission, ruling by majority vote (it eventually proved to be a majority of three English commissioners against two Americans) judgment of all claims "whether of principal or of interest." Second, the spoliations commission was not made subordinate in jurisdiction to the rules outlined in the Project, but the principle of taking enemy property from neutral ships was written into the treaty itself. Third, Grenville did not secure the attempted rectification of the northwest boundary line; this question was disposed of by a formula which admitted of its postponement without prejudice to the contentions of either party. Finally, English manufactures and products did not acquire a backdoor *free-trade* entrance into the American West. The last two points reflected the far-sighted ambitions of traders and frontier officials who looked to the time when both Indians and fur-bearing animals should have disappeared from the region of the Great Lakes and the Mississippi Valley, when that vast domain, filled with an English-speaking population, would form a valuable market for English products imported by the St. Lawrence and Great Lakes, and by a communication therefrom to the "navigable waters" of the Mississippi. Their acceptance by the United States would have been a serious embarrassment to the tariff revenue and a heavy servitude on sovereignty. There is no indication that they were pressed vigorously by Grenville. Jay, at any rate, deserves credit for resisting them as a matter of principle.

One should note, however, that, subject to general prohibitions and tariffs on either side, trade across the frontier by land and inland navigation was opened to either party reciprocally: further, there was nothing in Article III to forbid British goods from being imported across the frontier into the United States (subject to most-favored-nation tariff or to general prohibitions); this allowed a backdoor entrance but not a free-trade entrance into the United States via Canada; again, British ships might carry goods from the ocean up the Mississippi to American customers (subject to general tariffs and prohibitions) in as ample a manner as to American Atlantic ports, but American ships could not take American goods, or any goods, up the St. Lawrence to Canada from the sea.

If Great Britain did not secure in full all of the desirable but partially impossible advantages, the treaty contained everything else that was desired, as well as an abundance of advantages not stipulated in the Project. The fur trade with the Indians south of the American boundary was safeguarded and the reciprocity equivalent for American citizens north of the line was emasculated by the exception of the territories within the dominions of the Hudson's Bay Company. By a curious impertinence Article II of the treaty permitted the United States to extend its own settlements within its own territory, before the date stipulated for evacuation, "to any part within the said boundary line except within the precincts or jurisdiction of the said posts." Permanent freedom of passage over the portages inter-

lacing the boundary line satisfied the demands of the
North West traders by securing the best route to the
fur preserves of the Far West. In providing for the
adjudication and assumption by the United States
Government of the pre-war debts the treaty did not
specifically deny the British claim to interest from the
date of contract of the debts, without reference to suspension during time of war. Great Britain secured
compensation for spoliations by French privateers fitted
out in American harbors, the right to have her warships hospitably received, and a guaranty that British
naval officers on shore should be treated "with the respect due their commissions." British privateers might
be admitted into American harbors with their prizes,
and neither party should so receive privateers or prizes
of the other's enemy (nothing in the treaty, however,
was to contravene previous stipulations between the
United States and other powers). Great Britain secured a ten-year guaranty against any future tariff and
tonnage discrimination—the great bugbear which the
Ministry had been trying to destroy for four years—
and the right to levy countervailing duties in England
on American goods and ships to the extent of wiping
away the difference in duty encountered by British and
by American ships in American harbors. Thus at one
stroke was the purpose of the American navigation
laws of 1789 and 1790 neutralized—though the benefits of neutral carriage continued during the war to give
to American carrying interests the same advantages
which the now frustrated shipping policy had been designed to achieve. And this privilege of countervailing
duties was granted despite the fact that the light and
Trinity dues on foreign shipping in English harbors

more than balanced any discrimination in the United States against foreign vessels. Even the concession to American shipping in the West Indies would have proven advantageous to England by releasing badly needed tonnage from the trade between the islands and the United States and diverting it to European use, while at the same time it would have delivered over to British ships the European carriage of the principal West Indian products, whatever their nationality.[2] The commercial articles of the treaty merely set a seal on already satisfactory conditions, and did this in return for very desirable guaranties.

Now consider the negotiation and the treaty from the American point of view.

Jay's instructions, as we have seen, laid down only two "immutable" conditions: (a) no deviation "from our treaties or engagements with France"; (b) no treaty of commerce without an entrance for American ships of at least limited tonnage into the British West Indies. Hamilton's statement to Hammond had indicated as the indispensable basis of any friendly adjustment the evacuation of the posts and indemnification for the Caribbean spoliations. Hamilton's letters to Jay had outlined the terms which in the last resort might be accepted: evacuation of American territory, indemnification for spoliations not justifiable by the Order of June 8, 1793, or the Rule of 1756; if necessary the acceptance, for a limited period, of the existing commercial relations, without a treaty of commerce.

These indispensable conditions Jay succeeded in writing into the treaty, and a very little more: namely, reciprocal trading privileges with Indians in Canada

2. Mahan, *Sea Power and the War of 1812*, I, 96.

exclusive of the territory of the Hudson's Bay Company, a mixed commission to settle the northeastern boundary, direct trading privileges with the British East Indies. Article XIII legalized an American trade with the British East Indies hitherto enjoyed on British sufferance, as a carriage incidental to the American China trade. It proved to be of much more advantage to the United States than doubtless either party realized at the time of making the treaty. During the long years of European war that followed, British courts interpreted an article to allow an American carriage between British Indian ports and neutral European countries by a circuitous voyage between India and the United States.[3] Outside of these privileges and of the conventional articles regarding pirates, privateers, extradition, consuls, etc., the United States secured no commercial concessions other than those enjoyed before the treaty. The one strictly limited privilege of entry into the West Indies was rejected by the Senate because of the onerous conditions attached, which prevented exportation of molasses, sugar, coffee, or cotton from the United States. The restraints which this twelfth article would have placed on American exportations of West Indian products would have cut off the re-exportation not only of English but also of French and all other foreign West Indian products, and incidentally it would have prevented for the period of the war then in existence between Great Britain and France the development of American domestic cotton export, the prospective importance of which nobody then appreciated.

3. Holden Furber, "The Beginnings of American Trade with India, 1784–1812," *New England Quarterly,* XI (1938), 235–65.

Jay was Chief Justice of the United States as well as Plenipotentiary Extraordinary to Great Britain. The Constitution had made treaties the law of the land and the federal courts were adjudicating cases involving British debts in a way consistent with the terms of the treaty of peace. Hammond had admitted that there was no cause for complaint against the federal courts in any district except that of Virginia. It is true that over half of all the debts were lodged in that state and that delays prevented the adjudication of a test case until 1793, when it was decided that British creditors might recover all *bona fide* debts except those paid, by state law, into the state treasury during the war. This construction and the matter of acceptable legal evidence as to the existence of a debt remained the sole complaint. In 1796 the Supreme Court of the United States, on appeal from the Virginia district, reversed the lower court's judgment of 1793 on state confiscation of debts during the war.[4] Hammond had written Grenville, at the time the case was in the District Court, that if Jay were on the bench a favorable decision would have been certain.[5] All cases of debts were appealable to the Supreme Court.

As a negotiator Jay should have upheld the sufficiency of the judicial court over which he presided at home by insisting on its competence to interpret the treaty and on the sufficiency of its justice. He could have taken this position with candor and honor and could

4. Hammond to Grenville, June 8, 1792, P.R.O.,F.O., 4, 15; Hammond to Grenville, Dec. 4, 1792, ibid., 4, 16; Hammond to Grenville, No. 1, Jan. 30, 1793, ibid., 5, 1; Ware, Administrator of Jones v. Hilton, III *Dallas* 199, for decision of U. S. Supreme Court in 1796 and complete review of the whole question of British debts in American courts. See Appendix IV in this volume.

5. See note 8, ch. 10.

have maintained it without derogation from the opinions he had expressed when as Secretary for Foreign
Affairs of the Continental Congress he condemned
the infraction of the treaty by the several states. He
could have stressed the increased powers of the new
federal Government and the increased jurisdiction of
its courts. Particularly could he have insisted on this
when he had a valuable equivalent to set over against
the British debts: namely, the claims of American
owners for indemnity for slaves carried away by the
British army. If there is little moral justification, from
the twentieth-century point of view, for the Negro
claims, one is nevertheless constrained to wonder why
Jay so readily threw this weapon out of his armory.
A proper use of it might have brought a public recognition of that satisfaction with the justice of the new
federal courts which the British Minister at Philadelphia had already privately expressed in his dispatches.
Jay's explanations[6] of the use he made of these Negro
claims are not very impressive diplomatically. Jay con-
sented to the stipulation that British claimants need not
exhaust the resources of American justice—at least in
some instances, i.e., British claims for damages promised by the United States on account of captures by
French privateers fitted out in American ports, or by
French privateers in American territorial waters—

6. "In considering the treaty, it will doubtless be remembered, that
there must be two to make a bargain. We could not agree about the
negroes. Was that a good reason for breaking up the negotiation? I
mentioned in a former letter, that I considered our admission into the
islands as affording compensation for the detention of the posts and
other claims of that nature. In that way we obtain satisfaction for the
negroes though not in express words." Jay to Randolph, London,
Feb. 6, 1795, *A.S.P.,F.R.*, I, 518.

before appealing to a mixed debts commission at Philadelphia.

Jay's Treaty failed to secure recognition of the principles of international maritime law which the United States under the Government of the Confederation had written into all of its treaties with friendly foreign powers or allies—France, The Netherlands, Prussia, Sweden—principles which accorded with the definitions of the First Armed Neutrality. On the contrary, the first treaty ratified by the Senate expressly acquiesced in an abeyance of the principles of those treaties. The United States accepted the *consolato del mare* outright, for the duration of the war, in place of the doctrine of free ships free goods; acquiesced in the British Admiralty's definitions of contraband, with pre-emption of foodstuffs, *after*[7] the date of ratification of the treaty; and yielded to the operation of the Rule of 1756 though not accepting it in principle, a concession which was to strengthen tremendously the prestige of that arbitrary dictum. Rights of convoy, rules for visitation and search to prevent undue vexations, specific definition of noncontraband, definition of blockade: all of these liberal principles of former treaties were deserted in Jay's anxiety to secure his minimum of concessions from England in other fields.

Nor was he successful in inserting an article protecting American seamen from impressment. This was not a part of his instructions, to be sure, but it had been the subject of many conversations between Grenville and Thomas Pinckney, the regular minister at London, and was one of the chief objects of Pinckney's diplo-

7. See Appendix V.

macy.[8] The apparent willingness of Grenville early in
the Jay negotiations to accede to such a regulation
seems to have disappeared after he heard from Hammond that there was no chance of the United States'
joining another Armed Neutrality. The nominally reciprocal article to which Jay agreed, which stipulated
that the naval officers of either party—the presence and
deportment of English naval officers in American ports
did not always stimulate public friendliness toward
their persons—should be treated "with the respect due
their commissions," was really one-sided. As an equivalent for it he was unable to incorporate in the treaty his
proposal making such officers amenable to the law of
the land and especially to writs of *habeas corpus* for
the delivery of American citizens detained on their
ships. It is difficult to explain the presence of such unnecessarily humiliating provisions as are found in this
Article XXIII.

Finally, Jay was unable to get recognition of the
principle that Indians dwelling within the territory of
one party should not be interfered with by the other
party. Grenville would not consent to the proposal that
each Government strive to restrain its Indians from
hostility against the other. Nor would he agree not to
use Indian allies in case of war with the United States.
He likewise rejected the proposal, which Hamilton had
formulated, for the absolute limitation of naval armaments on the Great Lakes and the prospective limitation of land armaments on the international frontier.
These well-meant American proposals which have long

8. See Pinckney's dispatches, and Jefferson's instructions to him in
State Dept., Instructions, I and II, and Dispatches, England, I–III.

since been accepted and which for over one hundred years have been a noble example to the world and a step toward even greater limitations, were in 1794 in advance of their time.

The British refusal to agree to these last principles undoubtedly was connected with the hope of the Foreign Office that there might yet be a chance to set up the neutral Indian barrier state before the actual evacuation of the posts in June, 1796, by the terms of the new treaty.[9] The day after the signature of the treaty Grenville instructed Hammond again to bring forward the mediation proposal. This time he was to propose the subject to Hamilton, not to Randolph, the Secretary of State. Should Mr. Hamilton and the American Government not be inclined to any public stipulation in the premises "such an Arrangement might be settled between him and yourself by a secret Understanding or Agreement to be communicated to Lord Dorchester and Lieut. Governor Simcoe. It is particularly desirable for Reasons with which you are not unacquainted that this Matter should be adjusted in the Manner I have mentioned before the Evacuation of the Posts takes

9. The posts were not evacuated until several weeks after the date stipulated in the treaty, June 1, 1796. Major John Bigelow, *Breaches of Anglo-American Treaties* (New York, 1917), p. 17, attributes this delay to dissatisfaction with the terms of the American Treaty of Greenville with the Indians, which was signed before Jay's Treaty. He says "it appears that the original tardiness of Great Britain in providing for the surrender of the posts was another case of her holding them as security for the observance of the treaty by the United States." This guess is correct, but not in the sense surmised by Major Bigelow. A perusal of the correspondence between Grenville and the British Minister in America shows that it was feared that the opposition in the House of Representatives might nullify the treaty ratified by the Senate. The British delayed evacuation, against this contingency.

place." [10] Supplementary instructions were sent to Dorchester and Simcoe.[11] But the French captured the *Tankerville* packet which bore the several dispatches. Before duplicates of the correspondence in the sunken mail-pouch finally arrived in July, 1795, General Anthony Wayne had gathered in the fruits of his victories in a preliminary peace with the Indians, and was even then engaged in negotiating final terms of peace with them. Hammond was already packing his belongings for return to England.

Despite efforts which Wayne alleged were made by the Canadian Indian Department to prevent the Indians from making peace,[12] the Treaty of Greenville was signed with the western tribes on August 3, 1795. It ceded to the United States most of the present State of Ohio, leaving to the natives a broad strip of land along the shore of Lake Erie between the Maumee and Cuyahoga Rivers.[13] Sixteen strategic points in the Northwest Territory were also given up for military' posts, with a right of way to them across Indian lands. Wayne's campaign and his inexorable Indian diplomacy broke the back of the native confederacy and opened the way for the settlement of most of Ohio. The Treaty of Greenville proved the precursor of numerous other Indian cessions during the next fifteen years, by which Indian title to the greater part of the Northwest Territory was extinguished preparatory to opening the lands for government survey. But neither Wayne's

10. Grenville to Hammond, Nov. 20, 1794, P.R.O.,F.O., 115, 3; Mayo, *Instructions,* p. 72.

11. Portland to Dorchester and Simcoe, Nov. 19, 1794, P.R.O.,F.O., 95, 512.

12. Wayne to the Secretary of War, Dec. 23, 1794, *A.S.P.,I.A.,* I, 547.

13. See map, p. 152.

victories nor Jay's Treaty entirely put an end to British intrigues in the American West. The notorious Blount affair of 1796–97 showed that Pitt continued to weigh the possibilities of an alliance with the men of the western waters against Spanish Louisiana, even while the treaty with the United States was before the Senate for ratification.[14] But it must be acknowledged that this was the last serious British intrigue in the West. Wayne's operations checked but did not stop the exasperating support which the Canadian Indian Department gave to its former *protégés*. Nor did the neutral barrier state project die the early death which its chances for success should have indicated. It recurred in the maps and plans of the Foreign Office at intervals until the negotiations at Ghent in 1815 marked its final demise. Tecumseh's confederation of 1811 and his relations with the British, their alliance with the Indians in the War of 1812, the vital strategical importance of the Great Lakes during that conflict, the renewal at Ghent of the neutral barrier project, the resurrection there of the rectification proposal to bring Canada south to the "navigable waters" of the Mississippi, all testify that British ambitions in the American West did not cease with the ratification of Jay's Treaty.

It cannot be said positively whether Hammond actually made proposals to Hamilton to adopt secretly the principle of mediation. Hammond wrote before sailing, in August, 1795, that he had arranged for a final conference with Hamilton and Jay on the subject.[15]

14. See F. J. Turner, "The Diplomatic Contest for the Mississippi Valley," *Atlantic Monthly*, XCIII (1904), 676, 807.

15. Hammond to Grenville, Aug. 14, 1795, P.R.O.,F.O., 5, 9. The only inkling of the nature of this conversation with Hamilton which

Jay was then Governor of New York and Hamilton
had retired to private life, after waiting until the crisis
of the British negotiation and the Whiskey Rebellion
had been safely passed.[16] His resignation toward the
end of the year 1794 was caused by the necessity of
repairing a badly depleted private fortune and by
injured feelings due to the action of the House of Representatives in appointing a committee to report on
means of raising additional revenue instead of referring the matter to the Secretary of the Treasury, the
procedure previously followed. But as a private citizen
Hamilton's counsel weighed decisively with President
Washington throughout his Administration—as we
know, for example, from the history of the Farewell
Address. Indeed, it dominated President Adams's Cabinet in the first year of his Administration, as the second
President was to discover to his discomposure. Jay, too,
remained an active captain of Federalist cohorts. What
the result was of Hammond's final interview with these

the writer has been able to find is the following: "Mr. Hammond
told me that Colonel Hamilton told him the day before he left New
York that the demagogic party would have a majority in the house
of Representatives." Entry at London, Nov. 26, 1795, *Diary and Letters
of Gouverneur Morris*, II, 136.

16. One might wonder whether the Whiskey Rebellion had any
effect on the Jay-Grenville negotiations. It apparently did not. The
dispatches of Hammond to Grenville considered that the Government
could overcome the insurrection. He refused to give any encouragement to two different delegations of the insurrectionists who visited
him at Philadelphia. The treaty was signed by Grenville before news
had been received from Hammond of the extinction of the rebellion.
Thus it cannot be said that the show of increased vigor by the Government in putting down this insurrection had any influence on Grenville.
Nor is there any indication that he was impressed by the rebellion as
indicating any weakness of the federal Government. See Hammond to
Grenville, Aug. 29, Sept. 5, 28, Nov. 12, P.R.O.,F.O., 5, 5.

two high priests of Federalism we do not know. The Minister chose to report it orally.

Hammond's recall was the result of an exchange of private notes between Grenville and Jay immediately after the treaty was signed. Grenville professed a desire to eliminate the acrimonious correspondence that had been going on at Philadelphia and to remove the "influence of personal animosities and individual contests" which might endanger the work of conciliation just completed. The Secretary declared he could answer for Mr. Hammond's ceasing to use a tone similar to that emanating from the Department of State— through Randolph—and readily adopting a language better suited to the new situation. He hoped that the United States Government would reach a similar resolution; it was immaterial whether the sentiments were to be conveyed through Randolph or some other channel. Jay answered that his conviction that the mutual efforts of the two negotiators to restore "good humour and good will . . . should be continued beyond the date of the treaty" made him happy that their sentiments coincided in this respect. In turn he suggested that Hammond be transferred from Philadelphia.[17] So far as Randolph was concerned this problem was solved soon after Jay's return by Washington's dismissal of the Secretary of State because of his questionable relations with the French Minister.[18] It is not im-

17. Grenville to Jay (secret and confidential), Nov. 21, 1794, ibid., 95, 512; Jay to Grenville, November 22, 1794, *Corres. of J. Jay,* IV, 145.

18. The Fauchet "No. 10" dispatch of Oct. 31, 1794, and the previous dispatches to which it refers, are printed in Turner, *Corres. French Ministers.* The editor gives references to the literature on the subject. See also Channing, *Hist. U. S.,* IV, 144, notes 1 and 2.

"Randolph's Ruin" is an episode belonging to the history of the

possible that the exchange of notes between Jay and Grenville may have been a factor in determining Washington to call for Randolph's resignation. Hammond was duly recalled and promoted to the post of Undersecretary for Foreign Affairs.[19]

A question inseparable from any discussion of Jay's Treaty is its bearing on Franco-American relations. Article XXV, which provides for friendly reception of the privateers and ships of war and their prizes within the ports of each party, and which forbids shelter in the ports of one party to prizes taken by the enemies of the other, stipulates, among other things: "Nothing in this treaty contained shall, however, be construed or operate contrary to former and existing public treaties with other sovereigns or States." This proviso speaks obviously of the terms of the whole treaty, not of those particularly in Article XXV, which article was contrary to the Franco-American treaty of 1778 that allowed the reception of French prizes in American harbors and

---

ratification of Jay's Treaty rather than to the subject of the present study, the negotiation of that convention. The tendency of recent historians has been to acquit Randolph of any treachery toward his country or disloyalty to President Washington. See Dice Robbins Anderson in *Am. Secs. State*, II (1927), 149–55; Irving Brant in *Wm. and Mary Quar.*, 3rd Series, VII (April 1950); Alexander De-Conde, *Entangling Alliance* (1957) and Carroll and Ashworth in Vol. VII (1958) of Douglas S. Freeman's *George Washington*.

The following passage quoted from the French Minister Adet's dispatch of August 26, 1795, anent Fauchet's interview at Newport with Randolph and the efforts of the French Legation to exonerate the disgraced Secretary, throws light on Randolph's real attitude toward the fate of the treaty: "M. Randolph m'a assuré que si nous fournissions les moyens de se justifier, la Chambre de réprésentans s' opposeroit à l'exécution du traité." See Turner, p. 776.

19. Grenville to Hammond, private, Dec. 9, 1794, *Dropmore Papers*, II, 651.

forbade the reception therein of prizes captured from French subjects; and it was exhibited by itself, before the rest of the treaty was published, as evidence of good faith, to the French Government. It is significant, however, that the proviso is tucked away in the middle of Article XXV and not made a separate article by itself as it should have been if a wish for clarity were the dominating desire of the negotiators.

If it be said that nothing actually contained in the treaty was contrary to the Franco-American treaty, aside from this Article XXV—for which exception was expressly made—one must remember that the treaty specifically agreed for the period of the war to the British practice of taking enemy property from neutral ships. That the United States reserved itself in principle on this point was nothing to France. It was only in time of war, particularly in time of war with England, that the neutral code of the Franco-American treaty of 1778 could be esteemed of value to France. Nor by accepting compensation for illegal spoliation "under color" of the British Order-in-Council did the United States destroy the principle of those Orders. The question of principle was sunken for the period of the war. After the ratification of Jay's Treaty the situation continued to be governed by British Orders-in-Council according to the discretion of the Admiralty.[20]

20. Grenville interpreted the treaty's reference to contraband (i.e., "It is agreed that whenever such articles [namely provisions and other articles, not generally contraband], so becoming contraband, according to the existing law of nations, shall for that reason, be seized, the same shall not be confiscated" but pre-empted) to sanction the procedure of pre-emption followed under the Provision Order of June 8, 1793 (Grenville to Bond, chargé d'affaires at Philadelphia after Hammond's departure; Nov. 4, 1795, P.R.O.,F.O., 115, 4). A secret

Whatever reservations may be argued in theory, and whatever money compensation may have been received in fact for spoliations "under color," the United States by Jay's Treaty acquiesced in practice in the British system of maritime law. In so far as this was the case our conduct was helpful to England and harmful to France, our ally, who could with some show of reason accuse us of being in collusion with the hostile purposes of her enemy. The effect on France was so injurious that a recent French scholar has described the treaty as "almost equivalent to a treaty of alliance," a "submission for the period of the war to all British

---

Order-in-Council of April 25, 1795, in effect restored the instructions of the Provision Order of June 8, 1793, which, it will be remembered, had been quietly suspended during the negotiations with Jay. But Article VII of the Treaty gave the spoliation commission power to judge all alleged spoliations up to the time of ratification of the treaty, which occured Oct. 28, 1795. According to J. B. Moore, *International Arbitrations*, I, 310, the Order was revoked after it was given out to naval commanders and the American majority on the London spoliations commission decreed that compensation should be made for spoliations made under color of it as well as under the Orders existing before the treaty was signed. For further explanation of interpretations by this commission see Appendix V.

The secret order of April 25, 1795, was never published until an American student more than a century later secured a copy from the British archives. See Josiah T. Newcomb, "New Light on Jay's Treaty," *Amer. Jour. International Law*, XXVIII, 685–93, where the text is published. If anything, it was more severe than the Order of June 8, 1793, because it instructed naval officers to bring in not only all ships loaded with corn or other provisions suspected of proceeding to France or to ports occupied by the armies of France, but also all ships "which they shall have reason to believe are laden *on account of the said persons* [i.e. shippers under feigned names and destinations] *or any other of His Majesty's enemies.*" This last condition laid the cargoes, and even the ships wholly so laden, open to confiscation as enemy property rather than pre-emption as neutrally owned contraband.

claims." [21] This judgment is scarcely an accurate statement of the case.

Could Jay have had a better treaty? The writer has already suggested that he might have more ably defended the judicial competency of the American federal courts, and that there are certain expressions in the treaty unnecessarily humiliating to the United States. Jay's unsuccess as to the debts must also be regarded as one of the glaring deficiencies of the negotiation. Whether Grenville if harder pressed might have acceded to the American proposals as to the Indians and the regulation of the frontier is worthy of speculation. British territorial and commercial ambitions were strong in the American West, but not so important to England's economic and political prosperity as was the commerce of the Atlantic and the American market. It is the writer's opinion that if these proposals had been pushed hard enough they might have succeeded. As to the neutral code and American definitions of international maritime law, it was hopeless to expect that Britain would relinquish her position unless compelled to do so by armed force. On this point Jay had no illusions. "That Britain, at this period," he wrote, sending home the treaty, "and involved in war, should not admit principles, which would impeach the propriety of her conduct in seizing provisions bound to France, and enemy's property on board of neutral vessels, does not appear to me extraordinary. The articles, as they now stand, secure compensation for

21. R. Guyot, *Le Directoire et la paix de l'Europe, 1795–1799* (Paris, 1911), p. 558. This author, who takes the copy of the treaty in the *Moniteur* of Nov. 16, 1795, as his authority, does not notice that the West Indian Article was in part not ratified. He also overlooks the qualifying clause of Article XXV.

seizures, and leave us at liberty to decide whether they were made in such cases as to be warranted by the *existing* law of nations." But there was no limit on British naval operations after the ratification of the treaty.

The twelfth article, in the part not thrown out by the Senate, provided that after its termination, that is, in two years after the end of the war between Great Britain and France, the two parties should "endeavor to agree whether, in any, and in what cases neutral vessels shall protect enemy's property: and in what cases provisions and other articles, not generally contraband, may become such. But in the meantime their conduct shall be regulated by the articles hereinafter inserted on these subjects." Jay considered that this stipulation kept alive "the principles we contend for." [22] Suspended animation would have been a better way of describing the condition of those principles. Under the circumstances this was the best Jay could do—if he wanted any treaty at all. It would have been better for Britain to have gone to war with the United States than to have agreed to principles which would have sapped the strength of her arbitrary naval power.

One might naturally conclude that Jay did not make the most of the advantages afforded by the European situation upon his arrival in England, particularly the overtures of the armed neutrals. His early flirtations with Engeström mysteriously subsided. Whether this was due to caution on Jay's part or to communications from home not known to us, we cannot say. But this much is true: any action which he might have taken to display the apparition of another armed neutrality

22. Jay to Randolph, November 19, 1794, *A.S.P.,F.R.,* I, 503.

would have failed to scare concessions out of Grenville.
It would have failed because of the intimate relations
between the Foreign Office and America's most influential and powerful statesman. When Grenville learned
opportunely from Hamilton that the United States
would have nothing further to do with "entangling
alliances" in Europe, the rest of his work with Jay was
easy. Moreover, his superior intelligence service—it
had even furnished him with a copy of Jay's cipher[23]—
which kept him well and fairly accurately informed of
political conditions on the other side of the Atlantic as
well as across the Channel, gave him an enormous advantage over Jay, an advantage which he turned to
most profitable use. Grenville, in the writer's opinion,
was also a more able and a more experienced diplomat
than John Jay.

It must be admitted that Jay, in his desire for peace
and his nervous anxiety about unforeseen contingencies
which might endanger the whole negotiation, was induced to accept terms which might have been bettered
by an abler negotiator. One of the most brilliant writers
on American history has remarked: "That Mr. Jay's
treaty was a bad one few persons even then ventured to
dispute; no one would venture on its merits to defend
it now"; and that "there has been no moment since
1810 when the United States would have hesitated to
prefer war rather than peace on such terms." [24] Yes,
but not *before* 1810. Agreeing with Mr. Henry Adams
that the concessions of principle were enormous, we
must remember Admiral Mahan's statement that the
signature by England of any treaty at all with the

23. See above, p. 317.

24. Henry Adams, *The Life of Albert Gallatin* (Philadelphia, 1879),
p. 158.

United States at that time was an event of "epochal significance," a recognition of the existence of American nationality of far greater import than the technical recognition of independence forced from George III in 1783.[25]

The United States needed peace and commercial expansion more than anything. The new nationality was still in danger. The political and economic foundations of the American nation had been laid by the hands of genius, but those foundations in 1794 were by no means unshakeable. The power of the federal Government to hold the Union together under the Constitution depended on the financial system which Hamilton had created. The elixir of national credit which energized the Government depended almost wholly on imports, which a war or even commercial hostility with Great Britain would have destroyed. This is what has escaped the careful attention of historical students. This is why Anglo-American diplomacy between 1789 and 1794 was a period as critical for American nationality as was the "critical period" of the Confederation so ably described by John Fiske.

This danger is what Alexander Hamilton realized, with the clear eye of the *realpolitiker*. If study of the sources leads us to say—despite Sheffield's later persuasion that Grenville was completely duped by Jay in 1794![26]—that Jay was somewhat outplayed[27] by Eng-

25. Mahan, *Sea Power and the War of 1812*, I, 43.

26. "We have now a complete opportunity of getting rid of that most impolitic treaty of 1794, when Lord Grenville was so perfectly duped by Jay." Statement of Lord Sheffield in 1812, *The Diary and Correspondence of Lord Colchester* (3 vols. London, 1861), II, 409, quoted by Pellew, *John Jay*, p. 279.

27. Jefferson claims that Hamilton, when discussing the treaty with Talleyrand referred to it as an "execrable" one, and said that Jay

land's great Foreign Secretary, it must be recognized
that in 1794 the United States had far more at stake in
a war with Great Britain than did the latter nation.
The treaty of 1794 served to postpone hostilities to
another remove and to give the United States in the
meantime an opportunity to develop in population and
resources, and above all in consciousness of nationality,
to a degree which made possible in the War of 1812 a
more effective resistance than could have been afforded
in 1794. In case of war in 1794, how could American
credit have survived the loss of tariff revenue? Would
the United States have been able to retain the still
loosely attached back country? Could American nationality itself have survived?

Hamilton had well reflected on the situation when he
wrote to Washington during the crisis of 1794 that if
war should extend "to the total prohibition of her
[Britain's] commodities, however brought, it deprives
us of a supply for which no substitute can be found
elsewhere—a supply, necessary to us in peace, and
more necessary to us if we are to go to war. It gives a
sudden and violent blow to our revenue, which cannot
easily, if at all, be repaired from other sources. It will
be so great an interruption to commerce as may very
possibly interfere with the payment of duties which
have hitherto accrued, and bring the Treasury to an
absolute stoppage of payment—an event which would
*cut up credit by the roots.*" [28]

While Jay's reputation as a diplomat might have

---

was "an old woman for making it." Yet Hamilton had advised Jay
among all others for the mission, and in his "Camillus" letters was
the strongest advocate of its ratification. Jefferson, *Writings,* I, 274.

28. Hamilton, *Works,* IV, 528. Italics inserted.

been much greater if his services in that field had ceased with signature of the treaty of peace in 1782, it must be remembered that his was not the guiding hand in 1794. The terms of his treaty were the result of the powerful influence of Alexander Hamilton, to whom in the last analysis any praise or blame for the instrument must be given. It was the price paid by the Federalists for a peace which they believed indispensable to the perpetuation of American nationality.

More aptly the treaty might be called Hamilton's Treaty.

# APPENDICES

Memorial of Beckwith to Dundas,
June 20, 1792

To the Right Honorable Henry Dundas, One of His
Majesty's Principal Secretaries of State, etc., etc.

The Memorial of Brevet Lieutenant Colonel George
Beckwith

Most respectfully sheweth

That your memorialist has been twenty-one years in
the Army, and served the late war in North America
from 1776 to 1783 in a variety of public situations, and
amongst others, as an aide-de-camp to General Knyp-
hausen, who commanded the Foreign Forces, in which
situation he remained with his successor General Los-
berg, and afterwards as an Aid-de-camp to Lord Dorchester, in which capacity he continued to the close of
that war.

In 1781 he obtained the Rank of Major in the Army
for which he had the honor of being particularly recommended to The King as will appear from the copy of
Sir Henry Clinton's letter, hereunto annexed; and in
1786 he accompanied Lord Dorchester to America as
one of his Lordship's Aide-de-Camps.

In the spring of 1787, he was sent from Canada into
The United States, from whence he returned in three

months; the consequences of this journey will appear from his Lordship's correspondence on that subject.

In the Autumn of 1788, your memorialist made a second journey into The United States, and returned to Quebec in Two Months; a reference to Lord Dorchester's correspondence will best explain its effects and shew the nature of the Revolution which then took place in their government.

In October 1788, Your Memorialist returned to this Country on which occasion he had a letter of introduction to Lord Sydney and in consequence had the honor of having several conversations with his Lordship on American Affairs.

In the spring of 1789, he had many interviews with Lord Hawkesbury on the navigation, commerce and infant manufactures of The United States, having been directed to attend his Lordship for that purpose by The Duke of Richmond, to whom also, by His Grace's directions, Your Memorialist submitted statements of the political situation of that Country.

In the summer of 1789, he was honored by Lord Grenville with several conversations on American Affairs, and in the month of August of that year, he was the bearer of a message from his Lordship, to The Executive Government of The United States, on the subject of a discrimination of duties, an object then in agitation, and supported by a party in that Country; this message he delivered in the October following, at New York, which led to certain overtures on the part of their Government; these were communicated by Lord Dorchester.

In March, 1790, he was again sent from Canada into The States, at this period they had resolved to raise an

army; in obedience to his instructions, Your memorialist transmitted direct information to Lord Grenville
of their views on that subject, for which his Lordship
was pleased to express his thanks by a letter from Mr.
Bernard of the 3rd of August of the same year.

In July 1790, he was sent a fifth time into The
United States, upon an appearance of a War with
Spain, and amongst other objects was directed to sound
their dispositions upon the supposition of a rupture
actually taking place; on this occasion his overtures
were certainly amicably received, and a great degree of
cordiality manifested, during the course of our negotiations with The Court of Madrid: it is not necessary
nor would it be proper in Your Memorialist to attempt
to explain the importance of such cordiality, nor its
probable effects, if those negotiations had ended in
hostility. From this period he remained in The United
States one year and nine months, and in conformity to
his instructions, in a regular correspondence with Lord
Grenville, until the arrival of Mr. Hammond, His
Majesty's Minister Plenipotentiary, soon after which
he was withdrawn.

It is with much satisfaction Your Memorialist finds
that such services as he has been capable of rendering
have been favorably received, in compliance with Your
directions, he has endeavoured on this occasion to describe them in as narrow a compass as their nature and
his capacity will admit, and in obedience to Your com-
mands to mention his wishes, as they respect his further
prospects in life, he begs leave to say, that having for a
considerable period been employed by Lord Dorchester
in a particular line of Service, he is desirous of being
continued in it, if he shall be thought deserving of it?

Which is with the greatest deference humbly submitted London, June 20th, 1792.

GEO. BECKWITH[1]

Letter appended of Sir Henry Clinton to Lord George Germain, 29 Sept 1781

1. P.R.O.,F.O., 4, 12. A letter of Dorchester to Dundas of 8 December, 1791, is contained in the same folio. Dorchester in answer to Dundas's inquiry as to what would be a proper acknowledgment of Beckwith's services, recommends a Lieutenant-Colonelcy of a Regiment as a flattering mark of the royal favor.

# APPENDIX II

Project
of
Heads of Proposals
to be made to Mr. Jay[1]

Posts and Boundary

## I

The Posts to the Southward of the Lakes to be delivered up to the Americans, subject to the following Provisions—viz.

The actual Cession not to take place, 'till the Summer of 1796, in order to leave time for our Traders to remove their effects, and to make all the other arrangements consequent on the Delivery of the Posts.

The Cession is not to be considered as interrupting the usual course of Communication and Commerce between the Two Canadas and the Indian Nations who are to the Southward and Eastward of the Lakes: But it shall be free to His Majesty's Subjects, and to the Indians, to pass and repass, with their Goods and Merchandizes; and His

1. MS in Grenville's private papers, Dropmore, England. The left column contains marginal emendations. Deletions by striking out, and by brackets, are reproduced as in the original MSS. The document is undated.

*Q.* If a reciprocal claim is made on the part of America for freedom of communication and commerce with the Indian Nations North of the Boundary or with the Two Canadas ought it to be admitted.

*Q.* Under what restrictions does the Commerce between the Canadas and the United States now rest under the provincial ordinance made by Ld. Dorchester in—

*Q.* As to those Carrying Places, which are on our Side of the Boundary Line, or may be made there?

And an unlimited freedom of inland trade and communication shall be established between the Two Canadas and the United States.

See Lord Dorchester's Suggestion to this Effect: but *Q* whether this is an object which ought to be brought forward?

at a point to be fixed
*Q.* By the best accounts it should seem that the Mississippi is not navigable for large vessels above the falls of

Majesty's Subjects shall be at liberty to hire or possess Houses and Ware Houses, within, or without the Jurisdiction of the Forts, in all parts of the territory now possessed, or which may here after be possessed by the United States: and every necessary facility and accommodation shall be given to them for that purpose by the officers of the United States stationed at the Posts.

The Passage of the Waters, and the Carrying Places, and roads adjoining thereto shall be Free: and no Impediment or Obstacle shall be given to the Free Passage of Goods and Merchandize, nor any Duty attempted to be levied on such Passage.

The whole course of the Boundary Line shall be distinctly ascertained by actual Survey, and Mapping, by officers to be appointed by the Two Governments.

The Boundary shall [include within the Canadian Limits the Island of "La Grande Isle" on Lake Champlain; and shall] be carried from Lake Superior to the Mississippi, so as to communicate with the navigable part of the said River; The Navigation of the Mississippi shall remain, as by the Treaty of Peace and the British shall be admitted to enter freely into

St. Anthony. (See Carver handb.)

Q. St. Croix—Two Rivers of that name—doubt which is the Boundary between Nova Scotia and New England.

Q. Also some question respecting an Island in the bay of Fundy.

## Debts

In all cases or questions arising from or touching the late Treaty of Peace or the present Treaty, the Courts of Law and Equity shall be bound to decide and adjudge according to the interests, tenor and true intent of the same. And in order to remove all disputes respecting the execution of the 4th Art of the Treaty of Peace.

in such cases where suits have not been already decided against the Parties in the Courts.

the Bays, Ports and Creeks on the American side, and to land and dwell there, for the purposes of their Commerce, in the same manner as in other parts of the United States.

## II

All Debts, due to the King's Subjects by any of the Inhabitants or Citizens of the United States shall from henceforth be recoverable from the Debtors, their Heirs or representatives in the Courts of Law in the said States, with Interest thereupon from the time of their being respectively contracted, and all Laws or Decisions to the contrary heretofore made shall be considered as Null and of no effect, in the same manner as if the same had never existed. A Commission shall be instituted in America, by the Nomination of Two Commissaries on each side, Q { with power to call to their assistance, as Joint Commissaries, one or Three more persons, of any Indifferent Nation or Nations: These Commissaries shall be sworn to hear and impartially determine by way of appeal or petition all Complaints respecting the Execution of this Article and, in those Cases where the Parties appealing shall appear to such Commissaries to be justly intitled to redress, or the execution of the 4th Article in the late Treaty of Peace. Such appeal shall Lay and be entertained as such in those cases where judgments have already been given in the Courts of the United States as in those where such judgment shall hereafter be given.

:

which, from whatever cause, they have not been able to procure in the Courts of the United States, the American Government shall take upon itself to make a full Compensation to such Parties, according to the Judgment of the Commissaries, and to the amount which shall be settled by such Commissaries.

And whereas by the lapse of time and the impediments which have arisen to the prosecution of suits of this nature, much legal evidence which might have been produced at the period of the Treaty of Peace or since that time, has now been destroyed or lost, the Creditors who shall be unable to prove their debts by strict legal evidence may be received to Petition the said Commissioners who shall receive such Evidence (of whatever nature) as shall be tendered to them by the parties so applying, and shall judge equitably and impartially according to the circumstances of the case whether the claim is satisfactorily substantiated, and whether the said debt should be allowed in the whole or in part.

In all cases where the said Commissaries shall pronounce in favor of the parties appealing or petitioning, the Government of America shall make itself responsible for the payment of the debt so allowed, reserving to itself such measures as it may be proper to adopt with respect to its own Citizens.

N.B. The amount of money paid into the Treasuries was about £400,000, calculated according to the usual rate of exchange.

## Neutral Code

### III

With respect to the Neutral Commerce of Great Britain or America with European Nations, it may be agreed, that the Principles to be observed by Great Britain towards America, and reciprocally by America towards Great Britain, shall always be the same as shall be observed towards the most favoured Neutral Nations of Europe; with the Exception only of such particular Privileges, as may occasionally be granted by Special Treaty to particular European Nations, and subject also to such Modifications, as may occasionally be established by Special Treaty between Great Britain and the United States, for their mutual convenience. Vessels captured or detained on Suspicion of carrying Enemies property, or of carrying to the Enemy any of *the Articles which are called* "Contraband of War" shall be brought to the nearest or most convenient Port; and sufficient Regu-

*Q.* a more particular enumeration of these? What should in that case be said about Provisions?

lations shall be adopted, to prevent Delay in deciding the Cases of all Ships so brought in for adjudications, and in the Payment of any Indemnification, adjudged, or agreed to be paid to the Masters or Owners of such Ships.

The present Situation of the West Indies prevents the necessity of any prospective regulation as to the Neutral Commerce in that part of the world; but, as Complaints have been made, respecting what has already passed there, it may be agreed, that a Commission shall be appointed, in the Form above proposed with respect to the Debts, in order to enquire into the Cases of Capture or Condemnations of American Ships in the West Indies; and that, when any such Capture or Condemnation shall appear to have been irregular and contrary to the Laws of Nations, Indemnification shall be made by the British Government; who shall, however, have the right to call upon Individuals to proceed by Appeal, in such Cases where the Commissioners shall judge it reasonable. To facilitate this proceeding, and to prevent Doubts respecting the Rules by which these Cases are to be examined, it may be agreed, that the said Commission shall proceed on the following Principles—viz.—

This will be unnecessary at least in the first instance if the appeals can be opened in those cases where there has hitherto been an omission on the part of the Americans in not appealing.

First—That all Enemies
property, on board neutral vessels, and all Naval and Military Stores bound to the Ports
of the Enemy, or destined for
their use, shall be considered
as Lawfull Prize.

Secondly—that all Vessels,
having False Clearances or colourable Papers, shall be considered as Lawfull Prize, they
and their Cargoes.

Thirdly—That all Commodities, the growth and Produce of the French West India
Islands, shipped in the said Islands, and bound to the United
States (other than such Articles as might before the war
have been lawfully carried
from the said Islands to the
United States) shall be considered as Lawfull Prize.

Fifthly—That all Goods or
Merchandize, found on board
Neutral Ships bound to the
said Islands other than such
Articles as the said Vessels
might lawfully have imported
there before the War, shall be
considered as Lawfull Prize.

Sixthly—That Compensation shall be made for all
Losses by Capture. Detention
or Condemnation, not falling
under the above mentioned
Principles; but that no Compensation shall be made, for
the Detention of the Vessels,
whose Cargoes were Lawfull
Prize; except it shall be
proved, that such Detention

was unnecessarily and injuriously protracted.

Treaty of Commerce                IV

A Treaty of Commerce to be made between the Two Nations, and to last for a limited Term of years.

This Treaty to establish the following Principles—

First—That no Distinction shall exist in the Ports of Either, by which Greater Duties shall be paid, on any Article imported there by the other, than on the like Article imported by any other Nation.

Secondly—That no Distinctions of Tonnage, or other Duties, shall exist, by which the Ships of One Party shall pay, in the Ports of the Other, more than the Vessels of other Nations, or than the Vessels of the Party into whose Ports such Vessels shall come.

Thirdly—That no new Prohibition shall be laid, in either Country, on the Importation of any Article, the Growth, Produce or Manufacture of the other, nor shall any Article, being of the Growth, Produce or Manufacture of any other Country, be prohibited to be imported into one Country by the Ships of the other, which is not now so prohibited.

Fourthly—These Regulations to extend to the Euro-

Navigation Act
Fisheries
W. India Produce

pean Dominions of Great Britain only.

[*Q.*—What may be fit to be proposed, or agreed to, either permanently, or as a temporary measure, with respect to the Commerce between America and the West Indies, so as, if possible, to give America an Interest in our retaining the newly acquired Colonies?]

Fifthly—In case of any alledged Infraction of these articles, the Others not to be suspended, or in any respect infringed, 'till after regular application made, and notice given to that effect, to the other party.

Sixthly—The usual Article to be inserted from the Old Treaties of Navigation and Commerce, that, in case of Rupture, all just Debts shall be recovered, and all persons be at Liberty, to depart etc.

V

All Complaints or Causes of Uneasiness, not included in the above Proposals, to be entirely done away and obliterated.

Other Complaints

This article is however not to suspend the cause of proceeding in the Courts or respecting individual cases of alledged grievance, which cases are on the contrary to be decided according to the term

of the treaties and the principles of the Laws of Nations.

*Q.* the individual cases of
Loyalists, confiscated Es-
tates, etc.
*Q.* also individual cases of
Captures    by    privateers
fitted out in America etc.
*Q.* Sale of prizes.

# Comparison of Jay's Draft of September 30, 1794, with the Treaty Signed by Jay and Grenville on November 19, 1794

The following document, a draft of a treaty submitted by Jay on September 30, is to be found in P.R.O.,F.O., 95, 512. Those portions of the draft which are identical with the final treaty are underlined. Those portions which are similar in content to corresponding sections of the treaty but not identical in language are underlined with broken line. Differences between articles of Jay's draft and corresponding articles of the treaty are indicated by footnotes. Material in Jay's draft not included in the treaty is not underscored.

Article XVI and the final article of the treaty have no corresponding parts in the draft. The other articles of the treaty are taken from Jay's draft or represent modifications, in greater or less degree, of articles proposed in the draft. The greatest differences between the draft and the treaty, it should be noted, consist in articles of the draft omitted altogether in the treaty.

Treaty of Amity and Commerce made and concluded by and between His Britannic Majesty and the Presi-

dent of the United States of America, on the part and
behalf of the said States, by and with the advice and
consent of the Senate thereof—

His Britannic Majesty and the United States of
America, being desirous by a Treaty of Amity and
Commerce, to terminate their differences in such a
manner, as without drawing the merits of them into
question,[1] shall produce mutual content[2] and good understanding. And also to regulate the Commerce[3] between their respective countries, territories and inhabitants,[4] in such a manner as to render the same reciprocally beneficial and satisfactory. They have respectively named their Plenepotentiaries, and given them
full powers to treat of and conclude the said Treaty.
That is to say His Britannic Majesty has named for his
Plenepotentiary . . . and the President of the said
United States, by and with the advice and consent of
the Senate therof, hath appointed for their Plenepotentiary . . . who have agreed on and concluded the following articles, viz:

1st. There shall be a firm, inviolable and universal
Peace and a true and sincere Friendship between His
Britannic Majesty, His heirs and Successors, and the
United States of America, and between their respective

1. The treaty reads: "as, without reference to the merits of their
respective claims and pretensions."
2. The treaty substitutes "satisfaction" for "content."
3. The treaty interposes "and navigation."
4. The treaty substitutes "people" for "inhabitants."

countries, Territories, cities, Towns and People, and Inhabitants of every degree,[5] without exception of Persons or Places.

2nd. His Majesty will withdraw all his Troops and Garrisons from all Posts and Places within the boundary lines assigned by the Treaty of Peace to the United States. This Evacuation shall take place on or before the first day of June 1796, and all the proper measures shall in the interval be taken by concert between the Government of the United States, and His Majesty's Governor General in America, for settling the previous arrangements which may be necessary respecting the delivery of the said Posts.[6]

All Settlers and Traders within the Precincts or jurisdiction of the said Posts, shall continue to enjoy unmolested, all their property of every kind, and shall be protected therein. They shall be at full liberty to remain there, or to remove with all [7] their effects, and also to sell their Lands, Houses, or Effects, or to retain the property thereof.[8] Such of them as shall continue to reside there for the purposes of their Commerce, shall not be compelled to become citizens of the United States or to take any oath of allegiance to the Govern-

5. Doubtless this expression was dropped in the treaty because of the possibility of its including Indians.

6. The treaty permits the United States to extend settlements anywhere within the boundaries of the United States, except, pending evacuation, "within the precincts of jurisdiction of any of the said posts."

7. The treaty interposes "or any part of."

8. The treaty adds "at their discretion."

ment thereof, but they shall be at full liberty so to do, if they think proper; and they shall make and declare their election within one year after the evacuation aforesaid. All the other Settlers[9] who shall continue there after the expiration of the said year,[10] shall be considered as having elected to become citizens of the United States.

It shall at all times be free to the Indians dwelling within the Boundaries of either of the parties,[11] to pass and repass with their own proper goods and effects, and to carry on their commerce within or without the jurisdiction of either of the said parties, without hindrance or molestation, or being subjected to any imposts whatever—but goods in bales (Peltries excepted) shall not be considered as goods belonging bona fide to Indians—Provided however that this privilege shall be suspended with respect to those Tribes, who may be at war and while they may be at war, with the party within whose Jurisdiction they may either dwell, or attempt to come—But neither of the contracting Par-

9. The treaty substitutes "all persons."

10. The treaty interposes "without having declared their intention of remaining subjects of His Britannic Majesty."

11. See Article III of the treaty, which reads "on either side of the boundary line, freely to pass and repass by land or inland navigation, into the respective territories of the two parties, on the continent of America (the country within the limits of the Hudson's Bay Company only excepted) and to navigate all the lakes, rivers and waters thereof, and freely to carry on trade and commerce with each other." This provision occurs in Article IX of Jay's draft, and thus would have been limited in duration to twelve years. Inclusion within Article III made it permanent in the treaty.

ties will form any political connextions, nor hold any
Treaties with Indians dwelling within the boundaries
of the other—They will with good faith endeavour to
restrain their respective Indians from war, and the
better to prevent it, they will make every future indian
war a common cause so far as to prohibit and prevent
any supplies of ammunition or arms being given or sold
even by indian traders to the belligerent tribe or tribes
or to any individuals of them—

In case it should happen (which God forbid) that
war should exist between the said parties, they mutually
engage to abstain not only from inviting, but also from
permitting any Indians to join in it; but on the contrary
will reject their offers of aid and receive no assistance
from them; nor shall they be allowed under any pretence or in any capacity, to attend or resort to the
armies or detachments of either of the said parties—

No armed vessels shall be kept by either of the
parties on the lakes and water thro' which the boundary
line between them passes—It being their earnest desire
to render mutual justice, confidence, and goodwill, a
sufficient Barrier against encroachment and aggression.

Under the influence of these motives, they will as
soon as circumstances shall render it seasonable, enter
into arrangements for diminishing or wholly withdrawing all military force from the Borders—

3d. Whereas it is questioned and uncertain, whether
the River Mississippi does extend so far to the northward, as to reach or intersect the[12] due west line from
the Lake of the Woods, which is mentioned in the
Treaty of Peace, and consequently whether the north-

12. The treaty substitutes "a" for "the."

ern and western lines of the United States do or do not
close in that corner, and in the latter case how they
ought to be closed, which questions it would be premature to discuss and endeavour to settle, while the parties
remain uninformed of the actual extent and other material circumstances of the said River.

Wherefore it is agreed that all discussions on these
subjects shall be postponed, untill an accurate survey
of the said River shall be made—Such a survey of the
River Mississippi, beginning at the distance of one
degree of latitude below and from the Falls of St.
Anthony, and proceeding thence to its source or head,
shall be made. The said survey shall comprehend the
course, width & depth of the said River, the Falls and
Rapids which may be found therein; and an account of
the intervals where it may be navigable, and for what
Vessels; and of all such other matters and things, as
it may be interesting to both or either of the said parties
to be informed of. It shall also comprehend similar
surveys and accounts of all the principal Branches or
Streams, which empty into the said River, above the
said place of beginning. The Lake of the Woods shall
also be surveyed—the most northwestern point thereof
shall be ascertained and described; and the Latitude
and Longitude thereof, as well as the Latitude and
Longitude of the Head or Source of the Mississippi,
and of the said principal Branches of Streams, shall be
correctly taken and fixed.

This work shall be performed and executed by and
under the direction of three Commissioners, whereof
one shall be appointed by his Majesty, one by the
President of the United States with the advice and con-

COMPARISON OF JAY'S DRAFT WITH TREATY 397

sent of the Senate, and the third by those two. In case those two should not be able to agree in such appointment then each of them shall propose a person, and of the two so proposed, one shall be taken by lot in the presence of both the proposers, and the one so taken shall be the *third* Commissioner—

The said *two first appointed* Commissioners shall as soon as may be after *being duly notified* meet at Philadelphia; and before they proceed to execute any part of their commission shall take the following Oath or Affirmation before any one of the National or State Judges viz.

"I A.B. one of the Commissioners appointed to make the surveys directed in and by the (    ) Article of the Treaty of Amity and Commerce between his Britannic Majesty and the United States of America, do solemnly swear (or affirm) that I have no personal interest in the issue of those surveys, and that I will faithfully and diligently, impartially and carefully make the said surveys, according to the directions of the said article, and to the best of my skill and understanding— And I do also solemnly swear (or affirm) that I will sincerely endeavour to agree with my colleague in the appointment of a third Commissioner, that I will propose only such person or persons as I shall judge to be qualified for that place—and that I will not oppose but will favor the appointment of that one among those whom we shall propose, whom I shall really think the best qualified for the same."

When the said third Commissioner shall be appointed, he shall before he proceeds to act, take the Oath or Affirmation first above mentioned—

The said third Commissioner shall always preside,

and every question that may come before the board,
shall be decided by plurality of voices, openly given
*that is not by Ballot*—

They shall appoint one chief clerk, and also such
assistant clerks as they may judge from time to time to
be necessary, each of whom before he does any act in
that capacity shall take the following oath or affirmation before any one of the said commissioners who are
hereby severally authorised to administer the same, viz

"I A.B. appointed clerk (or assistant clerk) to the
commissioners appointed in pursuance of the (     )
article of the Treaty of Amity and Commerce between
His Britannic Majesty and the United States of America, to make the surveys therein directed, do solemnly
swear (or affirm) that I am not personally interested
in the said surveys and that I will do the duties of the
said place with fidelity care and diligence according to
the best of my skill and understanding."

The said commissioners shall appoint such Astronomers and Surveyors, as they shall judge necessary; and
shall administer to them respectively an Oath or
Affirmation purporting that they have no personal interest in the said surveys and that they will respectively
perform the duties to be assigned to them by the said
Commissioners, with fidelity care and diligence—

The said Commissioners shall decide on the allowances and compensation to be made to the several persons whom they shall employ as aforesaid, and to all
others whom they may occasionally employ; but these
compensations or allowances shall be confined to the
time or times during which the said persons shall be in
actual service—

When their Business shall be finished, the said Commissioners shall deliver to the Minister of His Majesty at Philadelphia for the use of his Majesty, a chart representing the said surveys, a statement of their accounts, and a journal of their proceedings which shall contain such remarks, facts and circumstances, as shall tend to explain the said chart, and as shall in their opinion be necessary to convey and preserve the information intended to be acquired by the execution of their commission. They shall also on the same day, deliver exact duplicates of the said chart statement and journal, for the use of the United States, to their Secretary of State at his Office—

Arrangements shall be taken by concert between the Government of the United States and His Majesty's Governor General in America, to afford proper protection, facilities and supplies to the said Commissioners—

The whole expense of executing this commission shall be paid in equal moieties by his Majesty and the United States—necessary advances of money shall from time to time be made, and his Majesty's Minister at Philadelphia, and the Secretary of the Treasury of the United States, shall be respectively authorised and enabled to make such advances, in equal proportions.—

Whenever any one of the said commissioners shall die, or in the opinion of the other two signified by writing under their hands, become disqualified by sickness or otherwise for service, the place of such commissioner shall be supplied by another to be appointed in the same manner that he was, and to take the same oaths that he did and to perform the same duties that were encumbent on him—and his Majesty will authorize his Minister with the United States, to make such appointments as this Treaty assigns to his Majesty—

The said Commissioners shall be paid for their services at the rate of ———— per annum while on actual service. They shall also be provided with necessary supplies while actually on service, but while absent from the said surveys or service they shall bear their own expenses, and receive no Salary nor Compensation.

And to the end that this survey may not be interrupted by the Indian Tribes in the vicinity, the Government of the United States will by concert with His Majesty's Governor of upper Canada take the necessary measures for explaining the object of the same to those Indians; and unite their efforts in composing their apprehensions and in restraining them from interrupting the progress and completion of the work—[13]

4th. Although the Boundaries of the United States as delineated by the Treaty of Peace are hereby recognized and admitted, Yet as the Parties differ as to which is the River intended by the said Treaty, and therein called the River St Croix, which forms a part of the Boundary therein described—

It is agreed that the said question shall be referred to the final decision of three Commissioners to be appointed exactly in the same manner,[14] and to take the

13. This article of the draft should be compared with Article IV of the treaty, which provides that the two parties shall "take measures in concert" for a joint survey of the upper Mississippi, but appoints no commission. After the survey the two parties are to proceed "by amicable negotiation to regulate the boundary line in that quarter."

14. Article IV of the treaty refers the final decision of the identity of the St. Croix to a commission of three chosen in the same way as provided in the Jay draft.

same oaths (mutatis mutandis) before any respectable Magistrate, as is prescribed in the preceeding Article relative to the Commissioners therein mentioned— They shall meet at Quebec, Halifax, etc.

They shall appoint a clerk, and if necessary, assistant clerks, Astronomers and Surveyors—They shall in like manner administer to them the same oaths (mutatis mutandis) they shall make them allowances and compensations on the like principle of actual service, and they themselves shall receive the same compensations with those commissioners, and while actually on duty shall be allowed their reasonable Expences—

They shall direct such surveys as they shall judge proper, and may adjourn to such place or places as they may think expedient. They shall hear and receive whatever Testimony and Evidences shall be offered to them by the parties, and without improper precipitation or delay, shall by writing [15] under their hands, attested by their Clerk decide which is the River St. Croix intended by the Treaty—The said written decision shall contain a description of the said River, and the Latitude and Longitude of its mouth and of its source—They shall deliver duplicates of this writing and of statements of their accounts and of the journal of their proceedings, to the agent of his Majesty and to the agent of the United States, who shall be respectively appointed and authorized to manage the business on their respective parts and behalf.—

The expence of executing this Business shall be paid in equal moieties by both parties, and the necessary

15. The treaty uses the words "declaration under their hands and seals."

advances shall be made in like manner as the advances mentioned in the preceeding article are provided for— And the said commissioners shall be authorised to employ all such persons as they shall deem necessary and proper in the Business committed to them by this article—

5th. Whereas complaints have been made by divers Merchants and other citizens of the United States, that during the course of the war in which his Majesty is now engaged, they have sustained considerable losses and damage, by reason of irregular or illegal captures and condemnations of their Vessels and other property under colour of authority or commissions from his Majesty, and that from various circumstances belonging to the said cases, adequate compensation for the said losses and damages, cannot now be actually obtained had and received by the ordinary course of judicial proceedings It is agreed that in all such cases where adequate compensation cannot for whatever reason or cause be now actually obtained had and received by the said Merchants and others[16] for the said losses and damages, full and complete satisfaction for the same will be made by the British Government to the said Complainants.[17]

16. The treaty interposes the words "in the ordinary course of justice." This article V of Jay's draft is embodied in article VII of the treaty.

17. The treaty adds another sentence to this paragraph: "But it is distinctly understood that this provision is not to extend to such losses or damages as have been occasioned by the manifest delay or negligence, or wilful omission of the claimant."

That for this purpose five Commissioners shall be appointed and authorized (to meet and act in London) in manner following viz. Two of them shall be appointed by his Majesty, two of them by the President of the United States by and with the advice and consent of the Senate, and the fifth by the unanimous voice of the other four.

When the said first four Commissioners shall meet, they shall before they proceed to act, respectively take the following Oath or Affirmation—viz.

"I A.B. one of the Commissioners appointed in pursuance of the        article of the Treaty of amity and commerce between His Britannic Majesty and the United States of America do solemnly swear (or affirm) that I will honestly diligently impartially and carefully hear, and according to justice and equity and the best of my judgment decide all such complaints as under the said article shall be preferred to the said commissioners, and that I will forbear to act as a commissioner in any case in which I may be personally interested. And I do further solemnly swear (or affirm) that I will sincerely endeavour to agree with my colleagues in appointing a proper person to be the fifth Commissioner[18]

In case the said four Commissioners should not agree in such choice, then the said fifth commissioner shall be appointed by lot in the manner directed in the third article of this Treaty and when appointed shall take the

18. See Article VI of treaty.

first of the before mentioned Oaths or Affirmations.[19]

Three of the said Commissioners shall constitute a Board and have power to do any act appertaining to the said commission provided that one of the commissioners named on each side, and the fifth commissioner shall be present, and all decisions shall be made by the majority of the voices of the Commissioners then present.

In case of death sickness or necessary absence, the places of such Commissioners respectively shall be supplied in the same manner as such Commissioners were first appointed, and the new ones shall take the same Oath or Affirmation and do the same duties.[20]

They shall appoint a Clerk and administer to him an Oath (or Affirmation) faithfully and impartially and diligently to do his duty—

Eighteen months from the day on which the said Commissioners shall form a Board and be ready to proceed to Business are assigned for the reception of complaints and applications but they are nevertheless authorised for once to prolong that term to a further period in case it shall appear to them to be reasonable and proper.

The said Commissioners in awarding such sums as

19. The manner of selecting the commission, prescribed in Article VI of the treaty, is the same as proposed by Jay's draft, except in case of lack of unanimous choice of the fifth commissioner a method is provided of selecting him by lot from two candidates, one appointed by each party through its duly appointed commissioners.

20. This paragraph embodied in a separate article, Article VII, in the treaty.

shall appear to them to be justly and equitably due to the said complainants, in pursuance of the true intent and meaning of this article, are empowered to take into their consideration and to determine all claims according to the merits of the several cases, due regard being had to all the circumstances thereof, and as equity and justice shall appear to them to require, and the said Commissioners shall have power to examine all persons on oath touching the premises and also to receive in evidence according as they think most consistent with equity and justice all written depositions or books or papers or copies of extracts thereof. Every such Deposition, book, paper, copy or extract being duly authenticated according to the legal forms now respectively existing in the two countries, or in such other manner as the said Commissioners shall see cause to prescribe and require.[21]

The award of the said Commissioners or of any three of them as aforesaid, shall in all cases be final and conclusive both as to the justice of the claim, and to the amount of the sum to be paid to the complainant or claimant—And his Majesty undertakes to cause the same to be paid to such claimants without deductions in specie, and at such time or times and at such place or places as shall be awarded by the said commissioners, and on condition of such releases to be given by the

21. The rules of procedure for the commission provided in Article VI of the treaty, also apply to the commission under Article VII. They are the same as devised in Jay's draft.

claimant of his demands against individuals as by the
said Commissioners may be directed.

And whereas certain merchants and others his
Majesty's subjects complain that in the course of the
war they have sustained loss and damage by reason of
the capture of their Vessels and Merchandize within
the limits and jurisdiction of the said States or by
vessels, armed in ports of the said States.

It is agreed that all such cases[22] shall be and hereby
are referred to the Commissioners before mentioned,
and they are authorized to proceed in like manner relative to those as to the other cases committed to them.
And the United States undertake to pay to the complainants or claimants in specie without deductions,
the amount of the sum to be awarded to them respectively by the said commissioners, at the times and places
which in such awards shall be specified, and on condition
of such releases to be given by the Claimant of his demands against individuals, as the said awards may
direct.

And it is further agreed that not only existing cases
of both descriptions, but also all such as shall exist at
the time of exchanging the Ratifications of this Treaty
shall be considered as being within the provisions, intent
and meaning of this article—

6th. Whereas it is alleged by divers british mer-

22. The treaty interposes "where restitution shall not have been
made agreeably to the tenor of the letter from Mr. Jefferson to Mr.
Hammond, dated at Philadelphia, September 5, 1793, a copy of which
is annexed to this treaty."

chants and others his Majesty's subjects that debts to a considerable amount which were bona fide contracted before the peace, still remain owing to them by citizens or inhabitants of the United States, and that by the operation of various lawful impediments since the peace, not only the full recovery of the said debts has been delayed, but also the[23] security thereof has been in several instances impaired and lessened; so that by the ordinary course of judicial proceedings the British creditors cannot obtain and actually have and receive full and adequate compensation for the losses and damages which they have thereby sustained. It is agreed that in all such cases where full compensation for such losses and damages cannot for whatever reason (other than insolvency not imputable to the said impediments and delays) be actually obtained had and received by the said creditors in the ordinary course of justice, the United States will make full and complete satisfaction for the same to the said creditors. And that for this purpose five Commissioners shall be appointed & authorized exactly in the manner directed with respect to those mentioned in the preceding article and shall take the same Oaths or Affirmations (mutatis mutandis) and proceed as is therein directed. The same term of eighteen months is also assigned for the reception of claims and they are in like manner authorized for once to prolong it to a more distant period. They shall

23. The treaty interposes "value and."

receive testimony books, papers and evidence in the
same latitude, and exercise the like discretion and
powers respecting the subject, and shall decide the
claims in question whether they respect principal or
interest, or ballances of either, according to the merits
of the several cases, and to justice, equity and good
conscience, having due regard to all the circumstances
thereof—

The award of the said Commissioners shall in all
cases be final and conclusive, both as to the justice of the
claim, and to the amount of the sum to be paid to the
claimant, and the United States undertake to cause the
same to be paid to such claimants without any deductions, in specie, at such place or places and at such time
or times, after the first day of June, 1796 as shall be
awarded by the said Commissioners and on condition
of such assignments by the said claimants of their demands against individuals to the United States, or of
such releases of their said demands to individuals, as the
said Commissioners may think proper to direct—

The said Commissioners shall meet at Philadelphia,
but shall have power to adjourn at their discretion to
any other place or places in the United States—

It is further agreed that the Commissioners mentioned in this and in the preceding article shall be paid
at the rate of ——— per annum for the first eighteen
months and at the rate of ——— per annum for the
residue of the time they may sit. No allowances whatever shall be made to them on account of expences—

Their clerks shall each be paid at the rate of ———
per annum for the whole time of their service—

These expences shall be paid in equal shares by both
the parties,[24] and they will provide that the said salaries
shall be paid quarterly to be computed from the day of
the first meeting to do business—They will also provide
that on the said first day of meeting one hundred
pounds sterling be paid in advance and on account to
each of the said Commissioners, and fifty pounds sterling to each of the clerks—

7th. It is agreed that British Subjects who now hold
lands in the Territories of the United States, and
American Citizens who now hold lands in the Dominions of his Majesty shall continue to hold them according to the nature and tenure of their respective Estates
and Titles therein, and may grant and sell and devise
the same, as, and to whom they please, in like manner
as if they were natives—And that neither they nor
their heirs or assigns shall, so far as may respect the
said lands and legal remedies incident thereto, be regarded as aliens—[25]

8th. Neither the debts due from individuals of the
one nation to individuals of the other, nor shares or
monies which they may have in the public funds, or in
the public or private Banks, shall ever in any event of
war or national differences be sequestered or confiscated

24. Article VIII of the treaty provides for joint payment of the
expenses of the commissions, "the same being previously ascertained
and allowed by a majority of the commissioners."

25. See Article IX of treaty.

—it being both unjust and consequently impolitic that debts and engagements contracted and made by individuals having confidence in each other, and in their respective Governments, should ever be destroyed or impaired by national authority, on account of national differences and discontents.[26]

It is agreed between His said Majesty and the United States of America that there shall be reciprocal and entirely perfect liberty of navigation and commerce between their respective people in the manner, under the limitations, and on the conditions specified in the following Articles viz.[27]

9th. It shall be free to his Majesty's subjects and to the citizens of the United States[28] to pass and repass into their respective Territories and Countries on the Continent of America (the country within the limits of the Hudson's Bay company only excepted) and to navigate all the Lakes Rivers and waters thereof, and freely to carry on trade and commerce with each other, and with the Indians dwelling within the boundaries of the said contracting parties.[29] But the navigation of His Majesty's Rivers to or from the Sea shall not be open to vessels of the United States—nor shall the Rivers of the United States be open to british vessels from the

26. See Article X of treaty.
27. See Article XI of treaty.
28. The treaty interposes "freely." See Article III.
29. The treaty allows Indians and traders to cross the line for purposes of trade.

Sea further than to the usual ports near the sea into which they have heretofore been admitted. But the River Mississippi shall according to the treaty of peace continue to[30] be open to both parties, and [31] all the Ports and Places on its eastern side may freely be restored to and used by both parties in as ample a manner as any of the Atlantic ports or places of the United States or any of the ports or places of his Majesty in Great Britain—

All Goods and Merchandizes (whose importation into his Majesty's said American dominions shall not be entirely prohibited) may freely for the purposes of Commerce be carried into the same, by American citizens, in any manner except by sea, and shall be subject only to the same duties as in like cases would be payable by his Majesty's subjects. And on the other hand, all Goods and Merchandizes (whose importation into the United States shall not be entirely prohibited) may freely for the purposes of commerce be carried into the same from his Majesty's said Territories by British subjects, in any manner except by Sea, and shall be subject only to the same duties as in like cases would be payable by American citizens. Peltries may always be freely carried (except by sea) from one side to the other without paying any duty or impost, and all other goods whose exportation may not be entirely

30. The treaty reads, Article III, "shall be entirely open."
31. The treaty interposes "it is further agreed."

prohibited, may also be freely carried paying Duties as
aforesaid.

No higher or other Tolls or Rates or Ferriage than
what are or shall be payable by natives, shall be demanded or exacted on either side.

As this Article is particularly intended and calculated
to render in a great degree the local advantages of each
common to both, and thereby to promote a disposition
favourable to friendship and good neighbourhood, it
is agreed that the respective Governments will constantly[32] promote this amicable intercourse, by causing
speedy and impartial justice and necessary protection
to be done and extended to all who may be concerned
therein[33]

10th. His Majesty consents that it shall and may be
lawful, during the time hereinafter limited, for the
citizens of the United States, to carry to any of his
Majesty's Islands and Ports in the West Indies, from
the United States in their own vessels, not being above
the burthen of             tons, any Goods or Merchandizes being of the growth, manufacture or produce of
the said States, which it is, or may be lawful to carry to
the said islands or ports from the said States in british
vessels—And that the said American vessels and their

32. The treaty substitutes "mutually" for "constantly."
33. It should be observed that Article IX of Jay's draft was limited
to twelve years' duration. By placing these provisions for land and
inland water commerce in Article III of the treaty they were made
permanent instead of temporary. The importance of this change cannot be overemphasized.

cargoes shall pay there no other or higher duties or charges than shall be payable by british vessels in similar circumstances.[34] And that it shall be lawful for the said american citizens to purchase load and carry away in their said vessels to the United States from the said islands and ports all such articles being of the growth manufacture or produce of the said islands, as may by law be carried from thence to the said States in british vessels, and subject only to the same duties and charges on Exportation, to which British vessels are or shall be subject in similar circumstances—It is his Majesty's intention that american vessels shall, as to the articles which may lawfully [be] exported or imported to or from the said Islands and the United States, as well as with respect to duties and charges shall be exactly on the same footing on which British vessels now are, and that any extension or amplification of the priviledges of the latter shall immediately extend to the former. Provided always that the said american vessels do carry and land their cargoes in the United States *only*—it being expressly agreed and declared that during the continuance of this article, the United States will prohibit the carrying any Sugar Coffee or Cotton[35] in American vessels, either from his Majesty's islands or from the United States to any part of the world except the United States—reasonable sea stores excepted—

34. The treaty reads, Article XII, "in the ports of the United States."
35. The treaty adds, Article XII, molasses and cocoa.

It is agreed that this article and every matter and thing therein contained, shall continue to be in force during the continuance of the war in which his Majesty is now engaged and also for two years from and after the day of the signature of the preliminary Articles of peace by which the same may be terminated

And it is further agreed that at the expiration of the said term, the two contracting [parties] will treat further concerning their Commerce in this respect, according to the situation in which his Majesty may then find himself with respect to the West Indies, and with a view to such arrangements as may best conduce to the mutual advantage and extension of commerce[36]

11th. There shall be between all the dominions of his Majesty in Europe and the Territories of the United States a reciprocal and perfect liberty of commerce and navigation. And it is agreed that this navigation and commerce shall continue to be exactly on the same footing in every respect on which they now stand, except that in cases where any other nation or nations now are or hereafter shall be admitted by either party to greater priviledges or favours, the same shall immediately become common to the other party, who shall enjoy the same priviledge or favor freely, if the concession was gratuitously made, or on allowing the same

36. Article XII of the treaty adds these sentences: "and the said parties will then also renew their discussions, and endeavor to agree whether, if any, and what, cases neutral vessels shall protect enemy's property; and in what cases provisions and other articles, not generally contraband, may become such. But, in the meantime, their conduct towards each other in these respects shall be regulated by the Articles hereinafter inserted on those subjects."

equally valuable compensation if the concession was made in consideration of compensation—Neither of the parties will in future lay any other or higher duties or imports on each others vessels and merchandizes, than what they shall lay on the like vessels and merchandizes of all other nations—nor shall they lay any prohibitions on any kind of merchandize without extending it to the same kind of merchandize to whatever nation belonging.[37]

The people and inhabitants of the two countries respectively shall have liberty freely and securely, and without hindrance or molestation to come with their ships and cargoes to the lands countries cities ports places and rivers within the dominions and territories aforesaid—to enter into the same, to resort thereto, and to remain and reside there without any limitation of time—also to hire and possess houses and warehouses for the purposes of their commerce and generally that the merchants and traders on each side shall enjoy the most complete protection and security for their commerce—but subject always as to what respects

37. The treaty adds, Article XV, this important reservation: "But the British Government reserves to itself the right of imposing on American vessels, entering into the British ports in Europe, a tonnage duty equal to that which shall be payable by British vessels in the ports of America; and also such duty as may be adequate to countervail the difference of duty now payable on the importation of European and Asiatic goods, when imported into the United States in British or in American vessels." The United States agreed for twelve years not to impose any new or additional duties on British vessels, nor to increase the existing tariff discrimination on imports in British vessels as compared with American.

this article to the general laws and statutes of the two countries respectively.

12th. In consideration that the United States agree not to lay any duties or imposts on the exportation of any of their commodities produce or manufactures in british vessels, His Majesty agrees that masts ship-timber staves, boards plank and spars may be imported into his said dominions duty free from the United States in American vessels, and also that the duty on the importation of Rice from the United States shall be reduced to ———— per hundred and that on whale oil to ———— and that Salt may be imported into the United States in their vessels from Turks Island duty free[38]

13th. It shall be free for the two contracting parties respectively, to appoint Consuls for the protection of Trade, to reside in the dominions and territories afore-said, and who shall enjoy those liberties and rights which belong to them by reason of their function—But before any consul shall act as such, he shall be in the usual forms approved and admitted by the party to whom he is sent, and it is hereby declared to be lawful and proper that in case of illegal or improper conduct towards the laws and government, a consul may either be punished according to law if the laws will reach the case, or be dismissed or even sent back—the offended Government assigning to the other their reasons for the same—

38. A marginal comment, apparently written in the Foreign Office, reads: "N.B. The Constitution forbids duties on exportation."

Either of the parties may except from the residence of Consuls, such particular places as such party shall judge proper to be so excepted—[39]

14th. His Majesty consents that american vessels trading to Asia shall be hospitably received and treated, in all his Asiatic Ports and Dominions; and may freely import into the same any of the productions and manufactures of the United States, and purchase and carry from thence any of the productions or manufactures of those countries directly to the United States, but not directly to any part of Europe. This Article shall be of the same duration with the Article respecting the West Indies.[40]

15th. It shall be lawful for all the subjects of his Majesty and the citizens of the United States, to sail with their ships with perfect security and liberty no distinction being made who are the proprietors of the merchandizes laden thereon from any port whatever to the countries which are now or shall be hereafter at war with His Majesty or the United States. It shall likewise be lawful for them respectively to sail and traffic with their ships and merchandizes, with the same liberty and security, from the countries ports and

39. This is Article XVI of the treaty.

40. See Article XIII of the treaty which specified this privilege, limited to such exports and imports as were not prohibited by law. It added an inhibition to import from the British East Indies, in time of war, military stores, naval stores, or rice; excluded American vessels from the coasting trade of the British East Indies; and prohibited American citizens from settling in those dominions without the consent of the British Government. Stop for refreshment was allowed American vessels at St. Helena Island. American vessels were to pay no higher duties or charges than British vessels.

places of those who are enemies of both, or of either party, and to pass directly, not only from the places of the enemy aforementioned to neutral places, but also from one place belonging to an Enemy to another place belonging to an enemy, whether they be under the jurisdiction of the same or of several Sovereigns or Governments. And as everything shall be deemed to be free which shall be found on board the Ships belonging to the said subjects or citizens aforesaid, altho' the whole lading or part thereof should belong to the enemies of the contracting parties (contraband goods always excepted) so it is also agreed that the same liberty be extended to persons who are on board a free ship, to the end, that altho' they be enemies to both or to either party, they may not be taken out of such free ship, unless they are soldiers actually in the service of the enemies and on their voyage for the purpose of being employed in a military capacity in their fleets or armies.

This liberty of navigation and Commerce shall extend to all kinds of merchandizes, excepting those only which are specified in the following article, and which are described under the name of contraband.[41]

16th. Under the name of contraband or prohibited goods shall be comprehended Arms, Cannon, Harquebusses, Mortars, Petards, Bombs, Grenades, Saucisses, Carcasses, carriages for cannon, Musket Rests, Bandoliers, Gunpowder, Match, Salt-Petre, Ball, Pikes, Swords, Headpieces, Helmets, Cuirasses, Halberds,

---

41. Same as Article XXIII of the Treaty of Amity and Commerce of 1778 with France.

Javelins, Holsters, Belts, Horses and Harness, and all other like kind of arms and warlike implements fit for the use of Troops.[42]

These Merchandizes which follow shall not be reckoned among Contraband Goods. That is to say—All sorts of cloth, and all other manufactures of Wool, Flax, Silk, Cotton, or any other materials, all kinds of wearing apparel, together with the articles of which they are usually made—Gold, Silver coined or un-coined—Tin, Iron, Lead, Copper, Brass, Coals—as also Wheat and Barley and Flour, and every kind of corn and Pulse—Tobacco and all kinds of Spices— Salted and Smoked Flesh, Fish, Cheese, Butter, Beer, Cyder, Oil, Wines, Sugar, Salt, and all kinds of provisions whatever which serve for sustenance and food to mankind—All kinds of Cotton, Flax, Hemp, Cordage, Cables, Sails, Sailcloth, Tallow, Pitch, Tar, Rosin, Anchors, and any parts of Anchors, Ship masts, Planks, Timber of all kinds of Trees and all other things proper either for building or repairing Ships. Nor shall any other Goods whatever which have not been worked into the form of any Instrument or Furniture for warlike use, by land or by sea, be reputed contraband, much less such as have been already wrought and made up for any other purpose—All which things shall be deemed goods not contraband—As likewise all others which are not herein before and particularly enumerated and described as contraband—So that they may be freely carried by the respective subjects and citizens of the contracting parties even to places belonging to an enemy excepting only such places as are besieged

42. The treaty says, Article XVIII, "all other implements of war."

blocked up or invested,[43] and whereas it frequently happens that vessels sail for a Port or place belonging to an Enemy without knowing that the same is either besieged blockaded or invested. It is agreed that every vessel so circumstanced may be turned away from such port or place, but she shall not be detained nor her cargo, if not contraband, be confiscated; unless after notice she shall again attempt to enter—but she shall be permitted to go to any other Port or place she may think proper. Nor shall any vessel or goods of either party, that may have entered into such port or place, before the same was besieged blockaded or invested by the other, and be found therein after the Reduction or surrender of such place, be liable to confiscation, but shall be restored to the owners or Proprietors thereof. And whereas corn grain or other Provisions can only be considered as contraband on occasions and in Cases when a well-founded Expectation exists of reducing an Enemy by the want thereof It is agreed that in all such Cases, the said articles shall not be confiscated [44] but that the captors, or in their Default the Government under whose authority they act, shall pay to the masters or owners of such vessels, the full value of all such articles, with a reasonable mercantile Proffit thereon,

43. The treaty, Article XVIII, did not accept Jay's proposed definition of foodstuffs when contraband, but stated that whenever "provisions and other articles not generally contraband," do become such "according to the law of nations," they should be pre-empted at full value, with grant of freight and demurrage.

44. Up to here this paragraph corresponds with Article XXIV of the Treaty of 1778 with France.

together with the Freight, and also the Demurrage incident to their Detention.

17th. To the end that all manner of dissentions and
quarrels may be avoided and prevented on both sides
—It is agreed that in case either of the contracting
parties should be engaged in war, the vessels belonging
to the subjects or citizens of the other, shall be furnished with Sea Letters or Passports, expressing the
name, property, and bulk of the Ship or Vessel and
also the name and place of abode of the Master or
Commander, that it may appear thereby, that the said
Ship really belongs to such subjects or citizens—Which
passports shall be made out and granted according to
the form annexed to the present Treaty. They shall
likewise be renewed every year, if the Ship happens to
return home within the space of a year.

It is also agreed that such Ships when laden, are to be
provided not only with passports as above mentioned
but also with certificates containing the several particu-
lars of the cargo, the place from whence the Ship
sailed, and whither she is bound; so that it may be
known whether she carries any of the prohibited or
contraband goods specified in the preceding article
Which certificates shall be prepared by the officers
of the place from whence the Ship set sail in the accustomed form. And if any one shall think fit to express
in the said certificates the name of the person to whom
the goods belong, he may freely do so.[45]

18th. The Merchant Ships of either of the parties
coming to any of the coasts of either of them, but
without being willing to enter into port, or being
entered, yet not willing to land their cargoes or break

45. Same as Article XXV of treaty with France of 1778.

bulk, shall not be obliged to give an account of their
lading; unless suspected on sure evidence, of carrying
contraband Goods to the enemies of either of the
contracting parties.[46]

In case the said Merchant Ships shall meet with any
Men of War or Privateers of either of the contracting
parties, either on the Coast or on the High Seas, the
said men of War & Privateers are to remain out of
cannon shot, and to send their boats to the Merchant
Ship which may be met with, and shall enter her to
the Number of two or three men only, to Whom the
master or commander of such ship or vessel, shall
show his passport containing the proof of the property
of the ship, made out according to the form annexed to
this present Treaty; And the Ship which shall exhibit
the same, shall have liberty to continue her voyage, and
it shall be wholly unlawful to molest or search her, or
to chase or compel her to alter her course.[47]

But such of the said merchant Ships as may be bound
for a port at enmity with the other contracting party,
concerning whose voyage, and the sort of goods on
board, there may be just cause of suspicion, shall be
obliged to exhibit, as well on the high seas as in the
Ports and Havens, not only her passports, but also
her certificates expressing that the goods are not of
the kind which are contraband as specified in the
———— article of this Treaty.[48]

If on exhibiting the above-mentioned Certificates
containing a list of the Cargo, the other party should
discover any goods of that kind which are declared

46. Same as Article XXVI of treaty with France of 1778.
47. Same as Article XXVII of treaty with France of 1778.
48. Same as Article XII of treaty with France of 1778.

contraband or prohibited by this treaty, and which are designed for a port subject to the enemy of the said party, it shall be unlawful to break up or open the Hatches, Chests, Bales or other Vessels found on board such Ship, or to remove even the smallest parcel of Goods, unless the lading be brought on shore in the presence of the Officers of the Court of Admiralty, and an inventory made by them of the said goods. Nor shall it be lawful to sell, exchange or alienate the same in any manner, unless after lawful process shall have been had against such prohibited goods and the Judges of the Admiralty shall, by sentence pronounced, have confiscated the same Saving always as well the Ship itself, as all the other goods found therein, which by this Treaty are accounted free; neither may they be detained on pretence of their being mixed with prohibited goods, much less shall they be confiscated as lawful prize. And if when only part of the cargo shall consist of contraband goods, the master of the Ship shall consent and offer to deliver them to the captor who has discovered them; in such case the captor, after having received those goods as lawful prize, shall forthwith release the ship and not hinder her by any means from prosecuting her voyage to the place of her destination.[49]

19th. It is agreed that whatever shall be found to be laden by the respective subjects or citizens of either of the said parties on any ship belonging to the enemies of the other, altho' the same be not contraband goods, shall be confiscated in the same manner as if it belonged to the enemy himself—Excepting always those goods

49. Same as Article XIII (except for last sentence) of treaty with France of 1778.

which were put on board such ship before the declaration of war, or the general order for reprizals, or even after such declaration or order, if it were done within the times following, that is to say—if they were put on board such ship in any port or place, within the space of two months after such declaration, or order for Reprizals, between Archangel, St. Petersburg, and the Scilly Islands, and between the said Islands and the City of Gibraltar of ten weeks in the Mediterranean Sea and of eight months in any other country or place in the world. So that the goods whether contraband or not, which were put on board any ship belonging to an enemy as aforesaid before the war, or after the declaration of the same or of the general order for reprizals, within the times and limits above mentioned shall not be liable to confiscation, but shall be restored without delay to the proprietors demanding the same. Provided nevertheless, that if the said merchandizes be contraband, it shall not be anyways lawful to carry them after being so restored, to the ports belonging to the enemy—[50]

20th. And the more abundant care may be taken for the Security of the respective subjects and citizens of the contracting parties, and to prevent their suffering injuries by the men of war or privateers of either party, all commanders of ships of war and privateers, and all other the said subjects and citizens shall forbear doing any damage to those of the other party or committing any outrage against them and if they act to the con-

50. Practically the same as Article XIV of treaty with·France of 1778.

trary, they shall be punished, and shall also be bound in their persons and estates to make satisfaction and reparation for all damages and the interest thereof, of whatever nature the said damages may be.

For this cause all commanders of privateers, before they receive their commissions, shall hereafter be obliged to give before a competent judge, sufficient security by at least two responsible sureties who have no interest in the said privateer, each of whom together with the said commander shall be jointly and severally bound in the sum of fifteen hundred pounds sterling, or if such a ship be provided with above one hundred and fifty seamen or soldiers, in the sum of three thousand pounds sterling, to satisfy all damages and injuries which the said privateer or her officers or men or any of them may do or commit during their Cruize contrary to the tenor of this Treaty, or to the laws and instructions for regulating their conduct—and further that in all cases of aggressions thereof, the said commissions shall be revoked and annulled—

It is also agreed that whenever a judge of a Court of Admiralty of either of the parties, shall pronounce sentence against any vessel or goods or property belonging to the subjects or citizens of the other party, a formal and duly authenticated copy of all the proceedings in the cause, and of the said sentence, shall be delivered gratis to the commander of the said vessel [51]

51. Article XIX of the treaty.

before the said sentence shall be executed— And this
the said judge shall do on pain of forfeiting his commission—

21st. When the Quality of the Ship Goods and
Master shall sufficiently appear, from such passports
and certificates, it shall not be lawful for the commanders of men of war or privateers, to exact any further
proof, under any pretext whatever. But if any merchant
ship shall not be provided with such passports or certificates, then it may be examined by a proper judge, but in
such manner as, if it shall be found, from other proofs
and documents, that it truely belongs to the subjects or
citizens of one of the contracting parties, and does not
contain any contraband goods designed to be carried to
the enemy of the other, it shall not be liable to confiscation, but shall be released together with its cargo, in
order to proceed on its voyage— If the master of the
ship named in the passports, should happen to die, or
be removed by any other cause, and another put in his
place, the Ships and Goods laden thereon, shall nevertheless be equally secure, and the passports shall remain
in full force—

22d. It is further agreed that both the said contracting parties shall not only refuse to receive any
Pirates into any of their ports, havens, or towns, or
permit any of their inhabitants to receive protect harbor conceal or assist them in any manner, but will bring
to condign punishment all such Inhabitants as shall
be guilty of such acts or offences. And all their ships
with the goods or merchandizes taken by them and
brought into the ports of either of the said parties, shall

be seized, as far as they can be discovered, and shall be restored to the owners of their factors or agents duly deputed and authorised in writing by them (proper evidence being first given in the court of admiralty for proving the property) even in case such effects should have passed into other hands by sale, if it be proved that the buyers knew, or might have known that they had been piratically taken[52]

It is likewise agreed and concluded that the subjects and citizens of the two nations, shall not do any acts of hostility or violence against each other; nor accept commissions or instructions so to act from any foreign Prince or State, enemies to the other party nor shall the enemies of one of the parties be permitted to invite or endeavour to enlist in their military service, any of the subjects or citizens of the other party; and the laws against all such offences and aggressions shall be punctually executed—And if any subject or citizen of the said parties respectively shall accept any foreign commission or letters of marque for arming any vessel to act as a privateer against the other party, and be taken by the other party, it is hereby declared to be lawful for the said party to treat and punish the said subject or citizen having such commission or letters of marque as a pirate—[53]

It is expressly stipulated that neither of the said contracting parties will order or authorize any acts

52. Article XX of the treaty.
53. Article XXI of the treaty.

of reprizal against the other on complaints of injuries
or damages until the said party shall first have presented to the other a statement thereof, verified by
competent proof and evidence and demanded justice,
and satisfaction, and the same shall either have been
refused, or unreasonably delayed—[54]

Not only the merchant ships but also the ships of war
of either of the contracting parties shall be hospitably
received in the ports of the other, and their Officers
shall be treated with that decorum and respect which
friendly nations owe to each other—[55] But the said
officers as well as all others shall be amenable to the
laws of the land, and shall take care so to govern and
regulate the conduct of the men under their command,
as that they behave peaceably and inoffensively; and
particularly that a Habeas Corpus issued by the proper
magistrate directed to any of the said officers, commanding him forthwith to bring any particular person
duly described by his name or otherwise, before such
magistrate shall be punctually obeyed by such officers—

And all magistrates duly authorised to issue such
writs, on complaint that any subject or citizen of either
of the said parties, other than the one to whom the
said man of war belongs, hath been impressed and is
unlawfully detained on board thereof, shall issue a
Habeas Corpus to the officer having the command of
the said man of war, and thereby order him to have
such person or persons so said to have been impressed,
before the said Magistrate, at a time and place therein

54. Article XXII of the treaty.
55. The treaty, Article XIII, substitutes for this clause the words
"with that respect which is due to the commissions which they bear."

to be specified, which writ shall be obeyed— And the said Magistrate shall then proceed to inquire into the merits of the case, and shall do therein as to him shall appear to be just and right, either remanding the said person or persons, if the complaint be groundless, or discharging him if it be well founded— And in the latter case, the said Officer shall deliver forthwith to the said person or persons, whatever arrears of wages may be due, and whatever Effects or Property he or they may have on board— All which shall be done uprightly and with good faith—

23d. It shall not be lawful for any foreign Privateer, (not being subjects or citizens of either of the said parties) who have commissions from any other prince or state, in enmity with either nation, to arm their Ships in the ports of either of the said parties, nor to sell what they have taken, nor in any other manner to exchange the same, nor shall be allowed to purchase more provisions than shall be necessary for their going to the nearest port of that prince or state from whom they obtained their commissions.[56]

It shall be lawful for the Ships of war and privateers belonging to the said parties respectively so far and so far only as shall not be repugnant to former treaties made in this respect with other sovereigns or states to carry whithersoever they please the ships and goods taken from their enemies without being obliged to pay any fee to the officers of the admiralty or to any Judges whatever—Nor shall the said prizes when they arrive

56. Article XXIV of the treaty.

at and enter the ports of the said parties, be detained or
seized—neither shall the searchers or other officers of
those places, visit or take cognizance of the validity of
such prizes, nor shall the said prizes be unladen or
break bulk, but they shall hoist sail and depart as
speedily as may be and carry their said prizes to the
places mentioned in their Commissions or patents
which the Commanders of the said ships of war or
Privateers shall be obliged to shew—No shelter or
refuge shall be given in their ports to such as have
made prize upon the subjects or citizens of either of
the said parties, but if forced by stress of weather, or
the dangers of the sea to enter therein, particular care
shall be taken to hasten their departure and to cause
them to retire as soon as possible. And further that
while the said parties continue in amity, neither of them
will in future make any Treaty that shall be inconsistent
with this article—[57]

24th. Neither of the said parties shall permit the
ships or goods belonging to the subjects or citizens of
the other to be taken within cannon shot of the coast,
nor in any of the bays ports or rivers of their territories, by ships of war or others having commission
from any prince republic or state whatever. But in
case it should so happen, the party whose territorial
rights shall thus have been violated, shall make full and
ample satisfaction for the vessel or vessels so taken,

57. Article XXI, paragraph one, of the treaty.

whether the same be vessels of war or merchant vessels.—[58]

If at any time a Rupture should take place (which God forbid) between His Majesty and the United States, the merchants and others of the two nations, residing in the dominions of the other, shall have the priviledge of remaining and continuing their trade therein so long as they behave peaceably and commit no offence against the laws; and in case their conduct should render them suspected, and the respective Governments should think proper to order them to remove, the term of twelve months from the publication of the order shall be allowed them for that purpose to remove with their families effects and property, but this favor shall not be extended to those who shall act contrary to the established laws. And for greater certainty it is declared, that such rupture shall not be deemed to exist while negotiations for accommodating differences shall be depending, nor until the respective Ambassadors or Ministers shall be recalled or sent home on account of such differences, and not on account of personal misconduct, according to the nature and degrees of which, both parties retain their rights either to request the recall or immediately to send home the Ambassador or Minister of the other; and that without prejudice to their mutual Friendship and Good understanding.—[59]

58. The treaty substitutes Article XXV, paragraph two, "shall use his utmost endeavors to obtain . . . full and ample satisfaction . . ."
59. Article XXVI of the treaty.

25th. It is further agreed that his Majesty and the United States on mutual requisitions, by them respectively or by their respective ministers or officers authorized to make the same, will deliver up to justice all persons who being charged with Murder or Forgery committed within the jurisdiction of either, shall seek an asylum within any [of] the countries of the other, and that on such evidence of criminality, as according to the laws of the place where the fugitive or person so charged shall be found, would justify his apprehension and commitment for Tryal, if the offence had there been committed. The expence of such apprehension and delivery shall be born and defrayed by those who make the requisition and receive the fugitive.[60]

It is agreed that the first eight [61] articles of this Treaty shall be permanent And that all the subsequent articles[62] shall be limited in their duration to twelve years to be computed from the day on which this Treaty shall be ratified by the President of the United States by and with the advice and consent of the Senate thereof.[63] But whereas the tenth Article will expire by its own limitation at the end of two years from the signing the preliminary articles of the peace which are to terminate the present war in which his

60. Where the 26th article of the draft would naturally follow occurs a large blank.
61. The first ten articles of the treaty are permanent.
62. The treaty here interposes "except the twelfth [article].
63. The treaty stipulates "to be computed from the day on which the ratifications of this treaty shall be exchanged."

Majesty is engaged, It is agreed that proper measures shall by concert be seasonably taken for bringing the subject of that article into amicable treaty and discussion, so early before the expiration of the said term, as that new arrangements on that head may, by that time, be perfected and ready to take place. But if it should unfortunately happen that His Majesty and the United States should not be able to agree on such new arrangements, in that case all the Articles of this Treaty except the first eight shall then cease and expire together.

Endorsement

In Mr. Jay's

30 Sept 1794

F. O., 95, 512.

# American Law and British Creditors

The American records of the Foreign Office abound in memorials and representations of British creditors for redress. These poured in with greater frequency when it became known that negotiations had been opened with Jay in 1794. The case of the creditors is well summed up in one of their numerous papers submitted to the Cabinet on March 16, 1794. It recapitulates the nature of the trade as it existed before the war, the substance of former memorials, and asserts that the private rights of British merchants trading to North America before 1776 had been sacrificed by the following:

(a) The prohibitory law of 1775 (cutting off intercourse with the American Colonies) ; (b) the emancipation of America by the Peace of 1783, thus giving up the dominion of laws made by Parliament for the encouragement and security of trade in America; (c) delay in insisting on the due performance of Article IV of the Treaty of Peace; (d) withholding the forts claimed by the Americans. Since these sufferings and losses originated entirely from the legislative restrictions and political system of their own Government, they claimed compensation as an act of justice.[1]

1. Brief statement of the case of the British Merchants, etc., P.R.O., F.O., 95, 512.

Pitt had a conference with a committee of the Glasgow merchants, July 15, 1794, in which they represented the amount of debts remaining unpaid as "near £3,000,000 sterling," an amount much in excess of the statement made in 1792, which Hammond said was greatly exaggerated. They claimed nineteen years' interest. In answer to a question by Pitt how much interest they would be willing to renounce upon being secured that no legal impediments to the recovery of debts would thereafter obtain, they were willing to renounce if necessary the whole interest. They claimed that in Virginia not less than £275,000 had been paid into the treasury of that state during the war, in Maryland £148,000.[2]

The decision of the federal court of the Virginia district in 1793 allowed validity of *bona fide* debts, excepting those sequestered during the war, and the sequestrations were in 1796 declared illegal by the Supreme Court,[3] so that if the British creditors had not been secured by the treaty they would have been safe in the American federal courts.

Grenville asked the Committee of Merchants (July 23, 1794) if the alternatives were presented of the payment of a round sum by the American Government in liquidation of all British claims previous to the peace, or the adoption of measures for opening the courts of law in America—without impediment, with appeal to some special court or commission instituted so as to remedy difficulties arising from embarrassments of legal evidence and unfavorable disposition of the mass

2. Memorandum desired by Mr. Pitt, July 3, 1794, P.R.O.,F.O., 95, 512.

3. Ware, Administrator of Jones, *v.* Hylton, III *Dallas,* 285.

of the people of the community, which alternative the creditors would prefer.[4] The Committee replied it would accept a round sum, equal to the amount of debts esteemed good, January 1, 1776, with ten years' interest, the whole estimated at £2,000,000.[5] This Grenville deemed far in excess of any sum which might reasonably be recovered, "even if the Treaty had been fulfilled by the United States in all its parts and without delay." [6] It is worth noting, as significant that the British creditors themselves had some faith in the ultimate justice of American courts, that in consenting to a round sum they desired to reserve the right to pursue their entire claims by legal process.

The chief grievance, aside from the sequestration of debts as an act of war, was the difficulty of procuring evidence of legal value. The jurisdiction of the federal courts took no cognizance of debts under $500. As most of the business of the British merchants in Virginia had been of retail nature, dispersed by local factors, a great part of the debts was composed of separate sums under $500, of which the state courts refused to take cognizance, on the ground that no compensation had been given for negroes carried off by the British army.[7] Often no accounts were kept other than those of the factor, for the planter was accustomed to pay at the end of the year when his crop receipts came in. The only proof of indebtedness that in many instances could be produced was the wholly *ex*

4. Grenville to Messrs. Moleson & Nutt, July 23, 1794, P.R.O.,F.O., 95, 512.
5. Moleson & Nutt to Grenville, Aug. 25, 1794, ibid.
6. Grenville to Moleson & Nutt, Aug., 1794, ibid.
7. Glasford to Grenville, Glasgow, July 29, 1794, ibid.

*parte* evidence of the factor's accounts, which an ordinary court of law would refuse.[8] The fact that the merchants engaged in the trade neglected to take such caution as would secure their debt by common law could not be made a serious argument against the American courts, which applied, generally speaking, the common law of England. The provision of article six of the treaty of 1794, proposed by Grenville to provide for such debts, gave the Commission power to "receive in evidence, according as they may think most consistent with equity and justice all written Depositions, or Books, or Papers, or Copies, or Extracts thereof, every such Deposition, Book or Paper, or Copy or Extract, being duly authenticated, either according to the legal forms now respectively existing in the two Countries, or in such other manner as the said Commissioners shall see cause to require or allow." This provision gave to British creditors in America a greater distress on debtors than the American state laws would to an American citizen, or than a British creditor in England would enjoy, since it admitted *ex parte* evidence if the Commissioners chose to accept it.

8. Gilbert Hamilton and Robert Findlay to Pitt, London, July 21, 1794; enclosing extract of a letter from Petersburg, Va., Dec. 10, 1793, ibid.

# Summary of the Proceedings of the Joint Commissions Provided by Articles VI and VII of Jay's Treaty

The joint commissions provided under Articles VI and VII of Jay's Treaty were appointed as follows: two commissioners by each party to the treaty, and these four to appoint a fifth; in case the four could not agree upon a fifth, each side to present one name and the fifth to be chosen by lot from these two. It was also provided that three of each commission's members should constitute a board and "have power to do any act pertaining to the said commission, provided that one of the commissioners named on each side, and the fifth commissioner shall be present."

When the Debts Commission met at Philadelphia it was necessary to appoint the fifth commissioner by lot. A British subject was chosen. Thus constituted with a majority of British members the Commission proceeded to lay down principles which the American minority would not accept; such as refusal to suspend interest during the war, and inclusion within the purview of Article VI of debts confiscated from Loyalists by acts of attainder. After much wrangling the two American Commissioners availed themselves of the proviso which necessitated the presence of a commissioner of each party to form a board, and withdrew. This made it impossible for the Commission to continue its work. John Marshall, then Secretary of State, defended the procedure of the United States by claiming that the majority of the Commission had attempted to extend its jurisdiction far beyond the limits of the treaty. Lord Grenville, in retaliation, withdrew both British Commissioners from the Spoliations Commission, then sitting at London.

The Debts Commission never met again. The dispute was compromised by the Convention of January 8, 1802, by which Article VI of the Treaty of 1794 was annulled, and the United States agreed to pay to the British Government the lump sum of £600,000 sterling, in three annual installments, in satisfaction of what the United States might have been liable to pay under that article. A sum of $2,664,000, exchange value in dollars, was duly appropriated and paid. By Article II of the Convention, Article IV of the treaty of peace, so far as respected its future operation, was confirmed, so that creditors on either side should in the future meet with no lawful impediments to recovery. The matter was thus finally left to the American courts, from jurisdiction of which Jay should never have allowed it to escape.

The fifth commissioner of the Spoliations Commission, sitting at London, was also selected by lot. That commission was composed of three Americans and two Englishmen. One of the first cases to come before it involved the finality of the highest British court of appeal for admiralty cases—the Lords Commissioners of Appeals. Unlike the Philadelphia Commission, the

London Commission could not take cognizance of claims until the resources of British law courts had been exhausted; but the American members held that, the resources of British courts having been finally exhausted by a decision of the Lords Commissioners of Appeals, claimants could then apply to the Commission, otherwise practically all the claims would be excluded from the Commission's cognizance. The two English Commissioners, refusing to assent to this interpretation, withdrew and thus paralyzed the Commission's powers. Acting upon the advice of the Lord Chancellor, Loughborough, Grenville adopted the principle that the opinions of the Lords Commissioners of Appeals were final so far as vesting of property titles was concerned; but that Article VII of Jay's Treaty allowed claimants to go before the mixed Commission for claims for money compensation because of decisions of the British admiralty courts. He instructed the British Commissioners to resume attendance at the sessions. The work of the Commission then proceeded until the British Commissioners were withdrawn in retaliation for the withdrawal of the American Commissioners from the Philadelphia Debts Commission. Following the settlement of the debts question by the Convention of 1802, the London Commission convened again, in accordance with a provision of that convention, and proceeded to adjudicate all remaining claims.

The three American Commissioners at London held that by the "existing law of nations" foodstuffs were not to be considered contraband, and the Commission granted compensation on that basis. One infers from Mr. Justice John Bassett Moore's summary of the Commission's labors that this grant of compensation did not invalidate the Orders-in-Council under color of authority of which pre-emption of provisions had been made; it merely granted compensation for a procedure which the mixed Commission held to be contrary to the existing law of nations.

The United States in accepting this compensation without destroying the principle of the provision orders did exactly what it would have done, for example, if it had accepted Germany's offer to make money compensation for American lives lost by the torpedoing of the *Lusitania,* Germany at the same time defending the principle of sinking passenger ships without warning.

The London Commission wound up its business on February 24, 1804. A summary of its awards shows that American claimants received £2,330,000 which at the exchange rate of $4.44 to the pound sterling (the rate adopted by the Convention of 1802) was equivalent to $10,345,200. British claims to the amount of $143,428 were allowed.

Balancing money received in final settlement of spoliation and debt claims by both parties we have:

| | |
|---|---|
| Received by the United States | $10,345,200 |
| Received by Great Britain | 2,807,428 |
| Balance in favor of the United States | $ 7,537,772 |

The above is based on the study of the Commissions presented in Volume I of John Bassett Moore's *History and Digest of the International Arbitrations to which the United States Has Been a Party,* pp. 270–349. This page of my text contains important corrections of the corresponding page of the first edition of this book. My apologies to the late Mr. Justice Moore.

APPENDIX VI

A.

# Definitive Treaty of Peace and Independence

The following text is from the definitive edition of Hunter Miller's
*Treaties and other International Acts of the United States of America*
(8 vols. Washington, 1931–48), II, 151–57.

*Definitive Treaty of Peace, signed at Paris September
3, 1783. Original in English.
Ratified by the United States January 14, 1784.
Ratified by Great Britain April 9, 1784. Ratifications
exchanged at Paris May 12, 1784. Proclaimed January
14, 1784.*

In the Name of the most Holy & undivided Trinity.

It having pleased the divine Providence to dispose
the Hearts of the most Serene and most Potent Prince
George the third, by the Grace of God, King of Great
Britain, France & Ireland, Defender of the Faith, Duke
of Brunswick and Lunebourg, Arch Treasurer, and
Prince Elector of the Holy Roman Empire &cᵃ. and of
the United States of America, to forget all past Misunderstandings and Differences that have unhappily
interrupted the good Correspondence and Friendship
which they mutually wish to restore; and to establish

such a beneficial and satisfactory Intercourse between
the two Countries upon the Ground of reciprocal Advantages and mutual Convenience as may promote and
secure to both perpetual Peace & Harmony, and having
for this desirable End already laid the Foundation of
Peace & Reconciliation by the Provisional Articles
signed at Paris on the 30ᵗʰ of Novʳ. 1782. by the Commissioners empower'd on each Part, which Articles
were agreed to be inserted in and to constitute the
Treaty of Peace proposed to be concluded between the
Crown of Great Britain and the said United States, but
which Treaty was not to be concluded until Terms of
Peace should be agreed upon between Great Britain &
France, And his Britannic Majesty should be ready to
conclude such Treaty accordingly: and the Treaty between Great Britain & France having since been concluded, His Britannic Majesty & the United States of
America, in Order to carry into full Effect the Provisional Articles abovementioned, according to the Tenor
thereof, have constituted & appointed, that is to say
His Britannic Majesty on his Part, David Hartley
Esqʳ, Member of the Parliament of Great Britain; and
the said United States on their Part, John Adams Esqʳ,
late a Commissioner of the United States of America
at the Court of Versailles, late Delegate in Congress
from the State of Massachusetts and Chief Justice of
the said State, and Minister Plenipotentiary of the said
United States to their High Mightinesses the States
General of the United Netherlands; Benjamin Franklin
Esqʳᵉ late Delegate in Congress from the State of
Pennsylvania, President of the Convention of the sᵈ
State, and Minister Plenipotentiary from the United
States of America at the Court of Versailles: John Jay

Esq.$^{re}$ late President of Congress, and Chief Justice of
the State of New-York & Minister Plenipotentiary
from the said United States at the Court of Madrid; to
be the Plenipotentiaries for the concluding and signing
the Present Definitive Treaty; who after having reciprocally communicated their respective full Powers have
agreed upon and confirmed the following Articles.

## ARTICLE 1$^{st}$

His Britannic Majesty acknowledges the s.$^{d}$ United
States, viz. New-Hampshire Massachusetts Bay,
Rhode-Island & Providence Plantations, Connecticut,
New York, New Jersey, Pennsylvania, Delaware,
Maryland, Virginia, North Carolina, South Carolina
& Georgia, to be free sovereign & Independent States;
that he treats with them as such, and for himself his
Heirs & Successors, relinquishes all Claims to the
Government Propriety & Territorial Rights of the
same & every Part thereof.

## ARTICLE 2$^{d.}$

And that all Disputes which might arise in future on
the Subject of the Boundaries of the said United States,
may be prevented, it is hereby agreed and declared,
that the following are and shall be their Boundaries,
Viz. From the North West Angle of Nova Scotia, viz.
That Angle which is formed by a Line drawn due
North from the Source of Saint Croix River to the
Highlands along the said Highlands which divide those
Rivers that empty themselves into the River S.$^{t}$ Law-
rence, from those which fall into the Atlantic Ocean, to
the Northwestern-most Head of Connecticut River:
Thence down along the middle of that River to the

forty fifth Degree of North Latitude; From thence by
a Line due West on said Latitude until it strikes the
River Iroquois or Cataraquy; Thence along the middle
of said River into Lake Ontario; through the Middle
of said Lake until it strikes the Communication by
Water between that Lake & Lake Erie; Thence along
the middle of said Communication into Lake Erie;
through the middle of said Lake, until it arrives at the
Water Communication between that Lake & Lake
Huron; Thence along the middle of said Water-Com-
munication into the Lake Huron, thence through the
middle of said Lake to the Water Communication between that Lake and Lake Superior, thence through
Lake Superior Northward of the Isles Royal & Phe-
lipeaux to the Long Lake; Thence through the Middle
of said Long-Lake, and the Water Communication between it & the Lake of the Woods, to the said Lake of
the Woods; Thence through the said Lake to the most
Northwestern Point thereof, and from thence on a due
West Course to the River Mississippi, Thence by a
Line to be drawn along the Middle of the Said River
Mississippi until it shall intersect the Northernmost
Part of the thirty first Degree of North Latitude.
South, by a Line to be drawn due East from the Determination of the Line last mentioned, in the Latitude
of thirty one Degrees North of the Equator to the
middle of the River Apalachicola or Catahouche.
Thence along the middle thereof to its Junction with
the Flint River; Thence strait to the Head of S$^t$.Mary's
River, and thence down along the middle of S$^t$ Mary's
River to the Atlantic Ocean. East, by a Line to be
drawn along the Middle of the River S$^t$ Croix, from
its Mouth in the Bay of Fundy to its Source; and from

its Source directly North to the aforesaid Highlands, which divide the Rivers that fall into the Atlantic Ocean, from those which fall into the River S$^t$. Lawrence; comprehending all Islands within twenty Leagues of any Part of the Shores of the United States, & lying between Lines to be drawn due East from the Points where the aforesaid Boundaries between Nova Scotia on the one Part and East Florida on the other, shall respectively touch the Bay of Fundy and the Atlantic Ocean, excepting such Islands as now are or heretofore have been within the Limits of the said Province of Nova Scotia.

## ARTICLE 3$^d$.

It is agreed that the People of the United States shall continue to enjoy unmolested the Right to take Fish of every kind on the Grand Bank and on all the other Banks of New-foundland, also in the Gulph of S$^t$ Lawrence, and at all other Places in the Sea where the Inhabitants of both Countries used at any time heretofore to fish. And also that the Inhabitants of the United States shall have Liberty to take Fish of every Kind on such Part of the Coast of New-foundland as British Fishermen shall use, (but not to dry or cure the same on that Island) And also on the Coasts Bays & Creeks of all other of his Britannic Majesty's Dominions in America, and that the American Fishermen shall have Liberty to dry and cure Fish in any of the unsettled Bays Harbours and Creeks of Nova Scotia, Magdalen Islands, and Labrador, so long as the same shall remain unsettled but so soon as the same or either of them shall be settled, it shall not be lawful for the said Fishermen to dry or cure Fish at such Settlement, without a previous Agreement for that purpose with the Inhabitants, Proprietors or Possessors of the Ground.

## ARTICLE 4th

It is agreed that Creditors on either Side shall meet with no lawful Impediment to the Recovery of the full Value in Sterling Money of all bona fide Debts heretofore contracted.

## ARTICLE 5th

It is agreed that the Congress shall earnestly recommend it to the Legislatures of the respective States to provide for the Restitution of all Estates, Rights and Properties which have been confiscated belonging to real British Subjects; and also of the Estates Rights and Properties of Persons resident in Districts in the Possession of his Majesty's Arms, and who have not borne Arms against the said United States. And that Persons of any other Description shall have free Liberty to go to any Part or Parts of any of the thirteen United States and therein to remain twelve Months unmolested in their Endeavours to obtain the Restitution of such of their Estates Rights & Properties as may have been confiscated. And that Congress shall also earnestly recommend to the several States, a Reconsideration and Revision of all Acts or Laws regarding the Premises, so as to render the said Laws or Acts perfectly consistent, not only with Justice and Equity, but with that Spirit of Conciliation, which, on the Return of the Blessings of Peace should universally prevail. And that Congress shall also earnestly recommend to the several States, that the Estates, Rights and Properties of such

last mentioned Persons shall be restored to them, they
refunding to any Persons who may be now in Possession, the Bonâ fide Price (where any has been given)
which such Persons may have paid on purchasing any
of the said Lands, Rights or Properties, since the Confiscation.

And it is agreed that all Persons who have any
Interest in confiscated Lands, either by Debts, Mar-
riage Settlements, or otherwise, shall meet with no
lawful Impediment in the Prosecution of their just
Rights.

## ARTICLE 6th

That there shall be no future Confiscations made nor
any Prosecutions commenc'd against any Person or
Persons for or by Reason of the Part, which he or they
may have taken in the present War, and that no Person
shall on that Account suffer any future Loss or Damage, either in his Person Liberty or Property; and that
those who may be in Confinement on such Charges at
the Time of the Ratification of the Treaty in America
shall be immediately set at Liberty, and the Prosecutions so commenced be discontinued.

## ARTICLE 7th

There shall be a firm and perpetual Peace between
his Britannic Majesty and the said States and between
the Subjects of the one, and the Citizens of the other,
wherefore all Hostilities both by Sea and Land shall
from henceforth cease: All Prisoners on both Sides
shall be set at Liberty, and his Britannic Majesty shall
with all convenient speed, and without causing any
Destruction, or carrying away any Negroes or other

Property of the American Inhabitants, withdraw all his Armies, Garrisons & Fleets from the said United States, and from every Port, Place and Harbour within the same; leaving in all Fortifications the American Artillery that may be therein: And shall also Order & cause all Archives, Records, Deeds & Papers belonging to any of the said States, or their Citizens, which in the Course of the War may have fallen into the Hands of his Officers, to be forthwith restored and deliver'd to the proper States and Persons to whom they belong.

### ARTICLE 8th

The Navigation of the River Mississippi, from its source to the Ocean shall for ever remain free and open to the Subjects of Great Britain and the Citizens of the United States.

### ARTICLE 9th

In Case it should so happen that any Place or Territory belonging to great Britain or to the United States should have been conquer'd by the Arms of either from the other before the Arrival of the said Provisional Articles in America it is agreed that the same shall be restored without Difficulty and without requiring any Compensation.

### ARTICLE 10th

The solemn Ratifications of the present Treaty expedited in good & due Form shall be exchanged between the contracting Parties in the Space of Six Months or sooner if possible to be computed from the Day of the Signature of the present Treaty. In Witness whereof we the undersigned their Ministers Plenipotentiary have in their Name and in Virtue of our Full Powers signed with our Hands the present Definitive Treaty, and caused the Seals of our Arms to be affix'd thereto.

Done at Paris, this third Day of September, In the Year of our Lord one thousand seven hundred & eighty three.

D HARTLEY   JOHN ADAMS   B FRANKLIN   JOHN JAY
[Seal]      [Seal]      [Seal]      [Seal]

## NOTES

There are two originals of this treaty in the Department of State file; in trifles, such as punctuation, they are not literally identical; the provisions of the one reproduced are in the handwriting of William Temple Franklin. With each original, following the signatures, are copies of the full powers of David Hartley, dated May 14, 1783, and of John Adams, Benjamin Franklin, John Jay, Henry Laurens, and Thomas Jefferson, dated June 15, 1781; these are certified "to be authentic" by George Hammond, Secretary to the British Commission, and by William Temple Franklin, Secretary to the American Commission. The certificate of the example from which the text here printed is taken is undated; the other is dated at Paris September 3, 1783.

The treaty was signed at Paris for the reason that David Hartley, the representative of Great Britain, refused to go to Versailles for the purpose (Wharton, Diplomatic Correspondence, VI, 674, 740).

No facsimile of the United States instrument of ratification is available; the original instrument has not been found in the British archives; it is copied in 135 C. C. Papers, I; also in Wharton, Diplomatic Correspondence, VI, 756. Certain objections, which Franklin called "trivial and absurd," were made to its form (see Diplomatic Correspondence, 1783–1789, I, 380–84) but were not pressed. The British instrument of ratification is copied in Wharton, Diplomatic Correspondence, VI, 757–58, note. The original is in the treaty file.

Neither in the British archives nor in those of the Department of State has been found any protocol or other similar record of the exchange of ratifications. The date is reported in the letter of Franklin of May 12, 1784 (Diplomatic Correspondence, 1783–1789, I, 379–80).

The treaty was laid before Congress on December 13, 1783. As to the non-attendance of six States, see proceedings of December 23, 1783 (Journals, XXV, 836). The period allowed by Article 10 of the treaty for the exchange of ratifications was six months from the date of signature; no objection was made by Great Britain to the necessary prolongation of the term (Wharton, Diplomatic Correspondence, VI, 789–90; other letters on the point, Thomson to the American Commissioners January 5, 1784, Hartley to Carmarthen March 22, 1784, Carmarthen to Hartley March 25, 1784, are copied in Bancroft's Transcripts, Hartley's Negotiations, II, 167–75, NYPL).

The proclamation is copied in Wharton, Diplomatic Correspondence, VI, 755.

The original proclamation is in the Library of Congress. A facsimile thereof is in the Department of State file. It is a folio broadside, bearing the imprint, "Annapolis: Printed by John Dunlap, Printer for the United States in Congress assembled." The seal is affixed at the upper left corner; just below is the signature of Thomas Mifflin; and about halfway down, in the margin, is the signature of Charles Thomson, Secretary.

## Note Regarding the Alternat

The form of the treaty was the subject of some correspondence between Fox, Secretary of State for Foreign Affairs, and Hartley. Copies of the letters are in Bancroft's Transcripts, Hartley's Negotiations, II, 53, 57, NYPL. On August 21, 1783, Fox wrote to Hartley:

One thing only I must remind you of in point of form. When a treaty is signed between two Crowned Heads in order to prevent disputes about precedency, the name of the one stands first in one instrument and that of the other in the other but when the Treaty is between a crowned Head and a Republic, the name of the Monarch is mentioned first in each instrument. I believe if you will inquire upon this subject among the *Corps Diplomatique,* you will find this to have been the constant practice.

Hartley replied as follows under date of September 1:

The treaties are drawn out for signature as you have expressed it viz: giving precedence to the Crowned Head. The American Ministers never had a thought of disputing the priority or equality of rank & therefore I have had no occasion to mention the subject.

# Jay's Treaty (Treaty of Amity, Commerce, and Navigation), 1794

The following text is set up from the definitive edition of Hunter Miller's *Treaties and other International Acts of the United States of America*, II, 245–67.

*The Jay Treaty. Treaty of Amity, Commerce, and Navigation, signed at London November 19, 1794, with additional article. Original in English.*
*Submitted to the Senate June 8, 1795. Resolution of advice and consent, on condition, June 24, 1795. Ratified by the United States August 14, 1795. Ratified by Great Britain October 28, 1795. Ratifications exchanged at London October 28, 1795. Proclaimed February 29, 1796.*

Treaty of Amity Commerce and Navigation, between His Britannick Majesty;—and The United States of America, by Their President, with the advice and consent of Their Senate.

His Britannick Majesty and the United States of America, being desirous by a Treaty of Amity, Commerce and Navigation to terminate their Differences in such a manner, as without reference to the Merits of

Their respective Complaints and Pretensions, may be the best calculated to produce mutual satisfaction and good understanding: And also to regulate the Commerce and Navigation between Their respective Countries, Territories and People, in such a manner as to render the same reciprocally beneficial and satisfactory; They have respectively named their Plenipotentiaries, and given them Full powers to treat of, and conclude, the said Treaty, that is to say; His Brittanick Majesty has named for His Plenipotentiary, The Right Honourable William Wyndham Baron Grenville of Wotton, One of His Majesty's Privy Council, and His Majesty's Principal Secretary of State for Foreign Affairs; and The President of the said United States, by and with the advice and Consent of the Senate thereof, hath appointed for Their Plenipotentiary The Honourable John Jay, Chief Justice of the said United States and Their Envoy Extraordinary to His Majesty, who have agreed on, and concluded the following Articles

## ARTICLE 1.

There shall be a firm inviolable and universal Peace, and a true and sincere Friendship between His Britannick Majesty, His Heirs and Successors, and the United States of America; and between their respective Countries, Territories, Cities, Towns and People of every Degree, without Exception of Persons or Places.

## ARTICLE 2.

His Majesty will withdraw all His Troops and Garrisons from all Posts and Places within the Boundary Lines assigned by the Treaty of Peace to the United States. This Evacuation shall take place on or before

the first Day of June One thousand seven hundred and
ninety six, and all the proper Measures shall in the
interval be taken by concert between the Government
of the United States, and His Majesty's Governor
General in America, for settling the previous arrangements which may be necessary respecting the delivery
of the said Posts: The United States in the mean Time
at Their discretion extending their settlements to any
part within the said boundary line, except within the
precincts or Jurisdiction of any of the said Posts. All
Settlers and Traders, within the Precincts or Jurisdiction of the said Posts, shall continue to enjoy, unmolested, all their property of every kind, and shall be
protected therein. They shall be at full liberty to remain there, or to remove with all or any part of their
Effects; and it shall also be free to them to sell their
Lands, Houses, or Effects, or to retain the property
thereof, at their discretion; such of them as shall continue to reside within the said Boundary Lines shall
not be compelled to become Citizens of the United
States, or to take any Oath of allegiance to the Government thereof, but they shall be at full liberty so to
do, if they think proper, and they shall make and declare their Election within one year after the Evacuation aforesaid. And all persons who shall continue there
after the expiration of the said year, without having
declared their intention of remaining Subjects of His
Britannick Majesty, shall be considered as having
elected to become Citizens of the United States.

## ARTICLE 3.

It is agreed that it shall at all Times be free to His
Majesty's Subjects, and to the Citizens of the United

States, and also to the Indians dwelling on either side
of the said Boundary Line freely to pass and repass by
Land, or Inland Navigation, into the respective Territories and Countries of the Two Parties on the
Continent of America (the Country within the Limits
of the Hudson's Bay Company only excepted) and to
navigate all the Lakes, Rivers, and waters thereof, and
freely to carry on trade and commerce with each other.
But it is understood, that this Article does not extend
to the admission of Vessels of the United States into the
Sea Ports, Harbours, Bays, or Creeks of His Majesty's
said Territories; nor into such parts of the Rivers in
His Majesty's said Territories as are between the
mouth thereof, and the highest Port of Entry from the
Sea, except in small vessels trading bonâ fide between
Montreal and Quebec, under such regulations as shall
be established to prevent the possibility of any Frauds
in this respect. Nor to the admission of British vessels
from the Sea into the Rivers of the United States,
beyond the highest Ports of Entry for Foreign Vessels
from the Sea. The River Mississippi, shall however,
according to the Treaty of Peace be entirely open to
both Parties; And it is further agreed, That all the
ports and places on its Eastern side, to whichsoever of
the parties belonging, may freely be resorted to, and
used by both parties, in as ample a manner as any of
the Atlantic Ports or Places of the United States, or
any of the Ports or Places of His Majesty in Great
Britain.

All Goods and Merchandize whose Importation into
His Majesty's said Territories in America, shall not
be entirely prohibited, may freely, for the purposes of
Commerce, be carried into the same in the manner

aforesaid, by the Citizens of the United States, and such Goods and Merchandize shall be subject to no higher or other Duties than would be payable by His Majesty's Subjects on the Importation of the same from Europe into the said Territories. And in like manner, all Goods and Merchandize whose Importation into the United States shall not be wholly prohibited, may freely, for the purposes of Commerce, be carried into the same, in the manner aforesaid, by His Majesty's Subjects, and such Goods and Merchandize shall be subject to no higher or other Duties than would be payable by the Citizens of the United States on the Importation of the same in American Vessels into the Atlantic Ports of the said States. And all Goods not prohibited to be exported from the said Territories respectively, may in like manner be carried out of the same by the Two Parties respectively, paying Duty as aforesaid

No Duty of Entry shall ever be levied by either Party on Peltries brought by Land, or Inland Navigation into the said Territories respectively, nor shall the Indians passing or repassing with their own proper Goods and Effects of whatever nature, pay for the same any Impost or Duty whatever. But Goods in Bales, or other large Packages unusual among Indians shall not be considered as Goods belonging bonâ fide to Indians.

No higher or other Tolls or Rates of Ferriage than what are, or shall be payable by Natives, shall be demanded on either side; And no Duties shall be payable on any Goods which shall merely be carried over any of the Portages, or carrying Places on either side, for the purpose of being immediately reimbarked, and carried to some other Place or Places. But as by this Stipulation it is only meant to secure to each Party a free passage across the Portages on both sides, it is agreed, that this Exemption from Duty shall extend only to such Goods as are carried in the usual and direct Road across the Portage, and are not attempted to be in any manner sold or exchanged during their passage across the same, and proper Regulations may be established to prevent the possibility of any Frauds in this respect.

As this Article is intended to render in a great Degree the local advantages of each Party common to both, and thereby to promote a disposition favourable to Friendship and good neighbourhood, It is agreed, that the respective Governments will mutually promote this amicable Intercourse, by causing speedy and impartial Justice to be done, and necessary protection to be extended, to all who may be concerned therein.

### ARTICLE 4.

Whereas it is uncertain whether the River Mississippi extends so far to the Northward as to be intersected by a Line to be drawn due West from the Lake of the woods in the manner mentioned in the Treaty of Peace between His Majesty and the United States, it is agreed, that measures shall be taken in Concert between His Majesty's Government in America, and the Government of the United States, for making a joint Survey of the said River, from one Degree of Latitude below the falls of S$^t$ Anthony to the principal Source or Sources of the said River, and also of the parts adjacent thereto, And that if on the result of such Survey it should appear that the said River would not be intersected by such a Line as is above mentioned; The two Parties will thereupon proceed by amicable negotia-

tion to regulate the Boundary Line in that quarter as
well as all other Points to be adjusted between the said
Parties, according to Justice and mutual Convenience,
and in Conformity, to the Intent of the said Treaty.

## ARTICLE 5.

Whereas doubts have arisen what River was truly
intended under the name of the River S$^t$ Croix mentioned in the said Treaty of Peace and forming a part
of the boundary therein described, that question shall
be referred to the final Decision of Commissioners to
be appointed in the following Manner—Viz—

One Commissioner shall be named by His Majesty,
and one by the President of the United States, by and
with the advice and Consent of the Senate thereof, and
the said two Commissioners shall agree on the choice
of a third, or, if they cannot so agree, They shall each
propose one Person, and of the two names so proposed
one shall be drawn by Lot, in the presence of the two
original Commissioners. And the three Commissioners
so appointed shall be Sworn impartially to examine and
decide the said question according to such Evidence as
shall respectively be laid before Them on the part of
the British Government and of the United States. The
said Commissioners shall meet at Halifax and shall
have power to adjourn to such other place or places as
they shall think fit. They shall have power to appoint
a Secretary, and to employ such Surveyors or other
Persons as they shall judge necessary. The said Commissioners shall by a Declaration under their Hands
and Seals, decide what River is the River S$^t$ Croix intended by the Treaty. The said Declaration shall contain a description of the said River, and shall partic-

ularize the Latitude and Longitude of its mouth and
of its Source. Duplicates of this Declaration and of the
Statements of their Accounts, and of the Journal of
their proceedings, shall be delivered by them to the
Agent of His Majesty, and to the Agent of the United
States, who may be respectively appointed and authorized to manage the business on behalf of the respective
Governments. And both parties agree to consider such
decision as final and conclusive, so as that the same
shall never thereafter be called into question, or made
the subject of dispute or difference between them.

## ARTICLE 6.

Whereas it is alledged by divers British Merchants
and others His Majesty's Subjects, that Debts to a considerable amount which were bonâ fide contracted
before the Peace, still remain owing to them by Citizens
or Inhabitants of the United States, and that by the
operation of various lawful Impediments since the
Peace, not only the full recovery of the said Debts has
been delayed, but also the Value and Security thereof,
have been in several instances impaired and lessened,
so that by the ordinary course of Judicial proceedings
the British Creditors, cannot now obtain and actually
have and receive full and adequate Compensation for
the losses and damages which they have thereby sustained: It is agreed that in all such Cases where full
Compensation for such losses and damages cannot,
for whatever reason, be actually obtained had and received by the said Creditors in the ordinary course of
Justice, The United States will make full and complete
Compensation for the same to the said Creditors; But
it is distinctly understood, that this provision is to ex-

tend to such losses only, as have been occasioned by
the lawful impediments aforesaid, and is not to extend
to losses occasioned by such Insolvency of the Debtors
or other Causes as would equally have operated to
produce such loss, if the said impediments had not
existed, nor to such losses or damages as have been
occasioned by the manifest delay or negligence, or will-
ful omission of the Claimant.

For the purpose of ascertaining the amount of any
such losses and damages, Five Commissioners shall be
appointed and authorized to meet and act in manner
following—viz—Two of them shall be appointed by
His Majesty, Two of them by the President of the
United States by and with the advice and consent of the
Senate thereof, and the fifth, by the unanimous voice
of the other Four; and if they should not agree in such
Choice, then the Commissioners named by the two
parties shall respectively propose one person, and of the
two names so proposed, one shall be drawn by Lot in
the presence of the Four Original Commissioners.
When the Five Commissioners thus appointed shall
first meet, they shall before they proceed to act respectively, take the following Oath or Affirmation in the
presence of each other, which Oath or Affirmation,
being so taken, and duly attested, shall be entered on
the Record of their Proceedings,—viz.—I. A: B: One
of the Commissioners appointed in pursuance of the 6.<sup>th</sup>
Article of the Treaty of Amity, Commerce and Navigation between His Britannick Majesty and The United
States of America, do solemnly swear (or affirm) that
I will honestly, diligently, impartially, and carefully
examine, and to the best of my Judgement, according
to Justice and Equity decide all such Complaints, as

under the said Article shall be preferred to the said
Commissioners: and that I will forbear to act as a
Commissioner in any Case in which I may be personally
interested.

Three of the said Commissioners shall constitute a
Board, and shall have power to do any act appertaining
to the said Commission, provided that one of the
Commissioners named on each side, and the Fifth Commissioner shall be present, and all decisions shall be
made by the Majority of the Voices of the Commissioners then present. Eighteen Months from the Day
on which the said Commissioners shall form a Board,
and be ready to proceed to Business are assigned for
receiving Complaints and applications, but they are
nevertheless authorized in any particular Cases in
which it shall appear to them to be reasonable and just
to extend the said Term of Eighteen Months, for any
term not exceeding Six Months after the expiration
thereof. The said Commissioners shall first meet at
Philadelphia, but they shall have power to adjourn
from Place to Place as they shall see Cause.

The said Commissioners in examining the Complaints and applications so preferred to them, are im-
powered and required in pursuance of the true intent
and meaning of this article to take into their Consideration all claims whether of principal or interest, or
balances of principal and interest, and to determine the
same respectively according to the merits of the several
Cases, due regard being had to all the Circumstances
thereof, and as Equity and Justice shall appear to them
to require. And the said Commissioners shall have
power to examine all such Persons as shall come before
them on Oath or Affirmation touching the premises;

and also to receive in Evidence according as they may think most consistent with Equity and Justice all written Depositions, or Books or Papers, or Copies or Extracts thereof. Every such Deposition, Book or Paper or Copy or Extract being duly authenticated either according to the legal Forms now respectively existing in the two Countries, or in such other manner as the said Commissioners shall see cause to require or allow.

The Award of the said Commissioners or of any three of them as aforesaid shall in all Cases be final and conclusive, both as to the Justice of the Claim, and to the amount of the Sum to be paid to the Creditor or Claimant.—And the United States undertake to cause the Sum so awarded to be paid in Specie to such Creditor or Claimant without deduction; and at such Time or Times, and at such Place or Places, as shall be awarded by the said Commissioners, and on Condition of such Releases or assignments to be given by the Creditor or Claimant as by the said Commissioners may be directed; Provided always that no such payment shall be fixed by the said Commissioners to take place sooner then twelve months from the Day of the Exchange of the Ratifications of this Treaty.

## Article 7.

Whereas Complaints have been made by divers Merchants and others, Citizens of the United States, that during the course of the War in which His Majesty is now engaged they have sustained considerable losses and damage by reason of irregular or illegal Captures or Condemnations of their vessels and other property under Colour of authority or Commissions from His Majesty, and that from various Circumstances belong-

ing to the said Cases adequate Compensation for the
losses and damages so sustained cannot now be actually
obtained, had and received by the ordinary Course of
Judicial proceedings; It is agreed that in all such Cases
where adequate Compensation cannot for whatever
reason be now actually obtained, had and received by
the said Merchants and others in the ordinary course
of Justice, full and Complete Compensation for the
same will be made by the British Government to the
said Complainants. But it is distinctly understood, that
this provision is not to extend to such losses or damages
as have been occasioned by the manifest delay or
negligence, or wilful omission of the Claimant.

That for the purpose of ascertaining the amount of
any such losses and damages Five Commissioners shall
be appointed and authorized to act in London exactly
in the manner directed with respect to those mentioned
in the preceding Article, and after having taken the
same Oath or Affirmation (mutatis mutandis). The
same term of Eighteen Months is also assigned for the
reception of Claims, and they are in like manner authorised to extend the same in particular Cases. They
shall receive Testimony, Books, Papers and Evidence
in the same latitude, and exercise the like discretion,
and powers respecting that subject, and shall decide the
Claims in question, according to the merits of the
several Cases, and to Justice Equity and the Laws of
Nations. The award of the said Commissioners or any
such three of them as aforesaid, shall in all Cases be
final and conclusive both as to the Justice of the Claim
and the amount of the Sum to be paid to the Claimant;
and His Britannick Majesty undertakes to cause the

same to be paid to such Claimant in Specie, without any
Deduction, at such place or places, and at such Time or
Times as shall be awarded by the said Commissioners
and on Condition of such releases or assignments to be
given by the Claimant, as by the said Commissioners
may be directed.

And whereas certain merchants and others, His
Majesty's Subjects, complain that in the course of the
war they have sustained Loss and Damage by reason
of the Capture of their Vessels and Merchandize taken
within the Limits and Jurisdiction of the States, and
brought into the Ports of the same, or taken by Vessels
originally armed in Ports of the said States:

It is agreed that in all such cases where Restitution
shall not have been made agreeably to the tenor of the
letter from M^r Jefferson to M^r Hammond dated at
Philadelphia September 5^th 1793. A Copy of which is
annexed to this Treaty, the Complaints of the parties
shall be, and hereby are referred to the Commissioners
to be appointed by virtue of this article, who are hereby
authorized and required to proceed in the like manner
relative to these as to the other Cases committed to
them, and the United States undertake to pay to the
Complainants or Claimants in specie without deduction the amount of such Sums as shall be awarded to
them respectively by the said Commissioners and at the
times and places which in such awards shall be specified,
and on Condition of such Releases or assignments to
be given by the Claimants as in the said awards may be
directed: And it is further agreed that not only the
now existing Cases of both descriptions, but also all
such as shall exist at the Time, of exchanging the

Ratifications of this Treaty shall be considered as being within the provisions intent and meaning of this article.

## ARTICLE 8.

It is further agreed that the Commissioners mentioned in this and in the two preceding articles shall be respectively paid in such manner, as shall be agreed between the two parties, such agreement being to be settled at the Time of the exchange of the Ratifications of this Treaty. And all other Expences attending the said Commissions shall be defrayed jointly by the Two Parties, the same being previously ascertained and allowed by the Majority of the Commissioners. And in the case of Death, Sickness or necessary absence, the place of every such Commissioner respectively, shall be supplied in the same manner as such Commissioner was first appointed, and the new Commissioners shall take the same Oath, or Affirmation, and do the same Duties.

## ARTICLE 9.

It it agreed, that British Subjects who now hold Lands in the Territories of the United States, and American Citizens who now hold Lands in the Dominions of His Majesty, shall continue to hold them according to the nature and Tenure of their respective Estates and Titles therein, and may grant Sell or Devise the same to whom they please, in like manner as if they were Natives; and that neither they nor their Heirs or assigns shall, so far as may respect the said Lands, and the legal remedies incident thereto, be regarded as Aliens.

## ARTICLE 10.

Neither the Debts due from Individuals of the one Nation, to Individuals of the other, nor shares nor monies, which they may have in the public Funds, or in the public or private Banks shall ever, in any Event of war, or national differences, be sequestered, or confiscated, it being unjust and impolitick that Debts and Engagements contracted and made by Individuals having confidence in each other, and in their respective Governments, should ever be destroyed or impaired by national authority, on account of national Differences and Discontents.

## ARTICLE 11.

It is agreed between His Majesty and the United States of America, that there shall be a reciprocal and entirely perfect Liberty of Navigation and Commerce, between their respective People, in the manner, under the Limitations, and on the Conditions specified in the following Articles.

## ARTICLE 12.

His Majesty Consents that it shall and may be lawful, during the time hereinafter Limited, for the Citizens of the United States, to carry to any of His Majesty's Islands and Ports in the West Indies from the United States in their own Vessels, not being above the burthen of Seventy Tons, any Goods or Merchandizes, being of the Growth, Manufacture, or Produce of the said States, which it is, or may be lawful to carry to the said Islands or Ports from the said States in British Vessels, and that the said American Vessels shall be subject there to no other or higher Tonnage Duties or Charges, than shall be payable by British Vessels, in the Ports of the United States; and that the Cargoes of the said American Vessels, shall be subject there to no other or higher Duties or Charges, than shall be payable on the like Articles, if imported there from the said States in British vessels.

And His Majesty also consents that it shall be lawful for the said American Citizens to purchase, load and carry away, in their said vessels to the United States from the said Islands and Ports, all such articles being of the Growth, Manufacture or Produce of the said Islands, as may now by Law be carried from thence to the said States in British Vessels, and subject only to the same Duties and Charges on Exportation to which British Vessels and their Cargoes are or shall be subject in similar circumstances.

Provided always that the said American vessels do carry and land their Cargoes in the United States only, it being expressly agreed and declared that during the Continuance of this article, the United States will prohibit and restrain the carrying any Melasses, Sugar, Coffee, Cocoa or Cotton in American vessels, either from His Majesty's Islands or from the United States, to any part of the World, except the United States, reasonable Sea Stores excepted. Provided also, that it shall and may be lawful during the same period for British vessels to import from the said Islands into the United States, and to export from the United States to the said Islands, all Articles whatever being of the Growth, Produce or Manufacture of the said Islands, or of the United States respectively, which now may, by the Laws of the said States, be so imported and exported. And that the Cargoes of the said British vessels, shall be subject to no other or higher Duties or Charges, then shall be payable on the same articles if so imported or exported in American Vessels.

It is agreed that this Article, and every Matter and Thing therein contained, shall continue to be in Force, during the Continuance of the war in which His Majesty is now engaged; and also for Two years from and after the Day of the signature of the Preliminary or other Articles of Peace by which the same may be terminated

And it is further agreed that at the expiration of the said Term, the Two Contracting Parties will endeavour further to regulate their Commerce in this respect, according to the situation in which His Majesty may then find Himself with respect to the West Indies, and with a view to such Arrangements, as may best conduce to the mutual advantage and extension of Commerce. And the said Parties will then also renew their discussions, and endeavour to agree, whether in any and what cases Neutral Vessels shall protect Enemy's property; and in what cases provisions and other articles not generally Contraband may become such. But in the mean time their Conduct towards each other in these respects, shall be regulated by the articles hereinafter inserted on those subjects.

## ARTICLE 13.

His Majesty consents that the Vessels belonging to the Citizens of the United States of America, shall be admitted and Hospitably received in all the Sea Ports and Harbours of the British Territories in the East Indies: and that the Citizens of the said United States,

may freely carry on a Trade between the said Territories and the said United States, in all articles of
which the Importation or Exportation respectively to
or from the said Territories, shall not be entirely prohibited; Provided only, that it shall not be lawful
for them in any time of War between the British
Government, and any other Power or State whatever, to export from the said Territories without
the special Permission of the British Government
there, any Military Stores, or Naval Stores, or
Rice. The Citizens of the United States shall pay for
their Vessels when admitted into the said Ports, no
other or higher Tonnage Duty than shall be payable
on British Vessels when admitted into the Ports of the
United States. And they shall pay no other or higher
Duties or Charges on the importation or exportation
of the Cargoes of the said Vessels, than shall be payable on the same articles when imported or exported in
British Vessels. But it is expressly agreed, that the
Vessels of the United States shall not carry any of the
articles exported by them from the said British Territories to any port or Place, except to some Port or
Place in America, where the same shall be unladen, and
such Regulations shall be adopted by both Parties, as
shall from time to time be found necessary to enforce
the due and faithfull observance of this Stipulation: It
is also understood that the permission granted by this
article is not to extend to allow the Vessels of the
United States to carry on any part of the Coasting
Trade of the said British Territories, but Vessels going
with their original Cargoes, or part thereof, from one
port of discharge to another, are not to be considered
as carrying on the Coasting Trade. Neither is this

Article to be construed to allow the Citizens of the said
States to settle or reside within the said Territories, or
to go into the interior parts thereof, without the permission of the British Government established there;
and if any transgression should be attempted against
the Regulations of the British Government in this
respect, the observance of the same shall and may be
enforced against the Citizens of America in the same
manner as against British Subjects, or others trans-
gressing the same rule. And the Citizens of the United
States, whenever they arrive in any Port or Harbour in
the said Territories, or if they should be permitted in
manner aforesaid, to go to any other place therein,
shall always be subject to the Laws, Government and
Jurisdiction, of what nature, established in such Harbour, Port or Place according as the same may be: The
Citizens of the United States, may also touch for refreshment, at the Island of S$^t$ Helena, but subject in all
respects to such regulations, as the British Government
may from time to time establish there.

## ARTICLE 14.

There shall be between all the Dominions of His
Majesty in Europe, and the Territories of the United
States, a reciprocal and perfect liberty of Commerce
and Navigation. The people and Inhabitants of the
Two Countries respectively, shall have liberty, freely
and securely, and without hindrance and molestation,
to come with their Ships and Cargoes to the Lands,
Countries, Cities, Ports Places and Rivers within the
Dominions and Territories aforesaid, to enter into the
same, to resort there, and to remain and reside there,
without any limitation of Time: also to hire and pos-

sess, Houses and warehouses for the purposes of their
Commerce; and generally the Merchants and Traders
on each side, shall enjoy the most complete protection
and Security for their Commerce; but subject always, as
to what respects this article, to the Laws and Statutes
of the Two Countries respectively.

## ARTICLE 15.

It is agreed, that no other or higher Duties shall be
paid by the Ships or Merchandize of the one Party in
the Ports of the other, than such as are paid by the
like vessels or Merchandize of all other Nations. Nor
shall any other or higher Duty be imposed in one
Country on the importation of any articles, the growth,
produce, or manufacture of the other, than are or
shall be payable on the importation of the like articles
being of the growth, produce or manufacture of any
other Foreign Country. Nor shall any prohibition be
imposed, on the exportation or importation of any
articles to or from the Territories of the Two Parties
respectively which shall not equally extend to all other
Nations.

But the British Government reserves to itself the
right of imposing on American Vessels entering into
the British Ports in Europe a Tonnage Duty, equal to
that which shall be payable by British Vessels in the
Ports of America: And also such Duty as may be
adequate to countervail the difference of Duty now
payable on the importation of European and Asiatic
Goods when imported into the United States in British
or in American Vessels.

The Two Parties agree to treat for the more exact

equalization of the Duties on the respective Navigation of their Subjects and People in such manner as may be most beneficial to the two Countries. The arrangements for this purpose shall be made at the same time with those mentioned at the Conclusion of the 12th Article of this Treaty, and are to be considered as a part thereof. In the interval it is agreed, that the United States will not impose any new or additional Tonnage Duties on British Vessels, nor increase the now subsisting difference between the Duties payable on the importation of any articles in British or in American Vessels.

## ARTICLE 16.

It shall be free for the Two Contracting Parties respectively, to appoint Consuls for the protection of Trade, to reside in the Dominions and Territories aforesaid; and the said Consuls shall enjoy those Liberties and Rights which belong to them by reason of their Function. But before any Consul shall act as such, he shall be in the usual forms approved and admitted by the party to whom he is sent, and it is hereby declared to be lawful and proper, that in case of illegal or improper Conduct towards the Laws or Government, a Consul may either be punished according to Law, if the Laws will reach the Case, or be dismissed or even sent back, the offended Government assigning to the other, Their reasons for the same.

Either of the Parties may except from the residence of Consuls such particular Places, as such party shall judge proper to be so excepted.

## ARTICLE 17.

It is agreed that, in all Cases where Vessels shall be captured or detained on just suspicion of having on board Enemy's property or of carrying to the Enemy, any of the articles which are Contraband of war; The said Vessel shall be brought to the nearest or most convenient Port, and if any property of an Enemy, should be found on board such Vessel, that part only which belongs to the Enemy shall be made prize, and the Vessel shall be at liberty to proceed with the remainder without any Impediment. And it is agreed that all proper measures shall be taken to prevent delay, in deciding the Cases of Ships or Cargoes so brought in for adjudication, and in the payment or recovery of any Indemnification adjudged or agreed to be paid to the masters or owners of such Ships.

## ARTICLE 18.

In order to regulate what is in future to be esteemed Contraband of war, it is agreed that under the said Denomination shall be comprized all Arms and Implements serving for the purposes of war by Land or Sea; such as Cannon, Muskets, Mortars, Petards, Bombs, Grenades Carcasses, Saucisses, Carriages for Cannon, Musket rests, Bandoliers, Gunpowder, Match, Saltpetre, Ball, Pikes, Swords, Headpieces Cuirasses Halberts Lances Javelins, Horsefurniture, Holsters, Belts and, generally all other Implements of war, as also Timber for Ship building, Tar or Rosin, Copper in Sheets, Sails, Hemp, and Cordage, and generally whatever may serve directly to the equipment of Vessels, unwrought Iron and Fir planks only excepted, and all the above articles are hereby declared to be just objects of Confiscation, whenever they are attempted to be carried to an Enemy.

And Whereas the difficulty of agreeing on the precise Cases in which alone Provisions and other articles not generally contraband may be regarded as such, renders it expedient to provide against the inconveniences and misunderstandings which might thence arise: It is further agreed that whenever any such articles so becoming Contraband according to the existing Laws of Nations, shall for that reason be seized, the same shall not be confiscated, but the owners thereof shall be speedily and completely indemnified; and the Captors, or in their default the Government under whose authority they act, shall pay to the Masters or Owners of such Vessels the full value of all such Articles, with a reasonable mercantile Profit thereon, together with the Freight, and also the Demurrage incident to such Detension.

And Whereas it frequently happens that vessels sail for a Port or Place belonging to an Enemy, without knowing that the same is either besieged, blockaded or invested; It is agreed, that every Vessel so circumstanced may be turned away from such Port or Place, but she shall not be detained, nor her Cargo, if not Contraband, be confiscated; unless after notice she shall again attempt to enter; but She shall be permitted to go to any other Port or Place She may think proper: Nor shall any vessel or Goods of either party, that may have entered into such Port or Place before the same was besieged, blockaded or invested by the other, and be found therein after the reduction or surrender of such place, be liable to confiscation, but shall be restored to the Owners or proprietors thereof.

## ARTICLE 19.

And that more abundant Care may be taken for the security of the respective Subjects and Citizens of the Contracting Parties, and to prevent their suffering Injuries by the Men of war, or Privateers of either Party, all Commanders of Ships of war and Privateers and all others the said Subjects and Citizens shall forbear doing any Damage to those of the other party, or committing any Outrage against them, and if they act to the contrary, they shall be punished, and shall also be bound in their Persons and Estates to make satisfaction and reparation for all Damages, and the interest thereof, of whatever nature the said Damages may be.

For this cause all Commanders of Privateers before they receive their Commissions shall hereafter be obliged to give before a Competent Judge, sufficient security by at least Two responsible Sureties, who have no interest in the said Privateer, each of whom, together with the said Commander, shall be jointly and severally bound in the Sum of Fifteen hundred pounds Sterling, or if such Ships be provided with above One hundred and fifty Seamen or Soldiers, in the Sum of Three thousand pounds sterling, to satisfy all Damages and Injuries, which the said Privateer or her Officers or Men, or any of them may do or commit during their Cruize contrary to the tenor of this Treaty, or to the Laws and Instructions for regulating their Conduct; and further that in all Cases of Aggressions the said Commissions shall be revoked and annulled.

It is also agreed that whenever a Judge of a Court of Admiralty of either of the Parties, shall pronounce sentence against any Vessel or Goods or Property belonging to the Subjects or Citizens of the other Party a formal and duly authenticated Copy of all the proceedings in the Cause, and of the said Sentence, shall if required be delivered to the Commander of the said Vessel, without the smallest delay, he paying all legal Fees and Demands for the same.

## ARTICLE 20.

It is further agreed that both the said Contracting Parties, shall not only refuse to receive any Pirates into any of their Ports, Havens, or Towns, or permit any of their Inhabitants to receive, protect, harbour conceal or assist them in any manner, but will bring to condign punishment all such Inhabitants as shall be guilty of such Acts or offences.

And all their Ships with the Goods or Merchandizes taken by them and brought into the port of either of the said Parties, shall be seized, as far as they can be discovered and shall be restored to the owners or their Factors or Agents duly deputed and authorized in writing by them (proper Evidence being first given in the Court of Admiralty for proving the property,) even in case such effects should have passed into other hands by Sale, if it be proved that the Buyers knew or had good reason to believe, or suspect that they had been piratically taken.

## ARTICLE 21.

It is likewise agreed that the Subjects and Citizens of the Two Nations, shall not do any acts of Hostility or

Violence against each other, nor accept Commissions
or Instructions so to act from any Foreign Prince or
State, Enemies to the other party, nor shall the Enemies
of one of the parties be permitted to invite or endeavour to enlist in their military service any of the
Subjects or Citizens of the other party; and the Laws
against all such Offences and Aggressions shall be punctually executed. And if any Subject or Citizen of the
said Parties respectively shall accept any Foreign Commission or Letters of Marque for Arming any Vessel
to act as a Privateer against the other party, and be
taken by the other party, it is hereby declared to be
lawful for the said party to treat and punish the said
Subject or Citizen, having such Commission or Letters
of Marque as a Pirate.

## ARTICLE 22.

It is expressly stipulated that neither of the said Contracting Parties will order or Authorize any Acts of
Reprisal against the other on Complaints of Injuries
or Damages until the said party shall first have presented to the other a Statement thereof, verified by
competent proof and Evidence, and demanded Justice
and Satisfaction, and the same shall either have been
refused or unreasonably delayed.

## ARTICLE 23.

The Ships of war of each of the Contracting Parties,
shall at all times be hospitably received in the Ports of
the other, their Officers and Crews paying due respect
to the Laws and Government of the Country. The
officers shall be treated with that respect, which is due
to the Commissions which they bear. And if any Insult

should be offered to them by any of the Inhabitants, all offenders in this respect shall be punished as Disturbers of the Peace and Amity between the Two Countries.

And His Majesty consents, that in case an American Vessel should by stress of weather, Danger from Enemies, or other misfortune be reduced to the necessity of seeking Shelter in any of His Majesty's Ports, into which such Vessel could not in ordinary cases claim to be admitted; She shall on manifesting that necessity to the satisfaction of the Government of the place, be hospitably received, and be permitted to refit, and to purchase at the market price, such necessaries as she may stand in need of, conformably to such Orders and regulations as the Government of the place, having respect to the circumstances of each case shall prescribe. She shall not be allowed to break bulk or unload her Cargo, unless the same shall be bonâ fide necessary to her being refitted. Nor shall be permitted to sell any part of her Cargo, unless so much only as may be necessary to defray her expences, and then not without the express permission of the Government of the place. Nor shall she be obliged to pay any Duties whatever, except only on such Articles, as she may be permitted to sell for the purpose aforesaid.

## ARTICLE 24.

It shall not be lawful for any Foreign Privateers (not being Subjects or Citizens of either of the said Parties) who have Commissions from any other Prince or State in Enmity with either Nation, to arm their Ships in the Ports of either of the said Parties, nor to sell what they have taken, nor in any other manner to

exchange the same, nor shall they be allowed to purchase more provisions than shall be necessary for their
going to the nearest Port of that Prince or State from
whom they obtained their Commissions.

## ARTICLE 25.

It shall be lawful for the Ships of war and Privateers
belonging to the said Parties respectively to carry
whithersoever they please the Ships and Goods taken
from their Enemies without being obliged to pay any
Fee to the Officers of the Admiralty, or to any Judges
whatever; nor shall the said Prizes when they arrive at,
and enter the Ports of the said Parties be detained or
seized, neither shall the Searchers or other Officers of
those Places visit such Prizes (except for the purpose of
preventing the Carrying of any part of the Cargo
thereof on Shore in any manner contrary to the established Laws of Revenue, Navigation or Commerce)
nor shall such Officers take Cognizance of the Validity
of such Prizes; but they shall be at liberty to hoist Sail,
and depart as speedily as may be, and carry their said
Prizes to the place mentioned in their Commissions or
Patents, which the Commanders of the said Ships of
war or Privateers shall be obliged to shew. No Shelter
or Refuge shall be given in their Ports to such as have
made a Prize upon the Subjects or Citizens of either of
the said Parties; but if forced by stress of weather or
the Dangers of the Sea, to enter therein, particular care
shall be taken to hasten their departure, and to cause
them to retire as soon as possible. Nothing in this
Treaty contained shall however be construed or operate
contrary to former and existing Public Treaties with
other Sovereigns or States. But the Two parties agree,

that while they continue in amity neither of them will in future make any Treaty that shall be inconsistent with this or the preceding article.

Neither of the said parties shall permit the Ships or Goods belonging to the Subjects or Citizens of the other to be taken within Cannon Shot of the Coast, nor in any of the Bays, Ports or Rivers of their Territories by Ships of war, or others having Commission from any Prince, Republic or State whatever. But in case it should so happen, the party whose Territorial Rights shall thus have been violated, shall use his utmost endeavours to obtain from the offending Party, full and ample satisfaction for the Vessel or Vessels so taken, whether the same be Vessels of war or Merchant Vessels.

## ARTICLE 26.

If at any Time a Rupture should take place (which God forbid) between His Majesty and the United States, the Merchants and others of each of the Two Nations, residing in the Dominions of the other, shall have the privilege of remaining and continuing their Trade so long as they behave peaceably and commit no offence against the Laws, and in case their Conduct should render them suspected, and the respective Governments should think proper to order them to remove, the term of Twelve Months from the publication of the order shall be allowed them for that purpose to remove with their Families, Effects and Property, but this Favor shall not be extended to those who shall act contrary to the established Laws, and for greater certainty it is declared that such Rupture shall not be deemed to exist while negotiations for accommodating Differences shall be depending nor until the respective Ambassa-

dors or Ministers, if such there shall be, shall be recalled, or sent home on account of such differences, and
not on account of personal misconduct according to the
nature and degrees of which both parties retain their
Rights, either to request the recall or immediately to
send home the Ambassador or Minister of the other;
and that without prejudice to their mutual Friendship
and good understanding.

## ARTICLE 27.

It is further agreed that His Majesty and the United
States on mutual Requisitions by them respectively or
by their respective Ministers or Officers authorized to
make the same will deliver up to Justice, all Persons
who being charged with Murder or Forgery committed
within the Jurisdiction of either, shall seek an Asylum
within any of the Countries of the other, Provided that
this shall only be done on such Evidence of Criminality
as according to the Laws of the Place, where the Fugitive or Person so charged shall be found, would justify
his apprehension and commitment for Tryal, if the
offence had there been committed. The Expence of such
apprehension and Delivery shall be borne and defrayed
by those who make the Requisition and receive the
Fugitive.

## ARTICLE 28.

It is agreed that the first Ten Articles of this Treaty
shall be permanent and that the subsequent Articles
except the Twelfth shall be limited in their duration to
Twelve years to be computed from the Day on which
the Ratifications of this Treaty shall be exchanged, but

subject to this Condition that whereas the said Twelfth Article will expire by the Limitation therein contained at the End of two years from the signing of the Preliminary or other Articles of Peace, which shall terminate the present War, in which His Majesty is engaged; It is agreed that proper Measures shall by Concert be taken for bringing the subject of that article into amicable Treaty and Discussion so early before the Expiration of the said Term, as that new Arrangements on that head may by that Time be perfected and ready to take place. But if it should unfortunately happen that His Majesty and the United States should not be able to agree on such new arrangements, in that Case, all the Articles of this Treaty except the first Ten shall then cease and expire together.

Lastly. This Treaty when the same shall have been ratified by His Majesty, and by The President of the United States, by and with the advice and Consent of Their Senate, and the respective Ratifications mutually exchanged, shall be binding and obligatory on His Majesty and on the said States, and shall be by Them respectively executed and observed with punctuality, and the most sincere regard to good Faith. And Whereas it will be expedient in order the better to facilitate Intercourse and obviate Difficulties that other Articles be proposed and added to this Treaty, which Articles from want of time and other circumstances cannot now be perfected; It is agreed that the said Parties will from Time to Time readily treat of and concerning such Articles, and will sincerely endeavour so to form them, as that they may conduce to mutual convenience, and tend to promote mutual Satisfaction and Friendship; and that the said Articles after having been duly ratified, shall be added to, and make a part of this Treaty.

In Faith whereof We the Undersigned, Ministers Plenipotentiary of His Majesty The King of Great Britain; and the United States of America, have signed this present Treaty, and have caused to be affixed thereto, the Seal of Our Arms.

Done at London, this Nineteenth Day of November, One thousand seven hundred and ninety Four.

GRENVILLE [Seal]                    JOHN JAY [Seal]

[Annexed Copy of the Letter Mentioned in Article 7]

PHILADELPHIA *Sept<sup>r</sup> 5<sup>th</sup> 1793.*

SIR, I am honored with yours of August 30.<sup>th</sup> Mine of the 7.<sup>th</sup> of that Month assured you that measures were taken for excluding from all further Asylum in our Ports Vessels armed in them to Cruize on Nations with which we are at Peace; and for the restoration of the Prizes the Lovely Lass, Prince William Henry, and the Jane of Dublin, and that should the measures for restitution fail in their Effect, The President considered it as incumbent on the United States to make compensation for the Vessels.

We are bound by our Treaties with Three of the Belligerent Nations, by all the means in our Power to protect and defend their Vessels and Effects in our Ports, or waters, or on the Seas near our Shores and to recover and restore the same to the right owners when taken from them. If all the means in our Power are used, and fail in their Effect, we are not bound, by our Treaties with those Nations to make Compensation.

Though we have no similar Treaty with Great Britain, it was the opinion of the President that we should use towards that Nation the same rule, which, under this Article, was to govern us with the other Nations; and even to extend it to Captures made on the High Seas, and brought into our Ports; if done by Vessels, which had been armed within them.

Having for particular reasons, forbore to use all the means in our power for the restitution of the three vessels mentioned in my Letter of August 7.<sup>th</sup> The President thought it incumbent on the United States to make Compensation for them; and though nothing was said in that Letter of other Vessels taken under like Circumstances and brought in after the 5.<sup>th</sup> of June, and before the date of that Letter, yet when the same forbearance had taken place it was and is his opinion that Compensation would be equally due.

As to Prizes made under the same Circumstances, and brought in after the date of that Letter the President determined, that all the means in our power, should be used for their restitution. If these fail as we should not be bound by our Treaties to make Compensation to the other Powers, in the analogous Case, he did not mean to give an opinion that it ought to be done to Great Britain: But still if any Cases shall arise subsequent to that date, the circumstances of which shall place them on similar ground with those before it, the President would think Compensation equally incumbent on the United States.

Instructions are given to the Governors of the different States to use all the means in their Power for restoring Prizes of this last description found within their Ports. Though they will of course take measures to be informed of them, and the General Government has given them the aid of the Custom-house Officers for this purpose, yet you will be sensible of the importance of multiplying the Channels of their Information as far as shall depend on yourself, or any person under your direction, in order that the Governors may use the means in their power, for making restitution. Without knowledge of the Capture they cannot restore it. It will always be best to give the notice to them directly: but any information which you shall be pleased to send to me also, at any time, shall be forwarded to them as quickly as distance will permit.

Hence you will perceive Sir, that, The President contemplates restitution or Compensation in the Case before the 7th August, and after that date restitution if it can be effected by any means in our power: And that it will be important that you should substantiate the fact, that such prizes are in our Ports or waters.

Your List of the Privateers illicitly armed in our ports, is, I believe Correct.

With respect to losses by detension, waste Spoilation sustained by vessels taken as before mentioned between the dates of June 5th and August 7th it is proposed as a provisional measure, that the Collector of the Customs of the district, and the British Consul, or any other person you please, shall appoint persons to establish the Value of the Vessel and Cargo, at the time of her Capture and of her arrival in the port into which She is brought, according to their value in that Port. If this shall be agreeable to you, and you will be pleased to signify it to me with the Names of the Prizes understood to be of this description Instructions will be given accordingly to the Collector of the Customs where the respective Vessels are.

I have the Honor to be &c

(Signed)     THO. JEFFERSON.

### ADDITIONAL ARTICLE

It is further agreed between the said contracting parties, that the operation of so much of the twelfth Article of the said Treaty as respects the trade which his said Majesty thereby consents may be carried on between the United States and his Islands in the West Indies, in the manner and on the terms and conditions therein specified, shall be suspended.

### NOTES

There is no signed original of the Jay Treaty in the Department of State file.

That John Jay sent two originals of this treaty to the United States is clear from his despatches. That only two originals were transmitted seems equally certain. If a third original had been transmitted, the records of the time would mention it; but they do not.

The first of the two originals which Jay did send went from Falmouth by the packet *Tankerville,* which had been detained a week or more for the purpose of taking the treaty. Jay wrote on November 19, 1794, the date of signature:

The long expected Treaty accompanies this letter;—a probability of soon concluding it has caused the Packet to be detained for more than a week. (D.S., 1 Despatches, Great Britain, No. 22, duplicate.)

And on November 21 he wrote:

On the 19.$^{th}$ Inst. a Treaty was signed. The next Day it was, together with my Letters to you N.$^o$ 21–22–& 23, dispatched to the Packet at Falmouth, which had been detained. (Ibid., No. 24.)

The example sent by the packet was lost; it is reported to

have been "cast into the sea to escape French hands" (Conway, Omitted Chapters of History Disclosed in the Life and Papers of Edmund Randolph, 233–34, 293). Grenville wrote of the unfortunate "loss" of the packet, misspelled *Tankenville* (Correspondence and Public Papers of John Jay, 1794–1826, IV, 174). The press of the period recounts that the *Tankerville,* on account of bad weather, did not sail from Falmouth until December 14, and that she was taken by a French brig near the West Indies and burned (the Evening Mail, London, December 3–5 and 15–17, 1794, and April 20–22, 1795).

As to the second original, Jay wrote in his despatch of November 21:

I now send you duplicates of them all, by Mʳ. [David] Blaney, a Gentleman of Virginia, recommended to me by Gov. Lee. The earliest advices from you will be expedient.

That only two originals were sent by Jay appears from his letter of December 10, 1794 (D.S., 1 Despatches, Great Britain, No. 26, duplicate), from which the following is extracted:

As the Treaty concluded on the 19ᵗʰ of last month, was sent by the Packet, and a Duplicate was committed to the Care of Mʳ. Blaney who sailed in a Vessel for Virginia commanded by Capᵗⁿ Vickary, I flatter myself it will arrive before you receive this Letter. . . . The Treaty may possibly not arrive so soon, as that the Ratification will reach this place before my Departure;—especially, as not only the Packet but also Mʳ. Blaney were detained a considerable Time by contrary Winds.

# NOTE ON MANUSCRIPT SOURCES

(See comment in Preface, pp. viii–ix)

The following descriptions of manuscripts are as they lay when the researches for the first edition of this work were undertaken. For possible variations in current archival designations, see M. S. Giuseppi, *A Guide to the Manuscripts Preserved in the British Record Office* (2 vols. London, 1923–24); Grace Gardner Griffin, *A Guide to the Manuscripts Relating to American History in British Depositories, Reproduced for the Division of Manuscripts in the Library of Congress* (Washington, 1946); and *National Archives Guide* (Washington, 1948).

Helpful as have been the general and special works dealing with the period, the writer has based the foregoing narrative on the sources. The backbone of the sources for Jay's Treaty is the great collection of unprinted public papers and official correspondence of the British Foreign and Colonial Offices, now deposited in the Public Record Office at London; the public papers and diplomatic correspondence of the United States Government, both printed and unprinted; the manuscripts, both in transcript and original, in the collections of the Canada Archives at Ottawa; and the correspondence and state papers of the French Foreign Office, preserved in the Archives of the Ministry of Foreign Affairs, Quai d'Orsay, Paris. In addition to these principal sources other valuable collections, public and private, have been used, as enumerated below.

The papers of the Colonial Office dealing with Canada are of the utmost importance for American history, for by correlating them with the correspondence of the Department of State and of the Foreign Office the complex history of Anglo-American frontier diplomacy can be brought into clear relief. The Colonial Office papers transcripts in the Canada Archives were used initially. The writer has checked these by examining the originals in the Colonial Office papers in London. Because the Canadian transcripts are more available to the American student and have the additional advantage of being helpfully calendared this correspondence has been referred to as Canadian Archives (C.A.) with the series number and volume number of the official archivist following. Occasionally, however, it has been found necessary to refer to the original document as a Colonial Office document in the Public Record Office (P.R.O.,C.O.). Other records of the Colonial Office have been used, in addition to the Canada correspondence, and these are documented as Colonial Office (for example, P.R.O.,C.O., Jamaica). Besides the transcripts a great many original document in the Canada Archives have been used.

The records of the Foreign Office, besides comprising the dispatches to the British ministers, consuls, and other agents in the United States, with enclosures, contain all the official communications exchanged between the two governments, both in the United States and in England. Copies of these also exist in the archives of the Department of State at Washington. Frequently the contemporary European correspondence of the Foreign Office helps to explain phases of Great Britain's American policy not elsewhere revealed. It should be noted here that in one or two instances volumes of F.O. documents were still sealed against perusal.

The reports of the French ministers in the United States are of value to Anglo-American history because they present the incisive scrutiny of a third party. Where French diplomacy enters into the complications of Anglo-American relations, as it does so greatly after February 1, 1793, the value of these reports is too obvious to need comment. The correspondence of the French ministers and instructions to them have been edited by Professor Turner, a printed source that includes everything but a few enclosures, as comparison with the original manuscripts at the Quai d'Orsay shows.

A source of great aid in revealing the complications of the abortive Armed Neutrality of 1794 and its relation to Anglo-American negotiations is the correspondence of the French agent in Denmark, Philippe de Grouvelle, preserved in the Archives des Affaires Étrangères at Paris. The writer has read both the Danish and the Swedish correspondence of the Committee of Public Safety with much profit (Arch. Aff. Étrang., Danemark, Suède). He has also secured transcripts of the correspondence of the Swedish Foreign Office relating to the Swedish invitation to the United States to accede to the Dano-Swedish Convention of 1794 (Swedish Royal Archives, Anglica).

The unprinted papers of John Jay, preserved in the New York Historical Society's collection as well as in the Butler Library of Columbia University, have been used. There are some comparatively unimportant papers relating to the Jay mission which were not given to the Senate with the treaty and have not been printed in any of the publications of American state papers. These documents, now in the archives of the Department of State, have been examined, as have the dispatches and instructions of Thomas Pinckney during his London mission, 1791–1795.

The unprinted Hamilton and Jefferson papers now in the Library of Congress were examined (the Jefferson Papers with the help of the official calendar) for any material relative to the Jay negotiation such as might supplement the well-known printed "Writings" of these men. Little if any new material of this nature was located.

For key to abbreviations of documents ·see front of book.

## A. RECORDS OF THE BRITISH
### FOREIGN OFFICE

1. America

Series 4, Volumes 4 to 16 inclusive. Cited as Public Record Office, Foreign Office, Series 4, Volumes 4, 5, 6, or 7, etc., abbreviated, for example, as P.R.O.,F.O., 4, 5.

Volumes 4 to 11 inclusive consist of dispatches from the British consuls and secret agents in the United States during the Confederation, with relevant enclosures, dealing with alleged infractions of the treaty of peace and disputes arising therefrom, boundary controversies, Indian relations, commercial matters, consular business, and political information of many kinds. Volume 12 contains, with enclosures, the correspondence of George Beckwith, the informal agent of the British Government, under the direction of Lord Dorchester, Governor General of Canada. Beckwith made several trips to the United States between 1788 and 1794. The volume contains letters, and one memorial to Government reciting his past services, June 20, 1792. This piece supplements very effectively the Beckwith correspondence in the Canadian Archives. Volumes 13 to 16 contain the dispatches of George Hammond, first British Minister to the United States, and of the consuls, with instructions to them from Whitehall, together with relevant enclosures, from 1791 until January, 1793.

Series 5, Volumes 1 to 13 inclusive, contains the correspondence to and from Hammond and the consuls, with copies of captured French correspondence, enclosures, etc., covering the whole field of political and commercial relations of Great Britain with America. Volumes 3, 7, and 12, contain domestic papers relating to the United States, including official correspondence with Thomas Pinckney, United States Minister in London.

These papers are duplicated in part in Series 115, Volumes 1 to 4, inclusive, being the archives of the British legation at Philadelphia. Often the enclosures alluded to in the drafts of instructions to Hammond preserved in Series 4 and 5, are not enclosed; these are always to be found in Series 115. The ink of this series is badly faded, and parts are illegible.

2. Miscellaneous

Series 95, Volume 7, contains duplicates of three of Beckwith's letters, in F.O., 4, 12, and a few copies of full powers, etc., relating to the negotiations of 1794.

Series 95, Volume 512, abbreviated as F.O., 95, 512, contains the correspondence between Jay and Grenville during the negotiations. Among other documents of importance is a draft of a treaty, proposed by Jay on September 30, 1794.

3. Russia

Series 65, Volumes 26 and 27, contains correspondence of Charles Whitworth, Minister at St. Petersburg, relative to the abortive Armed Neutrality of 1794.

4. Prussia

Series 64, Volume 29, dispatches of George H. Rose, *Chargé d'Affaires* at Berlin, relative to attitude of Prussia in 1794 and an account of an interview with Count Finkenstein on American affairs and the Baltic States.

5. Holland

Series 37, Volume 56, contains a précis of secret correspondence from Copenhagen, relative to French diplomacy in Denmark and Sweden in 1794.

6. Denmark

Series 22, Volumes 18 and 19. Correspondence of David Hailes, *Chargé d'Affaires* at Copenhagen, and J. Mitchell,

Consul, relative to the Convention with Sweden of March, 1794.
7. Sweden
Series 73, Volume 17. Dispatches from Lord Henry Spencer touching on relations with Denmark.
See *List of Indexes to the Foreign Office Records* (London, H.M. Stationery Office, 1914) for useful catalogue of Foreign Office Records. Sources cited here follow the terminology of this catalogue.

## B. RECORDS OF THE BRITISH COLONIAL OFFICE

1. Canada
The original dispatches for the period 1789 to 1795 are at the Public Record Office, Chancery Lane, London. These have been used to check transcripts of the same in the Canadian Archives. Occasionally Colonial Office (P.R.O.,C.O.) papers have been documented as such for lack of Canadian duplicates. Otherwise the Canadian correspondence is cited as Canadian Archives (C.A.).
2. Other American Colonies
Some of the correspondence with other colonies than Canada has been found useful, for example, Jamaica. It is documented as such, under proper serial number (P.R.O.,C.O., Jamaica 137, 92–95). Frequent searches have been made in the other American colonial correspondence without noteworthy result. Explanations are given in footnotes.

## C. CHATHAM PAPERS

Containing correspondence and public papers of William Pitt, preserved at the Public Record Office. Bundles 343 and 344 have, among other miscellaneous papers, material relating to Pitt's conferences with Miranda at the time of the Nootka controversy, and documents illustrative of British projects against West Florida in that year. Bundles 287 and 288 contain schedules and statistics of imports and exports of Great Britain, classified according to foreign countries, useful material for the study of British-American commerce.

## D. PRIVATE PAPERS OF LORD GRENVILLE

Preserved at the estate of Mr. J. B. Fortescue at Dropmore, England. Though unsuccessful in his efforts to see these papers because of conditions prevailing during the First World War, the investigator in 1921 was helped by an influential intermediary in securing transcripts of several documents dealing with the Jay negotiations and not printed in the Historical Manuscripts Commission's edition of *The Manuscripts of J. B. Fortescue, Esq., preserved at Dropmore* (3 vols. London, 1892–99), cited as *Dropmore Papers*. These pieces, seven in number, are as follows: Jay's notes to Grenville of Aug. 6 and Sept. 30, 1794; Grenville's copy of his note to Jay of Oct. 7, 1794; Project of Heads of Proposals to be made to Mr. Jay; a treaty "Project" with marginal comments dictated by Grenville for Jay's reference; a piece endorsed "Copy of Mr. Jay's Counter Project"; and a proposed "article Directing a Survey of the Mississippi."

## E. PRIVY COUNCIL REGISTER

Contains many Orders-in-Council and Reports of Committees relating to American affairs. Most of the more important ones have already been printed, however; for example, the Reports of the Committee on Trade on the Petition of the West Indian Planters in 1783; on Commerce between the United States and Great Britain, 1791 (reprinted in *Collection of Interesting and Important Reports and Papers on Navigation and Trade,* 1807); and on the Memorial of Levi Allen for a Commercial Treaty between Vermont and Great Britain, 1791 (*A.H.R.,* VIII, 78–86).

For more detailed indication of the above documents (with the exception of F.O., Prussia, Sweden, Russia, Denmark, and Holland) see Paullin and Paxson's *Guide to the Materials in London Archives for the History of the United States since 1783* (Washington, 1914).

## F. ARCHIVES AT WASHINGTON, D. C.

1. Library of Congress, MSS Division
   i. Hamilton Papers.
   ii. Jefferson Papers.

Little unpublished material of importance to this essay was discovered in these collections.

iii. Washington Papers.

These were examined for the author for unprinted material relating to the mission of Gouverneur Morris to England in 1790–1791. Only one such letter was found here (listed as "247, fol. 33056").

2. Department of State Records (now in National Archives)

i. Bureau of Rolls and Library, Washington Papers, Vol. 20.

Contains two unpublished letters relating to the Morris Mission ("fol. 340 and fol. 349").

ii. Diplomatic Archives (Bureau of Indexes and Archives). Dispatches, France, 3, B.

Contains three unpublished letters relating to the Morris Mission.

Instructions to U. S. Ministers, Vols. I-III.

Contains instructions of the Secretary of State to Thomas Pinckney, United States Minister to the Court of St. James's, 1791–1795; and to the Plenipotentiary Extraordinary, John Jay. Most of the instructions to Pinckney are unpublished.

Dispatches from Ministers, Vols. I-III.

These contain the dispatches of Pinckney, the regular Minister, as well as of Jay, the Plenipotentiary Extraordinary. The few Jay dispatches not printed are not as important as the printed letters sent in to the Senate in 1795 with the treaty. Their chief value consists in showing Jay's well-restrained contempt for the ability and judgment of his nominal superior, Secretary of State Edmund Randolph. The Pinckney dispatches are many of them unpublished, and, so far as the investigator is aware, have been little used by historical students. They throw some light on the Swedish proposal of 1794 to the United States and on early impressment disputes. There is also material connected with Washington's unsuccessful effort to secure the release of General Lafayette from an Austrian prison in 1794.

For general description of archives at Washington see Van Tyne and Leland's valuable *Guide to the Archives of the Government of the United States* (2d ed. Washington, 1907), and A. C. McLaughlin's *Re-*

*port on the Diplomatic Archives of the Department of State* (Washington, 1906). These earlier publications are now (1962) long since superseded by *Guide to National Archives* (Washington, 1948).

## G. CANADIAN ARCHIVES

1. Transcripts from England
    Series Q. Lower Canada.
    Volumes 23 to 78 inclusive are useful for the subject of this study. Some numbers are in two distinct volumes, as 61–1, and 61–2. These transcripts, numbering over sixty volumes, comprise the full correspondence of the Colonial Office with British North America, from the treaty of 1783 to the evacuation of the frontier posts in 1796, containing the dispatches and public papers with countless enclosures of the Governors, Lieutenant Governors and administrators of Lower Canada (Quebec) during those years; a source of inestimable value and richness, indispensable for a study of British-American frontier history, especially for Indian affairs, the project of the neutral Indian barrier state, and the question of the military posts. Some of the maps enclosed in the originals are only to be found in the Public Record Office, or the libraries of the Foreign and Colonial Offices, at London, or not at all. Among the maps removed to the Colonial Office Library at Whitehall is the Indian boundary map agreed on at the conference of Dorchester with the Indians, Aug. 17, 1791. Still other maps, for example, a map of the disputed townships near Lake Champlain, are in the Map Room of the Canada Archives at Ottawa.
    Series Q. Upper Canada.
    Upon the division of Quebec into Upper and Lower Canada by the Act of 1791, a similar series of separate correspondence with the Government of Upper Canada developed. This consists, in Series Q, of the volumes from No. 278 on. Volumes 278 to 282–2 inclusive have been used in this study. They are especially valuable for revealing the activities of Governor Simcoe during the establishment of the new colony. He was in constant communication with Hammond, and the letters between these two, and between Whitehall and Upper Canada, throw great light on the frontier situation, especially the incident of the occupation of the Miamis fort in

1794, relations with the Indians, attempts to mediate between the natives and the United States, etc.

Both the Upper Canada and the Lower Canada documents were calendared by the late Archivist of the Dominion, Dr. Douglas Brymner, particularly in *Reports on Canadian Archives* for 1890 and 1891, a work of greatest aid to the student in searching out from this mass of documents those relating to his subject. Dr. Brymner in introductions to these two annual *Reports* printed copious extracts from some of the more important documents. A few documents relating to Vermont are printed in Note C in the introduction to the *Report* for 1889. There are some documents, however, which are most important to the student of the frontier diplomacy, which are merely mentioned in the Calendar, without summary of their contents. Among these are such important pieces as the famous speech of Lord Dorchester to the Indian Delegation, February 10, 1794, and the Requisitions made by Captain Stevenson, in the name of Lieutenant-Governor Simcoe, July 31, 1793. Hence it is not always possible to use the Calendar as an infallible guide. But see the now printed *The Correspondence of Lieut. Governor John Graves Simcoe, with Allied Documents Relating to His Administration of Upper Canada* (5 vols. Toronto, 1923–31), cited as *S.P.*

Many of the papers have been printed in *Michigan Pioneer Collections,* Volumes 20, 24, and 25, but here again one cannot place full reliance, as only those documents considered relevant to Michigan history are printed. A great number are printed, nevertheless, and their incorporation in this easily accessible series is a great aid.

2. Original Collections

Series G, Volume I. Documents relative to Indian Affairs, Vermont, and Posts.

Series C. Miscellaneous records of the military secretary of Canada. Volume 247 of this series contains a wealth of material, in great part original and not duplicated in other series, relating to Indian affairs in 1793 and 1794, and to the American war in the Indian country. It is especially important for Wayne's campaign and its effect on British-American frontier relations. Volume 248, consisting of documents for the year 1795, is less important for this particular study.

Series M. Miscellaneous. Volume 107, correspondence of British officials in the neighborhood of Detroit, Indian speeches, etc. Most of the correspondence after 1789, of value here, is duplicated in enclosures to Series Q. Volumes 108 and 109 are valuable for material upon the Indian negotiations of 1793 and Wayne's campaign. Most of the more important ones are duplicated in Series Q.

Department of Indian Affairs. A carton of loose papers, marked "Sundries 1765–1793," contains a few papers of interest to this study, particularly some letters to and from Alexander McKee, deputy superintendent of Indian affairs at Detroit. Another unlabeled carton contains many papers dated from 1792–1796. These are particularly valuable for the situation at Detroit at the time of Wayne's victory at Fallen Timbers.

A great service for students has been rendered by Mr. David W. Parker's guides to the Canadian Archives: *Guide to the Materials for United States History in Canadian Archives* (Washington, 1913), and *Guide to the Documents in the Manuscript Room at the Public Archives of Canada* (Ottawa, 1913). The value of these guides cannot be overestimated, nor can enough thanks be given to the most thorough and scholarly author.

## H. ARCHIVES DES AFFAIRES ÉTRANGÈRES, PARIS

The correspondence of the French Foreign Office of 1793–1794, under the régime of the Committee of Public Safety.

1. Correspondence to and from Denmark (Arch. Aff. Étrang., Danemark, Vols. 169, 170).

    Contains the dispatches of the French agent at Copenhagen, Philippe de Grouvelle, as well as his instructions, and relevant enclosures, including decrees of the Committee of Public Safety, 1793–1795. This correspondence is intimately connected with Anglo-American relations, because of its connection in turn with the Scandinavian Armed Neutrality project of 1794.

2. Correspondence to and from the United States. Most of this (except a few enclosures) has been printed by Turner.

3. Correspondence to and from Sweden (Arch. Aff. Étrang., Suède, Vol. 286). Similar in character to the French Foreign Office's Danish correspondence, but scantier.

## I. SWEDISH ROYAL ARCHIVES
### TRANSCRIPTS

Transcripts were secured from the Swedish Royal Archives in Stockholm of the correspondence of the Foreign Office of the Swedish Kingdom with the Swedish Ministers in London and Copenhagen. They concern the United States and the abortive Armed Neutrality of 1794.

## J. JAY MSS IN THE NEW YORK
### HISTORICAL SOCIETY

These papers were received in 1847 from the Hon. Wm. Jay of Bedford. They consist of:
1. Instructions and official dispatches to Mr. Jay, 1794. These contain the same documents found in *A.S.P.,F.R.,* I, except two private letters of Randolph to Jay. One of Nov. 12, 1794, is in reply to Jay's private letters of Sept. 13, relative to dissatisfaction in England at the warmth conveyed in Randolph's draft of the Senate's expression of felicitation to the French Convention in 1794. Another letter of Randolph of Dec. 12 to Jay, concerning Messrs. Talleyrand, Beaumetz, and the Duc de La Rochefoucauld-Liancourt, French Royalists, who had been recommended to his country by Jay, and whom he did not receive for fear of offending the French Republic.
2. Papers connected with the negotiation of the treaty of 1794.
3. Papers respecting British spoliations and interference with the Indians, and the correspondence of Hammond with the American Government. These are the papers forwarded to Jay by Randolph from Philadelphia. They are alluded to but not published in *A.S.P., F.R.,* I.

## K. JAY-BANCROFT CORRESPONDENCE,
### NEW YORK PUBLIC LIBRARY

A correspondence between Mr. John Jay, grandson of the Chief Justice, and the historian, Dr. George Bancroft. It concerns chiefly the omission from the treaty of 1794 of an article for compensation for Negroes carried away. Appended are copies of several letters to Jay, and letters of Jay to John

Quincy Adams, Nov. 24, 1794, to Timothy Pickering, Oct. 14, 1795, explaining Articles 6 and 7 of the treaty, and a letter to Dr. Edward Bancroft of London (the former secret agent of the British Government), Oct. 30, 1795, explaining and commenting on the opposition to the Treaty.

## L. PRIVATE FAMILY CORRESPONDENCE OF JOHN JAY, FROM THE ISELIN COLLECTION NOW IN THE BUTLER LIBRARY, COLUMBIA UNIVERSITY.

Contains little of significance for the subject of this study.

## M. WETMORE PAPERS, MASSACHUSETTS HISTORICAL SOCIETY

A valuable set of commercial correspondence between British and American mercantile houses, illustrating the character of commerce between the two countries subsequent to the peace of 1783 and during the period of this study. The correspondence continues to 1808.

# Index